Racism without Racists

Racism without Racists

Color-Blind Racism and the Persistence of Racial Inequality in America

Fourth Edition

Eduardo Bonilla-Silva

ROWMAN & LITTLEFIELD PUBLISHERS, INC.
Lanham • Boulder • New York • Toronto • Plymouth, UK

Published by Rowman & Littlefield Publishers, Inc.
A wholly owned subsidiary of The Rowman & Littlefield Publishing Group, Inc.
4501 Forbes Boulevard, Suite 200, Lanham, Maryland 20706
www.rowman.com

10 Thornbury Road, Plymouth PL6 7PP, United Kingdom

British Library Cataloguing in Publication Information Available

Library of Congress Cataloging-in-Publication Data

Bonilla-Silva, Eduardo, 1962–
  Racism without racists : color-blind racism and the persistence of racial
inequality in America / Eduardo Bonilla-Silva.—Fourth edition.
    pages cm
  Includes bibliographical references and index.
  ISBN 978-1-4422-2054-6 (cloth : alk. paper)—ISBN 978-1-4422-2055-3 (pbk.
: alk. paper)—ISBN 978-1-4422-2056-0 (electronic) 1. Minorities—United
States—Social conditions. 2. Minorities—United States—Economic conditions. 3.
Racism—United States. 4. United States—Race relations. I. Title.
  E184.A1B597 2014
  305.800973—dc23   2013015714

∞™ The paper used in this publication meets the minimum requirements of
American National Standard for Information Sciences—Permanence of Paper
for Printed Library Materials, ANSI/NISO Z39.48-1992.

Printed in the United States of America

I do not have many real friends. I have plenty of acquaintances, but not many people that I truly trust. In my friendship kingdom, very few are allowed in. To them I dedicate this edition. Their names are irrelevant in mass communications like this one, but they all know who they are. These are the people that are indispensable to me. They all have been there for me during tough times such as the death of my brother, during a recent operation, when I have needed advice on work or life issues, or during the many times I have made mistakes in my life. My blood family is peculiar, but this, my other family, bonded by love and solidarity, counts as much as my "real" family. At the helm of my nonblood family is the only person who loves me "for real" and all the way, my wife, Mary Hovsepian. Countless people question why we are still together. The answer is that my Mary is a truly exceptional person. We have been together twenty-five years and, honestly, it feels like today is still 1988. Mary, I am not the best, but you and I together add to more than two. Thanks for loving me despite my silliness and volatility. I will try to be better to you in the next twenty-five years.

Contents

Acknowledgments   ix

Preface to the Fourth Edition   xiii

1   The Strange Enigma of Race in Contemporary America   1

2   The New Racism: The U.S. Racial Structure Since the 1960s   25

3   The Central Frames of Color-Blind Racism   73

4   The Style of Color Blindness: How to Talk Nasty about
    Minorities without Sounding Racist   101

5   "I Didn't Get That Job Because of a Black Man": Color-Blind
    Racism's Racial Stories   123

6   Peeking Inside the (White) House of Color Blindness: The
    Significance of Whites' Segregation   151

7   Are All Whites Refined Archie Bunkers? An Examination
    of White Racial Progressives   179

8   Are Blacks Color Blind, Too?   199

9   E Pluribus Unum, or the Same Old Perfume in a New Bottle?
    On the Future of Racial Stratification in the United States   225

10 Race Matters in Obamerica: The Sweet (but Deadly)
    Enchantment of Color Blindness in Black Face   255

11 "The (Color-Blind) Emperor Has No Clothes": Exposing the
Whiteness of Color Blindness   301

Selected Bibliography   317

Index   347

About the Author   363

Acknowledgments

The last words my mother told me before I left Puerto Rico in 1984 were: "Son, in the United States you need to walk and behave like a king." She also told me something to the effect that no matter what the "gringos" said about me, I always had to remember that "I was as good if not better than them." At the time, I did not understand her advice. Over twenty years later, I fully understand her enormous wisdom. In this country, racial "others" of dark complexion are always viewed as incapable of doing much; we are regarded and treated as secondary actors only good for doing beds in hotels or working in fast-food restaurants. Therefore, my mother's advice ("walk and behave like a king") helped me develop the much-needed emotional *coraza* (shield) to repel all the racial nonsense of "gringolandia" (Frida Kahlo was so right about this country!). Thanks *Mami!*

This *coraza* has come in handy in my sociological career, because at every step of the way, I have encountered people who have tried to block my path one way or another. Fortunately, I have also encountered along the way many people who have helped me in this, my second country. And, in truth, my experience with good and generous people has outweighed that with the bad ones. Many of the former have seen me without my *coraza* and know the real me. At my alma mater (UW–Madison), professors such as Pamela Oliver, Russell Middleton, and Erik Wright were exceedingly generous with me. So were professors Sam Cohn (now my colleague at Texas A&M), Gay Seidman, and Denis O'Hearn, all of whom I served with as a teaching assistant. Wright and Oliver were even kind enough to read and send me feedback on a working paper I wrote two years after leaving Wisconsin. The paper appeared in 1997 in *ASR* with the title "Rethinking Racism: Toward a Structural Interpretation." But the most important sociological force that affected me at Wisconsin was my adviser, Professor Charles Camic. He was the perfect adviser for me. Professor Camic was knowledgeable, kind, savvy, and had an uncanny understanding of the business side of sociology. Then and now, whenever I have a "big (sociological) issue" at hand, he is one of the first people I consult. Thanks, Chas, for being there for me. I hope I am able to repay you in some way.

At Michigan there were a number of colleagues who were very nice to me: Mark Chesler, Julia Adams, Howard Kimeldorf, Muge Gocek, Silvia Pedraza, Jim House, David Williams, and a few others. However, the people who helped me navigate that "peculiar institution" were professors Donald Deskins Jr., Alford Young II, and Carla O'Connor. These three colleagues were more than my colleagues: they were my friends and allies. Thanks Don, Al, and Carla! I hope the sociological gods allow us to work together one more time before our time expires.

At my sociological house, Texas A&M University, almost everyone has helped me. In my first year there, I received more feedback and love than I did at Michigan in five years! Thus, I thank the entire sociology department at A&M for providing me almost unconditional support. I hope I have not disappointed "y'all." Also deserving special mention are two former sociological Aggies, professors Benigno Aguirre (University of Delaware) and John Boies of the U.S. Census Bureau. They both enriched my sociological and nonsociological life. I miss having lunch with John and coffee with Benigno! Last but not least at A&M, my three outstanding graduate students, David G. Embrick (whom I owe many, many, many thanks for his steadfast loyalty and hard work), Paul Ketchum, and Karen Glover, helped me with some of the data and analysis and have supported me beyond the call of duty. Thanks for all your help and support, and I hope to read your own books soon!

Other people who have loved me *de gratis* in sociological Ameri*kkk*a are Joe R. Feagin, Hernán Vera, Judith Blau, Tukufu Zuberi, Hayward Horton, Ashley Doane, Gianpaolo Baiocchi, Joane Nagel, Margaret Andersen, Cedric Herring, Abel Valenzuela, Rogelio Saenz, Tyrone A. Forman, Amanda E. Lewis, Walter Allen, Eddie Telles, Michael O. Emerson, Paul Wong, Jose Padin, Veronica Dujon, Carla Goar, William Darity, Geoffrey Ward, Nadia Kim, Ramiro Martinez, Tom Guglielmo, Moon-Kie Jung, and Larry Bobo, among others. I also wish to thank the folks of the Association of Black Sociologists and the ASA Section on Racial and Ethnic Minorities for supporting me over the past five years.

The data for this book were gathered while I was a professor at Michigan. I thank all the people involved with the 1997 Survey of Social Attitudes of College Students (Amanda, Tyrone, and all the undergraduate students who helped me out!) and the 1998 Detroit-Area Study (DAS). The 1997 survey was done partly with funding from the ASA-NSF (National Science Foundation) Fund for the Advancement of the Discipline. The 1998 DAS was done with Michigan funds. However, I want to thank Jim House and Earl Lewis for funding the interview component for the 1998 DAS. Without those interviews, the 1998 DAS would have been just another run-of-the-mill survey on racial attitudes.

A significant amount of the drafting of this book was done while I was a visiting research fellow at the University of Houston Law Center in the fall of 2000, under the auspices of Professor Michael A. Olivas, director of the Institute for Higher Education Law and Governance. Michael generously hosted me when I was still an unproven commodity. Thanks, Michael. I owe you a lot! While I was in Houston, Professor Russell L. Curtis Jr. from the University of Houston Sociology Department provided me shelter and friendship. I will never forget our long discussions on almost every possible subject. Thanks, Russ!

The final drafting of this book was done at Stanford University, where I was invited to spend a year (2002–2003) as a Hewlett research fellow at the Research Institute for Comparative Studies of Race and Ethnicity, headed by Hazel R. Markus and George Fredrickson. I also wish to thank Leanne Issak, Awino Kuerth, and Dorothy Steele for helping me with all my silly problems during my time there.

This book benefited enormously from the incisive review of Professor Margaret Andersen from the University of Delaware. Maggie read this manuscript from beginning to end and made valuable suggestions that helped me make it a better—although still controversial—book. Thanks, Margaret, for doing such a terrific job!

Finally, I want to dedicate this book to five very special people in my life. First, to my brother, Pedro Juan Bonilla-Silva, who passed away in 2002. Pedro, I wish I had been able to tell you how much I love you, but a bit of machismo and a lot of family history prevented me from doing so. I will always regret that. Second, to my father, Jacinto Bonilla. I know I do not say it often, but I respect, admire, and love you. Third, to my sister, Karen Bonilla-Silva, the youngest, wisest, and nicest-looking in the Bonilla-Silva clan. Fourth, to my son, Omar Francisco Bonilla, who transcribed one of the DAS interviews quoted in this book. Omi, know that I love you and am very proud of your scholarly and artistic accomplishments. Finally, I dedicate this book to the love of my life, Mary Hovsepian. We have marinated our partnership for fifteen years (now, in 2013, twenty-five years) and it is still as sweet and strong as the first day we formalized it. Thanks, Mary. I am eagerly waiting to see what the next fifteen years bring us.

Preface to the Fourth Edition

I am so lonely tonight
If I could only hold you once more
If I could only kiss you once
If I could only see you one more time, one more time

Sam Cooke, a truly original African American singer, songwriter, and musical innovator, made popular a song in the 1950s entitled "One More Time." This is a classic love song where the male lover desperately wishes to see his (presumably female) sweetheart "one more time." In this new edition of *Racism without Racists*, like in Sam Cooke's song, I wish to engage my readers on the subject of racism in America "one more time." (Young readers may not know this popular culture reference, but I hope to inspire you to check out Sam Cooke online. Once you hear Sam Cooke, you will be hooked to his music for life, as he could sing with either a smoky voice or with a velvety, sweet tone. He was "the bomb" and thanks to technology, his image and voice will remain with us forever!)

But why do I need to engage you on this subject "one more time"? Fundamentally, I need to do so for two sociopolitical reasons and one purely related to this book as an intellectual product. Let me address first the sociopolitical reasons. Since the Obama phenomenon has become larger than life, particularly since his reelection in 2012, I thought there was a need to explain what has happened in the last four years (2008–2012), assess the balance and impact of his reelection, and see if my arguments from four years ago stood the test of history. In the third edition of the book I argued that Obama's election was not a miracle, but an expected outcome that reflected the sedimentation of the "new racism" regime that had emerged in the 1970s (for more on this regime, see chapter 2 in this edition). Specifically, I stated that Obama's election did not represent "racial progress" or signified a rupture with either the racial order or the dominant racial ideology at play in the nation, namely, color-blind racism. This argument was important, as Americans at the time (somewhat less so today) believed Obama's election had magically taken us to the racial Promised Land of honey and milk.

The second sociopolitical reason for reengaging readers is my belief that it is imperative to explain the coexistence in America of crude and vulgar antiminority sentiment and actions alongside the ideology (and its corresponding behaviors) I label in this book as color-blind racism. To anticipate the comments I will offer in chapters 2 and 11, (1) racial orders are never "pure," as elements of the past (and even of the future) often coexist with the dominant ways of conducting racial business, (2) coercion has always been central to the maintenance of racial domination,[1] and (3) despite the rise in racist violence, the practices I label as typical of the "new racism" period are still the *dominant* ones in America (more prevalent and central). On point 1, for example, think about how in the 1930s and 1940s, many of the practices and the ideology that would become central in the new racism period were evident. In Charles Johnson's book *Patterns of Negro Segregation* (1943) his interviews with whites reveal how many had already moved from the Jim Crow ideology to the tenets of color-blind racism as well as how many blacks were already talking and behaving as "new negros."[2] In terms of practices, for example, Northern cities had already developed racial ghettoes—a feature that would become central to the way of conducting racial business in the new-racism era. On point 2, as I will suggest in chapters 2 and 11, racist violence by police (from the brutal beatings of Rodney King to the murder of Amadou Diallo) or by "regular white folks" (from the brutal murder of Vincent Chin in the 1980s to the recent murder of Trayvon Martin by an "honorary white" Latino) has remained part of the landscape. This, again, is not surprising, as no system of domination can survive without violence in *the last instance*. Although as I have argued elsewhere (Bonilla-Silva 2011), successful domination (racial or otherwise) requires making the dominated believe, participate, and process their standing as normative, as this is the way things are, dominants need not only what Max Weber called the institutional "legitimate monopoly of violence" but also the violence of *their* masses in case of emergency.[3] Nevertheless, despite the ebb and flow of racial violence in the new-racism period—an ebb and flow usually related to the state of the economy in the nation—I maintain that racial domination is still fundamentally maintained through new practices (economic, political, social, and ideological) and we must focus on this fact if we wish to attain racial justice in America. The more we assume that the problem of racism is limited to the Klan, the Birthers, the Tea Party, or to the Republican Party, the less we understand that racial domination is a *collective* process (we are all in this game) and that the main problem nowadays is not the folks with the hoods, but the folks dressed in suits!

On the matter of this book as an intellectual product, I have been pressed by some users to incorporate a chapter dealing with the new racism, a matter that I mention in the first three editions and that I have addressed elsewhere extensively. I decided that since the book is used by many instructors as *the* book to address race matters in some courses, their demand was fair. Hence, I have included a chapter in this edition dealing with the new racism. The chapter in this edition is an update from a chapter that appeared in my first book, *White Supremacy and Racism in the Post–Civil Rights Era*.

Lastly, working on a revision of a book like this is a tedious job and I could not have done it without the able assistance of the "dynamic (sociological) duo," my two graduate students Victor E. Ray and Louise Seamster. They worked tirelessly to make this a successful revision and they did so during a beautiful yet tough period in their lives: while bringing to the world baby Malcolm. I thank both of them for their incredible work and, as usual, if there are any mistakes in the book, it is entirely their fault (okay, this is a joke!).

I hope readers like this new installment of my "sweet baby" (to keep the love-song style of the fifties going) and that, after you read it, you love it hard (if you *must* love, love hard or do not love at all). If you do not love my new installment, I will nonetheless thank you for listening to me "one more time."

Eduardo Bonilla-Silva
Durham, North Carolina

NOTES

1. Moon-Kie Jung, João H. Costa Vargas, and Eduardo Bonilla-Silva (eds.), State of White Supremacy: Racism, Governance, and the United States (Stanford, Calif.: Stanford University Press, 2011).

2. The term "new negro" was a term popularized during the Harlem Renaissance, albeit it emerged in the latter part of the twentieth century. It referred to blacks unwilling to submit to Jim Crow regulations. Johnson's book reveals that by the 1940s many middle-class blacks were ready for drastic change and were behaving accordingly.

3. On the subject of states and racist violence by the masses, see Rob Witte, *Racist Violence and the State* (London and New York: Longman, 1996).

1

⌇

The Strange Enigma of Race in Contemporary America

There is a strange kind of enigma associated with the problem of racism. No one, or almost no one, wishes to see themselves as racist; still, racism persists, real and tenacious

—Albert Memmi, *Racism*

RACISM WITHOUT "RACISTS"

Nowadays, except for members of white supremacist organizations,[1] few whites in the United States claim to be "racist." Most whites assert they "don't see any color, just people"; that although the ugly face of discrimination is still with us, it is no longer the central factor determining minorities' life chances; and, finally, that, like Dr. Martin Luther King Jr.,[2] they aspire to live in a society where "people are judged by the content of their character, not by the color of their skin." More poignantly, most whites insist that minorities (especially blacks) are the ones responsible for whatever "race problem" we have in this country. They publicly denounce blacks for "playing the race card," for demanding the maintenance of unnecessary and divisive race-based programs, such as affirmative action, and for crying "racism" whenever they are criticized by whites.[3] Most whites believe that if blacks and other minorities would just stop thinking about the past, work hard, and complain less (particularly about racial discrimination), then Americans of all hues could "all get along."[4]

But regardless of whites' "sincere fictions,"[5] racial considerations shade almost everything in America. Blacks and dark-skinned racial minorities lag well behind whites in virtually every area of social life; they are about three times more likely to be poor than whites, earn about 40 percent less than whites, and have about an eighth of the net worth that whites have.[6] They also receive an inferior education compared to whites, even when they attend integrated institutions.[7] In terms of housing, black-owned units comparable to white-owned ones are valued at 35 percent less.[8] Blacks and Latinos also have less access to the entire housing market because whites, through a variety of exclusionary practices by white realtors and homeowners, have been successful in effectively limiting their entrance into many neighborhoods.[9] Blacks receive impolite treatment in stores, in restaurants, and in a host of other commercial transactions.[10] Researchers have also documented that blacks pay more for goods such as cars and houses than do whites.[11] Finally, blacks and dark-skinned Latinos are the targets of racial profiling by the police, which, combined with the highly racialized criminal court system, guarantees their over-representation among those arrested, prosecuted, incarcerated, and if charged for a capital crime, executed.[12] Racial profiling on the highways has become such a prevalent phenomenon that a term has emerged to describe it: driving while black.[13] In short, blacks and most minorities are "at the bottom of the well."[14]

How is it possible to have this tremendous degree of racial inequality in a country where most whites claim that race is no longer relevant? More important, how do whites explain the apparent contradiction between their professed color blindness and the United States' color-coded inequality? In this book I attempt to answer both of these questions. I contend that whites have developed powerful explanations—which have ultimately become justifications—for contemporary racial inequality that exculpate them from any responsibility for the status of people of color. These explanations emanate from a new racial ideology that I label *color-blind racism*. This ideology, which acquired cohesiveness and dominance in the late 1960s,[15] explains contemporary racial inequality as the outcome of nonracial dynamics. Whereas Jim Crow racism explained blacks' social standing as the result of their biological and moral inferiority, color-blind racism avoids such facile arguments. Instead, whites rationalize minorities' contemporary status as the product of market dynamics, naturally occurring phenomena, and blacks' imputed cultural limitations.[16] For instance, whites can attribute Latinos' high poverty rate to a relaxed work ethic ("the Hispanics are mañana, mañana, mañana—tomorrow, tomorrow, tomorrow")[17] or residential segregation as the result of natural tendencies among groups ("Does a cat and a dog mix? I can't see it. You can't drink milk and scotch. Certain mixes don't mix.").[18]

Color-blind racism became the dominant racial ideology as the mechanisms and practices for keeping blacks and other racial minorities "at the bottom of the well" changed. I have argued elsewhere that contemporary racial inequality is reproduced through "new racism" practices that are subtle, institutional, and apparently nonracial.[19] In contrast to the Jim Crow era, where racial inequality was enforced through overt means (e.g., signs saying "No Niggers Welcomed Here" or shotgun diplomacy at the voting booth), today racial practices operate in a "now you see it, now you don't" fashion. For example, residential segregation, which is almost as high today as it was in the past, is no longer accomplished through overtly discriminatory practices. Instead, covert behaviors such as not showing all the available units, steering minorities and whites into certain neighborhoods, quoting higher rents or prices to minority applicants, or not advertising units at all are the weapons of choice to maintain separate communities.[20] In the economic field, "smiling face" discrimination ("We don't have jobs now, but please check later"), advertising job openings in mostly white networks and ethnic newspapers, and steering highly educated people of color into poorly remunerated jobs or jobs with limited opportunities for mobility are the new ways of keeping minorities in a secondary position.[21] Politically, although the civil rights struggles have helped remove many of the obstacles for the electoral participation of people of color, "racial gerrymandering, multimember legislative districts, election runoffs, annexation of predominantly white areas, at-large district elections, and anti-single-shot devices (disallowing concentrating votes in one or two candidates in cities using at-large elections) have become standard practices to disenfranchise" people of color.[22] Whether in banks, restaurants, school admissions, or housing transactions, the maintenance of white privilege is done in a way that defies facile racial readings. Hence, the contours of color-blind racism fit America's new racism quite well.

Compared to Jim Crow racism, the ideology of color blindness seems like "racism lite." Instead of relying on name calling (niggers, spics, chinks), color-blind racism otherizes softly ("these people are human, too"); instead of proclaiming that God placed minorities in the world in a servile position, it suggests they are behind because they do not work hard enough; instead of viewing interracial marriage as wrong on a straight racial basis, it regards it as "problematic" because of concerns over the children, location, or the extra burden it places on couples. Yet this new ideology has become a formidable political tool for the maintenance of the racial order. Much as Jim Crow racism served as the glue for defending a brutal and overt system of racial oppression in the pre–civil rights era, color-blind racism serves today as the ideological armor for a covert and institutionalized system in the post–civil rights era. And the beauty of this new ideology is that it aids in the maintenance of white privilege without fanfare, without naming those who it subjects and those who it rewards. It allows a president to state things such as, "I strongly support diversity of all kinds, including racial diversity in higher education," yet, at the same time, to characterize the University of Michigan's affirmation action program as "flawed" and "discriminatory" against whites.[23] Thus whites enunciate positions that safeguard their racial interests without sounding "racist." Shielded by color blindness, whites can express resentment toward minorities; criticize their morality, values, and work ethic; and even claim to be the victims of "reverse racism." This is the thesis I will defend in this book to explain the curious enigma of "racism without racists."[24]

WHITES' RACIAL ATTITUDES IN THE POST–CIVIL RIGHTS ERA

Since the late 1950s surveys on racial attitudes have consistently found that fewer whites subscribe to the views associated with Jim Crow. For example, whereas the majority of whites supported segregated neighborhoods, schools, transportation, jobs, and public accommodations in the 1940s, less than a quarter indicated they did in the 1970s.[25] Similarly, fewer whites than ever now seem to subscribe to stereotypical views of blacks. Although the number is still high (ranging from 20 percent to 50 percent, depending on the stereotype), the proportion of whites who state in surveys that blacks are lazy, stupid, irresponsible, and violent has declined since the 1940s.[26]

These changes in whites' racial attitudes have been explained by the survey community and commentators in four ways. First, are they *racial optimists*. This group of analysts agrees with whites' common sense on racial matters and believes the changes symbolize a profound transition in the United States. Early representatives of this view were Herbert Hyman and Paul B. Sheatsley, who wrote widely influential articles on the subject in *Scientific American*. In a reprint of their earlier work in the influential collection edited by Talcott Parsons and Kenneth Clark, *The Negro American*, Sheatsley rated the changes in white attitudes as "revolutionary" and concluded,

> The mass of white Americans have shown in many ways that they will not follow a racist government and that they will not follow racist leaders. Rather, they are engaged in the painful task of adjusting to an integrated society. It will not be easy for most, but one cannot at this late date doubt the basic commitment. In their hearts they know that the American Negro is right.[27]

In recent times, Glenn Firebaugh and Kenneth Davis, Seymour Lipset, and Paul Sniderman and his coauthors, in particular, have carried the torch for racial optimists.[28] Firebaugh and Davis, for example, based on their analysis of survey results from 1972 to 1984, concluded that the trend toward less antiblack prejudice was across the board. Sniderman and his coauthors, as well as Lipset, go a step further than Firebaugh and Davis because they have openly advocated color-blind politics as *the* way to settle the United States' racial dilemmas. For instance, Sniderman and Edward Carmines made this explicit appeal in their book, *Reaching beyond Race*:

> To say that a commitment to a color-blind politics is worth undertaking is to call for a politics centered on the needs of those most in need. It is not to argue for a politics in which race is irrelevant, but in favor of one in which race is relevant so far as it is a gauge of need. Above all, it is a call for a politics which, because it is organized around moral principles that apply regardless of race, can be brought to bear with special force on the issue of race.[29]

The problems with this optimistic interpretation are twofold. First, as I have argued elsewhere,[30] relying on questions that were framed in the Jim Crow era to assess whites' racial views today produces an artificial image of progress. Since the central racial debates and the language used to debate those matters have changed, our analytical focus ought to be dedicated to the analysis of the new racial issues. Insisting on the need to rely on old questions to keep longitudinal (trend) data as the basis for analysis will, by default, produce a rosy picture of race relations that misses what is going on on the ground. Second, and more important, because of the change in the normative climate in the post–civil rights era, analysts must exert extreme caution when interpreting attitudinal data, particularly when it comes from single-method research designs. The research strategy that seems more appropriate for our times is mixed research designs (surveys used in combination with interviews, ethnosurveys,[31] etc.), because it allows researchers to cross-examine their results.

A second, more numerous group of analysts exhibit what I have labeled elsewhere as the *racial pesoptimist* position.[32] Racial pesoptimists attempt to strike a "balanced" view and suggest that whites' racial attitudes reflect progress and resistance. The classical example of this stance is Howard Schuman.[33] Schuman has argued for more than thirty years that whites' racial attitudes involve a mixture of tolerance and intolerance, of acceptance of the principles of racial liberalism (equal opportunity for all, end of segregation, etc.) and a rejection of the policies that would make those principles a reality (from affirmative action to busing).[34]

Despite the obvious appeal of this view in the research community (the appearance of neutrality, the pondering of "two sides," and this view's "balanced" component), racial pesoptimists are just closet optimists. Schuman, for example, has pointed out that, although "White responses to questions of principle are . . . more complex than is often portrayed . . . they nevertheless do show in almost every instance a positive movement over time."[35] Furthermore, it is his belief that the normative change in the United States is real and that the issue is that whites are having a hard time translating those norms into personal preferences.

A third group of analysts argues that the changes in whites' attitudes represent the emergence of a *symbolic racism*.[36] This tradition is associated with the work of David Sears and his associate, Donald Kinder.[37] They have defined symbolic racism as "a blend of anti-black affect and the kind of traditional American moral values embodied in the Protestant Ethic."[38] According to these authors, symbolic racism has replaced biological racism as the primary way whites express their racial resentment toward minorities. In Kinder and Sanders's words,

> A new form of prejudice has come to prominence, one that is preoccupied with matters of moral character, informed by the virtues associated with the traditions of individualism. At its center are the contentions that blacks do not try hard enough to overcome the difficulties they face and that they take what they have not earned. Today, we say, prejudice is expressed in the language of American individualism.[39]

Authors in this tradition have been criticized for the slipperiness of the concept of "symbolic racism," for claiming that the blend of antiblack affect and individualism is new, and for not explaining why symbolic racism came about. The first critique, developed by Howard Schuman, is that the concept has been "defined and operationalized in complex and varying ways."[40] Despite this conceptual slipperiness, indexes of symbolic racism have been found to be in fact different from those of old-fashioned racism and to be strong predictors of whites' opposition to affirmative action.[41] The two other critiques, made forcefully by Lawrence Bobo, have been partially addressed by Kinder and Sanders in their book, *Divided by Color*. First, Kinder and Sanders, as well as Sears, have made clear that their contention is not that this is the first time in history that antiblack affect and elements of the American Creed have combined. Instead, their claim is that this combination has become *central* to the new face of racism. Regarding the third critique, Kinder and Sanders go at length to explain the transition from old-fashioned to symbolic racism. Nevertheless, their explanation hinges on arguing that changes in blacks' tactics (from civil disobedience to urban violence) led to an onslaught of a new form of racial resentment that later found more fuel in controversies over welfare, crime, drugs, family, and affirmative action. What is missing in this explanation is a materially based explanation for why these changes occurred. Instead, their theory of prejudice is rooted in the "process of socialization and the operation of routine cognitive and emotional psychological processes."[42]

Yet, despite its limitations, the symbolic racism tradition has brought attention to key elements of how whites explain racial inequality today. Whether this is "symbolic" of antiblack affect or not is beside the point and hard to assess, since, as a former student of mine queried, "How does one test for the unconscious?"[43]

The fourth explanation of whites' contemporary racial attitudes is associated with those who claim that whites' racial views represent a *sense of group position*. This position, forcefully advocated by Lawrence Bobo and James Kluegel, is similar to Jim Sidanius's "social dominance" and Mary Jackman's "group interests" arguments.[44] In essence, the claim of all these authors is that white prejudice is an ideology to defend white privilege. Bobo and his associates have specifically suggested that because of socioeconomic changes that transpired in the 1950s and 1960s, a *laissez-faire racism* emerged that was fitting of the United States' "modern, nationwide, postindustrial free labor economy and polity."[45] Laissez-faire racism "encompasses an ideology that blames blacks themselves for their poorer relative economic standing, seeing it as the function of perceived cultural inferiority."[46]

Some of the basic arguments of authors in the symbolic and modern racism[47] traditions and, particularly, of the laissez-faire racism view are fully compatible with my color-blind racism interpretation. As these authors, I argue that color-blind racism has rearticulated elements of traditional liberalism (work ethic, rewards by merit, equal opportunity, individualism, etc.) for racially illiberal goals. I also argue like them that whites today rely more on cultural rather than biological tropes to explain blacks' position in this country. Finally, I concur with most analysts of post–civil rights matters in arguing that whites do not perceive discrimination to be a central factor shaping blacks' life chances.

Although most of my differences with authors in the symbolic racism and laissez-faire traditions are methodological (see below), I have one central theoretical disagreement with them. Theoretically, most of these authors are still snarled in the prejudice problematic and thus interpret actors' racial views as *individual psychological* dispositions. Although Bobo and his associates have a conceptualization that is closer to mine, they still retain the notion of prejudice and its psychological baggage rooted in interracial hostility.[48] In contrast, my model is not anchored in actors' affective dispositions (although affective dispositions may be manifest or latent in the way many express their racial views). Instead, it is based on a materialist interpretation of racial matters and thus sees the views of actors as corresponding to their systemic location. Those at the bottom of the racial barrel tend to hold oppositional views and those who receive the manifold wages of whiteness tend to hold views in support of the racial status quo. Whether actors express "resentment" or "hostility" toward minorities is largely irrelevant for the maintenance of white privilege. As David Wellman points out in his *Portraits of White Racism*, "prejudiced people are not the only racists in America."[49]

KEY TERMS: RACE, RACIAL STRUCTURE, AND RACIAL IDEOLOGY

One reason why, in general terms, whites and people of color cannot agree on racial matters is because they conceive terms such as "racism" very differently. Whereas for most whites racism is prejudice, for most people of color racism is systemic or institutionalized. Although this is not a theory book, my examination of color-blind racism has etched in it the indelible ink of a "regime of truth"[50] about how the world is organized. Thus, rather than hiding my theoretical assumptions, I state them openly for the benefit of readers and potential critics.

The first key term is the notion of *race*. There is very little formal disagreement among social scientists in accepting the idea that race is a socially constructed category.[51] This means that notions of racial difference are human creations rather than eternal, essential categories. As such, racial categories have a history and are subject to change. And here ends the agreement among social scientists on this matter. There are at least three distinct variations on how social scientists approach this constructionist perspective on race. The first approach, which is gaining popularity among white social scientists, is the idea that because race is socially constructed, it is not a fundamental category of analysis and praxis. Some analysts go as far as to suggest that because race is a constructed category, then it is not real and social scientists who use the category are the ones who make it real.[52]

The second approach, typical of most sociological writing on race, gives lip service to the social constructionist view—usually a line in the beginning of the article or book. Writers in this group then proceed to discuss "racial" differences in academic achievement, crime, and SAT scores as if they were truly racial.[53] This is the central way in which contemporary scholars contribute to the propagation of racist interpretations of racial inequality. By failing to highlight the social dynamics that produce these racial differences, these scholars help reinforce the racial order.[54]

The third approach, and the one I use in this book, acknowledges that race, as other social categories such as class and gender, is constructed but insists that it has a *social* reality. This means that after race—or class or gender—is created, it produces real effects on the actors racialized as "black" or "white." Although race, as other social constructions, is unstable, it has a "changing same"[55] quality at its core.

In order to explain how a socially constructed category produces real race effects, I need to introduce a second key term: the notion of *racial structure*. When race emerged in human history, it formed a social structure (a racialized social system) that awarded systemic privileges to Europeans (the peoples who became "white") over non-Europeans (the peoples who became "nonwhite").[56] Racialized social systems, or white supremacy[57] for short, became global and affected all societies where Europeans extended their reach. I therefore conceive a society's racial structure as *the totality of the social relations and practices that reinforce white privilege.* Accordingly, the task of analysts interested in studying racial structures is to uncover the particular social, economic, political, social control, and ideological mechanisms responsible for the reproduction of racial privilege in a society.

But why are racial structures reproduced in the first place? Would not humans, after discovering the folly of racial thinking, work to abolish race as a category as well as a practice? Racial structures remain in place for the same reasons that other structures do. Since actors racialized as "white"—or as members of the dominant race—receive material benefits *the* from the racial order, they struggle (or passively receive the manifold *moving* wages of whiteness) to maintain their privileges. In contrast, those de- *way away* fined as belonging to the subordinate race or races struggle to change the status quo (or become resigned to their position). Therein lies the secret of racial structures and racial inequality the world over.[58] They exist because they benefit members of the dominant race.

If the ultimate goal of the dominant race is to defend its collective interests (i.e., the perpetuation of systemic white privilege), it should surprise no one that this group develops rationalizations to account for the status of the various races. And here I introduce my third key term, the notion of *racial ideology*. By this I mean *the racially based frameworks used by actors to explain and justify* (dominant race) or *challenge* (subordinate race or races) *the racial status quo.* Although all the races in a racialized social system have the *capacity* of developing these frameworks, the frameworks of the dominant race tend to become the master frameworks upon which *all* racial actors ground (for or against) their ideological positions. Why? Because as Marx pointed out in *The German Ideology*, "the ruling *material* force of society, is at the same time its ruling *intellectual* force."[59] This does not mean that ideology is almighty. In fact, as I will show in chapter 7, ideological rule is always partial. Even in periods of hegemonic rule,[60] such as the current one, subordinate racial groups develop oppositional views. However, it would be foolish to believe that those who rule a society do not have the power to at least color (pun intended) the views of the ruled.

Racial ideology can be conceived for analytical purposes as comprising the following elements: common frames, style, and racial stories (details on each can be found in chapters 3, 4, and 5). The frames that bond together a particular racial ideology are rooted in the group-based conditions and experiences of the races and are, at the symbolic level, the representations developed by these groups to explain how the world is or ought to be. And because the group life of the various racially defined groups is based on hierarchy and domination, the ruling ideology expresses as "common sense" the interests of the dominant race, while oppositional ideologies attempt to challenge that common sense by providing alternative frames, ideas, and stories based on the experiences of subordinated races.

Individual actors employ these elements as "building blocks . . . for manufacturing versions on actions, self, and social structures" in communicative situations.[61] The looseness of the elements allows users to maneuver within various contexts (e.g., responding to a race-related survey, discussing racial issues with family, or arguing about affirmative action in a college classroom) and produce various accounts and presentations of self (e.g., appearing ambivalent, tolerant, or strong minded). This loose character enhances the legitimating role of racial ideology because it allows for accommodation of contradictions, exceptions, and new information. As Jackman points out about ideology in general, "Indeed, the strength of an ideology lies in its loose-jointed, flexible application. *An ideology is a political instrument, not an exercise in personal logic:* consistency is rigidity, the only pragmatic effect of which is to box oneself in."[62]

Before I can proceed, two important caveats should be offered. First, although whites, because of their privileged position in the racial order, form a social group (the dominant race), they are fractured along class, gender, sexual orientation, and other forms of "social cleavage." Hence, they have multiple and often contradictory interests that are not easy to disentangle and that predict a priori their mobilizing capacity (Do white workers have more in common with white capitalists than with black workers?). However, because all actors awarded the dominant racial position, regardless of their multiple structural locations (men or women, gay or straight, working class or bourgeois), benefit from what Mills calls the "racial contract,"[63] *most* have historically endorsed the ideas that justify the racial status quo.

Second, although not every single member of the dominant race defends the racial status quo or spouts color-blind racism, *most* do. To explain this point by analogy, although not every capitalist defends capitalism (e.g., Frederick Engels, the coauthor of *The Communist Manifesto,* was a capitalist) and not every man defends patriarchy (e.g., *Achilles Heel* is an English magazine published by feminist men), *most* do in some fashion. In the same vein, although some whites fight white supremacy and do not endorse white common sense, *most* subscribe to substantial portions of it in a casual, uncritical fashion that helps sustain the prevailing racial order.

apathy contributes largely

HOW TO STUDY COLOR-BLIND RACISM

I will rely mostly on interview data to make my case. This choice is based on important conceptual and methodological considerations. Conceptually, my focus is examining whites' racial ideology, and ideology, racial or not, is produced and reproduced in communicative interaction.[64] Hence, although surveys are useful instruments for gathering general information on actors' views, they are severely limited tools for examining how people explain, justify, rationalize, and articulate racial viewpoints. People are less likely to express their positions and emotions about racial issues by answering "yes" and "no" or "strongly agree" and "strongly disagree" to questions. Despite the gallant effort of some survey researchers to produce methodologically correct questionnaires, survey questions still restrict the free flow of ideas and unnecessarily constrain the range of possible answers for respondents.[65]

Methodologically, I argue that because the normative climate in the post–civil rights era has made illegitimate the public expression of racially based feelings and viewpoints,[66] surveys on racial attitudes have become like multiple-choice exams in which respondents work hard to choose the "right" answers (i.e., those that fit public norms). For instance, although a variety of data suggest racial considerations are central to whites' residential choices, more than 90 percent of whites state in surveys that they have no problem with the idea of blacks moving into their neighborhoods.[67] Similarly, even though about 80 percent of whites claim they would not have a problem if a member of their family brought a black person home for dinner, research shows that (1) very few whites (fewer than 10 percent) can legitimately claim the proverbial "some of my best friends are blacks" and (2) whites rarely fraternize with blacks.[68]

Of more import yet is the insistence by mainstream survey researchers' on using questions developed in the 1950s and 1960s to assess changes in racial tolerance. This strategy is predicated on the assumption that "racism" (what I label here "racial ideology") does not change over time. If instead one regards racial ideology as in fact changing, the reliance on questions developed to tackle issues from the Jim Crow era will produce an artificial image of progress and miss most of whites' contemporary racial nightmares.

Despite my conceptual and methodological concerns with survey research, I believe well-designed surveys are still useful instruments to glance at America's racial reality. Therefore, I report survey results from my own research projects as well as from research conducted by other scholars whenever appropriate. My point, then, is not to deny attitudinal change or to condemn to oblivion survey research on racial attitudes, but to understand whites' new racial beliefs and their implications as well as possible.

DATA SOURCES

The data for this book come primarily from two similarly structured projects. The first is the 1997 Survey of Social Attitudes of College Students, based on a convenient sample of 627 college students (including 451 white students) surveyed at a large midwestern university (MU henceforth), a large southern university (SU), and a medium-sized West Coast university (WU). A 10 percent random sample of the white students who provided information in the survey on how to contact them (about 90 percent) were interviewed (forty-one students altogether, of which seventeen were men and twenty-four women and of which thirty-one were from middle- and upper-middle-class backgrounds and ten were from the working class).

Although the data from this study are very suggestive and, I believe, essentially right, the study has some limitations. First, it is based on a convenient, rather than a representative, sample, limiting the capacity for generalizing the findings to the white population at large. Nevertheless, it is worth pointing out that the bias in that sample is in the direction of *more* racial tolerance, since researchers have consistently found that young, college-educated whites are more likely to be racially tolerant than any other segment of the white population.[69] Another limitation of the study is that interviews were conducted only with white respondents. Thus, this data set does not allow us to examine whether or not their views are different from blacks'. Finally, due to budget constraints, the sample was small, albeit large when compared to most interview-based work.[70]

The second data source for this book is the 1998 Detroit Area Study (DAS). This data set overcomes many of the limitations of the college students' data set, since the former is based on a representative sample and includes a significant number of interviews with both white and black respondents. The 1998 DAS is a probabilistic survey of four hundred black and white Detroit metropolitan-area residents (323 whites and 67 blacks). The response rate was an acceptable 67.5 percent. As part of this study, 84 respondents (a 21 percent subsample) were randomly selected for in-depth interviews (sixty-six were whites and seventeen were blacks). The interviews were race matched, followed a structured interview protocol, were conducted in the respondents' homes, and lasted about one hour.

The major limitation of the 1998 DAS data set is that the respondents are black and white only. As the United States has become a multiracial society, one has to be concerned about the generalizability of an analysis based on findings on blacks and whites. Although I posit color-blind racism is the general ideology of the post–civil rights era, I realize that a fuller analysis should include the views of other people of color. Thus, I will bring to bear data from other sources in my conclusion to show how other people of color fit into the notion of color-blind racism. On a final note regarding the 1997 Survey of Social Attitudes of College Students and the 1998 DAS, I am well aware that some readers may question their continued validity. However, both survey research as well as interview-based research (e.g., Bush 2004; Gallagher 2002; etc.) done since have produced similar results, thus adding strength to my arguments in this book.

POLITICS, INTERPRETATION, AND OBJECTIVITY

Social scientific research is always a political enterprise. Despite the Enlightenment's dream[71] of pure objectivity, the problems we pose, the theories we use, the methods we employ, and the analyses we perform are social products themselves and to an extent reflect societal contradictions and power dynamics. This view has become more acceptable in the social sciences today than it was ten or twenty years ago.[72] Accordingly, it is harder for social scientists today to defend sociologist Max Weber's call for a separation between researcher, method, and data.[73]

My scholarly goals in this book are to describe the main components of color-blind racism and explain their functions and to use these components to theorize how future U.S. race relations might look. I hope this effort helps social analysts to get over the present impasse on the nature and meaning of whites' racial views. Yet, by accomplishing my scholarly goals, I also hope to attain a much larger and important political goal: uncovering the basic profile of the main ideology reinforcing contemporary racial inequality. By definition, then, my work is a challenge to post–civil rights white common sense; to the view that race no longer matters; and to anyone who believes that the problems afflicting people of color are fundamentally rooted in their pathological cultures.[74] More specifically, I want to advance an argument (the sophisticated nature of color-blind racism), an approach (analyzing racial ideology rather than "prejudice"), and a politics (fighting racial domination based on a group rights'[75] agenda) that assist scholars and activists alike in their research and struggle against color-blind nonsense. I also hope that this book will serve as a wake-up call to color-blind liberal and progressive whites and confused members of minority communities who may favor equal opportunity but not affirmative action, who believe discrimination is not an important factor shaping the life chances of people of color, or who still wonder if racial minorities do in fact have an inferior culture that accounts for their status in America. Nevertheless, recognizing the political nature of research is not a green light for sloppiness and one-sidedness or for relying on unsystematically gathered data to make broad generalizations. Hence, I support my arguments with systematic interview data and reference where my data or analysis differs from that of mainstream analysts so that readers can find alternative interpretations to mine.

Let me now say a word on the matter of interpretation. It is true that "the spoken word has always the residue of ambiguity, no matter how carefully we word the questions and how carefully we report or code the answers."[76] Hence, it is possible for others to read the data differently. To satisfy the intellectual concerns of those who doubt my interpretation, whenever possible I present cases that do not nicely fit my interpretation (particularly in chapter 8). Nevertheless, I do not eschew the dangerous but necessary role of the analyst. I will make a strong case for the view that most whites endorse the ideology of color blindness and that this ideology is central to the maintenance of white privilege. The alternatives to this interpretive role of analysts, which I see as more problematic, are timid descriptions usually accompanied by a forest of caveats in which actors' self-reports of events becomes the ultimate goal of the research itself. Although I do not deny that "people's accounts count,"[77] my goals are interpretive (what do people's accounts mean?) and political (what do people's accounts help accomplish in society). Description and data presentation without interpretation, without analysis, is like going to a beach without a swimsuit.

Does this mean that my interpretation is infallible because I have some degree of authority, which somehow confers me a special gaze? In truth, given the situational and partial character of all knowledge,[78] neither I, nor my potential critics hold the monopoly over the right way of interpreting data. All of us try our best to construct robust explanations of events and hope that in the tilted market of ideas (tilted toward the interpretations of the powerful) the most plausible ones achieve legitimacy.

But if research is political by nature and my interpretation of the data is guided by my theoretical and political orientation, how can readers ascertain if my interpretation is better than those of other analysts? That is, how can we avoid the trap of relativism,[79] of the idea that "all thinking is merely the expression of interest or power or group membership?"

My answer to these questions is that my explanations—as well as those of other analysts—ought to be judged like maps. Judge my cartographic effort of drawing the boundaries of contemporary white racial ideology in terms of its usefulness (Does it help to better understand whites' views?), accuracy (Does it accurately depict whites' arguments about racial matters?), details (Does it highlight elements of whites' collective representations not discussed by others?), and clarity (Does it ultimately help you move from here to there?).[80]

ONE IMPORTANT CAVEAT

The purpose of this book is not to demonize whites or label them "racist." Hunting for "racists" is the sport of choice of those who practice the "clinical approach" to race relations—the careful separation of good and bad, tolerant and intolerant Americans. Because this book is anchored in a structural understanding of race relations,[81] my goal is to uncover the collective practices (in this book, the ideological ones) that help reinforce the contemporary racial order. Historically, many good people supported slavery and Jim Crow. Similarly, most color-blind whites who oppose (or have serious reservations about) affirmative action, believe that blacks' problems are mostly their own doing, and do not see anything wrong with their own white lifestyle are good people, too. The analytical issue, then, is examining how many whites subscribe to an ideology that ultimately helps preserve racial inequality rather than assessing how many hate or love blacks and other minorities.

Even with this caveat, some readers may still feel discomfort while reading this book. Since color-blind racism is the dominant racial ideology, its tentacles have touched us all and thus most readers will subscribe to some—if not most—of its tenets, use its style, and believe many of its racial stories. Unfortunately, there is little I can do to ease the pain of these readers, since when one writes and exposes an ideology that is at play, its supporters "get burned," so to speak. For readers in this situation (good people who may subscribe to many of the frames of color blindness), I urge a personal and political movement away from claiming to be "nonracist" to becoming "antiracist."[82] Being an antiracist begins with understanding the institutional nature of racial matters and accepting that all actors in a racialized society are affected *materially* (receive benefits or disadvantages) and *ideologically* by the racial structure. This stand implies taking responsibility for your unwilling participation in these practices and beginning a new life committed to the goal of achieving real racial equality. The ride will be rough, but after your eyes have been opened, there is no point in standing still.

THE PLAN OF THE BOOK

Color-blind racism emerged as a new racial ideology in the late 1960s, concomitantly with the crystallization of the "new racism" as America's new racial structure. In chapter 2, I describe how this new racial regime emerged and outline its central practices and mechanisms in the social, economic, political, and social control areas.

Because the social practices and mechanisms to reproduce racial privilege acquired a new, subtle, and apparently nonracial character, new rationalizations emerged to justify the new racial order. The new dominant themes or frameworks of color-blind racism are the subject of chapter 3.

All ideologies develop a set of stylistic parameters; a certain way of conveying its ideas to audiences. Color-blind racism is no exception. In chapter 4, I document the main stylistic components of this ideology. In chapter 5, I delve into the story lines ("The past is the past" or "I didn't get a job or promotion—or was not admitted to a certain college—because a black man got it") and personal stories that have emerged in the post–civil rights era to provide color-blind racism's gut-level emotionality.

If we take seriously whites' self-profession to color blindness, one would expect significantly high levels of racial interaction with minorities in general and blacks in particular. Using the data from these two projects, in chapter 6, I examine whites' patterns of interracial interactions and conclude that they tend to navigate in what I label as a "white habitus" or a set of primary networks and associations with other whites that reinforces the racial order by fostering racial solidarity among whites and negative affect toward racial "others."

In chapter 7, I address "race traitors,"[83] or whites who do not endorse the ideology of color blindness. After profiling college students and DAS respondents who fit the racial progressive mold, I suggest white women from working-class origins are the most likely candidates to commit racial treason in the United States. Nevertheless, I also show that color-blind racism has affected even these progressive whites. If color-blind racism has affected racial progressives, has it affected blacks, too? Attempting to answer this question is the focus of chapter 8. Using DAS data, I contend that although blacks have developed an oppositional ideology, color-blind racism has affected blacks in a mostly indirect fashion. Rather than totally controlling blacks' field of ideas and cognitions, color-blind racism has confused some issues, restricted the possibility of discussing others, and, overall, blunted the utopian character of blacks' oppositional views. In chapter 9, I challenge the assertions that the United States is still organized along a biracial divide and posit that the United States is slowly moving toward a triracial or "plural" order similar to that found in many Latin American and Caribbean countries. In chapter 10, I examine the

Obama phenomenon and suggest it is not emblematic of post-racialism but part of the color-blind drama I examine in this book. In chapter 11, I conclude by assessing the implications of color-blind racism, of the Latin Americanization of racial stratification, and of *Obamerica* for the struggle for racial and social justice in this country.

NOTES

1. Even members of these organizations now claim that they are not racist, simply pro-white. For David Duke's discussion on this matter, see his website, www.duke.org.

2. Some, such as former president George H. W. Bush, use Dr. King's dictum to oppose affirmative action. Interestingly, when Bush was in Congress, he opposed most of the civil rights legislation advocated by King. Furthermore, few whites have ever read the speech in which King used this phrase. If they had, they would realize that his dream referred to the future, that he emphasized that the "Negro [was] still not free." King also emphasized that there could not be peace without justice. In his words, "There will be neither rest nor tranquility in America until the Negro is granted his citizenship rights. The whirlwinds of revolt will continue to shake the foundations of our nation until the bright day of justice emerges." See Martin Luther King Jr., *A Call to Conscience: The Landmark Speeches of Dr. Martin Luther King, Jr.*, edited by Clayborne Carson and Kris Shephard (New York: Intellectual Properties Management, in association with Warner Books, 2001).

3. These views have been corroborated in survey after survey. For instance, a recent nationwide survey found that 66 percent of whites thought the disadvantaged status of blacks in America was due to blacks' welfare dependency and 63 percent thought blacks lacked the motivation to improve their socioeconomic status. Tom W. Smith, "Intergroup Relations in Contemporary America," in *Intergroup Relations in the United States: Research Perspectives*, edited by Wayne Winborne and Renae Cohen, 69–106 (New York: National Conference for Community and Justice, 2000).

4. This phrase was made popular by Rodney King immediately after his first trial. Curiously, the phrase was provided to King by his white lawyer and a movie producer. See Houston A. Baker, "Scene . . . Not Heard," in *Reading Rodney King, Reading Urban Uprising*, edited by Robert Gooding-Williams, 38–50 (New York: Routledge, 1993), 45.

5. This term was coined in Joe R. Feagin and Hernán Vera, *White Racism: The Basics* (New York: Routledge, 1995), to refer to whites' myths about race in contemporary America, particularly their self-delusions.

6. See Melvin Oliver and Thomas Shapiro, *Black Wealth/White Wealth* (New York: Routledge, 1995). See also Juliane Malveaux, "Black Dollar Power: Economics in the Black Community," *Essence* 10 (October 1999): 88–92; John Goering (ed.), *Fragile Rights in Cities* (Lanham, Md.: Rowman & Littlefield, 2007), and Thomas M. Shapiro, *The Hidden Cost of Being African American: How Wealth Perpetuates Inequality* (London: Oxford University Press, 2004).

7. For a vivid description of the educational inequalities between blacks and whites, see Jonathan Kozol, *Savage Inequalities* (New York: Crown, 1992). For a discussion of resegregation and its consequences, see Gary Orfield, Susan Eaton, and the Harvard Project on School Desegregation, *Dismantling Desegregation: The Quiet Reversal of* Brown v. Board of Education (New York: New York Press, 1996). For a discussion of racial matters in "integrated" campuses, see Joe R. Feagin, Hernán Vera, and Nikitah Imani, *The Agony of Education: Black Students at White Colleges and Universities* (New York: Routledge, 1996); and chapter 2 in Roy Brooks, *Integration or Separation? A Strategy for Racial Equality* (Cambridge, Mass.: Harvard University Press, 1996).

8. William J. Collins and Robert A. Margo, "Race and the Value of Owner-Occupied Housing, 1940–1990," Working Papers Series (Annandale-on-Hudson, N.Y.: Bard College, Levy Economics Institute, August 2000).

9. Douglas Massey and Nancy E. Denton, *American Apartheid* (Cambridge, Mass.: Harvard University Press, 1993); John Yinger, *Closed Doors, Opportunities Lost: The Continuing Costs of Housing Discrimination* (New York: Russell Sage Foundation, 1995); Judith N. Desena, "Local Gatekeeping Practices and Residential Segregation," *Sociological Inquiry* 64, no. 3 (1994): 307–21.

10. Joe R. Feagin and Melvin Sikes, *Living with Racism: The Black Middle-Class Experience* (Boston: Beacon, 1994); Peter Siegelman, "Racial Discrimination in 'Everyday' Commercial Transactions: What Do We Know . . . ," in *A National Report Card on Discrimination in America: The Role of Testing*, edited by Michael Fix and Margery Austin Turner, chapter 4 (Washington, D.C.: Urban Institute, March 1999).

11. Oliver and Shapiro, *Black Wealth/White Wealth*; Siegelman, "Racial Discrimination."

12. Katheryn K. Russell, *The Color of Crime* (New York: New York University Press, 1998).

13. David A. Harris, *Driving While Black: Racial Profiling on Our Nation's Highways*, Special Report (New York: American Civil Liberties Union, June 1999).

14. Derrick Bell, *Race, Racism and American Law* (Boston: Little, Brown, 1992).

15. The work of William A. Ryan and Joel Kovel represent early efforts to understand the parameters of post–civil rights racial ideology. See William A. Ryan, *Blaming the Victim* (New York: Random House, 1976); Joel Kovel, *White Racism: A Psychohistory* (New York: Columbia University Press, 1985).

16. Melvin Thomas has found that this perspective deeply affects social science research on racial matters. Melvin Thomas, "Anything but Race: The Social Science Retreat from Racism," *African American Research Perspectives* 6, no. 1 (Winter 2000): 79–96.

17. This statement is from the top officer of a cart transport company in Chicago. William Julius Wilson, *When Work Disappears* (New York: Norton, 1996), 112.

18. These comments are from a resident of Canarsie, New York. Jonathan Rieder, *Canarsie: The Jews and Italians of Brooklyn against Liberalism* (Cambridge, Mass.: Harvard University Press, 1985), 58.

19. See my chapter with Amanda E. Lewis, "The 'New Racism': Toward an Analysis of the U.S. Racial Structure, 1960–1990s," in *Race, Nation, and Citizenship*, edited by Paul Wong, 100–150 (Boulder, Colo.: Westview, 1999). For a more re-

cent, updated version, see chapter 3 in my *White Supremacy and Racism in the Post Civil Rights Era* (Boulder, Colo.: Rienner, 2001).

20. For general findings on housing matters, see John Yinger, *Closed Doors*. For gatekeeping practices, see Judith A. Desena, "Local Gatekeeping Practices and Residential Segregation."

21. Bonilla-Silva, *White Supremacy*, 11–117.

22. Bonilla-Silva, *White Supremacy*, 100–101.

23. CBS, "Bush Enters Affirmative Action Fray," CBS.com, January 16, 2003. For a discussion of the contradiction between President Bush opposing affirmative action and his own affirmative action–like admission to Phillips Academy and Yale, see Ellis Henican, "When It Comes to Hypocrisy, He's Brilliant!" *Newsday*, January 17, 2003. In *Grutter v. Bollinger* et al., the Supreme Court decided that Michigan could use race as one factor among many in its admissions policy. Although President Obama has appointed Judge Sonia Sotomayor to the court, the court is still center-right and may further restrict affirmative action.

24. I must caution, however, that at no point in history have dominant groups, whether capitalists, men, or whites, proclaimed that their domination is rooted in unfairness and oppression or characterized their behavior as abominable. Hence, whether in the slavery, Jim Crow, or post–civil rights eras, whites have never acknowledged any wrongdoing. From a social-psychological standpoint, this makes perfect sense since, as William Ryan stated in his famous book, *Blaming the Victim*, "no one [wants to think] of himself as a son of a bitch" (20).

25. Howard Schuman et al., *Racial Attitudes in America* (Cambridge, Mass.: Harvard University Press, 1997).

26. For data on stereotypes, see Mark Peffley and Jon Hurwitz, "Whites' Stereotypes of Blacks: Sources and Political Consequences," in *Perception and Prejudice: Race and Politics in the United States*, edited by Jon Hurwitz and Mark Peffley, 58–99 (New Haven, Conn.: Yale University Press); John F. Dovidio and Samuel L. Gaertner, "Changes in the Expression and Assessment of Racial Prejudice," in *Opening Doors*, edited by Harry J. Knopke et al., 119–50 (Tuscaloosa: University of Alabama Press, 1991); Paul M. Sniderman and Edward G. Carmines, *Reaching Beyond Race* (Cambridge, Mass.: Harvard University Press, 1997). See also Anti-Defamation League, *Highlights from the Anti-Defamation League Survey on Racial Attitudes in America* (New York: Anti-Defamation League, 1993).

27. Paul B. Sheatsley, "White Attitudes toward the Negro," in *The Negro American*, edited by Talcott Parsons and Kenneth B. Clark, 303–24 (Boston: Beacon, 1966), 323.

28. Glenn Firebaugh and Kenneth E. Davis, "Trends in Antiblack Prejudice, 1972–1984: Region and Cohort Effects," *American Journal of Sociology* 94 (1988): 251–72; Paul M. Sniderman and Thomas Piazza, *The Scar of Race* (Cambridge, Mass.: Harvard University Press, 1993); Seymour Lipset, *American Exceptionalism* (New York: Norton, 1996); Sniderman and Carmines, *Reaching beyond Race*.

29. Sniderman and Carmines, *Reaching beyond Race*, 138.

30. Eduardo Bonilla-Silva and Tyrone Forman, "'I Am Not a Racist But . . .': Mapping White College Students' Racial Ideology in the USA," *Discourse and Society* 11, no. 1 (2000): 50–85.

31. For a discussion on this methodology, see Douglas S. Massey, R. Alarcon, J. Durand, and H. Gonzalez, *Return to Aztlan: The Social Process of International Migration from Western Mexico* (Berkeley: University of California Press, 1997).

32. See the introduction to Bonilla-Silva, *White Supremacy*.

33. See Tom W. Smith, "Measuring Inter-Racial Friendships: Experimental Comparisons" (paper presented at the 1999 American Sociological Association meeting in San Francisco).

34. The earliest statement of Schuman's paradoxical views can be found in Angus Campbell and Howard Schuman, *Racial Attitudes in Fifteen American Cities* (Ann Arbor, Mich.: Survey Research Center, June 1968).

35. Schuman et al., *Racial Attitudes in America*.

36. In truth, there are at least four versions of this tradition (symbolic, aversive, modern, and subtle racism). Yet, despite small differences, all of them make the claim that antiblack prejudice has gone underground and is now expressed symbolically through apparently nonracist means.

37. The foundational paper here was David O. Sears and Donald R. Kinder, "Racial Tensions and Voting in Los Angeles," in *Los Angeles: Viability and Prospects for Metropolitan Leadership*, edited by Werner Z. Hirsch (New York: Praeger, 1971).

38. Donald R. Kinder and David O. Sears, "Prejudice and Politics: Symbolic Racism versus Racial Threats to the Good Life," *Journal of Personality and Social Psychology* 40, no. 1 (1981): 414–31, 416.

39. David R. Kinder and Lynn M. Sanders, *Divided by Color: Racial Politics and Democratic Ideals* (Chicago: University of Chicago Press, 1996), 106.

40. Schuman et al., *Racial Attitudes in America*, 293.

41. Michael Hughes, "Symbolic Racism, Old-Fashioned Racism, and Whites' Opposition to Affirmative Action," in *Racial Attitudes in the 1990s*, edited by Steven A. Tuch and Jack K. Martin, 45–75 (Westport, Conn.: Praeger 1997).

42. Lawrence Bobo, James A. Kluegel, and Ryan A. Smith, "Laissez-Faire Racism: The Crystallization of a Kinder, Gentler, Antiblack Ideology," in *Racial Attitudes in the 1990s*, edited by Steven A. Tuch and Jack K. Martin, 15–44 (Westport, Conn.: Praeger, 1997), 21. For a similar critique, see chapter 1 in Mary R. Jackman, *The Velvet Glove: Paternalism and Conflict in Gender, Class, and Race Relations* (Berkeley: University of California Press, 1994).

43. This comment was made by Susanna Dolance, a graduate student at Michigan.

44. Jim Sidanius et al., "It's Not Affirmative Action, It's the Blacks," in *Racialized Politics*, edited by David O. Sears, Jim Sidanius, and Lawrence Bobo, 191–235 (Chicago: University of Chicago Press, 2000); Jackman, *The Velvet Glove*.

45. Bobo, Kluegel, and Smith, "Laissez-Faire Racism," 21. Philomena Essed has developed a similar argument and claims that in the modern world the dominant racial ideology is that of "competitive racism." See Philomena Essed, *Diversity: Gender, Color, and Culture* (Amherst: University of Massachusetts Press, 1996). See also my "'This Is a White Country': Racial Ideological Convergence among the Western Nations of the World-System," *Sociological Inquiry* 70, no. 2 (2000): 188–214.

46. Lawrence Bobo and James R. Kluegel, "Status, Ideology, and Dimensions of Whites' Racial Beliefs and Attitudes: Progress and Stagnation," in *Racial Attitudes in the 1990s*, 93–120 (Westport, Conn.: Praeger, 1997), 95.

47. John B. McConahay and J. C. Hough, "Symbolic Racism," *Journal of Social Issues* 32, no. 2 (1976): 23–46; John B. McConahay, "Modern Racism, Ambivalence, and the Modern Racism Scale," in *Prejudice, Discrimination, and Racism*, edited by John F. Dovidio and Samuel L. Gaertner (New York: Academic, 1986).

48. This critique of the prejudice problematic (and of Bobo's work) was issued first by Jackman, *The Velvet Glove*, 55–58.

49. David T. Wellman, *Portraits of White Racism*, 2d ed. (Cambridge: Cambridge University Press, 1993).

50. See Michel Foucault, *The Order of Things: An Archeology of the Human Sciences* (New York: Random House, 1973).

51. A few highly visible social scientists such as Charles Murray, Arthur Jensen, Pierre van den Berghe, and Edward O. Wilson still conceive of race as a biological or primordial category. However, they are in a minority and are severely criticized by most people in academia.

52. For an example of this view, see Yehudi O. Webster, *The Racialization of America* (New York: St. Martin's, 1992). However, this view is much more extensive and has been publicly stated by radical scholars such as Todd Gitlin. I have seen the growing influence of this stance among many "radical" scholars who now proclaim to be disillusioned with what they label as "identity politics" (in truth, they never got onboard with the radical gender and racial agendas of their minority and women's colleagues) and thus argue that gender and race are divisive categories preventing the unity of the working class.

53. For a biting critique of statistical racial reasoning, see Tukufu Zuberi, "Deracializing Social Statistics: Problems in the Quantification of Race," *Annals of the American Academy of Political and Social Science* 568 (2000): 172–85.

54. It is largely irrelevant whether these authors are "racist" (that is, hold negative views about racial minorities) or not. "That knowledge [that produced by race scholars unwilling to accept the centrality of racial stratification as the basic force behind the data they uncover], sometimes wittingly, sometimes unwittingly, operates to reinforce the fear and hatred of others by providing rationales for hierarchizing differences." Thomas L. Dunn, "The New Enclosures: Racism in the Normalized Community," in *Reading Rodney King, Reading Urban Uprising*, edited by Robert Gooding-Williams, 178–95 (New York: Routledge, 1993), 180.

55. I borrow this phrase from Michael G. Hanchard, *Orpheus and Power* (Princeton, N.J.: Princeton University Press, 1994). Too many postmodern-inspired readings on race insist on the malleability and instability of all social constructions. This, they believe, is the best antidote to essentialism. In my view, however, by focusing on the instability of race as a category, they miss its continuity and social role in shaping everyday dynamics. Even worse, in some cases, the views of some of these authors come close to those of right-wing scholars who advocate the elimination race as a category of analysis and discourse. From the perspective advanced in this book, the elimination of race from above without changing the material conditions that makes race a *socially* real category would just add another layer of defense to white supremacy.

56. I have argued in my work that race emerged as a category of human division in the fifteenth and sixteenth centuries as Europeans expanded their nascent world system. However, other analysts believe that the category has existed since

antiquity and cite evidence of "racism" from the Roman and Greek civilizations. Although I believe that they confuse xenophobia and ethnocentrism with what I call a racialized social system, our disagreement is not central to the point at hand.

57. Although many analysts resent this concept and think that is inappropriate, I am persuaded by the arguments advanced by philosopher Charles W. Mills. This notion forces the reader to understand the systemic and power elements in a racialized social system, as well as the historical reality that such systems were organized and are still ordained by Western logics. For a discussion on this matter, see my book, *White Supremacy,* or consult Charles W. Mills, *Blackness Visible* (Ithaca, N.Y.: Cornell University Press, 1998).

58. I have been criticized for holding this position (see my debate with Mara Loveman in the pages of the *American Sociological Review,* December 1999), yet the view that race relations have a material foundation has a long history in American sociology. This notion formed part of the classic work of W. Lloyd Warner, in *Social Class in America* (New York: Harper & Row, 1960), and John Dollard, in *Caste and Class in a Southern Town* (New York: Doubleday, 1957); later, it could be found in the work of Herbert Blumer, Hubert Blalock, Stokely Carmichael and Charles Hamilton, and Robert Blauner.

59. My emphasis. Karl Marx, *The German Ideology,* edited and with an introduction by C. J. Arthur (New York: International, 1985), 64.

60. Hegemonic rule means that dominant groups actively attempt to achieve the consent of the subordinated groups through a variety of means.

61. Margaret Wetherell and Jonathan Potter, *Mapping the Language of Racism* (New York: Columbia University Press, 1992), 91.

62. My emphasis. Jackman, *The Velvet Glove,* 69.

63. Black philosopher Charles W. Mills argues that with the advent of modern imperialism (the fifteenth and sixteenth centuries onward), whites developed a political, moral, and epistemological "racial contract" to maintain white supremacy over nonwhites. See *The Racial Contract* (Ithaca, N.Y.: Cornell University Press, 1997).

64. Volosinov, the great Russian psychologist, stated a long time ago that ideology, and even self-awareness and consciousness, are "always verbal [communicative], always a matter of finding some specifically suitable verbal complex." Vladimir N. Volosinov, *Freudianism: A Marxist Critique* (New York: Academic, 1976), 86. For treatises on how language is embedded in ideology, see Norman Fairclough, *Language and Power* (London: Longman, 1989), and *Critical Discourse Analysis: The Critical Study of Language* (London: Longman, 1995).

65. For an example of the efforts of survey researchers to craft better survey instruments, see Judith Tanur, ed., *Questions about Questions* (New York: Russell Sage Foundation, 1994).

66. Teun A. van Dijk, *Prejudice in Discourse* (Philadelphia: Benjamins, 1984). See also Howard Schuman et al., *Racial Attitudes in America.*

67. The specific wording of this survey question is "If a black family with about the same income as you moves into your neighborhood, would you mind it a little, a lot, or not at all?" See Schuman et al., *Racial Attitudes in America.*

68. For data on traditional social distance questions, see chapter 3 in Schuman et al., *Racial Attitudes in America.* For data on the limited level of white-black friendship,

see Mary R. Jackman and Marie Crane, "'Some of My Best Friends Are Black . . .': Interracial Friendship and Whites' Racial Attitudes," *Public Opinion Quarterly* 50 (Winter 1986): 459–86. For more recent data on whites' racial attitudes see Kristen Myers, *Racetalk: Racism Hiding in Plain Sight* (Lanham, Md.: Rowman & Littlefield, 2005), and Melanie Bush, *Breaking the Code of Good Intentions: Everyday Forms of Whiteness* (Lanham, Md.: Rowman & Littlefield, 2004). Data on limited fraternization between white and black college students will be provided in chapter 6.

69. Lawrence Bobo and Fred Licari, "Education and Political Tolerance: Testing the Effects of Cognitive Sophistication and Target Group Affect," *Public Opinion Quarterly* 53, no. 5 (Fall 1989): 285–308; Schuman et al., *Racial Attitudes in America.*

70. According to Steinar Kvale, *Interviews: An Introduction to Qualitative Research Interviewing* (London: Sage, 1996), most interview-based projects use between ten and fifteen subjects.

71. For a critique of the Enlightenment project as a racialized project, see Zygmut Bauman, *Modernity and Ambivalence* (Ithaca, N.Y.: Cornell University Press, 1991); David T. Goldberg, *Racist Culture: Philosophy and the Politics of Meaning* (Cambridge, Mass.: Blackwell, 1993).

72. See, for example, Norman K. Denzin and Yvonna S. Lincoln (eds.), *Handbook of Qualitative Research* (Thousand Oaks, Calif.: Sage, 2000). Yet, this critical approach can be found in Dollard, *Caste and Class*, and more definitely, in Myrdal. For example, Myrdal wrote more than sixty years ago, in addressing the idea that "hard facts" debunk biases:

> It must be maintained, however, that *biases in social science cannot be erased simply by "keeping to the facts" and by refined methods of statistical treatment of the data.* Facts, and the handling of data, sometimes show themselves even more previous to tendencies toward bias than does "pure thought." . . . When, in an attempt to be factual, the statements of theory are reduced to a minimum, biases are left a freer leeway than if they were more explicitly set forth and discussed. (my emphasis)

Gunnar Myrdal, *An American Dilemma: The Negro Problem and Modern Democracy* (New York: Harper & Brothers, 1944), 1041.

73. See Max Weber, "Objectivity in Social Science and Social Policy," edited and translated by Edward A. Shils and H. A. Finch (New York: Free Press, 1949).

74. I am aware that a few blacks and minority scholars and politicians—some working in very important jobs—endorse these views. However, as I argue in chapter 7, this segment of the black community is very small and does not represent the views of the community at large.

75. This controversial agenda will be developed in chapter 9. My argument is not new. For similar arguments, see Harold Cruse, *Plural but Equal: A Critical Study of Blacks and Minorities and America's Plural Society* (New York: Morrow, 1987); David Ingram, *Group Rights: Reconciling Equality and Difference* (Lawrence: University Press of Kansas, 2000); and, particularly, chapter 8, "Antiracist Strategies and Solutions," in Joe R. Feagin, *Racist America: Roots, Realities, and Future Reparations* (New York: Routledge, 2000).

76. Andrea Fontana and James H. Frey, "The Interview: From Structured Questions to Negotiated Text," in *Handbook of Qualitative Research,* edited by Norman K. Denzin and Yvonna S. Lincoln, 645–72 (Thousand Oaks, Calif.: Sage, 2000).

77. Terri L. Orbuch, "People's Accounts Count: The Sociology of Accounts," *Annual Review of Sociology* 23 (1997): 455–78. The position I am elaborating here has been marvelously captured by philosopher of science Brian Fay.

> So must we comprehend others in their own terms? *Yes,* in the sense that we cannot grasp intentional phenomena and their products as intentional without ascertaining what they mean for those engaged in them. But *No,* in the sense that explaining these phenomena often will require outstripping the conceptual resources of those being studied.

Brian Fay, *Contemporary Philosophy of Social Science* (Oxford, England: Blackwell, 1996), 134.

78. Situational because those in the business of interpreting the world, "whether they admit it or not, always have points of view, disciplinary orientations, social or political groups with which they identify." Joel L. Kinchelor and Peter McLaren, "Rethinking Critical Theory and Qualitative Research," in *Handbook of Qualitative Research*, edited by Norman K. Denzin and Yvonna S. Lincoln, 279–314 (Thousand Oaks, Calif.: Sage, 2000), 288. Partial because we can never capture either the totality of events affecting a process or the process itself.

79. Fay, *Contemporary Philosophy of Social Science,* 220.

80. This idea is also from Fay, *Contemporary Philosophy of Social Science.*

81. For a full elaboration, see my "Rethinking Racism."

82. I owe this idea to Eileen O'Brien, a sociology professor at the State University of New York–New Paltz.

83. I borrow this phrase from the journal *Race Traitors.*

2

〰️

The New Racism

The U.S. Racial Structure Since the 1960s

INTRODUCTION

The white commonsense view on racial matters is that racists are few and far between, that discrimination[1] has all but disappeared since the 1960s, and that most whites are color blind. This view, which emerged in the 1970s, has gone viral with the election of Barack Obama as president in 2008. Whites seem to be collectively shouting, "We have a black president, so we are finally beyond race!" (see chapter 10 for a discussion on Obama, the new racism, and color blindness). This new common sense is not totally without foundation (e.g., traditional racial practices and exclusion as well as Jim Crow–based racist beliefs have decreased in significance), but it is ultimately false. What has happened is that white supremacy in the United States (i.e., the racial structure of America) has changed. Today "new racism" practices have emerged that are more sophisticated and subtle than those typical of the Jim Crow era. Yet, as I will argue, these practices are as effective as the old ones in maintaining the racial status quo. In this chapter, I trace the evolution of these new structures of racial domination to show how racial inequality is perpetuated in a color-blind world. I begin this chapter with a brief description of how this new racial structure (the new racism) came about. Against this backdrop, I survey the evidence of how black-white racial inequality is produced and reproduced in the United States in four areas: social, political, social control, and economic. The evidence is perused from 1960 until the present with the goal of examining the mechanisms and practices that keep minorities "in their place." I conclude the chapter with a discussion of some of the social, political, and legal repercussions of the new racial structure of America.

The argument that race and racism have "decreased in significance" in contemporary America was made prominent in the late 1970s by black sociologist William Julius Wilson.[2] This view is consistent with survey data on white attitudes since the early 1960s[3] as well as with many demographic and economic studies comparing the status of whites and blacks in terms of income, occupations, health, and education that suggest that a remarkable reduction in racial inequality has occurred in America.[4]

A smaller number of social scientists, on the other hand, believe that race continues to play a role similar to the one it played in the past.[5] For these authors, little has changed in America in terms of racism and there is a general pessimism in the prospects of changing the racial status of minorities. Although this is a minority viewpoint in academia, it represents the perception of many members of minority communities, especially of the black community.

These opinions about the changing import of race and racism in the United States are based on a narrowly defined notion of racism. For these analysts, racism is fundamentally an ideological or attitudinal phenomenon. In contrast, as I stated in the previous chapter, I regard racism as a structure, that is, as a network of social relations at social, political, economic, and ideological levels that shapes the life chances of the various races. What social scientists define as racism is conceptualized in this framework as racial ideology. Racism (racial ideology) helps to glue and, at the same time, organize the nature and character of race relations in a society. From this vantage point, rather than arguing about whether the significance of race has declined, increased, or not changed at all, the issue at hand is assessing if a transformation has occurred in the *racial structure* of the United States. It is my contention that despite the profound changes that occurred in the 1960s, a new racial structure—the new racism for short—is operating, which accounts for the persistence of racial inequality.

The elements that comprise this new racial structure are

1. the increasingly *covert* nature of racial discourse and racial practices;
2. the avoidance of racial terminology and the ever-growing claim by whites that they experience "reverse racism";
3. the elaboration of a racial agenda over political matters that eschews direct racial references;
4. the invisibility of most mechanisms to reproduce racial inequality; and, finally,
5. the rearticulation of some racial practices characteristic of the Jim Crow period of race relations.

I begin this chapter with a brief description of how this new racial structure (new racism) came about. Against this backdrop, I survey the evidence of how black-white racial inequality is produced and reproduced in the United States in several areas: social, political, economic, and ideological. The evidence is perused from 1960 until the present with the goal of examining the mechanisms and practices that keep minorities "in their place." I conclude the chapter with a discussion of some of the social, political, and legal repercussions of the new racial structure of America.

Before I move forward, I must state one important caveat. Although I hold that the dominant form of racism now practiced is a subtle one, this does not mean I am blind to the vulgar explicit racism now in vogue among the "Tea Party" and others on the right. Racial regimes may change, but that transformation is never complete and remnants of the old-fashioned Jim Crow racism are clearly resurgent. This resurgence is important and clearly influences the life chances of people of color; however, I contend that it is not the core of the system and the practices responsible for reproducing racial domination today.

THE EMERGENCE OF A NEW RACIAL STRUCTURE IN THE 1960s

Blacks were kept in a subordinate position during the Jim Crow period of race relations through a variety of bluntly racist practices. At the economic level, blacks were restricted to menial jobs by the joint effort of planters, corporations, and unions. Hence it is not surprising that in 1890 87 percent of blacks worked as either agricultural workers or domestics or in personal service (see table 2.1 below). In the South, they were mostly tenant farmers and this was accomplished through vagrancy and apprenticeship laws, restrictions on the right of blacks to buy land and to work in certain occupations, debt imprisonment, and the convict lease system.[6] In the North, the exclusionary practices of managers and unions

Table 2.1. Distribution of Blacks by Occupations, 1890

Industry	Number	Percent
Agriculture	1,728,325	56.2
Domestic and Personal Service	956,754	31.1
Manufacturing	208,374	6.8
Trade and Transportation	145,717	4.8
Professionals	33,994	1.1

Source: Lorenzo J. Greene and Carter Godwin Woodson, *The Negro Wage* Earner (Washington, D.C.: Association for the Study of Negro Life and History, 1930), p. 37, table 10.

kept them in unskilled occupations with very little chance for occupational mobility.[7] Thus, rather than a split labor market, "most blacks in
the South between 1865 and 1900 were not yet in a position to compete
directly with whites for the same occupations."[8] As tenant workers, they
were "reduced to the status of a serf" and cheated by white landlords in a
variety of ways. As industrial workers in the North, they were located at
the bottom of the well with little chance for occupational mobility.

The economic position of blacks did not change much until well into
the twentieth century. It was not until after WWI, which created a labor
shortage in the industrial North, that many blacks migrated from the
South and joined the ranks of the working class.[9] Yet this transition from
agricultural to industrial jobs did not break the Jim Crow pattern of employment. Spero and Harris contend that although there was no wage
discrimination between blacks and whites in the North, blacks earned
less than whites because they were concentrated in low-skill jobs: The jobs
into which the Negroes went were usually those that native Americans
and Americanized foreign-born white labor did not want. This largely
accounts for the almost-spectacular increase in the proportion of Negroes
in the iron and steel foundries, where the work is dirty, hot, and unpleas-
ant.[10]

At the social level, the rules of the new racial order emerged slowly
given that the War and the Reconstruction (1865–1877) shook the rules
of racial engagement and challenged the place of blacks in society. The
transition from slavery to Jim Crow was characterized by inconsistency
and no generally accepted code of racial mores. Slavery did not require
either a very sophisticated and specific set of rules to preserve "social
distance" or an elaborate racial ideology (racism) because of the thorough
differences of status among the races. But as blacks became free, they
posed a threat to white supremacy. Slowly but surely segregationist laws
and practices emerged after 1865 and were solidified by the 1880s with
the enactment of Jim Crow laws all over the South. These laws involved
the disenfranchisement of blacks, racial separation in public accommodations, segregation in housing, schools, the workplace, and in other areas
to insure white supremacy. C. Vann Woodward describes the extent of
these laws in the following manner:

> The extremes to which caste penalties and separation were carried in parts of
> the South could hardly find a counterpart short of the latitudes of India and
> South Africa. . . . Curfew . . . separate phone booths . . . separate books and
> storage of books in public schools . . . South Carolina separated the mulatto
> caste of prostitutes, and even "Ray Stannard Baker found Jim Crow Bibles
> for Negro witnesses in Atlanta and Jim Crow elevators for Negro passengers
> in Atlanta buildings."[11]

Politically, blacks were virtually disenfranchised in the South and were almost totally dependent on white politicians in the North. In the South, poll taxes, literacy tests, and outright coercive strategies restrained their political options. In the North, black politicians were subordinate to white ethnic political machineries and did not represent much for their own communities.[12]

In terms of social control, blacks in the South were regulated by the actions of individual whites, violent racist organizations such as the Ku Klux Klan, mob violence in the form of lynching, and the lack of enforcement of the laws of the land by state agencies. In the North, blacks suffered less from these practices largely because they were extremely residentially segregated and, thus, did not pose a "threat" to whites. However, whenever blacks "crossed the line," whites erupted in violence such as during the race riots of the late 1910s.[13]

Finally, in consonance with the above practices, racial ideology during the Jim Crow period of race relations was explicitly racist. Without question, most whites believed that minorities were intellectually and morally inferior, that they should be kept apart, and that whites should not mix with any of them.[14]

The apartheid that blacks[15] experienced in the United States was predicated on (1) keeping them in rural areas, mostly in the South, (2) maintaining them as agricultural workers, and (3) excluding them from the political process. However, as blacks successfully challenged their socioeconomic position by migrating initially from rural areas to urban areas in the South and later to the North and West, by pushing themselves by whatever means necessary into nonagricultural occupations, and by developing political organizations and movements like Garveyism, the NAACP, CORE, the National Urban League, the Southern Regional Council, and the CIC, the infrastructure of racial apartheid began to crumble.[16] Among the other factors leading to the abolition of the segregationist order, the most significant were the participation of blacks in World War I and World War II, which patently underscored the contradiction between fighting for freedom abroad and lacking it at home; the Cold War, which made it a necessity to eliminate overt discrimination at home in order to sell the United States as the champion of democracy; and a number of judicial decisions, legislative acts, and presidential decrees that transpired since the 1940s.[17]

The aforementioned political, social, and economic processes occurred in a fast-changing U.S. political economy. From 1920 until 1940, the North expanded its industrialization process at a furious pace. After WWII the South industrialized at an even more dramatic pace. Many Northern industries moved South in search of lower production costs and have continued doing so.[18] Hence today over 70 percent of the Southern labor force is engaged in nonagricultural pursuits. This industrialization process provided the pull factor for blacks to move from the rural South, which, coupled with the push factor of escaping the violence of Jim Crow and the demise in agricultural jobs, created the optimal conditions for the "great migration."[19] Although the 1.8 million blacks who migrated between 1910 and 1940 from the South to the North and West faced severe racial practices and economic constraints from white workers, labor unions, and whites in general, the North provided them expanded opportunities in all realms of life. This great migration continued between 1940 and 1970 as 4.4 million more blacks left the South.[20]

The impact of this migration was enormous on the overall condition of blacks. By 1970 blacks were geographically diffused throughout the United States; 80 percent were urban dwellers and had achieved a higher rate of urbanization than whites; they had increased their education and developed a small but thriving middle class; social and political organizations flourished and became training ground for many black leaders; by virtue of their new geographic dispersion, blacks increasingly became a national group; and they were able to develop a new consciousness, new attitudes, and a new view on how to deal with racial discrimination, characterized by Gunnar Myrdal as the "protest motive."[21]

Even in the South, the social, political, and cultural condition of blacks improved somewhat with the early process of industrialization. And, after the 1960s, even their economic condition changed as the top business elite abandoned all-out discrimination because of the adverse economic effects created by violence and protest demonstrations. According to Melvin M. Lehman, this pattern was reinforced by northern industrial capital that had penetrated the South, making the "southern system of brutality, social discrimination, and legalized (or extra-legalized) persecution . . . more and more economically and politically dysfunctional."[22]

To be clear, neither urbanization nor industrialization were nonracial "rational" progressive forces in themselves. Both northern and southern capitalists accommodated racial practices in their hiring, company policies, and daily activities. In the case of southern capitalists, industrialization became a necessity with the progressive decline of its agricultural economy. Although southern capitalists were able to maintain Jim Crow and industrialization for over fifty years (1890s to 1950s), by the mid-1950s it became clear that they could not coexist peacefully. Blacks in the North had acquired enough political muscle to push the federal government to do something about their civil rights. After the *Brown* decision of 1954 and its rejection by most of the South, instability and protests spread all over the South. Such instability was anathema for attracting capital. Therefore, the business elite, reluctantly and gradually, developed an accommodation with the new policies. In the North, the accommodation began much earlier in the 1920s, 1930s, and particularly after WWII, and involved the subordinate incorporation of blacks in industry. This accommodation, although progressive, maintained the view that blacks were inferior workers and kept them in the bottom of the occupational hierarchy. The views of northern managers were typified by a "progressive" manager who in the 1950s commented that "Negroes, basically and as a group, with only rare exceptions, are not as well trained for higher skills and jobs as whites. They appear to be excellent for work, usually unskilled, that requires stamina and brawn—and little else. They are unreliable and cannot adjust to the demands of the factory."[23] Views like this continue to plague American capitalists in the post-1960 period.[24] What industrialization and urbanization did for blacks was to provide a new context for struggle that made the southern Jim Crow system impossible to maintain in the face of black opposition. (Interested parties should see the similarities between this case in the United States and the collapse of Apartheid in South Africa. There the enlightened segment of the business elite decided to meet with leaders of the ANC in the late 1980s to discuss a possible solution to the sociopolitical crisis. They did so because of the pressure of international economic sanctions, anti-divestment campaigns, and boycotts to South African products.[25] Hence, for the elite, that matter was not black and white but green!)

These demographic, social, political, and economic factors and the actions of blacks made change almost inevitable. But ripe conditions are not enough to change any structural order. Hence, the racial order had to be *directly* challenged if it was going to be effectively transformed. That was the role fulfilled by the civil rights movement and the other forms of mass protest by blacks (so-called race riots) that took place in the 1960s and 1970s. Organized and spontaneous challenges were the catalysts that brought down overt segregation.

Yet the demise of Jim Crow did not mean the end of racism in America. Many analysts noted that "racism" (as usually defined) and race relations acquired instead a new character since the 1960s. They point to the increasingly covert nature of racial discourse and racial practices; the avoidance of racial terminology in racial conflicts by whites; and the elaboration of a racial agenda over political matters (e.g., state intervention, individual rights, responsibility, etc.) that eschews direct racial references.[26] In the following sections I describe the typical discriminatory practices of the post–civil rights era.

INTERRACIAL SOCIAL INTERACTION DURING THE NEW RACISM PERIOD

In all areas of social life blacks and whites remain mostly separate and disturbingly unequal. A close examination of research in the areas of

housing, education, and everyday social interaction reveals startlingly
little progress since the 1960s.

Residential Segregation

U.S. Census 2000 data indicates that residential segregation has declined
for the third straight decade. During the 1990s, segregation declined in 272
metropolitan statistical areas and increased in 19 areas; however, black-
white segregation remained high in the older Rust-Belt metropolitan
areas and increased during the 1990s in the suburbs. Furthermore, blacks
are still more segregated than any other racial or ethnic group—segregation that they have experienced longer than any other group—and are
segregated at every income level.[27] The black poor, in particular, suffer
the greatest degree of "hypersegregation" from the rest of America, and
this pattern of extreme isolation has remained the same through the last
one-third century. In their book, *American Apartheid*, Massey and Denton
measure the block-level indices of residential segregation of thirty metropolitan areas from 1940 to 1980. The index of residential segregation
for the North is around 80 and for the South around 70 (an index of 100
indicates total segregation and one of 0, no segregation at all). Even with
a steady decline in most of the metropolitan areas included, levels are still
extremely high, especially in the northern cities. In addition the level of
black isolation has improved little since the 1970s. The average level of
isolation was close to 66 percent in 1980 and no metropolitan area had an
isolation index under 50 percent. In 2000, national black isolation was 65
percent and remained 80 percent or higher in cities such as Detroit, Newark, and Chicago. Due to higher white flight of families with children to
segregated suburbs, white children are the most segregated (68.3 percent)
by neighborhood.[28]

    Some demographic data suggests that residential segregation is de-
clining. U.S. Census 2010 data indicates that residential segregation has
declined for the fourth straight decade. Although many of these types
of indices are used as if they were sophisticated measures, the reality
is otherwise, as these indices essentially rely on "simple numerical and
percentage comparisons of the numbers and proportions of persons in
each race/ethnicity group in a population."[29] Scholars have pointed to the
problem of unmeasured segregation because of the scale of census tracts.
More fundamentally, however, I suggest that "racial contacts" *do not*
mean substantive integration, since there are significant forms of racism
compatible with "physical closeness." The apparent "integration" noted
in some settings may have more to do with poverty and falling incomes
of poor whites or simply the restructuring of urban space than as a result
of meaningful racial integration.

The costs to blacks of residential segregation are high; they are likely to pay more for housing in a limited market, likely to have lower-quality housing, less likely to own their housing, likely to live in areas where employment is difficult to find, and likely to have to contend with prematurely depreciated housing.[30] Segregation makes it unlikely that poor blacks will be able to escape poverty. For instance, 72 percent of black Americans born into the lowest economic quartile of neighborhoods reside in poor areas as adults, compared with only 40 percent of whites.[31] Furthermore, race is also the most salient predictor of intergenerational downward residential mobility, with "the odds of downward mobility 3.6 times as large as the odds for whites."[32] The big difference is in how segregation is accomplished today. In the Jim Crow era the housing industry used overtly discriminatory practices such as real estate agents employing outright refusal or subterfuge to avoid renting or selling to black customers, federal government redlining policies, overtly discriminatory insurance and lending practices, and racially restrictive covenants on housing deeds in order to maintain segregated communities. In contrast, in the post–civil rights era, covert behaviors have replaced these practices and maintained the same outcome—separate communities.

Many studies have detailed the obstacles that minorities face from government agencies, real estate agents, money lenders, and white residents that continue to limit their housing options.[33] Housing audits done in many locations reveal that blacks and Latinos are denied available housing from 35 to 75 percent of the time depending on the city in question.[34] Turner, Struyk, and Yinger, in reporting the results of the Department of Housing and Urban Development's *Housing Discrimination Study*, found that blacks and Latinos experienced discrimination in approximately *half* of their efforts to rent or buy housing. Yinger, in a separate article, reported that the average incidence of discrimination for audit studies is 47 percent. These housing studies have shown that when paired with similar white counterparts, blacks are likely to be shown fewer apartments, be quoted higher rents, or offered worse conditions, and be steered to specific neighborhoods. Using a similar procedure in a 2000 audit of housing racial practices in twenty-three U.S. metropolitan areas, Turner and colleagues report that although there was improvement since the 1989 audit, whites continued to be given more information about potential rentals and were shown more available housing units in both the rental and sales markets. The study also showed a significant increase in geographic steering that perpetuated segregation, predominantly through real estate agent editorializing.[35]

In one study of lending practices done by the Kentucky Human Rights Commission, black and white testers with equal characteristics requested conventional mortgages for the same housing from ten of the top lending

institutions in Louisville, and while there were cases in which discrimination was apparent (blacks having trouble getting appointments, etc.),
in the eighty-five visits made to inquire about loans, none of the black
testers (with one exception) knew they were being discriminated against,
though *all* of them were. Blacks were given less information, less encouragement to return and apply for the loan, fewer helpful hints as to how
to successfully obtain a loan, and differential treatment in prequalify-
ing—sometimes being told they would not qualify when whites of the
same profile were told they would. Similar studies done in Chicago and
New York revealed discrimination in seven out of ten lending institutions in Chicago and in the one institution studied in New York City.[36]
National data from the Home Mortgage Disclosure Act shows that black
applicants are denied mortgages at least twice as frequently as whites
of the same income and gender. Finally, a study by the Federal Reserve
Bank of Boston found that after controlling for a number of variables,
blacks on average are denied loans 60 percent more times than whites.[37]
In an overview of mortgage loan practices during the 1990s, Turner and
Skidmore report that blacks received less information from loan officers,
were quoted higher interest rates, and suffered higher loan denial rates.
Much of the gain in home ownership among African Americans in the
1990s was achieved through subprime lenders who offer usurious rates,
due in large part to the continued practice of redlining of black neighborhoods by mainstream lenders. It is these same subprime mortgages that
have caused the recent mortgage crisis to impact minorities more severely
than whites.[38]

The racial practices of banks did not proceed in a color-blind fashion,
as black neighborhoods were actively targeted for higher-interest loans.
For instance, Wells Fargo recently settled a lawsuit with the NAACP for
$175 million. The suit alleged that customers were steered toward higher-
interest subprime loans—called "ghetto loans" for "mud people" within
the organization. Although Wells Fargo has been a high-profile fall guy
for this racist practice, the evidence suggests that banks routinely engage
in discriminatory lending. Further, this lending is not based upon blacks
having worse economic profiles, as higher-income blacks were more
likely to be steered toward subprime loans.[39]

Education

The history of black-white education in this country is one of substantive
inequities maintained through public institutions. While today many of
the traditional barriers to black advancement have been outlawed, the situation is by no means one of equity. Although scholars have documented

the narrowing of the gap in the *quantity* of education attained by blacks and whites, little has been said about the persisting gap in the *quality* of education received.[40] Still remaining (and in some cases worsening) high levels of de facto segregation are at least partly to blame for the gap in quality. However, tracking, differential assignment to special education, and other informal school practices are important factors too.

Over 30 percent of black students attend schools that are 95 percent or more nonwhite and over 30 percent of white students attend schools that are less than 95 percent white. In the 1998–1999 school year, 36.5 percent of blacks attended schools that were at least 90 percent nonwhite and 70.2 percent of blacks attended schools that were at least 50 percent nonwhite. Despite some progress during the period immediately after 1964, the level of school segregation for black students remains relatively high in all regions and has deteriorated in the Northeast and Midwest regions. The Civil Rights Project at Harvard University reports a trend beginning in 1986 toward resegregation of U.S. schools. As a consequence of resegregation during the decade of the 1990s, U.S. schools were more segregated in the 2000–2001 school year than in 1970. The relevance of this fact is that, as Gary Orfield has noted, "Segregated schools are still profoundly unequal." Inner-city minority schools, in sharp contrast to white suburban schools, lack decent buildings, are overcrowded, have outdated equipment—if they have equipment at all—do not have enough textbooks for their students, lack library resources, are technologically behind, and pay their teaching and administrative staff less, which produces, despite exceptions, a low level of morale. According to Jonathon Kozol these "savage inequalities," have been directly related to lower reading achievement and learning attained by black students and their limited computer skills.[41]

In integrated schools, blacks still have to contend with discriminatory practices. Oakes and her coauthors have found clear evidence of discriminatory practices in tracking within schools. Whites (and Asians) are considerably (and statistically significantly) more likely to be placed in the academic track than comparably achieving African American and Latino students.[42] Another study found that of the 1985 students who took the SAT, 65.1 percent of blacks compared to 81.2 percent of whites were enrolled in an academic track. No wonder black students tend to score lower on the SAT than white students. (As of early 2013, a new book by Amanda E. Lewis and John B. Diamond titled *Despite the Best Intentions: Why Racial Inequality Thrives in Good Schools* is about to be published by Oxford documenting exactly what happens in so-called integrated schools to minority students. So check this book out when it hits the bookstores.)

Other Areas of Social Life

A brief survey of research in other areas of social life reveals persistent discrimination, unequal treatment, and, in some cases, exclusion. In terms of intermarriage, blacks are less likely than any other racial or ethnic group to intermarry. This is one of the few areas where whites still openly express reservations in surveys.[43] In 1993, only 0.4 percent of all new marriages were black-white unions.[44] Furthermore, while a recent publication from the Pew Research Center stated that "a record 14.6 percent of all new marriages in the United States were between spouses of a different race or ethnicity," only 9 percent of whites married nonwhites in 2008.[45] Not only are over 90 percent of whites marrying other whites, but also additional research shows that intermarriage rates among Latinos and Asians has actually decreased since 1980.[46] In addition to whites' negative attitudes toward interracial relationships, the high level of residential segregation and the limited friendships between blacks and whites contribute to this low rate of intermarriage. Research by Jackman and Crane showed that only 9.4 percent of whites could name one good black friend. This led them to conclude that very few whites "could rightly claim that 'some of their best friends' are black."[47]

In the realm of everyday life, several recent works have attempted to examine the daily experiences blacks have with racism. In his interviews of middle-class blacks who have supposedly "made it," Ellis Cose repeatedly discovered a sense among these "successful blacks" that they were being continually blocked and constrained in ways that make it impossible to hold anyone accountable. Black executives, lawyers, and bankers repeatedly reported a feeling of being second class, of having a constant nagging sense that they were being treated differently despite doing everything they were supposed to do. In one series of examples Cose reports experiences of job tracking in which blacks are only given those jobs that dealt with "minority concerns" and that were seen as either unimportant or undesirable. Cose quotes many of his interviewees discussing the feeling of being susceptible to being "stripped of status at a moment's notice" by a store clerk, a cab driver, the waiter at a restaurant, a security guard, and so on.[48] Feagin and McKinney point out that the chronic stress and "justified rage" resulting from these mistreatments costs African Americans psychologically, creates loss of personal energy, and affects their physical health.[49]

In 1981 Howard Schuman and his coauthors replicated a 1950 study of restaurants in New York's Upper East Side and found a substantial amount of discrimination remained. Similar to the housing audits, the discrimination was of a subtle nature. Black patrons were refused use of the coatroom, they were seated in either isolated places or undesirable locations like near the kitchen, orders were reversed, and service workers were flustered by a black presence. A recent review of the literature on discrimination in the service industry shows that these practices continue. People of color are referred to using code words such as "Canadian," "cousins," "moolies," "black tops," and even "white people" to signal among servers that they are undesirable patrons. The problem doesn't end at nasty names, however, with servers unwilling to serve black patrons, extended waiting periods when tables are open, and instructions from managers to treat blacks poorly.[50] Importantly, much of the evidence of this type of behavior comes from reports from waiters, and people of color subjected to these racial practices are left to wonder if this behavior is indeed race-based. Lawrence Otis Graham reports in his book *Member of the Club* that in ten of New York's best restaurants he and his friends visited, they were stared at, mistaken for restaurant workers, seated in terrible spots, and buffered so as to avoid proximity to whites in most of them. Actually, Otis Graham reports that they were treated reasonably well in only two of the ten restaurants, one Russian and the other French. The suits recently filed against Denny's, Shoney's, and the International House of Pancakes seem to suggest that restaurants' racial practices discriminate against blacks of all class backgrounds.[51]

Joe R. Feagin and Melvin P. Sikes also document the dense network of discriminatory practices confronted by middle-class blacks in everyday life. Although they correctly point out that blacks face discriminatory practices that range from overt and violent to covert and gentle, the latter seem to be prevalent. In public spaces the discriminatory behavior described by black interviewees included poor service, special requirements applied only to them, surveillance in stores, being ignored at retail stores selling expensive commodities, receiving the worst accommodations in restaurants or hotels, being confused constantly with menial workers, along with the usual but seemingly less frequent epithets and overtly racist behavior.

More recently, a body of work on racial "microaggressions" chronicles how minorities can be subtly put down in many cross-race interactions. These may be a proto-typical example of the way the new racism operates, as microaggressions can be crimes of omission (i.e., an environment only displays symbols such as photos or reading material relevant to the dominant white culture) or of commission, as when one implies that a minority is unqualified for a job or admission to school, and is only present because of affirmative action. Importantly, the content of these messages is almost always devoid of overt racial appeals, allowing the perpetrator to maintain that they are neutral. This makes it very difficult for people of color to respond to this type of aggression. These microaggressions can have a serious affect on the lives of people of color, as this kind of hostility has been tied to a number of negative health outcomes.[52]

The Continuing Racial Economic Inequality

The economic life of blacks has always been influenced by structured racial inequality. A substantial body of literature on white-black employment differences has documented the influence of labor-market discrimination, wage differentials, occupational segmentation, as well as income and wealth inequalities and explaining racially differential economic outcomes.[53] Despite well-documented disparities between blacks and whites, many social scientists focused their attention on the growth of the black middle class. Some of them projected the "success" of this segment to the entire community, creating an image of general economic progress. To be sure, blacks have experienced significant progress in several areas of their economic life over the past four decades (the economic standing of black women vis-à-vis white women, the opening of jobs that were reserved for whites, the development of the significant middle class, etc.). Yet their overall economic situation relative to whites has not advanced much.[54]

THE POLITICAL STRUCTURE OF THE NEW RACIAL ORDER

Almost all commentators on black politics recognize that blacks became serious participants in "legitimate" politics very recently.[55] But since 1965, as blacks were able to register and vote, their representation in local and national political structures has increased dramatically. The data on this point is fairly clear. Whereas in 1970 there were only 1,460 black elected officials at all levels of the U.S. political system, by 1989 the total had increased to 7,226, and in the early 1990s their number reached 8,000.[56] Moreover, by 1990 "blacks held elective positions in every state except Idaho, Montana, and North Dakota."[57] In Congress there has been an increase in the number of African American elected officials from ten, or 1.9 percent of the members of Congress in 1970, to twenty-six, or 5.8 percent of the total in 1991. The 113th Congress has been hailed as the most diverse in history. However, the Senate has a total of five people of color, leaving the senate an overwhelmingly white body, with white men being 68 percent of the total in the house.[58] Furthermore, a point that I make below, among the people of color in Congress, several are antiminority minorities such as Florida's Marco Rubio and South Carolina's Tim Scott. As is the case with conservatives such as Supreme Court justice Clarence Thomas, these politicians are out of touch with the views, goals, and aspirations of most people of color.

Overall, the changes in this area give the impression of substantial progress and the beginning of a truly pluralist America.[59] The new political space that blacks have gained has without question provided them with some benefits. Today blacks have some direct—although small—influence in policies, have sensitized white politicians about the needs of blacks not only through their policy suggestions but also simply by their presence, and have established a direct link between government and citizenship. In terms of the cities where blacks have been elected as mayors, some commentators have pointed out that "African American–owned businesses expand, the rate of small business failure declines, and there are significant increases in both the number and proportions of African Americans employed in city government."[60] But despite these accomplishments, blacks remain a subordinate group in the political system. What follows is a discussion of the current limitations that blacks face in the political system.

good yes but still not truly good

Structural Barriers to the Election of Black Politicians

Racial gerrymandering, multimember legislative districts, election run-offs, annexation of predominantly white areas, at-large district elections, and anti-single-shot devices (disallowing concentrating votes in one or two candidates in cities using at-large elections) have become standard practices to disenfranchise blacks since 1965. All of these tactics attempt to either minimize the number of majority-black election districts or neutralize their electoral impact by diluting the black vote.[61] Except for gerrymandering (drawing districts so that minority coalitions waste their votes), the mechanisms have the facade of expanding democracy and being race-neutral. For instance, at-large districts were initially developed to weaken political machines by diluting the ethnic vote, but in recent times have become a way of diluting the black vote in cities.[62] All these procedures are effective because black representation is still dependent upon the existence of black districts. In the 2000 elections, unfair voting practices that turned away many black voters were reported in over a dozen U.S. states and similar voting irregularities in the 2004 elections disenfranchised voters in predominantly black communities. Similarly, in the 2012 elections right-wing groups attacked the voting rights of blacks through voter ID laws in a number of states. Since 2003, thirty-four states have implemented voter ID laws[63] that are similar to the poll taxes and literacy requirements under Jim Crow. Although it is claimed these laws are race-neutral, research from the University of Delaware showed that racial animus was the best predictor of support for the law, regardless of political party. Some of the legislatures, such as those in Florida and Pennsylvania, implemented these laws despite openly claiming that voter fraud was not a problem, but they hoped that their implementation would suppress black turnout, giving the election to Romney.[64]

Furthermore, the very structure of Congress and the rules of the game impose limits on what blacks can accomplish there even in the best of all possible scenarios. As John C. Berg has argued,

> Congress has an internal structure, and positions in this structure give an advantage to those who hold them, but this advantage is biased; it is not equally available to the powerless and the powerful. Throughout America's brief history, when representatives of oppressed groups have used the accommodationist strategy, that strategy has failed. They have climbed patiently up the ladder of congressional seniority and committee position, only to find that they could not use their new power to effect the changes most needed by their constituents.[65]

Underrepresentation among Elected and Appointed Officials

The best proof that there are still structural barriers to the election of blacks is the fact that despite their burgeoning rate of voter registration and participation since 1965, *black officials still represent 1 to 2 percent of all elected officials.*[66] Even more significant, blacks are substantially underrepresented even in places where they comprise 30 percent or more of the entire population.[67] The majority of cities with a population of fifty thousand or greater with black mayors in 2004 had more than a 40 percent black population.[68] Only three of the twelve largest cities with a 25 percent or more black population have black mayors. New York, Los Angeles, Chicago, Houston, and Dallas, which had black mayors in the 1990s, no longer do. Black appointees tend to be concentrated in the civil rights and social welfare bureaucracies and, in many of the remaining cases, are "sanitized" blacks like Justice Thomas or General Colin Powell.

Why are blacks so underrepresented? Because of the historical tendency of whites of only voting for or appointing white candidates. Thus the election and appointment of blacks seem to be circumscribed to locales in which blacks constitute a substantial segment of the population (40 percent or more) or to black candidates who "mainstream" or show "moderation."[69]

Although many whites would argue that this trend has ended with President Obama, the evidence suggests that Obama's ascendency to the presidency is in line with the historical trajectory of black politicians. See chapter 10 for an extended discussion of the Obama phenomenon.

The Limited Possibilities of Elected and Appointed Officials

What is the overall impact of black elected officials and appointees for the black community at large? In Congress, because of their relatively small numbers, blacks have a very limited role in creating policy. At best, they can shape aspects of legislation to soften the impact on poor minority communities and, so far, they have been able to curtail anti–civil rights legislation. The record of black appointees, who have been historically few, suggests that they tend to have an even more limited role in shaping policy. In addition, there is a disturbing trend of appointing antiblack blacks (a trend begun by President Carter), which fits well into our new racism argument.[70] By appointing conservative blacks to certain positions, the political system is *symbolically* integrated while maintaining policies and politics that keep blacks "in their place." WOWZA

The Limited Impact of Elected Black Mayors

Elected black mayors are in a political quandary because of the decline of political machines. This decline reduces significantly the "power" of the mayoral position since political machines allowed mayors in the past to dispense resources to their constituencies. Given that these political machines have been replaced by nonpartisan bureaucratic political structures, the likelihood of a black mayor being able to use his or her position for distributing resources has been seriously eroded.[71] Moreover, the financial crisis of cities limits drastically the projects that mayors can carry out as well as their overall independence from the dominant. Furthermore, since cities are controlled by the interests of white business elites, elected black mayors are increasingly captive to pro-growth policies based on making cities conducive to business investments. These policies usually imply neglecting the most pressing needs of racial minorities and the poor.[72] Moreover, despite the progressive impact that many have noted in the black community (appointment of blacks to various city positions, increase in the rate of black municipal employees, higher responsiveness to the needs of the poor, etc.), most of the benefits have not accrued to the black masses. More importantly, the election of black mayors, unlike those from white ethnic groups in the past, has not led to the institutionalization of "black control in the realms of public and private decision making."[73] Thus black mayors become "political managers" of cities in which the present economic, social, and political arrangements still benefit whites at large, and the elite in particular.

Electoral Participation as Entrapment

The subordinate incorporation of blacks into electoral politics has reduced their options to effect meaningful social change. Historically, blacks have advanced in this country through overt protest politics.[74] Hence the extension of universal suffrage to blacks has been a double-edged sword. On the one hand, it is one of the most enduring victories of the civil rights movement but on the other hand, it is progressively becoming an obstacle for further black progress. Because the number of blacks in significant decision-making bodies (House, Senate, etc.) is minuscule, because whites still vote largely for white candidates, and because blacks do not have enough economic and social resources to utilize formal political rights as effectively as whites, electoral politics are *restricting* the political options of blacks in the United States.

An example of how electoral politics restrict the options of blacks is the current political impasse experienced by blacks. They cannot vote Republican since that party has become increasingly a pro-white party; they cannot fully trust the Democratic party since it has shown in recent times a tremendous degree of ambivalence in its commitment to blacks as evidenced in the racialized discourse of many leaders on welfare, crime, government spending, and affirmative action; and the third-party option, advocated by many progressives, is still a farfetched idea with a very limited impact among black urban voters. The way out of this impasse seems to be through a return to mass protest but it is precisely that type of political activity that is incompatible with electoral politics. Hence what blacks need is what electoral participation limits.

Obama's election is perhaps the best illustration of this point. Since his election, many black politicians have complained that he has done little to further their legislative agenda. For instance, Maxine Waters, former chairperson of the Congressional Black Caucus, criticized Obama for ignoring the needs of black communities. These claims are backed up by empirical research, as the political scientist Daniel Gillian shows Obama has spoken less about race issues than any president since 1961.[75] Furthermore, it is clear that Obama's ability to address racial issues head on has been hugely constrained by the trap of electoral politics. The huge public outcries after his extremely mild comments on Henry Louis Gates's improper arrest and Trayvon Martin's murder show how quickly the media and public opinion turn against Obama for appearing concerned about racial profiling. (For a full discussion of Obama's place in the new racism order, see chapter 10.)

[handwritten margin note: Want black but not actually black]

"KEEPING THEM IN THEIR PLACE": THE SOCIAL CONTROL OF BLACKS SINCE THE 1960s

All domination is ultimately maintained through social-control strategies. For example, during slavery, whites used the whip, overseers, night patrols, and other highly repressive practices along with a number of paternalistic ones to keep blacks in their place. After slavery was abolished, whites felt threatened by free blacks; hence, very strict written and unwritten rules of racial contact (the Jim Crow laws) were developed to specify "the place" of blacks in the new environment of "freedom." And, as insurance, lynching and other terroristic forms of social control were used to guarantee white supremacy. In contrast, as the Jim Crow practices have subsided, the control of blacks has been chiefly attained through state agencies (police, criminal court system, FBI). Marable describes the new system of control as follows:

> The informal, vigilante-inspired techniques to suppress Blacks were no longer practical. Therefore, beginning with the Great Depression, and especially after 1945, white racists began to rely almost exclusively on the state apparatus to carry out the battle for white supremacy. Blacks charged with crimes would receive longer sentences than whites convicted of similar crimes. The police forces of municipal and metropolitan areas received a *carte blanche* in their daily acts of brutality against Blacks. The Federal and state government carefully monitored Blacks who advocated any kind of social change. Most important, capital punishment was used as a weapon against Blacks charged and convicted of major crimes. The criminal justice system, in short, became a modern instrument to perpetuate white hegemony. Extra-legal lynchings were replaced by "legal lynchings" and capital punishment.[76]

In the following sections of this chapter, I review the available data to see how well it fits Marable's interpretation of the contemporary system of control.

The State as Enforcer of Racial Order

The United States has the highest per capita incarcerated population in the world.[77] The incarceration rate has risen 600 percent in the past thirty years,[78] and race influences nearly every aspect of incarceration including arrest rates, conviction rates, the probability of post-incarceration employment, educational opportunities, and marriage outcomes. One in three black males born today can expect to spend some portion of his life behind bars, and Latinos have seen a 43 percent rise in their incarceration rates since 1990.[79] Data on arrest rates shows that the contrast between black and white arrest rates since 1950 has been striking. The black arrest rate increased throughout this period, reaching almost one hundred per one thousand by 1978 compared to thirty-five per one thousand for whites.[80] The 1989 data suggests that the arrest rate for blacks has stabilized at around eighty to ninety per one thousand.[81] The implications for the black community are astounding. Eight to nine percent of all blacks are arrested every year. This means that a substantial number of black families experience the "services" of the criminal justice system every year, directly (arrested or incarcerated) as well as indirectly (visit to jails, stops by police, etc.).

In terms of how many blacks are incarcerated, we find a pattern similar to their arrest rates. Although blacks have always been overrepresented in the inmate population, as can be seen in table 2.2, this overrepresentation has skyrocketed since 1960. By 1980, the incarceration rate of blacks was six times that of whites.

The statistics for black youth are even more depressing. Black youth aged ten to seventeen, who constitute 15 percent of American youth, account for 25 percent of arrests (Bishop 2005). Race differences exist at almost every stage of the juvenile justice process: black youth suffer racial profiling by police, higher rates of arrest, detention, and court referral, are charged with more serious offenses, and are more likely to be placed in larger public correctional facilities in contrast to small private group homes, foster homes, and drug and alcohol treatment centers.[82] "Almost one in four Black men aged 20 to 30 are under the supervision of the criminal justice system any given day."[83] The rate of incarceration of blacks for criminal offenses is over eight times greater than that of whites, with

Table 2.2. Percentage of U.S. Residents and Men in Prison or Jail, by Age, Race, and Education, 1980, 2000

All U.S. Residents, Men Aged 18–65	1980	2000
All U.S. Residents	0.2%	0.7%
Men Aged 18–65		
All	0.7	2.1
White	0.4	1.0
Hispanic	1.6	3.3
Black	3.0	7.9
Men Aged 20–40		
White	0.6	1.6
Hispanic	2.1	4.6
Black	4.8	11.5
Non-college Men Aged 20–40		
White	0.9	3.2
Hispanic	2.6	5.5
Black	6.0	17.0
High-School-Dropout Men Aged 20–40		
White	2.1	6.7
Hispanic	3.2	6.0
Black	10.7	32.4

Source: Bruce Western, "The Prison Boom and the Decline of American Citizenship," *Society* 44, no. 5 (2007): 30–36.

1 in 20 black men, in contrast to 1 in 180 white men, in prison.[84] Hence, given these statistics, it is not surprising that today there are more blacks aged twenty to twenty-nine under the supervision of the criminal justice system (incarcerated, on parole, or on probation) than in college.

This dramatic increase in black incarceration has been attributed to legislative changes in the penal codes and the "get tough" attitude in law enforcement fueled by white fear of black crime. Furthermore, the fact that blacks are disproportionately convicted and receive longer sentences than whites for similar crimes contributes to their overrepresentation among the penal population. For example, "according to the Federal Judicial Center, in 1990 the average sentences for blacks on weapons and drug charges were 49 percent longer than those for whites who had committed and been convicted of the same crimes—and that disparity has been rising over time."[85] Self-report data suggest about 14 percent of U.S. illegal drug users are black; however, blacks constitute 35 percent of those arrested, 55 percent of those convicted, and 74 percent of those incarcerated for drug possession.[86]

Official State Brutality against Blacks

Police departments grew exponentially after the 1960s, particularly in large metropolitan areas with large concentrations of blacks.[87] This growth has been related by various studies to black urban mobilization and rebellion in the 1960s.[88] Another way of measuring the impact of police departments on the life of blacks is surveying how blacks and whites rate police performance. Rosentraub and Harlow, in an article reviewing surveys on the attitudes of blacks and whites toward the police from 1960 through 1981, found that blacks consistently view the police in a much more negative light than do whites. Despite attempts in the 1970s and 1980s to reduce the friction between black communities and police departments by hiring more black police officers and, in some cases, even hiring black chiefs of police, "there has been little change in the attitudes of blacks toward the police, especially when the attitudes of black respondents are compared to those of white respondents." Blacks are also more inclined to believe that police misconduct occurs frequently and is common in their city and neighborhood.[89]

The level of police force used with blacks has always been excessive. However, since the police have become the more direct enforcer of the social control of blacks since the 1960s, their level of violence against blacks has skyrocketed. For example, in 1975 *46 percent of all the people killed by the police in official action were black.*[90] That situation has not changed much since. Robert Smith reported recently that of the people killed by the police, over half are black; the police usually claim that when they killed blacks it was "accidental" because they thought that the victim was armed although in fact the victims were unarmed in 75 percent of the cases; there was an increase in the 1980s in the use of deadly force by the police and the only ameliorating factor was the election of a sensitive mayor in a city; and in the aftermath of the King verdict, 87 percent of civilian victims of police brutality reported in the newspapers of fifteen American major cities were black, and 93 percent of the officers involved were white. Even the Rodney King incident, probably the most celebrated and visible case of police brutality in recent times, may hide the real extent of police brutality in America. While Americans became exhausted from watching the TV image of Rodney King being beaten by police officers, they did not know that during the 1980s, "18 citizens of Los Angeles died as a result of LAPD's use of the choke hold; 16 of them reportedly black," indicating that police brutality in Los Angeles was a common practice.[91]

More recently, on January 1, 2009, Bay Area Rapid Transit District police officers shot and killed Oscar Grant III. At the time of the shooting several videos show Mr. Grant was unarmed, lying face down, with an officer kneeling on his back. Mr. Grant was hardly in a position to struggle. Another officer who was on the scene has admitted under oath that Grant posed no threat to himself or "any other officer." Yet, this did not stop officer Mehserle from firing, point blank, into Grant's back. The bullet then ripped through Grant's body, ricocheted, and traveled back into him, lodging in his lung. Rather than seeking immediate medical care for Mr. Grant, they handcuffed him as he lay dying. Then the officers began grabbing cell-phones and video cameras from other travelers in the station, in an unfruitful attempt to destroy evidence of the crime.[92] This story did not immediately become national news. Rather, after videos of the attack appeared on YouTube, bloggers publicized the issue and local papers began to take notice. The police department was not terribly worried about the attack because they did not take the offending officer into custody until thirteen days later.[93] Officer Mehserle was convicted of involuntary manslaughter, but served just eleven months in prison.[94] To put it mildly, this is an extremely lenient sentence for a brazen, videotaped assassination.

A more mundane form of police brutality in the form of "stop and frisk" laws in New York city daily terrorize young people of color. Ostensibly aimed at finding weapons and drugs, nearly 90 percent of the stops are black and brown youth. This is despite the fact that, according to antiracist activist Tim Wise,[95] who is white,

> White high school students are seven times more likely than blacks to have used cocaine; eight times more likely to have smoked crack; ten times more likely to have used LSD and seven times more likely to have used heroin. . . . What's more, white youth ages 12-17 are more likely to sell drugs: 34 percent

more likely, in fact than their black counterparts. And it is white youth who are twice as likely to binge drink, and nearly twice as likely as blacks to drive drunk. And white males are twice as likely to bring a weapon to school as are black males.

The state-sanctioned abuse of blacks under the cover of enforcing drug laws is clearly not aimed at stopping drug distribution. Rather, it is a manifestation of how supposedly race-neutral laws can be applied at the discretion of officers and departments to control the black population.

Since the late 1990s, a new form of state-sanctioned social control has been written into law in numerous states. Promoted by the right-wing American Legislative Exchange Council, these so-called stand your ground or castle doctrine laws institutionalize racist vigilantism. Made famous through the tragic murder of Trayvon Martin, a seventeen-year-old black kid walking to his home, these laws are applied in a racist manner. Twenty states have adopted these laws since 2000 and murder rates in these states, counter to the expectations of advocates for these laws, have increased by 8 percent.[96] And, as one would expect in a racialized society, these laws have not been applied in a racially neutral manner:

> Whites who kill blacks in Stand Your Ground states are far more likely to be found justified in their killings. In non–Stand Your Ground states, whites are 250 percent more likely to be found justified in killing a black person than a white person who kills another white person; in Stand Your Ground states, that number jumps to 354 percent.[97]

Capital Punishment as a Modern Form of Lynching

The raw statistics on capital punishment seem to indicate racial bias *prima facie*: Of 3,984 people lawfully executed since 1930 (until 1980), 2,113 were black, over half of the total, almost five times the proportion of blacks in the population as a whole.[98] Blacks, who have made up about 13 percent of the population, have accounted for 52 percent of people executed in state or federal jurisdictions since 1930.[99] However, social scientific research on racial sentencing has produced mixed results. A number of authors have found a bias in sentencing,[100] but some have claimed that, as legal factors are taken into account, the bias disappears.[101] Yet recent research has suggested that "discrimination has not declined or disappeared but simply has become more subtle and difficult to detect."[102] Despite claims that discrimination has declined in significance, research shows that it may have simply gone underground. Others have pointed out that the discrimination experienced by blacks may occur at earlier stages. For instance, research by Radelet and Pierce suggests that homicides with white victims and black suspects are more likely to be upgraded to a more aggravated description by prosecutors. Hence, additive and linear models will tend to miss the effect of race.[103]

There is a substantial body of research showing that blacks charged of murdering whites are more likely to be sentenced to death than any other victim-offender dyad. Similarly, blacks charged of raping white women also receive the death sentence at a much higher rate. The two tendencies were confirmed by Spohn in a 1994 article using data for Detroit in 1977 and 1978: "Blacks who sexually assaulted whites faced a greater risk of incarceration than either blacks or whites who sexually assaulted blacks or whites who sexually assaulted whites; similarly, blacks who murdered whites received longer sentences than did offenders in the other two categories."[104] Data from 1976 to 1981, after the *Furman* statues were implemented, for the states of Arkansas, Florida, Georgia, Illinois, Mississippi, North Carolina, Oklahoma, and Virginia on people charged with homicide indicates that cases involving white victims are more likely to warrant the death penalty than cases involving black victims. Although the authors find a black suspect–white victim effect in Florida, Georgia, and Illinois, they claim that it disappears when they control for severity of the crime.[105] However, the most respected study on this matter carried out by Professor David C. Baldus to support the claim of Warren McClesky, a black man convicted of murdering a white police officer in 1978, found that there was a huge disparity in the imposition of the death penalty in Georgia.[106] The study found that in cases involving white victims and black defendants the death penalty was imposed 22 percent of the time, whereas in the white-black dyad, the death penalty was imposed in only 1 percent of the cases. *Even after controlling for a number of variables, blacks were 4.3 times as likely as whites to receive a death sentence.*[107] In a 1990 review of twenty-eight studies on death-penalty sentencing, twenty-three of them found that the fact that victims are white "influences the likelihood that the defendant will be charged with a capital crime or that death penalty will be imposed."

It should not surprise anyone that in a racist society, court decisions on cases involving the death penalty exhibit a race effect. Research on juries suggests that they tend to be older, more affluent, more educated, more conviction-prone, and more white than the average in the community.[108] Moreover, research on the process of selecting jurors for death-penalty cases suggests that the *voir dire* process (questions to select the jury) produces juries that are pro–death penalty.[109] This particular bias has been found to have a racial effect. Gregory D. Russell, in his *The Death Penalty and Racial Bias: Overturning Supreme Court Assumptions*, found indirect data (exhibited via surrogate measures) of racial bias among death-qualified jurors. This finding adds to our understanding of why there is a differential conviction rate for blacks and whites in cases involving the death penalty. As Russell explains,

> The evidence developed did suggest that juries composed of death-qualified jurors are more likely to be white, punitive, and authoritarian. Hence, they are more likely, on this evidence, to exhibit a tendency toward racially biased decisions. Will every juror or jury act in this manner? Of course not. The evidence simply suggests the probability that jurors so composed are more likely than not to be more predisposed to racially biased determinations than other juries, though the appearance of racial bias is quite idiosyncratic.[110]

The racial trends observed by research on the application of the death penalty will not abate any time soon. The 1986 Supreme Court decision *McClesky v. Kemp*, for example, stipulated that statistical evidence showing racial discrimination was not enough and argued further that evidence of discrimination would be valid only if the plaintiff could prove that a state "enacted or maintained the death penalty statute *because* of an anticipated racially discriminatory effect."[111] Given the new contours of the racial order, laws will not be written in ways to overtly discriminate against minorities. In this legal desert created by the Supreme Court, unless Congress enacts a law allowing statistical evidence as proof of discrimination, minorities sentenced to death will have no legal recourse of claiming discrimination. The first attempt to enact such a law (the Racial Justice Act in 1988) failed miserably in Congress. The second attempt during the 1993 discussion of Clinton's crime bill failed also. Meanwhile, the number of incarcerated blacks on death row has reached the 40 percent range.[112]

High Propensity to Arrest Blacks

Blacks complain that police officers mistreat them, disrespect them, assume that they are criminals, violate their rights on a consistent basis, and are more violent when dealing with them. Blacks and other minorities are stopped and frisked by police in "alarmingly disproportionate numbers."[113] Why is it that minorities receive "special treatment" from the police? Studies on police attitudes and on their socialization suggest that police officers live in a "cops' world" and develop a cop mentality. And that cops' world is a highly racialized one; minorities are viewed as dangerous, prone to crime, violent, and disrespectful.[114] Various studies have noted that the racist attitudes that police officers exhibit has an impact on their behavior toward minorities. Furthermore, other studies have suggested that police discretion and demographic bias contribute to the over-arrest of blacks. Extralegal subjective characteristics such as demeanor, appearance, and race have been found to influence the decision of police officers to arrest individuals as well as other stages in the individual's path through the criminal justice system.[115] In terms of demographic bias, research suggests that because black communities are overpatrolled, the officers patrolling these areas develop a stereotypical view of their residents as more likely to commit criminal acts and are more likely to "see" criminal behavior than in white communities.[116]

Thus, it is not surprising that blacks are disproportionally arrested compared to whites. It is possible to gauge the level of over-arrest endured by blacks by comparing the proportion of times that they are described by victims as the attackers with their arrest rates. Using this procedure, Farai Chideya contended that

> for virtually every type of crime, African-American criminals are arrested at rates above their commission of the acts. For example, victimization reports indicated that 33 percent of women who were raped said that their attacker was black; however, black rape suspects made up fully 43 percent of those arrested. The disproportionate arrest rate adds to the public perception that rape is a "black" crime.[117]

Using these numbers, the rate of over-arrest for blacks in cases of rape is 30 percent. As shocking as this seems to be, the rate for cases where the victim is white is even higher. Smith, Visher, and Davidson found that whereas the probability of arrest for cases in which the victim was white and the suspect black was 0.336, for cases of white suspects and black victims the probability dropped to 0.107. Blacks represent 65 percent of those exonerated for rape and half of the exonerations of men convicted of raping white women, even though less than 10 percent of rapes of white women are by black men.[118]

The enormous amount of anecdotal evidence on blacks detained, harassed, or illegally searched for looking "suspicious" is indicative of the racial consciousness and practices of white police officers. The following incidents are just a sample of recent cases of clearly racist policing:

1. In Florida in 1993, after a British tourist was killed, police officers rounded up black men aged fifteen to twenty-one in Jefferson County.
2. In 1992, all black men at the State University of New York Oneonta College were questioned as suspects after a white man was murdered by a black man.
3. Black professors at predominantly white institutions report incidents of police harassment and even being detained.[119] At the University of Michigan, Professor Aldon Morris was detained by the police because he was "confused" with a bank robber. He was not released

until white professors verified that he was indeed a professor, although he had shown the police officers his university identification.

4. In 1990 at Harvard, two black students running for a shuttle bus were detained after the description of a robbery went out over the police radio.

5. In 1994, the police department of Ann Arbor, Michigan, released a description of a serial rapist that fit a substantial proportion of the local black population. They later asked over one hundred black men to "collaborate" with the investigation by giving blood samples to see if they fit the DNA profile of the rapist.

6. Over four years, a New Jersey man driving from his home to his office was stopped by police over one hundred times.[120]

7. The Cambridge police department arrested Dr. Henry Louis Gates Jr., one of the most high-profile African American scholars in the county and director of Harvard's African American Studies Program, in his own home when he had committed no crime. A neighbor had called the police on him as he was outside his house because he had forgotten his keys.

Repression of Black Leaders and the Civil Rights Movement

Leaders of the black movement such as Elijah Muhammad, Malcolm X, Stokely Carmichael, Louis Farrakhan, Huey P. Newton, Bobby Seale, Ron Karenga, and Martin Luther King Jr. and organizations such as the Student Nonviolent Coordinating Committee (SNCC), the National Association for the Advancement of Colored People, Southern Christian Leadership Conference (SCLC), the Black Panthers, the Revolutionary Action Movement, and the MOVE Organization have been monitored by the FBI. Of particular significance was the six-year investigation (from 1962 to 1968) launched by the FBI against Martin Luther King Jr. given that King, unlike other black leaders of his time, was not advocating change through radical means. As David Garrow points out, "It is quite apparent that no other black leader came in for the intensive and hostile attention that Dr. King was subjected to in the mid-1960s."[121] Although initially the FBI claimed that the surveillance of King and the SCLC was because communists were involved in the organization—in this sense, it fitted the FBI organizational prerogatives—it soon delved into purely private matters of King's life with the explicit intent of discrediting him. Although many theories have been advanced for why King was singled out (J. Edgar Hoover's racism, racism in the bureau, Hoover's reaction to King's public criticism of the bureau in 1961, the conservatism of the bureau, and Hoover's as well as other top FBI agents' fascination with sexuality), the bottom line was that King, the most important black leader of this century, was carefully monitored by the FBI until his assassination.

The FBI persecution of leaders such as Elijah Muhammad and Malcolm X and their organization, the Nation of Islam, was less hostile and consistent than that of King and the SCLC because they were not mobilizing the black masses as King was. Only after Malcolm began making overtures to civil rights leaders and advocating militant political involvement did the FBI begin paying serious attention to him. After Malcolm's assassination in 1965—an assassination in which the FBI was apparently involved—the FBI launched a special offensive (the COINTELPRO against so-called black nationalist hate groups) to curb the spread of black nationalism by any means necessary.[122] By 1967, the FBI had over three thousand informants in black communities as part of this program and was conducting surveillance and playing "dirty tricks" on SNCC leader Stokely Carmichael and on the Black Panthers.[123] The FBI, through a smear campaign and other techniques, neutralized Stokely Carmichael, H. Rap Brown, Reverend Charles Koen of the Cairo United Front, and activist-comedian Dick Gregory.[124] Even seemingly less threatening groups such as black student unions on campuses around the nation were infiltrated by the FBI. By the time the COINTELPRO became known to the American people in 1971, radical black organizations had been all but dismantled.

Another area that indicates how social-control agents deal with the more politically dangerous threats posed by the black community is their handling of so-called riots. Balbus points out in his analysis of the 1960s rebellions in Los Angeles, Detroit, and Chicago that "justice" was carried out very swiftly because the "rioters" were black.

> Given that blacks are considered by many, including court authorities, to be "animals," and that their violent behavior was viewed by many as confirmation of their animality, flagrant violations of formal rationality were far less delegitimating than they would have been had they been committed against whites. It is simply the case—and no survey data are necessary to demonstrate this thesis—that Americans are far more likely to tolerate the incarceration of blacks for prolonged periods of time under inhuman conditions than they would be to tolerate similar indignities visited on whites.[125]

The number of people arrested in these rebellions is astounding. For instance, during the 1965 Watts riot in Los Angeles, four thousand people were arrested; during the Detroit riot of 1967, 7,200 people were arrested; during the Chicago riot of 1968 over 2,700 people were arrested; finally, in the 1992 L.A. rebellion, a staggering 9,456 people were arrested. This was due to a strategy of wholesale arrests, multiple charging, and extraordinarily high bonds developed with the intent of swiftly "controlling" riots. In the mid-1960s President Johnson authorized the FBI to expand its domestic intelligence, which "led to the designation of countless people as subversive or radicals in the FBI files." In addition, Congress passed the Riot Control Act in 1968, which provided that persons who traveled or used facilities of interstate commerce with the intent to incite a riot could be fined ten thousand dollars or incarcerated for five years, or both.[126]

Post–Civil Rights Social Control and the New Racism

The mechanisms by which blacks experience social control in the contemporary period are not overwhelmingly covert. Yet they share with the previous mechanisms discussed in this paper their invisibility. The mechanisms to keep blacks in "their place" are rendered invisible in three ways. First, because the enforcement of the racial order from the 1960s onward has been institutionalized, individual whites can express a detachment from the *racialized* way in which social control agencies operate in America. Second, because these agencies are *legally* charged with defending *order* in society, their actions are deemed neutral and necessary. Thus, it is no surprise that whites consistently support the police in surveys.[127] Finally, the white-dominated media depicts incidents that seem to indicate that racial bias is endemic to the criminal justice system as isolated. For example, cases that presumably expose the racial character of social-control agencies (e.g., the police beating of Rodney King, the police killing of Green, the acquittal or lenient sentences received by officers accused of police brutality, etc.) are viewed as "isolated" incidents and are separated from the larger social context in which they transpire. Ultimately, the emergence of the new racism does not mean that racial violence has disappeared as an enforcer of the racial order. Rather, these incidents are portrayed as nonracial applications of the law.

THE CONTINUING RACIAL ECONOMIC INEQUALITY

The economic life of African Americans has always been influenced by structured racial inequality. A substantial body of literature on white-black employment differences has documented the influence of labor market discrimination, wage differentials, occupational segmentation, as well as income and wealth inequalities in explaining racially differential economic outcomes.[128] Despite the well-documented disparities between blacks and whites, many social scientists have focused their attention on the growth of the black middle class.[129] Some of them have projected the "success" of this segment to the entire community, creating an image of general economic progress. To be sure, African Americans have experienced significant progress in several areas of their economic life over the past three decades (the economic standing of black women vis-à-vis white women, the opening of jobs that were reserved for whites, the development of a significant middle class, etc.). Yet their overall situation relative to whites has not advanced that much.[130] The following sections of this chapter highlight the economic status of blacks and the mechanisms that structure economic inequality at the economic level in the post–civil rights period.

Income and Wage Differentials

Studies analyzing differences in median income between blacks and whites have revealed some convergence; much of it has been attributed to the rising levels of educational attainment of African Americans, in particular among younger cohorts as well as affirmative action policies.[131] However, the empirical evidence regarding racial convergence in income is somewhat mixed. Several social scientists have found that the incomes of African Americans began rapid convergence with whites from World War II; but during the recession of the early 1970s, African Americans' income levels began to stagnate and the racial convergence ceased. By the 1990 a substantial black-white earnings gap had reemerged as the black-white family income ratio reached 0.56, a ratio hardly larger than the 0.55 of 1960. In 2003, the median black family income had only marginally improved to 61 percent of white median family income. Interestingly, the decline in blacks' income vis-à-vis whites has been attributed to the decline in enforcement of antidiscrimination laws and affirmative action policies by the federal government. Thus, while blacks made marked advancement from World War II to the early 1970s, their income relative to whites has progressed little over the last several decades.

Furthermore, analysts who focus on income convergence tend to mask serious trends affecting the African American population—like unemployment and underemployment and the decrease in the rate of labor-force participation—by making their comparisons based on full-time workers. Darity and Myers astutely observe that the exclusion of African Americans with zero incomes (i.e., the unemployed and the jobless) in social scientists' assessment of income differences between African Americans and whites masks the persistent racial fault line in economic life.[132] The gap in unemployment between African Americans and whites increased during the 1970s and the 1980s—the same period in which African Americans' incomes ceased converging with whites.[133] Even though the racial gap in employment decreased during the economic prosperity of the 1990s, the employment-to-population ratio for black men was 86 percent that of white men and black men were employed seven hours less per week than whites by 1999. Moreover, employment rates of blacks were much lower in some geographical areas. In 2003, only 52 percent of work-age black men in New York City were employed, "the lowest percent since the Bureau of Labor Statistics begin recording employment to population ratios in 1979."[134]

Income differences reflect to a large extent the different earning potential of blacks and whites in America. Black males in 1999 earned about 60 percent as much as white males; black females, who had per capita incomes 90 percent of white females in 1990, saw their incomes drop to 85 percent of white female income in 1999. This vast difference is attributed to blacks' lesser educational attainment, lesser rates of return for their education and their labor-market experience, and their concentration in the South, all directly related to the racial dynamics of this country.[135] Does the difference in earnings disappear when the comparison is blacks and whites with similar characteristics? The answer is no. Farley and Allen carried out such a comparison for 1980 and found the gap for black men to be 14 percent. Although this gap, known in the literature as the cost of being black, was better than the 19 percent gap of 1960s, the fact that the gap grew to 16 percent in 1985 does not give much hope. Thus, prior to a hasty conclusion that structured racial inequality has declined significantly based on the fact that the income of full-time male black and white workers has approached 73 percent in 1986 compared to 43 percent in 1940, we must examine other aspects of their economic life such as blacks' occupational distribution in order to provide a more accurate picture of their economic standing. More recently, Day and Newburger show that blacks earn less than whites at every educational level and, similarly, Grodsky and Pager find that even as blacks move up the occupational hierarchy, their income falls further behind their white peers.[136]

Occupational Mobility and Segmentation

One of the primary reasons why blacks' economic standing is much worse than whites is because of occupational race-typing. Although recent occupational data show that African Americans have made substantial progress in obtaining employment in occupational categories from which they previously were, for all practical purposes, excluded, they are still overrepresented among unskilled workers and underrepresented in higher-paying white-collar jobs. In 1960, whereas 60.4 percent of white men worked in blue-collar jobs, a whopping 76.7 percent of blacks did so.[137] The 2000 U.S. Census shows whites are still more likely than blacks to be employed in managerial and professional occupations: 35.43 percent of white males and 40.64 percent of white females compared to 21.65 percent of black males and 31 percent of black females. Blacks, in contrast, are disproportionately employed in service occupations: 20.23 percent of black males and 26.39 percent of black females compared to 10.85 percent of white males and 17.03 percent of white females. Within service occupations, black males are most likely to be employed in building and grounds cleaning and maintenance; black females, in health, personal, and food care. Black males are also disproportionately represented in production, transportation, and material moving (26.17 percent of blacks compared to 17.26 percent of whites). White males are more likely to hold construction jobs (17.26 percent of whites compared to 12.63 percent of blacks).

Two other factors point to the segmentation experienced by blacks in America. First, despite the apparent decline in underrepresentation of African Americans in managerial and professional occupations, those employed in these occupations have lower earnings than their white counterparts. Second, while the significance of race as a determinant of occupational mobility for African American men may have declined during the period of 1962 through 1973, other research suggests that their occupational mobility is less frequent than whites and more restricted in terms of destination.[138] Oliver and Shapiro note that "nearly two out of five blacks from lower blue-collar backgrounds remain stuck in unskilled and, for the most part, poorly paid jobs." Some mainstream researchers have attributed the racial differences in earnings to the existing educational gap between blacks and whites. However, Cotton found that racial differences among those employed in the managerial and professional occupations could not be explained by educational differences.[139] This is not surprising since research has consistently shown that black men earn less than white men in almost all occupations.[140]

Furthermore, as Collins points out, the relative opening of professional and managerial positions to blacks should not be mistaken for a decline in racial discrimination. While African Americans have succeeded in nontraditional occupations, their occupational mobility still exhibits a distinct racial pattern. Several studies have indicated that, for the most part, Jim Crow–type exclusion discrimination has been replaced with a new web of racial practices that limits their mobility and affects their everyday performance. One of the most pervasive of these practices is pigeonholing blacks in some positions, a practice reminiscent of typecasting blacks for "nigger jobs" during Jim Crow. For instance, Collins finds that many African American executives fill affirmative action, community relations, minority affairs, or public relations positions that were created during the 1960s and 1970s to respond to civil rights demands, positions than do not provide much mobility.[141]

Racial Practices in the Labor Market

Since the early 1960s social scientists have acknowledged that racial practices in the labor market are important causal factors in explaining the differential employment outcomes of blacks and whites. Yet, until recently, studies on labor-market discrimination assessed discrimination as the unexplained residual in black and white earnings after controlling for a number of variables. Although this measure is useful, it tends to underestimate the extent of discrimination by eliminating differences (e.g., in education and occupational status) that are themselves the product of discrimination racial practices.[142]

Since the 1990s, analysts have relied on a research strategy to *directly* assess the impact of discrimination. The technique used to examine labor-market discrimination is called an "employment audit," borrowed from the housing audit strategy, and consists of sending subjects matched in most characteristics except their race to find jobs. By adopting this approach, analysts have been able to estimate the *extent* as well as the *form* of discriminatory racial practices minorities endure in the labor market. Probably the most famous of these studies was one carried out by the Urban Institute in 1991. It was conducted on randomly selected employers in San Diego, Chicago, and Washington, D.C., and found that on average, white testers were significantly favored over black testers. In 20 percent of the audits, blacks were denied job opportunities, and in 31 percent of the audits Latinos were denied job opportunities. In Milwaukee, Wisconsin, Pager divided applicant testers with comparable resumes into four groups: whites without criminal record, whites with criminal record, blacks without criminal record, and blacks with criminal record. White applicants with a criminal record (17 percent) were more likely to be called back for an interview than black applicants without a criminal record (14 percent).[143]

Research indicates that blacks are discriminated against at all levels of the job process. In the search process, they are left behind because most employers rely on informal social networks to advertise their jobs. And since blacks are not part of those networks, they are left out in the cold. Not only does this hinder blacks in their efforts to gain middle-class jobs, but also, as Royster shows in her book *Race and the Invisible Hand*, networks of gatekeepers maintain white privilege in trade careers as well. Specifically, she shows how white students in a trade school who have similar credentials to their black counterparts (in fact, blacks students in the study are slightly *better*) are given preference by employers who clearly wish to hire their "own kind."[144]

Furthermore, recent examination of welfare leavers since the 1996 welfare reform laws indicate that white privilege operates even at low-level service jobs. Employers were less likely to hire black than white welfare leavers and paid the black welfare leavers they did hire less. At the job entry level, in addition to the practices mentioned above, blacks are screened out by tests and the requirement of a high school diploma.

These two practices were developed in the late 1950s and 1960s as substitutes for outright exclusion from jobs and were mentioned in the 1964 Civil Rights Act as practices that could have exclusionary results. They are discriminatory because the diploma and the tests are *not* essential to the job performance.

In terms of job promotion, blacks face a glass ceiling because they are pigeonholed in dead-end jobs. Research also suggests that blacks' exclusion from informal social networks restricts their opportunities to demonstrate criteria for promotion, such as loyalty, sound judgment, and leadership potential. Black professionals are also constrained regarding what emotions they can express even when confronted with outright racism in the workplace.[145] Moreover, Baldi and McBrier found that increased minority presence results in a negative effect on blacks. They suggest a group-threat process may be at work where white managers attempt to protect white workers in the face of increased minority presence.[146]

Wealth

The available data on wealth indicates that the disparities in this important area are greater than in any other economic area, and they are increasing. Blacks owned only 3 percent of U.S. assets in 2001, even though they constituted 13 percent of the U.S. population. In 2001, the median net worth of whites, $120,989, was over 6.3 times that of blacks, which was only $19,024. Calculation of mean net worth reveals that, in 2001, the average black family had 17 cents for every dollar of the average white family. Oliver and Shapiro report that the racial wealth gap increased from $60,980 in 1998 to $82,663 in 2002. This astounding inequality in wealth increased in 2009. Although all segments of the population except for the top 10 percent lost in the 2008 debacle, the financial crisis, given the vulnerable standing of people of color, led to an increase in the wealth gap between whites and blacks (twenty times) and whites and Latinos (eighteen times).[147]

A major reason for this disparity in wealth is inheritance and financial gifts from kin. The average financial legacy for white families in 2001 was ten times that of the average black family. Gittleman and Wolff examined factors affecting wealth accumulation from 1984 to 1994 and found no evidence of differences in saving behaviors after controlling for income. Had blacks had comparable inheritance, income, and portfolios during this period, they would have significantly narrowed the racial wealth gap. The researchers conclude, however, that it will be "extraordinarily difficult for blacks to make up significant ground relative to whites with respect to wealth" because of their much lower rates of inheritance, lower incomes, and the fact that much of their economic assets lie in home equity.[148]

Home equity is less among blacks than whites for several reasons. First, the long history of segregation and redlining ensures that black housing is concentrated in "less desirable" areas to the white mind. Further, housing stock in black areas appreciates much more slowly than similar housing in white locales, and in areas where the black population is growing, housing prices often fall. Whites are also likely to rate neighborhoods with high black populations as undesirable, promoting segregation.[149]

Managerial Views on Blacks

Recent research suggests that the views of white managers on blacks have not changed dramatically since the 1960s. Earlier studies were optimistic in predicting that managers would assume their social responsibilities toward blacks after years of exclusion.[150] Blacks have complained that they are bypassed by white managers for promotion, that they are not treated as equals, and that they endure a subtle hostility from their fellow workers and supervisors.[151] White employers and managers hiring for unskilled positions generally hold views that are more openly racist. In their interviews with Chicago and Cook county employers, Kirschenman and Neckerman and Wilson found that blacks were viewed as having a bad work ethic, as creating tensions in the workplace, as lazy and unreliable, as lacking leadership, and as having a bad attitude. For instance, a suburban drugstore manager said the following about blacks:

> It's unfortunate, but in my business I think overall [black men] tend to be viewed as dishonest. I think that's too bad but that's the image they have. (Interviewer: So you think it's an image problem?) Yeah, a dishonest, an image problem of being dishonest, mean and lazy. They are known to be lazy. They are [laughs]. I hate to tell you, but. It's all an image though. Whether they are or not, I don't know, but it's an image that is perceived. (Interviewer: I see. How do you think that image was developed?) Go look in the jails [laughs].[152]

Similarly, the chairman of a car transport company, when asked if there were differences in the work ethic of whites, blacks, and Latinos, stated,

> Definitively! I don't think, I know: I've seen it over a period of 30 years. I have it right in here. Basically, the Oriental is much more aggressive and intelligent and studious than the Hispanic. The Hispanics, except Cubans of course, they have the work ethnic [*sic*]. The Hispanics are mañana, mañana, mañana tomorrow, tomorrow, tomorrow. (Interviewer: You mentioned the case of native-born blacks.) They're the laziest of the bunch. (Interviewer: That would relate to your earliest remarks about dependability. What is the reason for that?) The parents are that way so, what the hell, they didn't have a role model to copy, that's part of it.[153]

In an investigation of the labor-market difficulties of urban minorities, Moss and Tilly studied the attitudes of employers toward prospective employees of entry-level, working-class jobs in the metropolitan areas of Atlanta, Boston, Detroit, and Los Angeles between 1992 and 1995. Most employers expressed greater concern about soft skills, such as social skills, which are subjectively determined, than about the hard skills of potential employees, and they found urban blacks, especially black males and inner-city residents, wanting in this respect. Moss and Tilly attributed the employers' racial bias to racial stereotypes, negative and racialized images of inner-city residents, and cultural differences, such as dress, vocabulary, and syntax.[154]

CONCLUSION

To sum up, blacks through their struggle have been able to gain access to the political system but that access has not translated itself into a significant influence. More blacks are elected to office and appointed to various positions than at any other time but that has a very limited impact on the status of the black masses. Moreover, a series of indirect barriers to the election of blacks, the rules of the game in Congress, and conditions in the cities of America where blacks have seemingly had more political success help to maintain them at bay and to preserve white political power almost intact. The changes in the racial dynamics at all levels, of which I have documented in this chapter only the social and economic, seem to amount to a reorganization—still incomplete and somewhat partial—of the racial structure of this country. This reorganization of the racial structure is incomplete because (1) not all the mechanisms and practices have settled, that is, have become institutionalized, and (2) we still have many legacies of the previous period affecting the life chances of blacks. On the first point, discrimination in the realm of education, for example, has not taken a definite institutional pattern in the contemporary period. Instead, there are various means (resegregation through white flight to the suburbs and to private schools, within-school segregation, tracking, etc.) to guarantee white advantages. On the second point, we still have old-fashioned racists, extra-legal violence, and an undeclared apartheid in the housing arena. Although many of these practices are manifestations of the legacies of slavery and Jim Crow in this country, the evidence reviewed here suggests that blacks and other minorities should fear less the angry men with white hoods and their traditional discriminatory practices than the men with suits and their "smiling discrimination."[155]

I agree with Pettigrew and Martin when they claim that "the greater subtlety of these new forms [of racial discrimination] pose new problems of remedy. They act at both the structural-institutional level focused on by sociologists, and the face-to-face situational level focused on by social psychologists."[156] Some of these problems that require remedy are as follows:

1. Detection of racial discrimination is extremely difficult for the party being discriminated against. Furthermore, too many progressive whites tend to explain away many of the claims of contemporary discrimination because

    > often the black is the only person in a position to draw the conclusion that prejudice is operating in the work situation. Whites have usually observed only a subset of the incidents, any one of which can be explained away by a nonracial account. Consequently, many whites remain unconvinced of the reality of subtle prejudice and discrimination, and come to think of their black co-workers as "terribly touchy" and "overly sensitive" to the issue. For such reasons, the modern forms of prejudice frequently remain invisible even to its perpetrators.[157]

    For example, when I, a black-looking Puerto Rican, am monitored in stores or asked numerous times by clerks, "May I help *you*?" (a way of letting me know they are checking me), I have limited legal recourse. How can I charge discrimination when the behavior seems to be "polite"? This is why some have referred to the new practices as "smiling discrimination."[158]

2. The standards that the Supreme Court has enacted recently on discrimination cases (plaintiffs carrying the burden of proof in discrimination cases and the denial of statistical evidence as valid proof of discrimination) help to preserve intact the contemporary forms for reproducing racial inequality in America. Unless the court becomes cognizant of the new character of racial discrimination and changes its current practice of requiring the "smoking gun" in cases, the court itself will be participating in covering up the far-reaching effects of racism in America.

3. Black leaders who continue to focus on the "old racism" will miss the most important manners by which racial inequality is being reproduced in America. It is vital that studies documenting the pervasive and comprehensive character of the new racism are done systematically.

4. Research that is still focused on the old racism will invariably find a decline in the significance of race. Research on racial practices has to become as sophisticated as the new racism. The studies carried out by the Urban Institute and the Department of Housing and Urban Development in which testers are sent out to various settings and

organizations are an example of what can be done. Unfortunately, that type of research does not enjoy the sympathy of our disciplines and has even been deemed "unethical." The web of discriminatory practices in the contemporary period is still not complete.

Hence it is still possible to mount an offensive to change its course. However, as I write this chapter, the prospects for such an offensive look bleak. First, the election of Obama, as I argue later in this volume, has narrowed the space for challenging race-based inequality. Nowadays whites believe racism has all but been defeated and thus it is much harder to challenge new and old-fashioned discrimination. Second, civil rights organizations such as the NAACP and the National Urban League continue to fight the enemies of the past, like the Ku Klux Klan or their Tea Party cousins, but not the contemporary structures and practices that are primarily responsible for post–civil rights racial inequality. The more these organizations fight "racists," the more they fail to highlight the new ways in which racial inequality is produced and reproduced, helping these practices sediment. Third, we may have missed the boat to challenge the system of "mass incarcerations"[159] and will pay dearly for doing so. If we do not work toward the development of a social movement to stop this tactic of social control, our collective chances for racial redemption are null. Unless this situation is reversed, the racial practices of the "new racism" will be institutionalized and minority folk will continue enduring a second-class existence in seemingly color-blind America.

NOTES

1. In prior versions of this chapter (Eduardo Bonilla-Silva and Amanda E. Lewis, "The 'New Racism': Toward an Analysis of the U.S. Racial Structure, 1960–1990s," in *Race, Nation, and Citizenship,* edited by Paul Wong, 100–150 [Boulder, Colo.: Westview, 1999]; Eduardo Bonilla-Silva, *White Supremacy and Racism in the Post–Civil Rights Era* [Boulder, Colo.: Rienner, 2001]; and Eduardo Bonilla-Silva and David Dietrich, "The Sweet Enchantment of Color-Blind Racism in Obamerica," *The ANNALS of the American Academy of Political and Social Science* 634 [March 2011]: 190–206) I used the disciplinarily accepted term "discrimination," but in this paper, where appropriate, I substitute with the notion of "racial practices." I do so because the notion of discrimination, married to the limiting prejudice problematic (Eduardo Bonilla-Silva, "Rethinking Racism," *American Sociological Review* 62, no. 3 [1997]: 465–80), does not allow us to capture normative, seemingly nonracial, kinder, and gentler forms of reproducing racial domination. Accordingly, by "racial practices" I refer to behaviors, styles, cultural affectations, traditions, and organizational procedures that help maintain white rule. Because many of these practices become routine ("That's the way things are!"), they are

not necessarily carried out with animosity and intent; that is, hostility and explicit expressions of racial cognitions and feelings about the "Other" need not be at the core of these practices. In fact, in contemporary America they tend *not* to be Jim Crow–like and are more in line with the hegemonic nature of post–civil rights racial domination (Michael Omi and Howard Winant, *Racial Formation in the United States* [New York: Routledge, 1994]; Bonilla-Silva, *White Supremacy and Racism in the Post–Civil Rights Era*).

2. This chapter revisits a chapter originally published in Paul Wong (ed.), *Race, Nation, and Citizenship* (Boulder, Colo.: Westview Press, 1999). The original chapter had numerous references, many of which were cut due to space constraints. I have also changed the parenthetical citations to endnotes. On the argument that race has become less important for the life chances of blacks, see William J. Wilson, *The Declining Significance of Race* (Chicago: University of Chicago Press, 1978).

3. Howard Schuman, Charlotte Steeh, and Lawrence Bobo, *Racial Attitudes in America: Trends and Interpretations* (Cambridge, Mass., and London: Harvard University Press, 1985). See also, Paul Sniderman and Thomas Piazza, *The Scar of Race* (Cambridge, Mass.: Harvard University Press, 1993).

4. See James P. Smith and Finnis R. Welch, *Closing the Gap, Forty Years of Economic Progress for Blacks* (Santa Monica, Calif.: Rand Corporation, 1986); See also Eric Grodsky and Devah Pager, "The Structure of Disadvantage: Individual and Occupational Determinants of the Black-White Wage Gap," *American Sociological Review* (2001): 542–67.

5. See Alphonso Pinkney, *The Myth of Black Progress* (Cambridge: Cambridge University Press, 1984); Charles V. Willie, *Caste and Class Controversy on Race and Poverty: Round Two of the Willie/Wilson Debate* (New York: General Hall, 1989).

6. See Lorenzo Greene and Carter G. Woodson, *The Negro Wage Earner* (New York: Association for the Study of Negro Life and History, 1930); George Fredrickson, *Black Image in the White Mind: The Debate on Afro-American Character and Destiny, 1817–1914* (New York: Evanston; San Francisco and London: Harper Torchbooks, 1973).

7. Philip S. Foner, *Organized Labor and the Black Worker, 1619–1981* (New York: International Publishers, 1981); Manning Marable, *How Capitalism Underdeveloped Black America* (Boston: South End Press, 1983).

8. George Fredrickson, *White Supremacy: A Comparative Study in American and South African History* (New York: Oxford University Press, 1981).

9. Gunnar Myrdal, *An American Dilemma* (New York, Toronto, and London: McGraw-Hill, 1964 [1944]).

10. Sterling D. Spero and Abraham L. Harris, *The Black Worker: The Negro and the Labor Movement* (New York: Atheneum, 1974).

11. C. Vann Woodward, *The Strange Career of Jim Crow*, 2d ed. (New York: Oxford University Press, 1966).

12. Ernest Patterson, *City Politics* (New York: Dood, Mead, 1974).

13. William M. Tuttle Jr., "Labor Conflict and Racial Violence: The Black Worker in Chicago, 1894–1919," in *Black Labor in America*, edited by Milton Cantor, 86–110 (Westport, Conn.: Negro Universities Press, 1970).

14. Thomas Gossett, *Race: The History of an Idea in America* (Dallas: Southern Methodist University Press, 1963).

15. In this chapter I limit the discussion to blacks and whites. However, see my discussion in chapter 10, where I expand the scope to all groups.

16. Florette Henri, *Black Migration: Movement North, 1900–1920* (New York: Anchor Press, Doubleday, 1975); Alferdteen Harrison, *Black Exodus: The Great Migration from the American South* (Jackson: University Press of Mississippi, 1991); Melvin M. Leiman, *Political Economy of Racism* (London and Boulder, Colo.: Pluto Press, 1992). Aldon Morris, *The Origins of the Civil Rights Movement: Black Communities Organizing for Change* (New York: The Free Press, 1984).

17. Woodward, *The Strange Career of Jim Crow*. See also Neil A. Wynn, *The Afro-American and the Second World War* (New York: Holmes and Meir, 1993).

18. Michael Reich, *Racial Inequality: A Political-Economic Analysis* (Princeton, N.J.: Princeton University Press, 1981). Bennett Harrison and Barry Bluestone, *The Great U-Turn: Corporate Restructuring and the Polarizing of America* (New York: Basic Books, 1988).

19. Leiman, *Political Economy*; Stewart Tolnay and E. M. Beck, "Rethinking the Role of Racial Violence in the Great Migration," in *Black Exodus: The Great Migration from the American South*, edited by Alferdteen Harrison, 20–35 (Jackson, Miss., and London: University of Mississippi Press, 1991). Ray Marshall, "Industrialisation and Race Relations in the Southern United States," in *Industrialisation and Race Relations: A Symposium*, edited by Guy Hunter, 61–96 (London and New York: Oxford University Press, 1965).

20. Leiman, *Political Economy*; Foner, *Organized Labor*; Tuttle, "Labor Conflict and Racial Violence"; Carole Marks, "The Social and Economic Life of Southern Blacks during the Migration," in *Black Exodus: The Great Migration from the American South*, edited by Alferdteen Harrison, 36–50 (Jackson, Miss., and London: University of Mississippi Press, 1991); Dernoral Davis, "Toward a Socio-Historical and Demographic Portrait of Twentieth-Century African Americans," in *Black Exodus: The Great Migration from the American South*, edited by Alferdteen Harrison, 1–19 (Jackson, Miss., and London: University of Mississippi Press, 1991).

21. Myrdal, *An American Dilemma*; Henri, *Black Migration*; Davis, "Toward a Socio-Historical and Demographic Portrait of Twentieth-Century African Americans."

22. Melvin M. Leiman, *Political Economy of Racism* (London and Boulder, Colo.: Pluto Press, 1992), 174.

23. Joseph J. Morrow, "American Negroes—a Wasted Resource," *Harvard Business Review* (1957): 65–74.

24. Joleen Kirschenman and Kathryn M. Neckerman, "'We'd Love to Hire Them, But. . .': The Meaning of Race for Employers," in *Race and Ethnic Conflict*, edited by Fred L. Pincus and Howard J. Erlich (Boulder, Colo.: Westview Press, 1994).

25. Naomi Klein, *The Shock Doctrine: The Rise of Disaster Capitalism* (New York: Metropolitan Books, 2007).

26. David T. Wellman, *Portraits of White Racism* (New York: Cambridge University Press, 1977); David O. Sears, "Symbolic Racism," in *Eliminating Racism: Profiles in Controversy*, edited by Phylis A. Katz and Dalmas A. Taylor, 53–84 (New York and London: Plenum Press, 1988). Thomas F. Pettigrew, "New Patterns of Prejudice: The Different Worlds of 1984 and 1964," in *Race and Ethnic Conflict*,

edited by Fred L. Pincus and Howard J. Erlich (Boulder, Colo.: Westview Press, 1994).

27. John R. Logan, "Ethnic Diversity Grows, Neighborhood Integration Lags," in *Redefining Urban and Suburban America: Evidence from Census 2000*, edited by Bruce Katz and Robert Lang (Washington, D.C.: Brookings Institution Press, 2003).

28. Douglas Massey and Nancy Denton, *American Apartheid: Segregation and the Making of the American Underclass* (Cambridge, Mass.: Harvard University Press, 1993); Sheryll Cashin, *Failures of Integration: How Race and Class are Undermining the American Dream* (New York: Public Affairs, 2004).

29. Steve H. Murdock and David R. Ellis, *Applied Demography: An Introduction to Basic Concepts, Methods, and Data* (Boulder, Colo.: Westview Press, 1991).

30. Reynolds Farley and Walter R. Allen, *The Color Line and the Quality of Life in America* (New York: Russell Sage Foundation, 1987); Margery A. Turner, Raymond Struyk, and John Yinger, *The Housing Discrimination Study* (Washington, D.C.: The Urban Institute, 1991); John Yinger, "Housing Discrimination and Residential Segregation as Causes of Poverty," in *Understanding Poverty*, edited by Sheldon H. Danziger and Robert H. Haveman, 359–91 (New York: Russell Sage Foundation, 2001).

31. Patrick Sharkey, "The Intergenerational Transmission of Context," *American Journal of Sociology* 113 (2008): 931–69.

32. Patrick Sharkey, "The Intergenerational Transmission of Context," *American Journal of Sociology* 113 (2008): 961.

33. George C. Glaster, "Racial Steering by Real Estate Agents: Mechanisms and Motives," *The Review of Black Political Economy* 19, no. 1 (Spring 1990): 39–61; Turner, Struyk, and Yinger, *The Housing Discrimination Study*.

34. Robert C. Smith, "'Politics' Is Not Enough: The Institutionalization of the African American Freedom Movement," in *From Exclusion to Inclusion: The Long Struggle for African American Political Power*, edited by Ralph C. Gomes and Linda Faye Williams, 97–126 (New York and London: Greenwood Press, 1992).

35. Margery A. Turner, Stephen L. Ross, George C. Glaster, and John Yinger, *Discrimination in Metropolitan Housing Markets: National Results from Phase 1 HDS* (Washington, D.C.: The Urban Institute, 2002).

36. Cathy Cloud and George Galster, "What Do We Know about Racial Discrimination in Mortgage Markets?" *The Review of Black Political Economy* 21 (1993): 101–20.

37. Robert C. Smith, *Racism in the Post–Civil Rights Era, Now You See It, Now You Don't* (New York: State University of New York Press, 1995); Melvin L. Oliver and Thomas Shapiro, *Black Wealth/White Wealth: A New Perspective on Racial Inequality* (New York: Routledge, 1995).

38. Jacob S. Rugh and Douglass Massey, "Racial Segregation and the American Foreclosure Crisis," *American Sociological Review* 75, no. 5 (2010): 629–51.

39. Karyn Lacy, "All's Fair? The Foreclosure Crisis and Middle-Class Black (In) Stability," *American Behavioral Scientist* 56 no. 11 (2012): 1565–80; Calvin Bradford, *Risk or Race? Racial Disparities in the Subprime Refinance Market* (Washington, D.C.: Center for Community Change, 2002).

40. Farley and Allen, *The Color Line and the Quality of Life in America*.

41. Gary Orfield, *Must We Bus? Segregated Schools and National Policy* (Washington, D.C.: Brookings Institution Press, 1978); Gary Orfield, "School Desegregation after Two Generations: Race, Schools and Opportunity in Urban Society," in *Race in America*, edited by Herbert Hill and James E. Jones (Madison: University of Wisconsin Press, 1993); Gary Orfield and Carol Ashkinaze, *The Closing Door: Conservative Policy and Black Opportunity* (Chicago: University of Chicago Press, 1991); Gary Orfield and Franklin Monfort, *Status of School Desegregation: The Next Generation* (Alexandria, Va.: National School Boards Association, 1992). Gary Orfield and Chungmei Lee, "Why Segregation Matters: Poverty and Educational Inequality," Harvard University, The Civil Rights Project, 2005.

42. Jeannie Oakes, Molly Selvin, Lynn Karoly and Gretchen Guiton, *Educational Matchmaking: Academic and Vocational Tracking in Comprehensive High Schools* (Santa Monica, Calif.: Rand, 1992).

43. Schuman, Steeh, and Bobo, *Racial Attitudes in America.*

44. Lawrence Otis Graham, *Member of the Club: Reflections On Life in a Racially Polarized World* (New York: HarperCollins, 1995).

45. Jeffery S. Passel, Wendy Wang, and Paul Taylor, "Marrying Out: One-in-Seven New U.S. Marriages Is Interracial or Interethnic," Pew Research Center, June 8, 2010, retrieved from www.pewtrusts.org/our_work_report_detail .aspx?id=59361 (accessed March 29, 2013).

46. Daniel T. Lichter, "U.S. Far From an Interracial Melting Pot," CNN Opinion, June 16, 2010, retrieved from www.cnn.com/2010/OPINION/06/14/lichter .interracial.marriage/index.html (accessed March 29, 2013).

47. Mary R. Jackman and Marie Crane, "'Some of My Best Friends Are Black . . .': Interracial Friendship and Whites' Racial Attitudes." *Public Opinion Quarterly* 50 (1986): 459–86.

48. Ellis Cose, *The Rage of a Privileged Class: Why Are Middle Class Blacks Angry? Why Should America Care?* (New York: HarperCollins, 1993).

49. Joe Feagin and Karen D. McKinney, *The Many Costs of Racism* (Lanham, Md.: Rowman & Littlefield, 2003).

50. Howard Schuman, Eleanor Singer, Rebecca Donovan, and Claire Selltiz, "Discriminatory Behavior in New York Restaurants: 1950 and 1981," *Social Indicators Research* 13, no. 1 (1983): 69–83; Zachary W. Brewster, "Racially Discriminatory Service in Full-Service Restaurants: The Problem, Cause, and Potential Solutions," *Cornell Hospitality Quarterly* 53, no. 4 (2012): 274–85.

51. Graham, *Member of the Club*; Joe R. Feagin and Melvin P. Sikes, *Living with Racism: The Black Middle-Class Experience* (Boston: Beacon Press, 1994).

52. Derald Wing Sue, Christina M. Capodilupo, Gina C. Torino, Jennifer M. Bucceri, Aisha M. B. Holder, Kevin L. Nadal, and Marta Esquilin, "Racial Microaggressions in Everyday Life: Implications for Clinical Practice," *American Psychologist* 62, no. 4 (2007): 271–86.

53. Oliver and Shapiro, *Black Wealth.*

54. Lui Meizhu, Barbara J. Robles, Betsy Leondar-Wright, Rose M. Brewer, and Rebecca Adamson, *The Color of Wealth: The Story Behind the U.S. Racial Wealth Divide* (New York: The New Press, 2006); William Darity Jr., Jeremiah Cotton, and Herbert Hill, "Race and Inequality in the Managerial Age," in *African Americans: Essential Perspectives*, edited by Wornie L. Reed, 33–80 (Westport, Conn.: Auburn House, 1993).

55. Patterson, *City Politics*; Marable, *How Capitalism Underdeveloped Black America*.

56. Clarence Lusane, *African Americans at the Crossroads: The Restructuring of Black Leadership and the 1992 Elections* (Boston: South End Press, 1994).

57. Pinkney, *The Myth of Black Progress*.

58. Theresa Chambliss, "The Growth and Significance of African American Elected Officials," in *From Exclusion to Inclusion: The Long Struggle for African American Political Power*, edited by Ralph C. Gomes and Linda Faye Williams (New York: Greenwood Press, 1992). Rosalind S. Helderman, "The 113th Congress Is the Most Diverse in History," *Washington Post*, January 3, 2013, retrieved from www.washingtonpost.com/politics/113th-congress-has-more-women-minorities-than -ever/2013/01/03/7d1aaf30-55e5-11e2-8b9e-dd8773594efc_story.html (accessed March 29, 2013).

59. For a critique of this view, see James Jennings, *The Politics of Black Empowerment: The Transformation of Black Activism in Urban America* (Detroit: Wayne State University Press, 1992).

60. Chambliss, "The Growth and Significance of African American Elected Officials"; Huey L. Perry, "The Evolution and Impact of Biracial Coalitions and Black Mayors in Birmingham and New Orleans," in *Racial Politics in American Cities*, edited by Rufus P. Browning, Dame Rogers Marshall, and David H. Tabb (New York: Longman, 1990).

61. Frank R. Parker, "Eradicating the Continuing Barriers to Effective Minority Voter Participation," in *From Exclusion to Inclusion: The Long Struggle for African American Political Power*, edited by Ralph C. Gomes and Linda Faye Williams (New York: Greenwood Press, 1992); Yvonne E. Moss, Wornie L. Reed, Alphonso Pinkney, James Turner, and Sidney Wilhelm, "Black Political Participation: The Search for Power," in *African Americans: Essential Perspectives*, edited by Wornie L. Reed (Westport, Conn.: Auburn House, 1993).

62. Edwin Dorn, *Rules and Racial Equality* (New Haven, Conn., and London: Yale University Press, 1979).

63. Suevon Lee, "Everything You've Ever Wanted to Know about Voter ID Laws," *ProPublica*, November 5, 2012, retrieved from www.propublica.org/ article/everything-youve-ever-wanted-to-know-about-voter-id-laws (accessed March 29, 2013).

64. Jamelle Bouie, "Pennsylvania Admits It: No Voter Fraud Problem," *Washington Post*, July 24, 2012, retrieved from www.washingtonpost.com/blogs/ plum-line/post/pennsylvania-admits-it-no-voter-fraud-problem/2012/07/24/ gJQAHNVt6W_blog.html (accessed March 29, 2013).

65. John C. Berg, *Class, Gender, Race, and Power in the U.S. Congress* (Boulder, Colo.: Westview Press, 1994).

66. Parker, "Eradicating the Continuing Barriers to Effective Minority Voter Participation."

67. Smith, "'Politics' Is Not Enough."

68. Phillip J. Thompson III, *Double Trouble: Black Mayors, Black Communities, and the Call for a Deep Democracy* (Oxford: Oxford University Press, 2006).

69. Chambliss, "The Growth and Significance of African American Elected Officials."

70. Smith, "'Politics' Is Not Enough."

71. William E. Nelson, "Black Mayoral Leadership: A Twenty-Year Perspective," in *Black Electoral Politics*, edited by Lucius Barker, 188–95 (New Brunswick, N.J., and London: Transaction Publishers, 1990), Moss et al., "Black Political Participation."

72. Thompson, *Double Trouble*.

73. Nelson, "Black Mayoral Leadership."

74. Charles Hamilton, *The Black Political Experience in America* (New York: Capricorn Books, 1973), Frances Fox Piven and Richard Cloward, *Poor People's Movements: Why They Succeed, How They Fail* (New York: Pantheon Books, 1979).

75. Ta-Nehisi Coates, "Fear of a Black President," *The Atlantic*, September 2012, retrieved from www.theatlantic.com/magazine/archive/2012/09/fear-of-a-black-president/309064 (accessed March 29, 2013).

76. Marable, *How Capitalism Underdeveloped Black America*.

77. Adam Liptak, "U.S. Imprisons One in 100 Adults, Report Finds," *New York Times*, February 29, 2008, retrieved from www.nytimes.com/2008/02/29/us/29prison.html (accessed March 29, 2013).

78. Devah Pager, "The Mark of a Criminal Record," *American Journal of Sociology* 108 (2003): 937–75.

79. Marc Mauer and Ryan S. King, "Uneven Justice: State Rates of Incarceration by Race and Ethnicity," The Sentencing Project, June 2007.

80. Gerald D. Jaynes and Robin M. Williams, *A Common Destiny: Blacks and American Society* (Washington, D.C.: National Academy Press, 1989).

81. Alfred N. Garwood, *Black Americans: A Statistical Sourcebook* (Boulder, Colo.: Numbers and Concepts, 1991).

82. Donna M. Bishop, "The Role of Race and Ethnicity in Juvenile Justice Processing," in *Our Children, Their Children: Confronting Racial and Ethnic Differences in American Juvenile Justice*, edited by Darnell F. Hawking and Kimberly Kempf-Leonard (Chicago and London: University of Chicago Press, 2005).

83. Derrick Bell, *Faces at the Bottom of the Well* (New York: Basic Books, 1992).

84. Renford Reese, *Prison Race* (Durham, N.C.: Carolina Academic Press, 2006).

85. Farai Chideya, *Don't Believe the Hype: Fighting Cultural Misinformation about African-Americans* (New York: Penguin Books, 1995).

86. Reese, *Prison Race*.

87. Pamela I. Jackson, *Minority Group Threat, Crime, and Policing* (New York; Westport, Conn.; and London: Praeger, 1989).

88. Allen E. Liska, Joseph J. Lawrence, and Michael Benson, "Perspectives on the Legal Order: The Capacity for Social Control," *American Journal of Sociology* 87 (1981): 413–26.

89. Mark S. Rosentraub and Karen Harlow, "Police Policies and the Black Community: Attitude toward the Police," in *Contemporary Public Policy Perspectives and Black Americans*, edited by Mitchell F. Rice and Woodrow Jones Jr., 107–21 (Westport, Conn., and London: Greenwood Press, 1984); Ronald Weitzer and Steven Tuch, "Race and Perception of Police Misconduct," *Social Problems* 51 (2004): 305–25.

90. Lawrence W. Sherman, "Execution without Trial: Police Homicide and the Constitution," *Vanderbilt Law Review* 33 (1980): 71–100.

91. Melvin Oliver, James H. Johnson, and Walter C. Farrell Jr., "Anatomy of a Rebellion: A Political-Economic Analysis," in *Reading Rodney King, Reading Urban Uprising*, edited by Robert Gooding-Williams, 117–41 (New York and London: Routledge, 1993).

92. Paul T. Rosynsky, "BART Officer Admits Oscar Grant III Posed No Threat before Mehserle Shot Him," *Oakland Tribune*, June 3, 2009, retrieved from www.highbeam.com/doc/1P2-20356411.html (accessed March 29, 2013).

93. Alternet staff, "Outrage in Oakland after Cop Kills Unarmed Man: Piecing Together the Story," *Alternet*, January 13, 2009, retrieved from www.alternet.org/story/119577/outrage_in_oakland_after_cop_kills_unarmed_man%3A_piecing_together_the_story?page=3%2C0 (accessed March 29, 2013).

94. Julianne Hing, "Remembering Oscar Grant on the Day of Johannes Mehserle's Release," *Colorlines*, June 14, 2011, retrieved from http://colorlines.com/archives/2011/06/remembering_oscar_grant_on_the_day_of_johannes_mehserles_release.html (accessed March 29, 2013).

95. Tim Wise, "School Shootings and White Denial," 2001, retrieved from www.timwise.org/2001/03/school-shootings-and-white-denial (accessed March 29, 2013).

96. Cheng Cheng and Mark Hoekstra, *Does Strengthening Self-Defense Law Deter Crime or Escalate Violence? Evidence from Castle Doctrine* (Cambridge, Mass.: National Bureau of Economic Research, 2012).

97. Sarah Childress, "Is There Racial Bias in 'Stand Your Ground' Laws?," *Frontline*, July 31, 2012, retrieved from www.pbs.org/wgbh/pages/frontline/criminal-justice/is-there-racial-bias-in-stand-your-ground-laws (accessed March 29, 2013).

98. Samuel R. Gross and Robert Mauro, *Death and Discrimination: Racial Disparities in Capital Sentencing* (Boston: Northeastern University Press, 1989).

99. David V. Baker, "The Racist Application of Capital Punishment to African Americans," in *Racial Issues in Criminal Justice: The Case of African Americans*, edited by Marvin D. Free Jr. (Westport, Conn.: Praeger, 2003); Reese, *Prison Race*.

100. Stephen Demuth and Darrell Steffensmeier, "Ethnicity Effects on Sentence Outcomes in Large Urban Courts: Comparisons among White, Black, and Hispanic Defendants," *Social Science Quarterly* 85 (2004): 994–1011.

101. Charles R. Pruitt and James Q. Wilson, "A Longitudinal Study of the Effect of Race in Sentencing," *Law and Society Review* 7 (1983): 613–35.

102. Cassia Spohn, "Crime and the Social Control of Blacks: Offender/Victim Race and the Sentencing of Violent Offenders," in *Inequality, Crime, and Social Control*, edited by George S. Bridges and Martha A. Myers, 249–68 (Boulder, Colo., San Francisco, and Oxford: Westview Press, 1994).

103. Spohn, "Crime and the Social Control of Blacks"; Michael L. Radelet and Glenn L. Pierce, "The Role of Victim's Race and Geography on Death Sentencing," in *From Lynch Mobs to the Killing State*, edited by Charles J. Ogletree Jr. and Austin Sarat (New York: New York University Press, 2006).

104. Spohn, *Crime and the Social Control of Blacks*.

105. Gross and Mauro, *Death and Discrimination*.

106. David C. Baldus, Charles A. Pulaski Jr., and George Woodworth, "Comparative Review of Death Sentences: An Empirical Study of the Georgia Experience," *Journal of Criminal Law & Criminology* 74 (1983): 661–753.

107. Bell, *Faces at the Bottom of the Well.*

108. Nijole Benokratis, "Racial Exclusion in Juries," *Journal of Applied Behavioral Science* 18 (1982): 29–47.

109. Craig Haney, "On the Selection of Capital Juries: The Biasing of the Death-Qualification Process," *Law and Human Behavior* 8 (1984): 121–32.

110. Gregory D. Russell, *The Death Penalty and Racial Bias: Overturning Supreme Court Assumptions* (Westport, Conn., and London: Greenwood Press, 1994).

111. Gross and Mauro, *Death and Discrimination.*

112. Lee P. Brown, "Crime in the Black Community," *The State of Black America,* edited by Janet Dewart, 95–113 (New York: National Urban League, 1988).

113. Bell, *Faces at the Bottom of the Well.*

114. John L. Cooper, *The Police and the Ghetto* (Port Washington, N.Y., and London: Kennikat Press, 1980).

115. Alan J. Lizote, "Extra-Legal Factors in Chicago's Criminal Courts: Testing the Conflict Model of Criminal Justice," *Social Problems* 25 (1978): 564–80.

116. Bishop, "The Role of Race and Ethnicity in Juvenile Justice Processing."

117. Chideya, *Don't Believe the Hype.*

118. Douglas Smith, Christy A. Visher, and Laura Davidson, "Equity and Discretionary Justice: The Influence of Race on Police Arrest Decisions," *Journal of Criminal Law and Criminology* 75 (1984): 234–49; Reese, *Prison Race.*

119. Smith, *Racism in the Post-Civil Rights Era*"; Feagin and Sikes, *Living with Racism.*

120. Joe R. Feagin, *Racist America: Roots, Current Realities, and Future Reparations* (New York and London: Routledge, 2001), 1.

121. David J. Garrow, *The FBI and Martin Luther King* (New York: Penguin Books, 1983).

122. Ward Churchill and Jim Vander Wall, *Agents of Repression: The FBI's Secret Wars against the Black Panther Party and the American Indian Movement* (Boston: South End Press, 1988).

123. Clayborne Carson, *Malcolm X: The FBI File* (New York: Carroll and Graf Editors, 1991).

124. Churchill and Wall, *Agents of Repression.*

125. Isaac D. Balbus, *The Dialectics of Legal Repression: Black Rebels before the American Criminal Courts* (New York: Russell Sage Foundation, 1974).

126. Oliver, Johnson, and Farrell, "Anatomy of a Rebellion"; Mary France Berry, *Black Resistance, White Law: A History of Constitutional Racism in America* (London: Allen Lane/Penguin Press, 1994).

127. Rosentraub and Harlow, "Police Policies and the Black Community."

128. Rosentraub and Harlow, "Police Policies and the Black Community."

129. Thomas Sowell, *Civil Rights: Rhetoric of Reality?* (New York: Morrow, 1984); William J. Wilson, *The Declining Significance of Race* (Chicago: University of Chicago Press, 1978).

130. Darity, Cotton, and Hill, "Race and Inequality in the Managerial Age."

131. Farley and Allen, *The Color Line and the Quality of Life in America*; Reynolds Farley, "The Common Destiny of Black and Whites: Observations about the Social and Economic Status of the Races," in *Race in America: The Struggle for Equality,* edited by Herbert Hill and James E. Jones Jr. (Madison, Wis.: University of Wisconsin Press, 1993); James J. Heckman and Brooks S. Payner, "Determining the

Impact of the Federal Antidiscrimination Policy on the Economic Status of Blacks: A Study of South Carolina," *American Economic Review* 79, no. 1 (1992): 138–72. Leonard A. Cole, *Blacks in Power: A Comparative Study of Black and White Elected Officials* (Princeton, N.J.: Princeton University Press, 1975).

132. William A. Darity Jr. and Samuel L. Myers, "Changes in the Black-White Income Inequality, 1968–1978: A Decade of Progress?," *The Review of Black Political Economy* 10 (1980): 365–92.

133. Jeremiah Cotton, "Opening the Gap: The Decline in Black Economic Indicators in the 1980s," *Social Science Quarterly* 70 (1989): 803–19.

134. Meizhu et al., *The Color of Wealth*.

135. Farley and Allen, *The Color Line and the Quality of Life in America*.

136. Jennifer Cheeseman Day and Eric Newburger, *The Big Payoff: Educational Attainment and Synthetic Estimates of Work-Life Earnings* (Washington, D.C.: U.S. Census Bureau, 2002); Grodsky and Pager, "The Structure of Disadvantage."

137. Reynolds Farley, *Blacks and Whites: Narrowing the Gap?* (Cambridge, Mass., and London: Harvard University Press, 1984). William O'Hare, Kelvin Pollard, Taynia Mann, and Mary Kent, "African Americans in the 1990s," *Population Bulletin* 46, no. 1 (1991).

138. Marshall Pomer, "Labor Market Structure, Intragenerational Mobility, and Discrimination: Black Male Advancement Out of Low-Paying Occupations, 1962–1973," *American Sociological Review* 51 (1986): 650–59. Jeffrey Waddoups, "Racial Differences in Intersegment Mobility," *Review of Black Political Economy* 20, no. 2 (1991): 23–43.

139. Cotton, "Opening the Gap."

140. Phillip Moss and Chris Tilly, *Stories Employers Tell: Race, Skill, and Hiring in America* (New York: Russell Sage Foundation, 2001).

141. Cose, *The Rage of a Privileged Class*; Sharon M. Collins, "The Making of the Black Middle Class," *Social Problems* 30 (1983): 369–82.

142. Thomas D. Boston, *Race, Class, and Conservatism* (Boston: Unwin Hyman, 1988).

143. Pager, "The Mark of a Criminal Record"; Devah Pager and Lincoln Quillian, "Walking the Talk? What Employers Say versus What They Do," *American Sociological Review* 70, no. 3 (2005): 355–80.

144. Deirdre A. Royster, *Race and the Invisible Hand: How White Networks Exclude Men from Blue-Collar Jobs* (Berkeley: University of California Press, 2003).

145. Adia-Harvey Wingfield, "Are Some Emotions Marked 'Whites Only'? Racialized Feeling Rules in Professional Workplaces," *Social Problems* 57, no. 2 (2010): 251–68.

146. Stéphane Baldi and Debra Branch McBrier, "Do the Determinants of Promotion Differ for Blacks and Whites?" *Work and Occupations* 24 (1997): 478–97.

147. Meizhu et al., *The Color of Wealth*; Paul Taylor, Rakesh Kochhar, Richard Fry, Gabriel Velasco, and Seth Motel, "Wealth Gaps Rise to Record Highs between Whites, Blacks and Hispanics," *Pew Research Center, Social and Demographic Trends*, retrieved from www.pewsocialtrends.org/files/2011/07/SDT-Wealth-Report_7-26-11_FINAL.pdf (accessed March 29, 2013).

148. Meizhu et al., *The Color of Wealth*; Maury Gittleman and Edward N. Wolff, "Racial Differences in Patterns of Wealth Accumulation," *Journal of Human Resources* 39 (2004): 193–227.

149. Maria Krysan, Mick P. Couper, Reynolds Farley, and Tyrone A. Forman, "Does Race Matter in Neighborhood Preferences? Results from a Video Experiment," *American Journal of Sociology* 115, no. 2 (2009): 527–59. Chenoa Flippen, "Unequal Returns to Housing Investments? A Study of Real Housing Appreciation among Black, White, and Hispanic Households," *Social Forces* 82, no. 4 (2004): 1523–51.

150. Herbert R. Northrup, "Industry's Racial Employment Policies," in *Employment, Race, and Poverty*, edited by Arthur M. Ross and Herbert Hill, 290–307 (New York: Harcourt, Brace, and World, 1967).

151. Graham, *Member of the Club.*

152. Kirschenman and Neckerman, "'We'd Love to Hire Them, But. . . .'"

153. William J. Wilson, *When Work Disappears: The World of the New Urban Poor* (New York: Random House, 1996).

154. Moss and Tilly, *Stories Employers Tell.*

155. Roy L. Brooks, *Rethinking the American Race Problem* (Berkeley: University of California Press, 1990).

156. Thomas F. Pettigrew and Joanne Martin, "Shaping the Organizational Context for Black American Inclusion," *Journal of Social Issues* 43, no. 1 (1987): 41–78.

157. Pettigrew and Martin, "Shaping the Organizational Context."

158. Brooks, *Rethinking the American Race Problem.*

159. Michelle Alexander, *The New Jim Crow: Mass Incarceration in the Age of Color Blindness* (New York: The New Press, 2010).

3

⌒

The Central Frames
of Color-Blind Racism

The master defense against accurate social perception and change is always and in every society the tremendous conviction of rightness about any behavior form which exists.

—John Dollard, *Class and Caste in a Southern Town*

If Jim Crow's racial structure has been replaced by a "new racism," what happened to Jim Crow racism? What happened to beliefs about blacks' mental, moral, and intellectual inferiority, to the idea that "it is the [black man's] own fault that he is a lower-caste . . . a lower-class man" or the assertion that blacks "lack initiative, are shiftless, have no sense of time, or do not wish to better themselves"[1]; in short, what happened to the basic claim that blacks are subhuman?[2] Social analysts of all stripes agree that most whites no longer subscribe to these tenets. However, this does not mean the "end of racism,"[3] as a few conservative commentators have suggested. Instead, a new powerful ideology has emerged to defend the contemporary racial order: the ideology of color-blind racism. Yet, color-blind racism is a curious racial ideology. Although it engages, as all ideologies do, in "blaming the victim," it does so in a very indirect, "now you see it, now you don't" style that matches the character of the new racism. Because of the slipperiness of color-blind racism, in this chapter, I examine its central frames and explain how whites use them in ways that justify racial inequality.

THE FRAMES OF COLOR-BLIND RACISM

Ideologies are about "meaning in the service of power."[4] They are expressions at the symbolic level of the fact of dominance. As such, the ideologies of the powerful are central in the production and reinforcement of the status quo. They comfort rulers and charm the ruled much like an Indian snake handler. Whereas rulers receive solace by believing they are not involved in the terrible ordeal of creating and maintaining inequality, the ruled are charmed by the almost magic qualities of a hegemonic ideology.[5]

The central component of any dominant racial ideology is its frames or *set paths for interpreting information*. These set paths operate as cul-de-sacs because after people filter issues through them, they explain racial phenomena following a predictable route. Although by definition dominant frames must *mis*represent the world (hide the fact of dominance), this does not mean that they are totally without foundation. (For instance, it is true that people of color in the United States are much better off today than at any other time in history. However, it is also true—facts hidden by color-blind racism—that because people of color still experience *systematic* discrimination and remain appreciably behind whites in many important areas of life, their chances of catching up with whites are very slim.) Dominant racial frames, therefore, provide the intellectual road map used by rulers to navigate the always rocky road of domination and, as I will show in chapter 6, derail the ruled from their track to freedom and equality.

Analysis of the interviews with college students and DAS respondents revealed that color-blind racism has four central frames and that these frames are used by an overwhelming majority of the white respondents. The four frames are *abstract liberalism, naturalization, cultural racism,* and *minimization of racism*. Of the four frames, abstract liberalism is the most important, as it constitutes the foundation of the new racial ideology. It is also the hardest to understand (What is *racial* about opposing busing or affirmative action, policies that clearly interfere with our American individualism?). Thus, I dedicate more space in this chapter to its discussion and to how it plays out in the color-blind drama.

In order to adequately understand the *abstract liberalism* frame, first we need to know what is liberalism. According to John Gray, liberalism, or "liberal humanism," is at the core of modernity; of the philosophical, economic, cultural, and political challenge to the feudal order. Although he acknowledges that liberalism has no "essence," he points out that it has a "set of distinctive features," namely, individualism, universalism, egalitarianism, and meliorism (the idea that people and institutions can be improved).[6] All these components were endorsed and placed at the core of the constitutions of emerging nation-states by a new set of actors: the bourgeoisies of early modern capitalism. When the bourgeoisie lauded freedom, they meant "free trade, free selling and buying"; when they applauded "individualism," they had in mind "the bourgeois . . . the middle-class owner of property"; "The ideas of religious liberty and freedom of conscience merely gave expression to the sway of free competition within the domain of knowledge."[7]

Hence, classical liberalism was the philosophy of a nascent class that as an aspiring ruling class expressed its needs (political as well as economic) as general societal goals. But the bourgeois goals were not extended to the populace in their own midst until the twentieth century.[8] Moreover, the liberal project was never inclusive of the countries that Spain, Portugal, France, Britain, the Netherlands, Italy, and later on, Germany used as outposts for raw materials and racialized workers (e.g., slaves). Although contemporary commentators debate the merits of liberal humanism as it pertains to current debates about race-based policies, muticulturalism, and "equality of results,"[9] many seem oblivious to the fact that *"European humanism* (and liberalism) *usually meant that only Europeans were human."*[10] Philosophers such as Kant stated that the differences between blacks and whites were "to be as great in regard to mental capacities as in colour." Voltaire, the great French philosopher, said on the same subject that "only a blind man is permitted to doubt that Whites, Blacks, and Albinoes . . . are totally different races." Lastly, even the father of modern liberalism, John Stuart Mill, author of *On Liberty*, justified nineteenth-century colonialism and supported slavery in antiquity and in certain nineteenth-century colonial situations.[11] To be clear, my intent here is not to vilify the founders of liberalism, but to point out that modernity, liberalism, and racial exclusion were all part of the same historical movement.

The liberal tradition informed the American Revolution, the U.S. Constitution, and "the leading American liberal thinker of this period, Thomas Jefferson."[12] And in the United States as in Europe, the exclusion of the majority of white men and all white women from the rights of citizenship and the classification of Native Americans and African Americans as subpersons accompanied the development of the new liberal nation-state.[13] Specifically, racially based policies such as slavery, the removal of Native Americans from their lands and their banishment to reservations, the superexploitation and degrading utilization of Mexicans and various Asian groups as contract laborers, Jim Crow, and many other policies were part of the United States' "liberal" history from 1776 until the 1960s.

Nevertheless, I would be remiss if I failed to acknowledge that, in both Europe and the United States, disenfranchised groups and progressive politicians used the liberal rhetoric to advance social and legal reforms (e.g., the civil rights movement, the National Organization of Women,

Liberal parties in Europe).[14] Thus liberalism, when extended to its seemingly logical conclusions ("Life, liberty, and the pursuit of happiness for *all*") and connected to social movements, can be progressive. My point, however, is less about social-reform liberalism (although I contend many reform organizations and many white reform-minded individuals[15] have adopted color-blind racism) than about how central elements of liberalism have been *rearticulated* in post–civil rights America to rationalize racially unfair situations.

The frame of *abstract liberalism* involves using ideas associated with political liberalism (e.g., "equal opportunity," the idea that force should not be used to achieve social policy) and economic liberalism (e.g., choice, individualism) in an abstract manner to explain racial matters. By framing race-related issues in the language of liberalism, whites can appear "reasonable" and even "moral," while opposing almost all practical approaches to deal with de facto racial inequality. For instance, the principle of equal opportunity, central to the agenda of the civil rights movement and whose extension to people of color was vehemently opposed by most whites, is invoked by whites today to oppose affirmative-action policies because they supposedly represent the "preferential treatment" of certain groups. This claim necessitates ignoring the fact that people of color are *severely* underrepresented in most good jobs, schools, and universities and, hence, it is an abstract utilization of the idea of "equal opportunity." Another example is regarding each person as an "individual" with "choices" and using this liberal principle as a justification for whites having the right of choosing to live in segregated neighborhoods or sending their children to segregated schools. This claim requires ignoring the multiple institutional and state-sponsored practices behind segregation and being unconcerned about these practices' negative consequences for minorities.

Naturalization **is a frame that allows whites to explain away racial phenomena by suggesting they are natural occurrences.** For example, whites can claim "segregation" is natural because people from all backgrounds "gravitate toward likeness." Or that their taste for whiteness in friends and partners is just "the way things are." Although the above statements can be interpreted as "racist" and as contradicting the color-blind logic, they are actually used to reinforce the myth of nonracialism. How? By suggesting these preferences are almost biologically driven and typical of all groups in society, preferences for primary associations with members of one's race are rationalized as nonracial because "*they* (racial minorities) do it too."

Cultural racism **is a frame that relies on culturally based arguments such as "Mexicans do not put much emphasis on education" or "blacks have too many babies" to explain the standing of minorities in society.**

This frame has been adequately discussed by many commentators and does not require much discussion.[16] During slavery and Jim Crow a central rationale for excluding racial minorities was their presumed biological inferiority. Even as late as 1940, a white newspaper editor in Durham, North Carolina, could confidently state that

> a Negro is different from other people in that he's an unfortunate branch of the human family who hasn't been able to make out of himself all he is capable of. He is not capable of being rushed because of the background of the jungle. Part of his human nature can't be rushed; it gets him off his balance. . . . You can't wipe away inbred character in one year or a hundred years. It must be nursed along. We look upon him for his lack of culture, as being less reliable, in business and unsafe socially. His passions are aroused easily.[17]

Today only white supremacist organizations spout things such as this in open forums. Yet, these biological views have been replaced by cultural ones that, as I will show, are as effective in defending the racial status quo.[18] For example, George McDermott, one of the white middle-class residents interviewed by Katherine Newman in her *Declining Fortunes*, stated,

> I believe in morality: I believe in ethics: I believe in hard work: I believe in all the old values. I don't believe in handouts. . . . So that the whole welfare system falls into that [category]. . . . The idea of fourteen-year-old kids getting pregnant and then having five children by the time they're twenty is absurd! It's ridiculous! And that's what's causing this country to go downhill.

And as Newman poignantly comments, "George does not see himself as racist. Publicly he would subscribe to the principle everyone in this society deserves a fair shake."[19] Color-blind racism is racism without racists!

Minimization of racism **is a frame that suggests discrimination is no longer a central factor affecting minorities' life chances ("It's better now than in the past" or "There is discrimination, but there are plenty of jobs out there").** This frame allows whites to accept facts such as the racially motivated murder of James Byrd Jr. in Jasper, Texas,[20] the brutal police attack on Rodney King, the Texaco case,[21] the 2005 lawsuit by black workers alleging that Tyson Foods maintained a "Whites Only" bathroom in one of their Alabama plants, the neglect and slow response by government officials toward a mostly black population during Hurricane Katrina, and many other cases and still accuse minorities of being "hypersensitive," of using race as an "excuse," or of "playing the infamous race card." More significantly, this frame also involves regarding discrimination exclusively as all-out racist behavior, which, given the way "new racism" practices operate in post–civil rights America (chapter 1), eliminates the bulk of racially motivated actions by individual whites and institutions by fiat.

Before proceeding to illustrate how whites use these frames, I need to clarify a few points about the data and how I present them. First, whites used these frames in combination rather than in pure form. This is understandable, since informal expressions of ideology are a constructive effort, a process of building arguments in situ. Therefore, the examples of how whites use a particular frame may be mixed with other frames. Second, the frames were verbalized by participants in various emotional tones, ranging from sympathy to absolute disgust and outrage toward minorities. This suggests whites with differing levels of sympathy toward minorities resort to the *same* frames when constructing their accounts of racial matters. I attempt to represent this range of emotion in the quotes. Third, because the college student and DAS samples represent two different populations, I present quotes from the two studies separately in the text. I do so to better identify differences in style or content among the two populations. Fourth, the quotes in the chapter were selected to embrace the variety of ways in which the frames are used by respondents. This implies that many outrageously racist quotes were left out for the sake of representing the variance in the samples. Fifth, the interviews were transcribed to be as close to what the respondents uttered as possible. Thus the transcripts include nonlexical expressions (umm, ahh, umhmm), pauses (indicated by ellipses when they are short and by a number in seconds in parentheses representing the duration of the pause when they are longer than five seconds), emphases (indicated by *italics* or, for notations of the respondent's tone, by italic letters in brackets), self-corrections (denoted by a short line, —), and other important discursive matters (laughs and changes in tone are indicated with italic letters in brackets). Whenever I have added words, they appear in brackets; the interviewers' interventions appear in brackets and in italic letters. However, to improve its readability, I edited the material lightly.

ABSTRACT LIBERALISM: UNMASKING REASONABLE RACISM[22]

Because of the curious way in which liberalism's principles are used in the post–civil rights era, other analysts label modern racial ideology "laissez-fare racism" or "competitive racism" or argue that modern racism is essentially a combination of the "American Creed" with antiblack resentment.[23] The importance of this frame is evident in that whites use it on issues ranging from affirmative action and interracial friendship and marriage to neighborhood and residential segregation. Because of the pivotal role played by this frame in organizing whites' racial views, I provide numerous examples below.

Rationalizing Racial Unfairness in the Name of Equal Opportunity

An archetype of how white students use the notion of equal opportunity in an abstract manner to oppose racial fairness is Sue, a student at SU.

When asked if minority students should be provided unique opportunities to be admitted into universities, Sue stated:

> I don't think that they should be provided with unique opportunities. I think that they should have the same opportunities as everyone else. You know, it's up to them to meet the standards and whatever that's required for entrance into universities or whatever. I don't think that just because they're a minority that they should, you know, not meet the requirements, you know.

Sue, like most whites, ignored the effects of past and contemporary discrimination on the social, economic, and educational status of minorities. Therefore, by supporting equal opportunity for everyone without a concern for the savage inequalities between whites and blacks, Sue's stance safeguards white privilege. Sue even used the notion of equal opportunity to avoid explaining why blacks tend to perform worse than whites academically: "I don't know . . . um, like I said, I don't see it as a group thing. I see it more as an individual [thing] and I don't know why as a whole they don't do better. I mean, as I see it, they have the same opportunity and everything. They *should* be doing equal."

College students are not the only ones who use this abstract notion of equal opportunity to justify their racial views. For example, Eric, a corporate auditor in his forties, and a very affable man who seemed more tolerant than most members of his generation (e.g., he had dated a black woman for three years, recognized that discrimination happens "a lot" and identified multiple examples, and even said that "the system is . . . is white"), erupted in anger when asked if reparations were due to blacks for the injuries caused by slavery and Jim Crow: "Oh tell them to shut up, OK! I had nothing to do with the whole situation. The opportunity is there, there is no reparation involved and let's not dwell on it. I'm very opinionated about that!" After suggesting that Jews and Japanese are the ones who really deserve reparation, Eric added, "But something that happened three God-damned generations ago, what do you want us to do about it now? Give them opportunity, give them scholarships, but reparations?"

Was Eric just a white with a "principled opposition" to government intervention (see chapter 1 for analysts who make this claim)? This does not seem to be the case since Eric, like most whites, made a distinction between government spending on behalf of victims of child abuse, the homeless, and battered women (whom whites deem as legitimate candidates for assistance) and government spending on blacks (whom whites deem as unworthy candidates for assistance). This finding was consistent with DAS survey results. For instance, whereas 64.3 percent of whites agreed that "we should expand the services that benefit the poor," only 39.6 percent (as opposed to 84 percent of blacks) agreed with the proposition "The government should make every effort to improve the social and economic position of blacks living in the United States." Furthermore, whereas 75.2 percent of white respondents approved of increasing federal spending for the environment and 59.7 percent for social security, only 31.7 percent approved such increases for programs to assist blacks. And when the question dealt with government programs that were not perceived as "racial" in any way,[24] the proportion of whites supporting the program increased even more.

"The Most Qualified . . .":
A Meritocratic Way of Defending White Privilege

Another tenet of liberalism whites use to explain racial matters is the Jeffersonian idea of "the cream rises to the top," or meritocracy (reward by merit). And whites seem unconcerned that the color of the "cream" that usually "rises" is white. For example, Diane, a student at SU, expressed her dissatisfaction about providing blacks unique opportunities to be admitted into universities: "I don't think you should admit anyone. It's gotta be, you've gotta be on the level to do it. If they were prepared beforehand to handle the college level to succeed in it, then there you go, anyone can." Diane then added, "They've gotta have the motivation to do well before you get there, I mean, I can't imagine being unprepared to go [to college] like just barely getting by in high school and then coming here to take the classes, you just can't go, 'OK, we want to put minorities in here so put anyone in,' you know." Diane also used the notion of meritocracy to explain her opposition to affirmative action.

> That's so hard. I still believe in merit, you know, I still believe in equality, you know. If you did have two people with the same qualifications, one's minority and one's not, you know, I'd want to interview them and just maybe a personality stands out that works with the job, I don't know. Just find something other than race to base it on, you know? Let that not be a factor if they qualify.

How could Diane maintain these views and remain "reasonable"? Diane could say these things and seem reasonable because she believes discrimination is not the reason why blacks are worse off than whites. Instead, she relied on the cultural racism frame to explain blacks' status. This view can be seen too in her response to a question on why blacks fare worse academically than whites: "I don't know why. Mine was a personal motivation so, you know, I don't know. I don't want to say they weren't personally motivated to get good grades, but that's what it was for me." Diane expanded on this matter and said, "Maybe some of them don't have parents to push them or . . . maybe the schools are not equal." She also speculated, "Maybe, you know, they've got in their mind that they can't succeed because they're a minority and they don't try, you know, no one there to tell them 'You can do it, it doesn't matter who you are.'"

Whites from the Detroit metro area used the meritocratic frame as extensively as college students. For instance Jim, a thirty-year-old computer software salesperson from a privileged background, explained in the following way his opposition to affirmative action:

> I think it's unfair top to bottom on everybody and the whole process. It often, you know, discrimination itself is a bad word, right? But you discriminate every day. You wanna buy a beer at the store and there are six kinda beers you can get, from Natural Light to Sam Adams, right? And you look at the price and you look at the kind of beer, and you . . . *it's a choice.* And a lot of that you have laid out in front of you, which one you get? Now, should the government sponsor Sam Adams and make it cheaper than Natural Light because it's brewed by someone in Boston? That doesn't make much sense, right? Why would we want that or make Sam Adams eight times as expensive because we want people to buy Natural Light? And it's the same thing about getting into school or getting into some place. And universities it's easy, and universities is a hot topic now, and I could bug you, you know, Midwestern University I don't think has a lot of racism in the admissions process. And I think Midwestern University would, would agree with that pretty strongly. So why not just pick people that are going to do well at Midwestern University, pick people by their merit? I think we should stop the whole idea of choosing people based on their color. It's bad to choose someone based on their color; why do we, why do we enforce it in an institutional process?

Since Jim posited hiring decisions are like market choices (choosing between competing brands of beer), he embraced a laissez-faire position on hiring. The problem with Jim's view is that discrimination in the labor market is alive and well (e.g., it affects black and Latino job applicants 30 to 50 percent of the time) and that most jobs (as many as 80 percent) are obtained through informal networks.[25] Jim himself acknowledged that being white is an advantage in America because "there's more people in the world who are white and are racist against people that are black than vice versa." However, Jim also believes that although blacks "perceive or feel" like there is a lot of discrimination, he does not believe there is much discrimination out there. Hence, by upholding a strict laissez-faire view on hiring and, at the same time, ignoring the significant impact of past and contemporary discrimination in the labor market, Jim can safely voice his opposition to affirmative action in an apparently race-neutral way.

"Nothing Should Be Forced upon People": Keeping Things the Way They Are

A central tenet of liberal democracies is that governments should intervene in economic and social matters as little as possible because the "invisible hand of the market" eventually balances states of disequilibrium. A corollary of this tenet, and part of the American mythology, is the idea that social change should be the outcome of a rational and democratic process and not of the government's coercive capacity.[26] During the Jim Crow era, the belief that racial change should happen through a slow, evolutionary process in "peoples' hearts" rather than through governmental actions was expressed in the phrase "you cannot legislate morality."[27] This old standpoint has been curiously reformulated in the modern era to justify keeping racial affairs the way they are. These ideas appeared occasionally in discussions on affirmative action, but most often in discussions about school and residential integration in America.

Sonny, a student at MU, explained in typical fashion her position on whether school segregation is the fault of government, whites, or blacks. As almost all the students, Sonny first stated her belief that school integration is in principle a good thing to have: "In principle, yeah, I think that's a good idea because like with, like with people interacting, they will understand each other better in future generations." But Sonny also, as most students, was not too fond of government attempts to remedy school segregation or, in her words, "I, I don't—I mean, it should be done if people want to do it. If people volunteer for it, and they want that part of their lives, then they should do it, but the government should not force people to bus if they don't want that." When asked to clarify her stance on this matter, she added, "I don't think the government should impose any legislation thinking that it will change people's hearts because people have to change them on their own. You can't force them to say, 'Well, OK, now that I have to bus my kid there, I like it.'"

DAS respondents were as adamant as students in arguing that it is not the government's business to remedy racial problems. For example, Lynn, a human resources manager in her early fifties, explained why there has been so little school integration since the 1954 *Brown v. Board of Education* decision:

> I don't and that's another one. *I do not believe in busing.* The reason I don't believe in busing, you know, I said I don't. I didn't encourage my children to play with the neighborhood kids. I still felt that going to school in your community was the key to developing a child's sense of community and I still believe that. One of the reasons, another reason I moved from where I was [was] that I didn't want my children to be bused. I didn't want to have them got on a bus, especially me working. So I don't think that is an answer.

> I think the answer is education and helping people learn to make a life for themselves and, you know, any type of social program that interacts, that provides interaction between races I think is excellent. But I'm just not a busing person.

Lynn wants equal opportunity in education as well as community schools, a position that sounds perfectly reasonable. However, one would expect Lynn to support doing something to make sure that communities throughout America are diverse, a policy that other things being equal would guarantee school integration. Yet, Lynn took a very strong laissez-faire, anti-government-intervention stance on this matter. Lynn answered as follows the question, "America has lots of all-white and all-black neighborhoods. What do you think of this situation?"

> I don't have a problem with all-white and all-black neighborhoods if that's the choice of the people, the *individuals*. But, if it's *forced* either way, if I'm a black person and I've come into the neighborhood and I want to live here and selectively denied that option, that's wrong. But, again, there still has to be some type of social interaction for growth and if the social interaction takes place then, the cross-integration will take place, I think.

When pressed about what she thought could be done specifically to increase the mixing of the races in neighborhoods, Lynn restated that this could only be achieved "through educating (people) and encouraging businesses." Lynn was not alone in having this abstract view on school and neighborhood integration. Only one of the white respondents who opposed busing in the interviews (69.7 percent of whites opposed busing in the survey) provided a specific proposal that if implemented would increase residential as well as school integration.[28]

Individual Choice or an Excuse for Racial Unfairness and Racially Based Choices?

Individualism[29] today has been recast as a justification for opposing policies to ameliorate racial inequality because they are "group based" rather than "case by case." In addition, the idea of individual choice is used to defend whites' right to live and associate primarily with whites (segregation) and for choosing whites exclusively as their mates. The problem with how whites apply the notion of individualism to our present racial conundrum is that a relation of domination-subordination still ordains race relations in the United States (see chapters 1 and 4 in my *White Supremacy and Racism in the Post–Civil Rights Era*). Thus, if minority groups face group-based discrimination and whites have group-based advantages, demanding individual treatment for all can only benefit the advantaged group.[30] And behind the idea of people having the right of making their own "choices" lays the fallacy of racial pluralism—the false assumption that all racial groups have the same power in the American polity. Because whites have more power, their unfettered, so-called individual choices help reproduce a form of white supremacy in neighborhoods, schools, and society in general.

Lynn, a human resources manager, used the notion of individualism in a very curious way. Although Lynn expressed her support for affirmative action because "there's still a lot of discrimination," she thinks that "there isn't as much discrimination as there used to be." Lynn also acknowledged white males have advantages in society and said "the white male is pretty much instilled" and "very much represses . . . um, people and other minorities." Nevertheless, when it came to the possibility of affirmative action affecting her, Lynn said,

> Um, because affirmative action is based on a group as a whole, but when it comes down to the individual, like if affirmative action were against me one time, like it would anger me. I mean, because, you know, *I* as an individual got ripped off and, you know, getting a job.

DAS respondents also used individualism to justify their racial views and race-based preferences. For example, Mandi, a registered nurse in her thirties, said she had no problems with neighborhood segregation. She justified her potentially problematic position by saying that people have the right to choose where and with whom they live.

> Umm, I think that people select a neighborhood to live in that they are similar to and people, you know, whatever similarities they *find* [*louder voice*], you know, it's race, economical level, religion, or, you know, whatever. When you are looking at somebody you don't know what, what denomination they are or what political preference they have, but you can tell right off in race. I think that they choose to live in a neighborhood that is their race.

NATURALIZATION: DECODING
THE MEANING OF "THAT'S THE WAY IT IS"

A frame that has not yet been brought to the fore by social scientists is whites' naturalization of race-related matters. Although the naturalization frame was the least-used frame of color-blind racism by respondents in these two projects, about 50 percent of DAS respondents and college students used it, particularly when discussing school or neighborhood matters, to explain the limited contact between whites and minorities, or to rationalize whites' preferences for whites as significant others. The word "natural" or the phrase "that's the way it is" is often interjected to normalize events or actions that could otherwise be interpreted as racially motivated (residential segregation) or racist (preference for whites as friends and partners). But, as social scientists know quite well, few things that happen in the social world are "natural," particularly things pertaining to racial matters. Segregation as well as racial preferences are produced through social processes and that is the delusion/illusion component of this frame.

The importance and usefulness of this frame can be illustrated with Sara, a student at MU who used the frame on three separate occasions. Sara, for example, used the frame to answer the question on black self-segregation.

> Hmm, I don't really think it's a segregation. I mean, I think people, you know, spend time with people that they are like, not necessarily in color, but you know, their ideas and values and, you know, maybe their class has something to do with what they're used to. But I don't really think it's a segregation. I don't think I would have trouble, you know, approaching someone of a different race or color. I don't think it's a problem. It's just that the people that I do hang out with are just the people that I'm with all the time. They're in my organizations and stuff like that.

Sara also used the naturalization frame to explain the paltry level of school integration in the United States.

> Well, I also think that, you know, where you are in school has to do with the neighborhood that you grow up in and, like, I grew up in mainly all-white communities so that community was who I was going to school with. And if that community had been more black, then that would be, I guess, more integrated and that would be just fine. I don't know if there's any way you can change the places in which people live because I think there *are* gonna be white communities and there are gonna be black communities and, you know, I don't know how you can get two communities like in the same school system.

The interviewer followed up Sara's answer with the question, "Why do you think there are white communities and black communities?" Sara's answer was, "Maybe like I said before, if people like to be with people that they're similar with and it means, you know—well, I don't think it has anything to do with color. I think it has to do with where they. . . ." Sara did not complete her thought as a light seems to have clicked on in her mind. She then proceeded to change her answer and acknowledged that race has a bearing on how people select neighborhoods: "Well, I guess it does [*laughs*]." The interviewer asked Sara if she thought her parents would move into an almost all-black neighborhood. Sara employed all sorts of rhetorical maneuvers (see chapter 4) to defend her parents by conveying the idea that racial considerations would have never been a criterion for selecting a neighborhood.

Finally Liz, a student at SU, suggested that self-segregation is a universal process or, in her own words: "I do think they segregate themselves, but I don't necessarily think it's on purpose. I think it's that, you know, *we all try to stay with our own kind* so, therefore, you know, *they get along better with their own people* or whatnot [my emphasis]." By universalizing segregation as a natural phenomenon, Liz was able to justify even her own racial preference for white mates. When asked if she had ever been attracted to minority people, Liz said,

> Um no, just because I wasn't really attracted to them, you know, I'm more attracted to someone that's like kinda more like me. But, you know, and I wouldn't say that, I mean, I like if he's good looking or not, you know, it's not that, it's just I'm more attracted to someone white, I don't know why [*laughs*].

DAS respondents naturalized racial matters too, but in general did it in a more crude fashion. For instance, Bill, a manager in a manufacturing firm, explained the limited level school integration:

> I don't think it's anybody's fault. Because people tend to group with their own people. Whether it's white or black or upper-middle class or lower class or, you now, upper class, you know, Asians. People tend to group with their own. Doesn't mean if a black person moves into your neighborhood, they shouldn't go to your school. They should and you should mix and welcome them and everything else, but you can't force people together. If people want to be together, they should intermix more. [*Interviewer: OK. So the lack of mixing is really just kind of an individual lack of desire?*] Well, individuals, it's just the way it is. You know, people group together for lots of different reasons: social, religious. Just as animals in the wild, you know. Elephants group together, cheetahs group together. You bus a cheetah into an elephant herd because they should mix? You can't force that [*laughs*].

[handwritten margin note: Uh nuh / Same thing]

Bill's unflattering and unfitting metaphor comparing racial segregation to the separation of species, however, was not the only crude way of using the naturalization frame. For example, Earl, a small-time contractor in his fifties, explained segregation in a matter-of-fact way.

> I think you're never going to change that! I think it's just kind of, you know, it's going to end up that way. . . . Every race sticks together and that's the way it should be, you know. I grew up in a white neighborhood, you know, most of the blacks will live in the black neighborhood. [*Interviewer: So you don't think there's anything wrong?*] No. Well, they can move, they still have the freedom to move anywhere they want anyway.

A significant number of DAS respondents naturalized racial matters in a straightforward manner. For example, Jim, a thirty-year-old computer software salesperson for a large company, naturalized school segregation as follows:

> Eh, you know, it's more of the human nature's fault. It's not the government's fault, right? The government doesn't tell people where to live. So as people decide where to live or where to move into or where they wanna feel comfortable, [they] move to where they feel comfortable. We all kinda hang out with people that are like us. I mean, you look at Detroit, we have a Mexican village, why do we have a Mexican village? Why aren't Mexican people spread out all over on metro Detroit? Well, they like being near other Mexican people; that way they could have a store that suited them close by them, you know, those sort of things probably together. So, it's more human nature that I would blame for it.

Despite whites' belief that residential and school segregation, friendship, and attraction are natural and raceless occurrences, social scientists have documented how racial considerations affect all these issues. For example, residential segregation is created by white buyers searching for white neighborhoods and aided by realtors, bankers, and sellers.[31] As white neighborhoods develop, white schools follow—an outcome that further contributes to the process of racial isolation. Socialized in a "white habitus" (see chapter 5) and influenced by the Eurocentric culture, it is no wonder whites interpret their racialized choices for white significant others as "natural." They are the "natural" consequence of a white socialization process.[32]

"THEY DON'T HAVE IT ALL TOGETHER": CULTURAL RACISM

Pierre-André Taguieff has argued that modern European racism does not rely on an essentialist interpretation of minorities' endowments.[33] Instead, it presents their presumed cultural practices as fixed features (hence, he labels it as the "biologization of racism") and uses that as the rationale for justifying racial inequality. Thus, Europeans may no longer believe Africans, Arabs, Asian Indians, or blacks from the West Indies are biologically inferior, but they assail them for their presumed lack of hygiene, family disorganization, and lack of morality.[34] This cultural racism frame is very well established in the United States. Originally labeled as the "culture of poverty"[35] in the 1960s, this tradition has resurfaced many times since, resurrected by conservative scholars such as Charles Murray and Lawrence Mead, liberals such as William Julius Wilson, and even radicals such as Cornel West.[36] The essence of the American version of this frame is "blaming the victim," arguing that minorities' standing is a product of their lack of effort, loose family organization, and inappropriate values.

Since there is little disagreement among social scientists about the centrality of this frame in the post–civil rights era, I focus my attention on highlighting what this frame allows whites to accomplish. I begin my illustration of this frame with two, clear-cut examples of college students who used it. The students agreed with the premise of the question, "Many whites explain the status of blacks in this country as a result of blacks lacking motivation, not having the proper work ethic, or being lazy. What do you think?" The first student is Kara, an MU student.

> I think, to some extent, that's true. Just from, like, looking at the black people that I've met in my classes and the few that I knew before college, not like they're—I don't want to say waiting for a handout, but to some extent, that's kind of what I'm like hinting at. Like, almost like they feel like they were discriminated against hundreds of years ago, now what are you gonna give me? You know, or maybe even it's just their background, that they've never, like maybe they're the first generation to be in college, so they feel like just that is enough for them.

The second quote is from Kim, a student at SU:

> Yeah, I totally agree with that. I don't think, you know, they're all like that, but, I mean, it's just that if it wasn't that way, why would there be so many blacks living in the projects? You know, why would there be so many poor blacks? If they worked hard, they could make it just as high as anyone else could. You know, I just think that's just, you know, they're raised that way and they see what their parents are like so they assume that's the way it should be. And they just follow the roles their parents had for them and don't go anywhere.

[handwritten margin note: assumption of same playing field]

When cultural racism is used in combination with the "minimization of racism" frame, the results are ideologically deadly. If people of color say they experience discrimination, whites, such as Kara and Kim, do not believe them and claim they use discrimination as an "excuse" to hide the central reason why they are behind whites in society: their presumed "laziness."

Although Kara and Kim used the cultural racism frame in a crude form, most students did not. They articulated their culture of poverty views in a gentler, at times even "compassionate," way. For example, Ann, a student at WU, inserted the frame in her answer to a question about why blacks as a group fare worse than whites academically.

Um, I guess I would have to say primarily family structure. Maybe it's not [being] able to support the child and, you know, in school and really encourage. It might be that it's a single-parent family and it's necessary [for them] to get out and get a job, you know, a full-time job and work a part-time job and still try to go to school. Maybe it's not encouraged as much for, like long term, it's mainly survival. I don't know, something, income; if the family is really skimping by it would be really far-fetched, well, it wouldn't be probably necessarily the first thing that a child from [such] a family would think of, you know, expensive college rather than paying the rent, you know what I mean [*laughs*]? So, I mean, you know, the priorities are different.

Although Ann's arguments seem "reasonable" (poor people may have a different set of priorities than other people based on their economic situation), her explanation is wanting because it avoids mentioning the institutional effects of discrimination in the labor, housing, and educational markets and the well-documented[37] impact that discrimination has on middle- and upper-middle-class blacks. More significantly, Ann's failure to recognize how old- and new-fashioned discrimination affects blacks' life chances is not an argumentative slip, but the way in which most whites construe the situation of blacks, as evidenced by how respondents in both samples used similar arguments in answering questions about blacks' status.

This kinder and gentler way of using the cultural frame was the preferred choice of students. For example, Jay, a student at WU, explained as follows why blacks have a worse overall standing than whites:

Hmm, I think it's due to lack of education. I think because if they didn't grow up in a household that afforded them the time to go to school and they had to go out and get jobs right away, I think it is just a cycle [that] perpetuates things, you know. I mean, I can't say that blacks can't do it because, obviously, there are many, many of them [that] have succeeded in getting good jobs and all that.

Jay, as most whites, admits to the "exceptional black." However, Jay immediately goes back to the gentle cultural argument:

So it's possible that the cycle seems to perpetuate itself because—I mean, let's say they go out and get jobs and they settle down much earlier than they would normally if they had gone to school and then they have kids at a young age and they—these kids—have to go and get jobs and so.

How did DAS respondents use this cultural frame? They relied on this frame as often as students did but were significantly more likely to use it in a straightforward and crude manner. The following two cases exemplify how most DAS respondents used this frame. First is Isaac, an engineer in his fifties. In response to the question comparing blacks' and whites' overall standing, Isaac argued that few blacks have the education to work as engineers. This led to the following exchange between Isaac and the interviewer:

> *Interviewer*: So you feel maybe there's a lack of interest in education that black people have?
>
> *Isaac*: They want to get a shortcut to make money. There's no urgency to get education. They want to make, to get money faster than whites. They don't want to take the time to get educated, they want to get money fast.
>
> *Interviewer*: So they also don't put the time into developing their educational skills?
>
> *Isaac*: Yeah the way you learn, the way you grow, is the way you become.
>
> *Interviewer*: Some people say that minorities are worse off than whites because they lack motivation, are lazy, or do not have the proper values to succeed in our society. What do you think?
>
> *Isaac*: Right now I think our minorities are lazy. They don't have the patience to keep going.

Ian, the manager of information security at an automotive company, explained why blacks are worse off than whites as follows: "The majority of 'em just don't strive to do anything, to make themselves better. Again, I've seen that all the way through. 'I do this today, I'm fine, I'm happy with it, I don't need anything better.' Never, never, never striving or giving extra to, to make themselves better."

Ian's perception of blacks as lazy emerged from his understanding of blacks as culturally deficient. This view was clearly expressed in his response to the question, "Do you think that the races are naturally different?"

> Well I think that genes have something, some play in this, but I think a lot of it is past history of the people and the way they're brought up. You look at Chinese, if you're gonna get ahead in China, you've gotta be very intellectual and you've gotta be willing to, uh, to fight for everything that you're gonna get. Ja–Japan is the same way. For a kid just to get into college, they gonna take two years of going through entrance exams to get in. Then you kinda look at the blacks' situation. It's like, "Well, because of slavery, I ought to be given this for nothing, so I don't have to work for it, just give it to me." So culture and their upbringing is the big part of this.

Although Ian came close to the old biological view ("Well, I think genes have something, some play in this"), overall he made use of the cultural frame to explain blacks' status (Asians do well because they "gotta be intellectual," whereas blacks believe that because of slavery they do not have to work).

MINIMIZATION OF RACISM: WHITES'
DECLINING SIGNIFICANCE OF RACE THESIS

When William Julius Wilson published *The Declining Significance of Race* in 1978, he made many whites in academia feel good about themselves. Wilson's main claim—that class rather than race was the central obstacle for black mobility—was an argument that had been brewing among whites for quite a while. Yet, whites believe that discrimination exists. For example, when white and black respondents in the DAS survey were given the statement, "Discrimination against blacks is no longer a problem in the United States," a high proportion of *both* groups (82.5 percent of whites and 89.5 percent of blacks) "disagreed" or "strongly disagreed" with that statement. Although whites and blacks believe discrimination is still a problem, they dispute its salience as a factor explaining blacks' collective standing. Thus, in response to the more specific statement, "Blacks are in the position that they are today as a group because of present day discrimination," only 32.9 percent of whites "agreed" or "strongly agreed" (compared to 60.5 percent of blacks). This means that in general whites believe discrimination has all but disappeared, whereas blacks believe that discrimination—old and new—is alive and well.

College students were more likely than DAS respondents to give lip service to the existence of discrimination. Because students for this study were taking social science courses at the time of the interviews, they may have become sensitized to the significance of discrimination as well as to the new character of contemporary discrimination. However, despite this sensitization, few believed discrimination and institutionalized racism are the reasons minorities lag behind whites in this society. In general, the students articulated their declining significance of race thesis in three ways. A plurality (eighteen of forty-one) used an indirect strategy of denial set by one of the following two phrases, "I am not black" or "I don't see discrimination" (see chapter 4 for an analysis of the functions of these phrases), others (nine of forty-one) minimized racism directly, and yet others (seven of forty-one) argued minorities make things look racial when they are not.

The following example illustrates how students used the indirect strategy of denial. The response of Mary, a student at SU, to the statement, "Many blacks and other minorities claim that they do not get access to good jobs because of discrimination and that when they get the jobs they are not promoted at the same speed as their white peers," was,

> I think before you really start talking about hiring practices and promotion practices, you have to look at credentials. I mean, you know, I've only really had one job. I worked for a general contractor so it was basically me in the

office all day with him, my boss. But I, in fact, you have to look at credentials. I mean, I don't know if, you know, a white person gets a job over a minority, I can't sit here and say, "Well, that's discrimination," because I don't know what the factors were. This person got a master's degree versus a bachelor's degree, or more in-depth training than this person, you know? I mean, I definitely do not doubt that [discrimination] happens, that minorities get passed over for promotions and that they are not hired based on their race. I have absolutely no doubt that it happens. I think that before you can sit there and start calling a lot of things discrimination, you need to look into the background, the credentials behind it.

Rather than stating "I don't believe minorities experience discrimination," Mary suggested they may not get jobs or promotions because they lack the credentials. And although Mary, as most whites, recognizes discrimination exists ("I definitely do not doubt that [discrimination] happens"), she clearly believes most claims are bogus ("I think that before you can sit there and start calling a lot of things discrimination, you need to look into the background, the credentials behind it").

The next example is of students who minimized the significance of racism directly. Andy, a student at WU, answered a question on whether discrimination is the central reason why blacks are behind whites today by saying, "I think they do." Yet his answer was wanting, since he could not provide a meaningful explanation of how discrimination affects minorities' life chances. More importantly, Andy's answers to the other questions minimized the salience of racism. For instance, his answer to the question of whether or not discrimination affects the chances of minorities getting jobs and promotions was, "I think that there's probably less than it used to be, but that it still happens. It's just in isolated places or, you know, it happens in different places, but in most jobs, I think it probably does not happen." When asked to elaborate, Andy stated he believes the reason why blacks do not get good jobs is, "if anything, it's probably education" because "you can't apply for certain jobs without a lot of education."

The last example is of students who argued blacks make situations racial that are not. Janet, an SU student, answered all the questions on discrimination by denying that discrimination is a salient factor in minorities' life chances and suggesting alternative interpretations. For instance, Janet's answer to the same question, on whether or not discrimination is the central reason why blacks lag behind whites, was, "I would say it depends on the individual. I'm sure there are some . . . that do and others [that] don't, so. . . ." When asked to clarify, she said, "Right. But I would say for the most part, most of them don't unless they make it out to be the case." When the interviewer asked Janet if she thought most claims of discrimination by minorities were a perception issue, she replied, "If they looked at it as a different way or something, they might see—might not see it as racism, you see what I'm saying? [*Interviewer: You are saying that they are seeing more than is actually out there?*] Right." When asked about discrimination in jobs, Janet answered in a blunt fashion:

> I would say that's a bunch of crap [*laughs*]. I mean, if they're qualified, they'll hire you and if you are not qualified, then you don't get the job. It's the same way with, once you get the job, if you are qualified for a promotion, you'll get the promotion. It's the same way with white, blacks, Asians, whatever. If you do the job, you'll get the job.

DAS respondents used similar argumentative strategies to deny the significance of discrimination. The strategy they used the most was direct minimization (eighteen of sixty-six), followed by outright denial (thirteen of sixty-six), stating that minorities make things racial (eleven of sixty-six), and indirect minimization (three of sixty-six). The remaining respondents (twenty of sixty-six) include a few who sincerely believe discrimination is important (see chapter 7) and others who denied the centrality of discrimination in their own peculiar way.

The first case exemplifies DAS respondents who minimized the significance of discrimination directly. Joann, a poor white woman in her fifties who works in a large chain store, answered the direct discrimination question by stating, "I don't see any in the store." When asked about discrimination against minorities in general, Joann said,

> I don't think it's as bad as it was. It probably needs improvement. What [society] needs is a knowledgeable crew and I think that is the truth there. I think that the work will have to be done up continually until we're all one big happy family. [*Interviewer: Do you foresee that happening?*] It wouldn't surprise me. My great-granddaughter might marry a black, I don't know. *I have no idea!*

The next case is an example of respondents who denied discrimination outright. It is worth pointing out that all the DAS respondents who used this strategy were from working- or lower-class backgrounds. Scott, a twenty-three-year-old drafter for a mechanical engineering company, answered the direct question on discrimination as follows:

> I don't—nowadays I don't, I don't really feel that way, I really don't at all. Maybe like when I was younger I would notice it, but right now I don't really feel that there's too much segregation anymore. If it is because of the person, you know, from their past experience. And, I mean, if you got a record, you're not gonna go too far, you know. So then they might feel like "Just being held back just because, you know, just 'cause I'm black."

The interviewer followed up Scott's answer with the question, "So you don't think that discrimination is a factor in most blacks' lives nowadays?" His answer was, "It might be just because of their past and their attitudes toward life. But if you just took it as everyday life and just went with it, no, I don't feel it at all, I don't see it. I don't practice it and my friends, all my friends [don't] practice it."

Next are examples of respondents who argued blacks make things racial that are not. Sandra, a retail salesperson in her early forties, explained her view on discrimination as follows:

> I think if you are looking for discrimination, I think it's there to be *found*. But if you make the best of any situation, and if *you don't use it as an excuse*. I think sometimes it's an excuse because people felt they deserved a job, whatever! I think if things didn't go their way I know a lot of people have a tendency to use prejudice or racism as whatever as an *excuse*. I think in some ways, *yes* there [are] people who are prejudiced. It's not only blacks, it's about Spanish, or women. In a lot of ways there [is] a lot of *reverse* discrimination. It's just what you wanna make of it.

Finally, I provide an example of respondents who used the indirect minimization strategy. Dave, an engineer in his forties who owns a small-time employment agency, answered the direct question on discrimination by saying, "[*laughs*] I don't know any blacks so I don't know. But, in general, I probably have to say it's true." When asked for clarification, Dave stated,

> Oh that's a hard one to just, well, I guess it comes down to stereotypes though like I said earlier. It just—some people may try to say that some blacks don't work as hard as whites. So, in looking for a job they may feel like they didn't get the job because they have been discriminated against because they were black, that's very possible. That may not really be, but as a person, they make the assumption.

Dave explained blacks' inferior status as compared to whites by suggesting that it "really comes down to individuals" and that he has "especially noted that if you want a job, [there are] jobs out there." In this reply Dave intimates his belief that racial discrimination is not a factor in the labor market since "[there are] jobs out there."

The last case is of DAS respondents who did not fit the overall strategies and used sui generis arguments to deny the significance of racial discrimination. Henrietta, a transsexual school teacher in his fifties, said the following in response to the question on discrimination:

> [*Nine-second pause*] Trying to be an unbiased observer because as a transsexual I am discriminated against. I think if people act responsible they will

not be discriminated against. People who are acting irresponsible, in other words, demanding things, ah, "I need this" or "You did this because of my skin color," yeah, then they will be discriminated against. People who are intelligent present themselves in a manner that is appropriate for the situation and will not be discriminated against.

Thus, Henrietta suggests that blacks who experience discrimination deserve so because they act irresponsibly or complain too much.

CONCLUSION

In this chapter I illustrated how whites use the four central frames of color-blind racism, namely, abstract liberalism, naturalization, cultural racism, and minimization of racism. These frames are central to the views of whites, young (college-student sample) and old (DAS respondents), and serve them as an interpretive matrix from where to extract arguments to explain a host of racial issues. More significantly, together these frames form an impregnable yet elastic wall that barricades whites from the United States' racial reality. The trick is in the way the frames bundle with each other, that is, in the wall they form. Whites, for example, would have a tough time using the abstract liberalism frame if they could not resort to the minimization of racism frame as well. Precisely because they use these frames the way children use building blocks, whites can say things such as "I am all for equal opportunity, that's why I oppose affirmative action" and also say "Everyone has almost the same opportunities to succeed in this country because discrimination and racism are all but gone." And if anyone dares to point out that in this land of milk and honey there is a tremendous level of racial inequality—a fact that could deflate the balloon of color blindness—they can argue this is due to minorities' schools, lack of education, family disorganization, or lack of proper values and work ethic. In short, whites can blame minorities (blacks in particular) for their own status.

But what if someone pokes holes in whites' color-blind story by pointing out that whites live mostly in white neighborhoods, marry and befriend mostly whites, interact mostly with whites in their jobs, and send their children to white schools or, if they attend mixed schools, make sure they take most of their classes with white children. Whites have two discursive options to avoid the potentially devastating effects of these arguments. They can resort to the abstract liberalism frame and say something like "I support integration, but I do not believe in forcing people to do anything that they do not want to do" or "People have the right to make their own individual choices and no one can interfere." Alternatively, they can naturalize the whiteness in which they live ("Blacks like living with blacks, and whites like living with whites . . . it's a natural thing"). As I documented in this chapter, whites mix and match arguments as they see fit. Therefore, someone can say, "Segregation is a natural thing" but also say that "I believe that no one has the right of preventing people from moving into a neighborhood." These frames then form a formidable wall because they provide whites a seemingly nonracial way of stating their racial views without appearing irrational or rabidly racist.

But if the ideological wall of color-blind racism were not pliable, a few hard blows would suffice to bring it down. That is why the flexibility of the frames is so useful. Color-blind racism's frames are pliable because they do not rely on absolutes ("All blacks are . . ." or "Discrimination ended in 1965"). Instead, color-blind racism gives some room for exceptions ("Not all blacks are lazy, but most are") and allows for a variety of ways of holding on to the frames—from crude and straightforward to gentle and indirect. Regarding the former, almost every white respondent in these studies mentioned the exceptional black ("Well, Robert, my black friend, is not like that"), agreed in principle with racially progressive notions ("I believe that school integration is great because we can learn so much from each other" or "Gee, I wish I could see the day when we have the first black president"), or even joined Martin Luther King Jr. in the dream of color blindness ("In two or three generations race will disappear and we will all just be Americans"). Regarding the latter, whites used the color-blind frames in crude ways, displaying resentment and anger toward minorities ("Blacks are God-damned lazy") or in compassionate ways ("It is terrible the way they live in those neighborhoods, with those schools, without fathers, with crime just around the corner . . . it saddens me whenever I see all that on TV").

The pliability of the color-blind wall is further enhanced by the style of color blindness. For instance, if whites find themselves in a rhetorical bind, such as having disclosed a personal taste for whiteness or a dislike for blackness, they can always utter a disclaimer such as, "I am not prejudiced," or "If I ever fall in love with a black person, the race thing will never be an obstacle for us getting together." They can tiptoe around the most dangerous racial minefields because the stylistic elements of color blindness provide them the necessary tools to get in and out of almost any discussion. I examine these tools in detail in the next chapter.

NOTES

1. John Dollard, *Caste and Class in a Southern Town*, 2d ed. (New York: Doubleday, 1949).

2. For discussions on the "defensive beliefs" that supported Jim Crow, see Dollard, *Caste and Class*; Gunnar Myrdal, *An American Dilemma: The Negro Problem and Modern Democracy* (New York: Harper Brothers, 1944); Allison Davis et al., *Deep South* (Chicago: University of Chicago Press, 1941); and Charles S. Johnson, *Patterns of Negro Segregation* (New York: Harper Brothers, 1943).

3. This is taken from the title of conservative commentator Dinesh D'Souza's book, *The End of Racism: Principles for a Multiracial Society* (New York: Free Press, 1995). This book is, among other things, a crude example of color-blind racism.

4. J. B. Thompson, *Studies in the Theory of Ideology* (Cambridge, UK: Polity, 1984).

5. All ideologies aspire to be hegemonic, to rule the hearts of rulers and ruled. However, only those that incorporate elements of the "common sense" of the oppressed (albeit in partial and refracted manner) can truly become hegemonic.

6. See John Gray, *Liberalism* (Minneapolis: University of Minnesota Press, 1986).

7. All these quotes are from *The Communist Manifesto*. See David McLellan (ed.), *Karl Marx: Selected Writings* (London: Oxford University Press, 1982). For a detailed intellectual assault at the farce of liberalism, see Karl Marx and Frederick Engels, *The German Ideology* (New York: International, 1985).

8. For a marvelous discussion of this point and of "racial capitalism," see Cedric J. Robinson, *Black Marxism: The Making of the Black Radical Tradition* (Chapel Hill: University of North Carolina Press, 2000).

9. Good examples of this trend are Andrea T. Baumeister, *Liberalism and the "Politics of Difference"* (Edinburgh: Edinburgh University Press, 2000), and Patrick Neal, *Liberalism and Its Discontents* (New York: New York University Press, 1997). Although Baumeister skillfully shows the tensions in traditional liberal discourse that foreshadow some of today's debates and provides a reasonable philosophical resolution based on "value pluralism," she fails to point out the exclusionary character of liberalism and the Enlightenment. Neal's account produces two interesting modifications of liberalism: the idea that liberal states cannot be neutral and the notion of "modus vivendi liberalism," which entails an open liberal approach to social issues. Yet, like Baumeister, Neal is silent about the racism of the founding fathers of liberalism and the meaning of their racial exclusions for today's liberal project.

10. Charles W. Mills, *The Racial Contract* (Ithaca, N.Y.: Cornell University Press, 1997), 27.

11. The quotes by Kant and Voltaire as well as the views of Mill on slavery and colonialism can be found in chapter 2 of David Theo Goldberg, *Racist Culture* (Cambridge, UK: Blackwell, 1993). See also Zygmunt Bauman, *Modernity and Ambivalence* (Ithaca, N.Y.: Cornell University Press, 1991).

12. Richard Bellamy, "Liberalism," in *Contemporary Political Ideologies*, edited by Roger Eatwall and Anthony Wright, 23–49 (Boulder, Colo.: Westview, 1993).

13. See Dana D. Nelson, *National Citizenship: Capitalist Citizenship and the Imagined Fraternity of White Men* (Durham, N.C.: Duke University Press, 1998), and chapter 5 in Howard Zinn, *A People's History of the United States* (New York: HarperCollins, 1980).

14. From a social movements perspective, "liberal groups are those that attempt to reform social systems for the purpose of giving all groups equal oppor-

tunities." Margaret L. Andersen, *Thinking about Women: Sociological Perspectives on Sex and Gender* (New York: Macmillan, 1988), 299.

15. For a scathing critique of color-blind "radicals" such as Todd Gitlin, Michael Tomasky, Richard Rorty, Jim Sleeper, Barbara Epstein, and Eric Hobsbawm, see chapter 4 in Robin D. G. Kelley, *Yo' Mama's Disfunktional: Fighting the Culture Wars in Urban America* (Boston: Beacon, 1997).

16. The classic statement on the subject still is William Ryan, *Blaming the Victim* (New York: Vintage, 1976).

17. Charles S. Johnson, *Racial Attitudes: Interviews Revealing Attitudes of Northern and Southern White Persons, of a Wide Range of Occupational and Educational Levels, toward Negroes* (Nashville, Tenn.: Social Science Institute, Fisk University, 1946), 153.

18. It is important to note that cultural racism was part and parcel of European and American racisms. My point is that this theme has supplanted biological racism in importance and effectiveness.

19. Katherine S. Newman, *Declining Fortunes: The Withering of the American Dream* (New York: Basic, 1993), 168.

20. James Byrd was a black man murdered by three white supremacist ex-convicts in 1998 in Jasper, Texas.

21. High-level Texaco executives were caught on tape saying some racially insensitive things about blacks and other minorities a few years back, which led them to settle a lawsuit brought by minority employees accusing the company of racial discrimination in pay and promotion.

22. I borrow the phrase "reasonable racism" from Jody David Armour, *Negrophobia and Reasonable Racism* (New York: New York University Press, 1997).

23. The former label is used in the works of Lawrence Bobo and his coauthors (see chapter 1) and the latter by Philomena Essed, in *Diversity: Gender, Color, and Culture* (Amherst: University of Massachusetts Press, 1996).

24. When the question at hand could be perceived as racial, white support declined significantly. Thus, for example, only 21 percent of whites agreed with the proposition to increase welfare spending.

25. The specific citations for these facts can be found in the introduction, or the reader can consult my chapter, coauthored with Amanda E. Lewis, "The 'New Racism': Toward an Analysis of the U.S. Racial Structure, 1960–1990s," in *Race, Nationality, and Citizenship*, edited by Paul Wong (Boulder, Colo.: Westview, 1999).

26. Bringing about social change in this country has never been a rational, civilized feat, particularly when racial considerations have been involved. Force and resistance have accompanied the most significant changes in America's political and racial order. We used force to achieve our independence from Britain, to keep the Union together, and to end state-sanctioned Jim Crow. An excellent little book on this subject is Irving J. Sloan, *Our Violent Past: An American Chronicle* (New York: Random House, 1970).

27. Southern sociologist Howard W. Odum took William Graham Sumner's idea of "mores" and suggested that racial conflicts must be solved through an evolutionary approach that he labeled "racial adjustments." In a similar vein, northern sociologist Robert E. Park argued that race contacts went through "race cycles" that ended in racial assimilation. See Howard W. Odum, *American Social*

Problems (New York: Holt, 1939), and Robert E. Park, *Race and Culture* (Glencoe, Ill.: Free Press, 1950).

28. One respondent suggested a tax-incentive policy to stimulate residential integration.

29. Despite its elitist origins in American history (see chapter 5 in Zinn, *A People's History of the United States*), the notion of individualism has been used by social reform movements such as the Jacksonian democracy movement of the nineteenth century, the civil rights movement of the 1950s and 1960s ("one man, one vote"), and the woman's suffrage movement of the early twentieth century ("one person, one vote") to advance truly inclusive democratic agendas.

30. David Ingram, *Group Rights: Reconciling Equality and Difference* (Lawrence: University Press of Kansas, 2000).

31. For a review, see chapter 4 in my *White Supremacy and Racism in the Post–Civil Rights Era* (Boulder, Colo.: Rienner, 2001).

32. On all these matters, see Beverly Daniel Tatum, *"Why Are All the Black Kids Sitting Together in the Cafeteria?": And Other Conversations about Race* (New York: Basic, 1997).

33. Most of the work of this important French scholar has not been published in English. A few of his pieces have appeared in *Telos* and, fortunately, the University of Minnesota Press translated his *La Force du préjugé: Essai sur le racisme et ses doubles*. Pierre-André Taguieff, *The Force of Prejudice: Racism and Its Doubles* (Minneapolis: University of Minnesota Press, 2001). See also Pierre-André Taguieff (ed.), *Face au racisme, Tome II: Analyse, hypothèses, perspectives* (Paris: La Découverte, 1991).

34. See my "'This Is a White Country': The Racial Ideology of the Western Nations of the World-System," *Research in Politics and Society* 6, no. 1 (1999): 85–102.

35. The culture of poverty argument was formally developed by anthropologist Oscar Lewis. His claim was that the poor develop a culture based on adaptations to their poverty status, which is then transmitted from generation to generation and becomes an obstacle for moving out of poverty. Although Lewis formulated his thesis as a class-based one, because the characters in his famous books, *The Children of Sánchez* (1961) and *La Vida* (1965), were Mexican and Puerto Rican, respectively, it was almost impossible not to interpret his argument as especially pertinent for understanding minorities' well-being in America. Lewis's argument was roundly condemned by many of his contemporaries, but it stuck in scholarly policy circles as well as among conservative politicians and a few "liberals" such as Senator Patrick Moynihan.

36. Charles A. Murray, *Losing Ground: American Social Policy, 1950–1980* (New York: Basic, 1984); Lawrence M. Mead, *Beyond Entitlement: The Social Obligations of Citizenship* (New York: Free Press, 1986); William Julius Wilson, *The Truly Disadvantaged: The Inner City, the Underclass, and Public Policy* (Chicago: University of Chicago Press, 1987); Cornel West, *Race Matters* (Boston: Beacon, 1993).

37. See Sharon Collins, *Black Corporate Executives: The Making and Breaking of a Black Middle Class* (Philadelphia: Temple University Press, 1997); Ellis Cose, *The Rage of a Privileged Class* (New York: HarperCollins, 1995); and Joe R. Feagin and Melvin Sikes, *Living with Racism: The Black Middle-Class Experience* (Boston: Beacon, 1994).

4

⟿

The Style of Color Blindness

How to Talk Nasty about Minorities without Sounding Racist

Subscribing to an ideology is like wearing a piece of clothing. When you wear it, you also wear a certain style, a certain fashion, a certain way of presenting yourself to the world. The style of an ideology refers to its peculiar *linguistic manners and rhetorical strategies* (or *race talk*),[1] to the technical tools that allow users to articulate its frames and story lines. As such, the style of an ideology is the thread used to join pieces of fabric into garments. The neatness of the garments, however, depends on the context in which they are being stitched. If the garment is being assembled in an open forum (with minorities present or in public venues), dominant actors will weave its fibers carefully ("I am not a racist, but . . .") and not too tight ("I am not black, so I don't know"). If, in contrast, the needlework is being done among friends, the cuts will be rough and the seams loose ("Darned lazy niggers").

I examine in this chapter the basic style of color blindness. At the core of my analysis is the idea that because the normative climate changed dramatically from the Jim Crow to the post–civil rights era, the language of color blindness is slippery, apparently contradictory, and often subtle.[2] Thus, analysts must excavate the rhetorical maze of confusing, ambivalent answers to straight questions; of answers speckled with disclaimers such as "I don't know, but . . ." or "Yes and no"; of answers almost unintelligible because of their higher-than-usual level of incoherence. This is not an easy task and the analyst can end up mistaking honest "I don't knows" for rhetorical moves to save face or nervousness for thematically induced incoherence. Cognizant of this possibility, I offer as much data as possible on each cited case.

101

Since a full discursive analysis of the stylistic components of color blindness is beyond the scope of this chapter,[3] I focus instead on showcasing five things. First, I document whites' avoidance of direct racial language to expressing their racial views. Second, I analyze the central "semantic moves" (see below) whites use as verbal parachutes to avoid dangerous discussions or to save face. Third, I examine the role of projection in whites' racial discourse. Fourth, I show the role of diminutives in color-blind race talk. Finally, I show how incursions into forbidden issues produce almost total incoherence in many whites. This last element is not part of the stylistic tools of color blindness but the result of talking about racially sensitive matters in a period in which certain things cannot be uttered in public. Nevertheless, because rhetorical incoherence appears often in whites' remarks, it must be regarded as part of the overall language of color blindness.

One concern for readers of this chapter may be whether I am attributing intentionality to whites as they piece together their accounts. That is, am I suggesting white respondents are "racists" trying to cover up their *real* views through these stylistic devices? First, readers need to be reminded that I see the problem of racism as a problem of power (see chapter 1). Therefore, the intentions of individual actors are largely irrelevant to the explanation of social outcomes. Second, based on my structural definition of "racism," it should also be clear that I conceive racial analysis as "beyond good and evil." The analysis of people's racial accounts is not akin to an analysis of people's character or morality. Lastly, ideologies, like grammar, are learned socially and, therefore, the rules of how to speak properly come "naturally" to people socialized in particular societies. Thus, whites construct their accounts with the frames, style, and stories available in color-blind America in a mostly unconscious fashion. As Stuart Hall has pointed out, "We all constantly make use of a whole set of frameworks of interpretation and understanding, often in a very practical unconscious way, and [those] things alone enable us to make sense of what is going on around us, what our position is, and what we are likely to do."[4]

CALLING BLACKS "NIGGER" SOFTLY: RACISM WITHOUT RACIAL EPITHETS

The literature about life in plantations, accounts from frontiersmen, or narratives from cattle ranchers show that whites used to talk about minorities in a straightforward matter. When people of color were property or regarded as secondary human beings, there was no reason to be concerned in talking about them. But the civil rights era shattered, among many things, the United States' norms about public discussions on race.

Hence using words such as "nigger" and "spic" and even saying things that sound or can be perceived as racist is deemed immoral. And because the dominant racial ideology purports to be color blind, there is little space for socially sanctioned speech about race-related matters. Does this mean that whites do not talk about minorities in public? As I showed in the previous chapter, whites talk about minorities in public, even in the somewhat formal venue of an interview sponsored by a major research university. But I also showed they talk in a very careful, indirect, hesitant manner and, occasionally, even through coded language.[5]

Almost all whites we interviewed avoided using traditional Jim Crow terminology to refer to blacks. Only one college student and six DAS respondents used terms such as "colored" or "Negroes" to refer to blacks and not a single one used the term "nigger" as a legitimate term. The student who used the term "colored" was Rachel, an MU student who had very conservative racial views. However, it was not clear whether or not she used the term as part of her normal repertoire. She used the term in her answer to a question about who were her friends in college:

> I wouldn't say mostly white. I'd say, it's probably a mix. 'Cause I have like a lot of Asian friends. I have a lot of colored friends,[6] you know, but it wasn't maybe not even the same, like, background either, I don't know. It's hard to tell, you know? From looking at somebody, so. . . .

From this statement, it is unclear whether she used the term in the old sense or wanted to say "people of color" and got confused.

All DAS respondents who used the term "colored" were sixty years of age or older. For example, Pauline, a retired woman in her late seventies, described the racial makeup of the schools she attended while growing up: "They were mixed, you know. [*Interviewer: Mixed of what?*] Well [*raises voice*] we had mostly colored and the white."

Although none of these older respondents were racial progressives, it would be a mistake to regard them as "Archie Bunkers," just because they used the racial language of the past. In truth, all these respondents were whites who have not fully absorbed the racial ideology and style of the post–civil rights era. Yet, based on what they said, some of these respondents seemed more open-minded than many younger respondents. For instance, when Pauline was asked if she had black friends while growing up, she said, "I always had black friends, even when I worked I had black friends. In fact, I had a couple of my best friends." Although many whites' self-reports on friendship with blacks are suspect (see chapter 5), based on Pauline's own narrative, she seems to have had real associations with blacks. For example, she played with black kids while growing up and remembered fondly her black coworker. More significantly, Pauline, who has a niece who is dating a black "gentleman," seemed less concerned than one would expect:

> I feel like it's none of my business. She's had trouble with ah, she's divorced. She's had a lot of trouble with her ex, and he's very, very abusive. This fellow she's going with is very kind. The kids like him so there you go. So maybe it's gonna be good for her and the kids. And for him too, who knows!

The fact that white youth do not use racial slurs as legitimate terms in *public* does not mean that they do not use these terms or denigrate blacks in *private*. For example, most college students acknowledged listening to or telling racist jokes with friends; six even told the jokes in the interviews. For example, Lynn, an MU student, told the following joke she heard back home:

> *Lynn*: Okay [*laughing*]. It was, it's terrible but, what do you call a car full of niggers driving off a cliff?
> *Interviewer*: What?
> *Lynn*: A good beginning.

Eric, another MU student, told the following joke: "It was, what do you call a black man, a black man in a, in a coat and a tie? And it was, the defendant or something. Yeah, it was the defendant. And that was probably a couple of weeks ago or something that I heard that."

In addition, racist terminology is current in the life of students and DAS respondents, as illustrated by the fact that more than half of them acknowledged that they have friends or close relatives who are "racist." For example, Lee, a WU student, acknowledged, "My father is pretty racist, so I heard everything, just about every racial slur you could possibly think of I heard it from him and I think that had an effect on me early." He also said that while his family was watching black TV shows such as *Sanford and Son* or *The Jeffersons,* his father would say things such as "Are we gonna watch the nigger shows?" Lee and his brothers would say, "Yeah," because it was "just kind of second nature." Although Lee believes he has been able to successfully repel his father's racist influence, he admitted that he had some Nazi leanings while growing up and that although "I wasn't a skinhead or anything, but, you know, every now and again, I would draw a swastika on my notebook or something."

READING THROUGH THE
RHETORICAL MAZE OF COLOR BLINDNESS

Because post–civil rights racial norms disallow the open expression of racial views, whites have developed a concealed way of voicing them.

Analysis of post–civil rights racial speech suggests whites rely on "semantic moves," or "strategically managed . . . propositions" whose meanings can be determined by the "content of speech act sequences,"[7] to safely state their views. For instance, most whites use apparent denials ("I don't believe that, but . . ."), claims of ignorance ("I don't know"), or other moves in the process of stating their racial views. The moves act as rhetorical shields to save face because whites can always go back to the safety of the disclaimers ("I didn't mean that because, as I told you, *I am not a racist*"). The data in this chapter will show whites often sandwich their racial statements between slices of nonracial utterances. In what follows I showcase the most common verbal strategies of post–civil rights racial speech.

"I Am Not Prejudiced, but . . ." and "Some of My Best Friends Are . . ."

Phrases such as "I am not a racist" or "Some of my best friends are black" have become standard fare of post–civil rights racial discourse. They act as discursive buffers before or after someone states something that is or could be interpreted as racist. Therefore, it was not surprising to find that four students and ten DAS respondents used phrases such as "I'm not prejudiced, but" in their answers. One example of how the respondents inserted this semantic move was Rhonda, a part-time employee in a jewelry store in her sixties. She used the move to safely express her highly racial views on why she thinks blacks are worse off than whites:

> Well, I'm gonna be, you understand I'm, I'm [not] prejudice or racial or whatever. They're always given the smut jobs because they would do it. Then they stopped, they stopped doing [them]. The welfare system got to be very, very easy. And I'm not saying all, there's many, many white people on welfare that shouldn't be. But if you take the percentage in the Tri-city country area, you will find that the majority are white, but all you see is the black people on welfare. But it's a graduation up. Thirty years ago they started it and they continued it, and they continued it, and they continued it. And it was easier to collect welfare from the state rather than go out and get a job. Why work if, if they gonna, if the government's gonna take care of you?

After Rhonda stated that, "I'm, I'm [not] prejudice or racial or whatever," she then gave her account on how she believes the welfare state has spoiled blacks. The ideological value of the "I am not a racist, but . . ." move is clear here.

The phrase "Some of my best friends are . . ." or its equivalent was used by eight students and twelve DAS respondents. Surprisingly, many respondents used it to refer to their Asian friends. For example, Eric, a student at MU, used this phrase after revealing that most of his friends while growing up were white. Specifically, when asked "Okay, and you say mostly whites, were there nonwhite friends along the way?" Eric answered, "Yeah I had a few. I, one of my best friends when I lived in New Jersey was Korean."

Jill, a salesperson in her thirties, used the "Some of my best friends are black" move in a rather odd way. In response to the question, "Have you ever dated racial minorities?" Jill said, "No, but I think one of my best friends is black."

The interviewer then asked Jill, "OK, can you talk a little bit about that relationship?" Jill answered,

> Yeah we worked together at Automotive Company and what happened is this man was very bright. He graduated first in his class in economics from Indiana University and he got a fellowship through Automotive Company, which probably helped because he was black. And I also know he got into Harvard because he had terrible GMAT scores, but he did get in. He didn't have terrible, he had in the high fives. He did get in and graduated from Harvard and now he's an investment banker. But you know what? He is a nice guy. What he lacks in intellect he makes up for in . . . he works so hard and he's always trying to improve himself. He should be there because he works harder than anybody I know.

One of Jill's "best friends," according to her own narrative, was "very bright" but had "terrible GMAT scores." Yet, she continued, he "did get in" Harvard, which he deserved because "he is a nice guy" who makes up for "what he lacks in intellect" with hard work (was her "best friend" "very bright" or lacking "in intellect"?). She also sprinkled the story with her veiled concerns about affirmative action (her commentary about Automotive Company helping him "because he was black"). Please also notice this "best friend" is never identified by name.

"I Am Not Black, So I Don't Know"

Since the aforementioned moves have become cliché (and thus less effective), color-blind racism has produced other semantic moves. These moves, as all the parts of any ideology, have developed collectively through a trial-and-error process and become resources available for the production of people's racial accounts.[8] One such move that appeared frequently among white college students but not among DAS respondents was the phrase "I am not black, so I don't know." After respondents interjected this phrase, they proceeded with statements that indicated they have strong views on the racial issue in question. For example, Brian, a student at SU, inserted the statement in response to the direct question on discrimination.

I don't know. I believe them. I don't know, I'm not a black person living so I don't hang out with a lot of black people, so I don't see it happen. But I do watch TV and we were watching the stupid talk shows—there's nothing else on—and there's people out there. And just that and just hearing the news and stuff. I'm sure it's less than it used to be, at least that's what everybody keeps saying so . . . I think it's less but I can't say. But I can't speak for like a black person who says they're being harassed or being prejudice or discriminated against.

Brian's statement can be broken down as follows. First, he stated "I'm not a black person," so he did not see discrimination happening. Second, he recognized that discrimination still happens. Third, he carefully stated his own view: "It's less than it used to be."

The second example is Liz, a student at MU. She also used the phrase in her answer to the direct question on discrimination:

Um, just because I'm not black, I'm not Hispanic, I don't really, don't understand. I don't go through it I guess. But then again, I've seen like racism on, you know, towards whites, scholarships and as far as school goes, which, I mean, which bothers me too. So I guess I can kind of understand.

Liz began her answer with the move and pondered whether or not she could understand minorities' complaints about discrimination because "I don't go through it I guess." But then she changed the topic to the issue of so-called reverse discrimination toward whites in "scholarships and as far as school goes," which "bothers me too." Thus Liz equalized the complaints about discrimination by all groups and concluded that, after all, "I guess I can kind of understand" minorities' claims about discrimination. In a specific question on whether or not blacks experience discrimination in jobs and promotions, Liz answered by avoiding the issue altogether: "Um, I just think that the best qualified should probably get the job and that, you know, like I wouldn't see why someone black wouldn't get a job over someone white who was more qualified or better suited for the job." Since Liz hinted that blacks lie when they make claims of discrimination, the interviewer asked her, "So when they say that [discrimination] happens to them, do you think they're lying or . . . ?" Liz proceeded to make a quick reversal to restore her image of neutrality:

I mean, I don't think they're lying, but I wouldn't, I mean, I guess in my little world, that everything is perfect, I wouldn't see why that would happen. But I guess that there are people who are, you know, racist who do, you know, would not promote someone black just because they're black, which I don't really understand, you know.

Liz's rhetorical back and forth (not understanding minorities' claims of discrimination and then claiming she does) and reversals (hinting that minorities lie when they claim to have experienced discrimination and then saying that discrimination happens) typify how dangerous are the waters of color blindness. Negotiating the seemingly contradictory views that "race does not matter" but, at the same time, that "race matters" a little bit for minorities and a lot for whites in the form of reverse discrimination is not an easy task.

"Yes and No, But . . ."

Another semantic move typical of color-blind racism is the "yes and no" strategy. After respondents insert this phrase and, apparently taking or examining all sides, they proceed to take a stand on the issue at hand. Students were more likely than DAS respondents to use this move, a finding that resonates with the fact, discussed in the previous chapter, that DAS respondents were more straightforward in the enunciation of the frames of color-blind racism. An example of how respondents used this move is Emily, a student at SU who answered a question about providing minorities special opportunities to be admitted into universities as follows:

> Unique opportunities, I don't know? There might be, I guess, some minorities do get schools [that] aren't as well funded as others. So, I would have to say yes and no. I think they should get an opportunity to come, but I also don't think they should allow other people to come. 'Cause that's sort of like a double-edged sword, maybe because you are discriminating against one group any way you do it and I don't believe in that, and I don't think you should discriminate against one group to give another a better chance. And I don't believe that's fair at all. But I also don't believe that it's fair they have to [attend a] school that can't teach as well or don't have the facilities to teach them like they should. I don't know. I'm kinda wishy-washy on that.

This "yes and no" answer can be interpreted as an expression of whites' ambivalence on a very "controversial" social policy.[9] However, Emily's answer to the direct question on discrimination clearly shows that she is decisively against affirmative action:

> I just have a problem with the discrimination, you're gonna discriminate against a group and what happened in the past is horrible and it should never happen again, but I also think that to move forward you have to let go of the past and let go of what happened. You know, and it should really start equaling out, um, 'cause I feel that some of it will go too far and it will swing the other way. One group is going to be discriminated against—I don't believe in that. I don't think one group should have an advantage over another, regardless of what happened in the past.

Thus, Emily opposes affirmative action as it is practiced because she interprets it as reverse discrimination. In turn, she favors programs that are not in place (expanding educational opportunities for minorities before college) or that would not change minorities' status in a significant way (equal opportunity).

Mark, an MU student, used the "yes and no" strategy to express his view on affirmative action:

> Yes and no. This is probably the toughest thing I have deciding. I really, 'cause I've thought about this a lot, but I can make a pro-con list and I still wouldn't like. I've heard most of the issues on this subject and I honestly couldn't give a definite answer.

Mark, who was taking a sociology course at the time of the interview, recognized minorities "don't have the same starting points and, if you are starting from so much lower, they should definitely be granted *some* additional opportunities to at least have an equal playing ground." But he immediately added, "I'm gonna be going out for a job next year, and I'll be honest, I'd be upset if I'm just as qualified as someone else, and individually, I'd be upset if a company takes, you know, like an African American over me just because he is an African American." Mark repeats this point when discussing three affirmative action–based hiring scenarios. When asked if he would support the hypothetical company's hiring decisions, Mark said, "If I'm that person, I'm not gonna support it. If I'm that majority getting rejected just because I'm a different race." Hence Mark's philosophical "yes and no" on affirmative action seems to disappear when the policy is discussed in practical terms.

It is important to point out that other respondents did not use the particular phrase "yes and no" but inserted similar buffer statements to safely express their reservations, objections, and at times, opposition to certain policies. For example, Brian, a student at SU, explained his stance on affirmative action: "Man, that's another one where [*laughs*] I kind of support and oppose it [*laughs*], you know? Uh pretty much the same thing I said before was that, I don't know, if I come, I don't know—somebody underqualified shouldn't get chosen, you know?" Brian opposed providing minorities unique opportunities to be admitted into universities and the hiring decisions in the three affirmative action hiring scenarios. This suggests Brian leans more toward the "against" than the "for" stance on affirmative action, regardless of his odd "I kind of support and oppose" stance.

One example of DAS respondents who used this strategy is Sandra. A retail person in her forties, Sandra used the move to voice her opposition to affirmative action. Sandra's answer to the question, "Are you for or against affirmative action?" was

> Yes and no. I feel someone should be able to have *something*, education, job, whatever, because they've earned it, they deserve it, they have the ability to do it. You don't want to put a six-year-old as a *rocket scientist*. They don't have the ability. It doesn't matter if the kid's black or white. As far as letting one have the job over another one just because of their race or their gender, I don't believe in that.

Sandra's "yes and no" answer on affirmative action seems like truly a strong "no," since she did not find any reason whatsoever for affirmative action programs to be in place. Her "yes and no" at the beginning was followed by a long statement on why affirmative action is wrong and thus she concluded by saying, "As far as letting one have the job over another because of their race or their gender [which is the way she interprets affirmative action policies], I don't believe in that."

Anything but Race

Another rhetorical move akin to the "I am not a racist, but" and "Some of my best friends are" is "Anything but race." This strategy involves interjecting comments such as "it's not a prejudice thing" to dismiss the fact that race affects an aspect of the respondent's life. Hence, this tool allows whites to explain away racial fractures in their color-blind story. For example, Ray, a student at MU, dismissed the notion that race had any bearing on the fact that he had no minority friends in high school:

> Yeah, I think, I think that as things got later on, I don't think there was any type of prejudice involved. I just think that we really didn't know these kids. You know what I mean? They lived in different neighborhoods, they went to different schools. Um, and there was never any effort made to exclude, and if anything, there was an effort made to cultivate these kids.

Sonny, a student at MU, also used this tool to explain why she did not have minority friends while growing up. Sonny revealed in the interview that she had Italian friends,[10] but suggested that "race never came into play" and that "most of my friends were just normal kids." After revealing that "one of my best friends is Indian" (Asian Indian), she pondered why she and her friends did not have blacks in their crowd:

> I mean, there was so many kids. I don't think we had any black friends. I don't know why. It kind of stuck together and I don't know, it wasn't that we, it wasn't that we wouldn't be like . . . allowing to black people. It's just

that there was never, like, an opportunity. There's no population like that around where we lived.

Both Ray and Sonny seemed to realize their almost-all-white networks violate their color-blind view of themselves. Thus, in their descriptions, they pointed out that this was a nonracial fact in their lives. My point here is not to accuse whites who do not have minority friends of being "racist" (see my definition of "racism" in chapter 1). Instead, I want to show that whites explain the product of racialized life (segregated neighborhoods, schools, and friendship networks) as nonracial outcomes and rely on the available stylistic elements of color blindness to produce such accounts.

As college students, DAS respondents used phrases in line with the "anything but race" strategy. For instance, Marge, an unemployed woman in her early fifties, used this rhetorical strategy in her response to the interracial marriage question:

> Very different than what I used to think, I think it doesn't have anything to do with racism. It has to do with how you will all be treated. Now, if it's just a matter of you and the other person and there's no families involved, no kids involved, and if you are living in an area [where people have] open minds, I think it's fine. But when you start dragging kids in, no matter how much you love or whether you are a racist or not, that's not the question, it's how those kids are going to be treated. And so my answer is if there are kids, you know, families in and all that involved, and you're living in a racially, you know, racist kind of area, no, I don't believe in marrying somebody of a different race. But if it's you two together and there's nobody else involved, then I say it's fine. But, you know, when you are dragging other people in, you have to think of them too.

Obviously, the phrase "I think it doesn't have anything to do with racism," and the carefully but long-winded statement afterwards, allowed Marge to oppose almost all kinds of interracial unions on a variety of apparently nonracial grounds (but see chapter 5).

"THEY ARE THE RACIST ONES": PROJECTION AS A RHETORICAL TOOL

Psychologists since Freud have argued that projection is part of our normal equipment to defend ourselves.[11] It is also an essential tool in the creation of a corporate identity (Us versus Them).[12] More pertinent to this section, projection helps all of us "escape from guilt and responsibility and affix blame elsewhere."[13] College students and DAS respondents projected racism or racial motivations onto blacks and other minorities as a way of avoiding responsibility and feeling good about themselves. The projections of college students appeared on a variety of issues (e.g., affirmative action, school and residential segregation, interracial friendship and marriage, and the work ethic of blacks), but most often on the hot issue of so-called black self-segregation. For example, Janet, a student at SU, answered a question on whether or not blacks self-segregate, as follows:

> I think they segregate themselves. Or, I mean, I don't know how everybody else is, but I would have no problem with talking with or being friends with a black person or any other type of minority. I think they've just got into their heads that they are different and, as a result, they're pulling themselves away.

The interviewer followed up Janet's answer with a question trying to ascertain whether or not Janet had tried to mingle with blacks, but Janet cut her off quickly with the following statement: "They're off to their own kind of little, own world."[14]

Janet projected once more in her answer to the interracial marriage question, but this time not onto blacks, but onto people who marry across the color line:

> I would feel that in most situations they're not really thinking of the, the child. I mean, they might not really think anything of it, *but* in reality I think most of the time when the child is growing up, he's going to be picked on because he has parents from different races and it's gonna ultimately affect the child and, and the end result is they're only thinking of them—of their own happiness, not the happiness of, of the kid.

By projecting selfishness onto people who intermarry ("they're not really thinking of the, the child"), Janet was able to voice safely her otherwise racially problematic opposition to intermarriage. Nevertheless, she admitted that if she or a member of her family ever became involved with someone from a different race, her family "would *not* like it *at all!* [*laughs*]."

Other examples of projection among students occurred when they discussed affirmative action. Although most students expressed open resentment on this subject, a few projected the idea that blacks feel "terrible" if they are hired because of their race. For instance, Rachel, the conservative MU student cited above, explained her position on affirmative action as follows:

> Affirmative action programs? Like I was saying, I think, I don't know if I do because, I mean, I think the only reason they, you know, established it was to make up for the 200 and some years of slavery. And it's just trying to,

like, for us it's just trying to like make up for the past. And on the blacks, on that end, I think they're kind of . . . I would feel bad, you know, because I'm getting in because of the color of my skin, not because of my merits. And I'd feel kind of inferior, you know, like I'd feel that the whole affirmative action system would inferiorize me. Just because maybe I'll get like, you know, a better placement, you know, in a school just because of the color of my skin. I don't know.

This argument appears quite often in whites' objections to affirmative action.[15] The rhetorical beauty of this projection is that it is couched as a "concern" on how blacks feel about affirmative action. Of course, because the market is heavily tilted toward whites, if someone ought to feel "inferior" about market decisions it should be whites, since they are the ones who receive preferential treatment "just because of the color of [their] skin."

DAS respondents projected racism and racial motivations onto blacks and minorities but at a slightly higher rate. Twenty-two of the sixty-six white respondents projected racism or racial motivations onto blacks on a variety of issues. For example Ann, an unemployed woman in her twenties, answered the question on whether blacks are hard to approach or are not welcomed by whites as follows: "I think that, I don't know—they live too much on the past, if you ask me. Some of 'em do. You know, I think blacks are more prejudiced against whites than whites are against blacks."

Francine, a homemaker in her late twenties, answered a question on why blacks and whites see the police and the criminal court system very differently in the following way: "Black people are just prejudiced. They just think that they're out to get them or something."

Pat, an orderly in a psychiatric hospital in her early thirties, balked at the idea of the government establishing programs on blacks' behalf to deal with the effects of discrimination:

On behalf of blacks? No, I think it's equaling out, I mean, if you want to go to school you can. I don't think there should be—Years back [the government] came out with a Negro College Fund. We don't have any United Caucasian Fund, I mean, I don't know why they separate themselves because they are allowed to go to the same schools and colleges and everything as white people. It should be all together. I don't think there should be *specials,* you know what I am saying? [*giggles and snorts*] No, I don't—it should all be the same for everybody. Everybody wants equal rights, equal this and equal this and that will equal everything out.

Beverly, a small-business owner and homemaker in her forties, projected the idea that blacks who are hired through affirmative action feel terrible. She stated that affirmative action is "unfair to black and white." When the interviewer asked her to explain what she meant, Beverly said,

"Because a lot of companies they know that they're hired [because they are black]. I mean, it's got to be in their mind, it would be in [my] mind, that's why I'm saying this. 'Was I hired because I was good or because I was black?'"

Racial projections bring to mind the famous statement by DuBois in *The Souls of Black Folk*, "How does it feel to be a problem?"[16] Whites freely lash out at minorities (*"They* self-segregate," *"They* take advantage of the welfare system," *"They* must feel terrible about affirmative action") and seldom exhibit self-reflexivity. Minorities are the problem; whites are not.

"IT MAKES ME A LITTLE ANGRY": THE ROLE OF DIMINUTIVES IN COLOR-BLIND RACE TALK

Because maintaining a nonracial, color-blind stance is key in the post–civil rights era, whites rely on diminutives to soften their racial blows. Hence, when they oppose affirmative action, few say, "I am against affirmative action." Instead, they say something such as, "I am just a little bit against affirmative action." Similarly, few whites who oppose interracial marriage state flatly, "I am against interracial marriage." Instead, they say something such as, "I am just a bit concerned about the welfare of the children."

About half of the college students and a quarter of DAS respondents used diminutives to cushion their views on issues such as interracial marriage and affirmative action. For instance, Andy, a student at WU, used diminutives twice to state his concerns on interracial marriage:[17]

> I would say I have a little bit of the same concern about the children just because it's more, I mean, would be more difficult on them. But, I mean, I definitely [*nervous laugh*] have no problem with any form of interracial marriage. That's just, just an extra hurdle that they would have to over, overcome with the children, but, but I—[it] wouldn't be a detriment to the kids, I don't think. That just makes it a little more difficult for them.

Mickey, a student at MU, used diminutives to make the potentially problematic claim that people at MU were oversensitive about matters regarding race or sexual orientation. Andy made his comments in response to a question about whether or not he participated in political activities on campus. After Andy stated in no uncertain terms that he did not participate in any political activity, the interviewer, curious about the tone of the answer, commented "You sounded pretty staunch in your no." To this Andy replied,

> Yeah, I just, I don't know. I think everybody, everybody here just seems like really uptight about that kind of stuff and, I mean, maybe it's just because

I never had to deal with that kind of stuff at home, but, you know, it seems like you have to watch everything you say because if you slip a little bit, and you never know, there's a protest the next day.

When asked to explain what kind of "little slips" he was referring to, Andy said,

Like, I mean, if you hear a professor say something, like a racial slur, or something just like a little bit, you know, a little bit outta hand, you know. I mean. I would just see it as like, you know, he was just, you took it out of context or something, but, you know, it's just little things like that. It's just, it's so touchy. Everything is so touchy it seems like around here. And I don't, like I don't like to get into debates about stuff and, you know, about cultures and stuff like that. 'Cause I've seen it, I've seen it around here, you know, plenty, you know, about like, with religious stuff and gay stuff and minority stuff. And it's just nothin' of that, I just don't like to get into that stuff.

Thus, Mickey uses the diminutives to state that people at MU are hypersensitive because they protest when a professor does "little things" like making "a racial slur" in class or making some insensitive religious or homophobic remarks.

DAS respondents also used diminutives, but consistent with what I have documented for other rhetorical tools and the frames of color blindness, they were less likely to use them. The following two examples illustrate how they used diminutives. First is Rita, an underemployed woman in her twenties. Rita stated her controversial belief that blacks are naturally different from whites as follows: "Well, I can't say that generally they all are, but a lot of the ones I've encountered are a little more aggressive, a little bit more high tempered, or whatever."

Obviously, the diminutives and her qualification that her view applies to most but not all blacks muted somewhat her otherwise traditional Jim Crow position.

Judy, a college professor in her forties who throughout the interview signified her "racial progressiveness," softened her opposition to affirmative action by using a diminutive. "I'm for it a little bit, not real dramatically. I think it's ah, I think is a temporary solution. I think it's bad when, if you have like, it's used for quotas."

"I, I, I, I DON'T MEAN, YOU KNOW, BUT . . .": RHETORICAL INCOHERENCE AND COLOR BLINDNESS

Rhetorical incoherence (e.g., grammatical mistakes, lengthy pauses, or repetition) is part of all natural speech. Nevertheless, the level of incoherence increases noticeably when people discuss sensitive subjects. Because the new racial climate in America forbids the open expression of racially based feelings, views, and positions, when whites discuss issues that make them feel uncomfortable, they become almost incomprehensible.[18]

Almost all the college students were incoherent when discussing certain racial issues, particularly their personal relationships with blacks. For example, Ray, the MU student cited above and a respondent who was very articulate throughout the interview, became almost incomprehensible when answering the question about whether he had been involved with minorities while in college:

> Um, so to answer that question, no. But I would not, I mean, I would not ever preclude a black woman from being my girlfriend on the basis that she was black. You know, I mean, you know what I mean? If you're looking about it from, you know, the standpoint of just attraction, I mean, I think that, you know, I think, you know, I think, you know, all women are, I mean, all women have a sort of different type of beauty, if you will. And I think that, you know, for black women, it's somewhat different than white women. But I don't think it's, you know, I mean, it's, it's, it's nothing that would ever stop me from like, I mean, I don't know, I mean, I don't if that's, I mean, that's just sort of been my impression. I mean, it's not like I would ever say, "No, I'll never have a black girlfriend," but it just seems to me like I'm not as attracted to black women as I am to white women, for whatever reason. It's not about prejudice, it's just sort of like, you know, whatever. Just sort of the way, way like I see white women as compared to black women, you know?

The interviewer followed up Ray's answer with the question, "Do you have any idea why that would be?" Ray replied, "I, I, I [*sighs*] don't really know. It's just sort of hard to describe. It's just like, you know, who you're more drawn to, you know, for whatever reason, you know?"

Mark, an MU student cited above, answered a direct question on interracial marriage in the following manner:

> I mean, personally, I don't see myself, you know, marrying someone else. I mean, I don't have anything against it. I just I guess I'm just more attracted to, I mean, others. Nothing like, I could not and I would never, and I don't know how my parents would—just on another side, I don't, like, if my parents would feel about anything like that.

Mark was one of three students who openly opposed interracial marriage. Acknowledging this seems to have rattled him emotionally, as his speech pattern became incongruous.

Another issue that made students feel seemingly uncomfortable was discussing their views on the matter of self-segregation. Ann, for example, a WU student, became very hesitant in her answer to the question of whether or not blacks self-segregate (remember, short lines [—] stand for self-corrections):

> Um, no, I don't think they segregate themselves, they just probably just, I guess probably they are, I don't know. Let's see, let's try to—Like we were trying—Like mutual friends, I suppose, maybe and probably maybe it's just your peers that you know, or maybe that they, they have more, more like activities, or classes and clubs, I don't really know, but I don't think it's necessarily conscious, I don't—I wouldn't say that I would feel uncomfortable going and talking to a whole group.

One potential reason why some whites get out of rhythm when discussing self-segregation is the realization that whatever they say about minorities can be said about them. Thus, as they explain their opinions on this issue, respondents make sure they provide nonracial explanations of why minorities may seemingly self-segregate (Ann suggesting friendship networks are based on people sharing similar interests).

DAS respondents were significantly less likely than students to become incoherent, but when they did, it was around the same issues. Dorothy, for instance, a retired automobile company worker in her seventies, who spoke clearly throughout the interview, seemed confused when addressing the topic of interracial marriage:

> Eh, well, I donno, but I, I, I feel that uh, I donno, I just feel like, that uh, you should [*low voice*] stick to your own race for marriage [*Interviewer: And why is that?*] Uh because I feel that there's uh proble—There would be problems on both sides. A girl would feel hurt if, if his parents, you know were. . . . [*End of Tape 1. Interviewer asked her to continue her answer.*] Yeah, I really do. Well, I donno—they have a different culture than we do, really and I think that his family would be, would probably be just as upset. I watch this on TV every day and see how, you know, how they, they have a different, I donno—I hear the men, I know I hear that the black men on TV say that the black women are so, you know, so wild and mad, you know, tempers, you know what I mean. And I just feel that's the limit. I donno, if my dau—If one of my daughters woulda, ah, married one, I would have accepted it because it's my daughter and I would, I wo—And I would have never be, I would never be nasty to them. Because I feel they're just as human as we are. If they treat me decent, I'm gonna treat them decent. That's my feelings!

Dorothy's incoherence "makes sense" in light of her opposition to interracial marriage. Because openly opposing interracial marriage is controversial and violates the notion of color blindness, Dorothy seemed compelled to qualify her answer and insert the profoundly awkward statement about the equality of the races ("they're just as human as we are").

Lynn, a human resource manager in her early fifties, became incoherent while stating her reservations about dating black men:

> I don't know. Just, well [*high pitched voice*] I think I would have been very uncomfortable, okay, I really do. I mean, it would just be, I [*raises voice*] wouldn't want to go out with a really dark Middle Eastern man, or Indian, or Oriental. I mean, I, I just would be uncomfortable. If they're closer to me in looks, okay. That's just always the way I felt. Not that I didn't like men of ethnic diversity, but I just—You have a certain taste, you know. I think I do.

As with college students, DAS respondents became nervous when discussing some matters other than interracial marriage. For example, Eric, an auditor for an automotive company, became anxious when discussing whether or not he associates with his black coworkers:

> Sure, sure, you can, it's—if you work in that environment the, the race is there obviously. I don't think it will ever go away, but I don't practice it and I see a lot of people who don't practice it. The, they, you know, but it's existing and I know that and I don't. Yeah, I, I, I, I go out with the black guys. I don't even care. It don't matter to me.

CONCLUSION

If the tales of color-blind racism are going to stick, whites need to be able to repair mistakes (or the appearance of mistakes) rhetorically. In this chapter I have documented the variety of tools available to whites to mend racial fissures, to restore a color-blind image when whiteness seeps through discursive cracks. Color-blind racism's race talk avoids racist terminology and preserves its mythological nonracialism through semantic moves such as "I am not a racist, but," "Some of my best friends are . . . ," "I am not black, but," "Yes and no," or "Anything but race." Thus, if a school or neighborhood is completely white, they can say "It's not a racial thing" or "It's economics, not race." They can also project the matter onto blacks by saying things such as "They don't want to live with us" or "Blacks are the really prejudiced ones."

But how can whites protect themselves against the charge of racism when they state positions that may be interpreted as racist? They can use diminutives as racial shock absorbers and utter statements such as "I am a little bit against affirmative action because it is terribly unfair to whites" or "I am a bit concerned about interracial marriage because the children suffer so much." And, as in the case of the frames of color-blind racism, whites mix and match the stylistic tools of color-blind racism. Hence, respondents could use a diminutive ("I am a little bit upset with blacks . . ."), followed by a projection (". . . because they cry racism for everything, even though they are the ones who are racist"), and balance out the statement with a semantic move at the end (". . . and I am not being racial about this, it's just that, I don't know").

The interviews also revealed that talking about race in America is a highly emotional matter. Almost all the respondents exhibited a degree of incoherence at some point or other in the interviews. Digressions, long pauses, repetition, and self-corrections were the order of the day. This incoherent talk is the result of talking about race in a world that insists race does not matter, rather than being a tool of color blindness. However, since it is so preeminent in whites' race talk, it must be included as part of the linguistic modalities of color-blind racism.

One final important point to make is that college students were more likely than DAS respondents to use semantic moves such as "I am not a racist, but," "Some of my best friends are . . . ," "Yes and no," and "I am not black, but." The students were also more likely to use diminutives to soften their racial views and to become incoherent when discussing sensitive racial matters. DAS respondents, however, were more likely to project than students. These findings match my findings in the previous chapter. Why is this the case? Preliminary analysis of survey and interview data from these two projects suggest that younger, educated, middle-class people are more likely than older, less-educated, working-class people to make full use of the resources of color-blind racism.

This means white youths are more adept at surfing the dangerous waters of America's contemporary racial landscape. This should not be surprising, since they are the cohort that has been ingrained from day one with the ideology of color blindness. However, it is worth noting that young, educated, middle-class DAS respondents are not too far off from their older, less-educated, working-class counterparts in their crudeness and lack of rhetorical sophistication. This may well mean that, as whites enter the labor market, they feel entitled to vent their resentment in a relatively straightforward manner. No need to sweeten the pill when you feel morally entitled to a job or promotion over all blacks, since you believe they are "not qualified," when you believe the taxes you pay are being largely wasted on "welfare-dependent blacks," when you are convinced that blacks use discrimination as an excuse to cover up for their own inadequacies.

In my substantiation of the frames and style of color blindness, many respondents inserted stories to make their points: stories about the mysterious "black man" who took "their job" or their "spot at Harvard." These stories provide the emotional glue and the seal of authenticity needed to validate strong racial claims. Without these stories, venting racial animosity would be untenable. I examine these stories and their functions in the next chapter.

NOTES

1. For a full discussion of the various stylistic components of a racial ideology, see chapter 3 in my *White Supremacy and Racism in the Post–Civil Rights Era* (Boulder, Colo.: Rienner, 2001).

2. There is no systematic research on whites' *private* racial discourse. I suspect the structured and formal nature of our interview process made it a public matter and thus signified to respondents to be cautious. However, community-based studies on whites and undercover observational studies suggest whites are more likely to use racialized language in private, white spaces. For examples of the former, see Jonathan Rieder, *Carnarsie: The Jews and Italians of Brooklyn against Liberalism* (Cambridge, Mass.: Harvard University Press, 1985), and John Hartigan Jr., *Racial Situations: Class Predicaments of Whiteness in Detroit* (Princeton, N.J.: Princeton University Press, 1999). For an example of the latter, see Lawrence Otis Graham, *Member of the Club* (New York: HarperCollins, 1995). Other notable studies on this subject include Kristen Myers, *Racetalk: Racism Hiding in Plain Sight* (Lanham, Md.: Rowman & Littlefield, 2005), and Melanie Bush, *Everyday Forms of Whiteness: Understanding Race in a "Post-Racial" World* (Lanham, Md.: Rowman & Littlefield, 2011). See also Leslie Houts Picca and Joe R. Feagin's *Two-Faced Racism, Whites in the Backstage and Frontsage* (New York: Routledge, 2007), where they document, using students' journals, the extensive level of racist interactions in college campuses.

3. For an example, see Eduardo Bonilla-Silva and Tyrone A. Forman, "'I Am Not a Racist but . . .': Mapping White College Students' Racial Ideology in the USA," *Discourse and Society* 11, no. 1 (2000): 50–85.

4. Stuart Hall, "The Narrative Construction of Reality," *Southern Review* 17, no. 2 (1984): 7.

5. For a discussion of coded racial discussions on government spending and taxes, see Tomas Edsall and Mary D. Edsall, *Chain Reaction: The Impact of Race, Rights, and Taxes on American Politics* (New York: Norton, 1992).

6. To help readers, all the rhetorical maneuvers used by respondents in this chapter are set in sans-serif type. It does not indicate any type of emphasis in tone of voice.

7. Teun van Dijk, *Communicating Racism: Ethnic Prejudice in Cognition and Conversation* (Amsterdam: Benjamins, 1987), 86.

8. On ideology, see Teun van Dijk, *Ideology: A Multidisciplinary Approach* (London: Sage, 1998).

9. Paul Sniderman and Thomas Piazza, *The Scar of Race* (Cambridge, Mass.: Harvard University Press, 1993); Seymour M. Lipset, *American Exceptionalism* (New York: Norton, 1996); Paul Sniderman and Edward G. Carmines, *Reaching Beyond Race* (Cambridge, Mass.: Harvard University Press, 1997).

10. Italians seem to have a tenuous claim to whiteness, since many "whites" mentioned them as examples of "minority friends" in the interviews.

11. For an excellent analysis of racial projection, see the classic book by Gordon W. Allport, *The Nature of Prejudice* (Garden City, N.Y.: Doubleday / Anchor, 1958).

12. For an excellent analysis of the creation of the antithetical figures of "barbarian" or "wild men" and "civilized men" in Europe and its central role in the

creation of the notion of "the other," see Roger Bartra, *Wild Men in the Looking Glass: The Mythic Origins of European Otherness* (Ann Arbor: University of Michigan Press, 1994).

13. Sam Keen, *Faces of the Enemy: Reflections of the Hostile Imagination* (New York: Harper & Row, 1986), 21.

14. On this matter and white college students' lack of self-reflexivity, see Joe R. Feagin and Nikitah Imani, *The Agony of Education* (New York: Routledge, 1996). On the so-called issue of self-segregation, see Beverly Daniel Tatum, *"Why Are All the Black Kids Sitting Together in the Cafeteria?": And Other Conversations about Race* (New York: Basic, 1997).

15. For a critique, see Bryan K. Fair, *Racial Caste Baby: Color Blindness and the End of Affirmative Action* (New York: New York University Press, 1997).

16. W. E. B. DuBois, *The Souls of Black Folk* (New York: Penguin, 1995), 44.

17. The question was, "twenty-five to thirty-five percent of whites oppose interracial marriage. Many claim they do not have any problem with minorities, but that they are concerned about what would happen to the children. What is your view on this delicate matter?" It is important to point out that we obtained similar "concerns about the children" from the DAS sample, even though we did not include the second part of the question. At any rate, my focus here is on whether or not respondents used diminutives while stating concerns over racially sensitive issues.

18. For a similar finding, see van Dijk, *Communicating Racism*.

5

⁓

"I Didn't Get That Job Because of a Black Man"

Color-Blind Racism's Racial Stories

Storytelling is central to communication. To a large degree, all communication is about telling stories.[1] We tell stories to our spouses, children, friends, and coworkers. Through stories we present and represent ourselves and others.[2] Stories have been defined as "social events that instruct us about social processes, social structures, and social situations."[3] We literally narrate status ("When we were at the Gold Golf Club . . ."), biases ("This guy, who was not even a member of the GG Club . . ."), and beliefs about the social order (". . . had the audacity of asking me out, even though he just drives a Cavalier"). Stories are also important because they help us reinforce our arguments; they assist us in our attempt of persuading listeners that we are "right."

Thus, the stories we tell are not random, as they evince the social position of the narrators and belong to what Moscovici labels as "social representations."[4] Storytelling often represents the most ideological moments; when we tell stories we tell them as if there were *only one way* of telling them, as the "of course" way of understanding what is happening in the world. These are moments when we are "least aware that [we] are using a particular framework, and that if [we] used another framework the things we are talking about would have different meaning."[5] This is also the power of storytelling—that the stories seem to lie in the realm of the given, in the matter-of-fact world. Hence stories help us make sense of the world but in ways that reinforce the status quo, serving particular interests without appearing to do so.

Not surprisingly, then, since stories are a normal part of social life, they are a central component of color-blind racism. In this chapter, I examine the stories people tell as they try to make sense of racial matters in contemporary America. While a number of authors have examined the racial stories people tell,[6] few have specifically focused on the storytelling itself or on the ideological functions of stories. In the pages that follow I delve into modern racial stories as told by college students and DAS respondents. These stories were not research-driven, since I did not probe for them in these projects. Instead, they emerged spontaneously in respondents' answers to questions, in their efforts to punctuate certain points or to underscore the salience of an issue, or as digressions in the middle of racially sensitive discussions.

I examine two kinds of stories in this chapter: *story lines* and *testimonies.* I define *story lines* as the *socially shared tales that are fable-like and incorporate a common scheme and wording.* Racial story lines are fable-like because, unlike testimonies (see below), they are often based on impersonal, generic arguments with little narrative content—they are the ideological "of course" racial narratives. In story lines characters are likely to be underdeveloped and are usually social types (e.g., the "black man" in statements such as "My best friend lost a job to a black man" or the "welfare queen" in "Poor black women are welfare queens"). Furthermore, story lines are social products, a fact revealed by the similar schemata employed by different storytellers in the execution of the story lines—for example, in the use of similar phrases and words (such as "the past is the past") in the accounts. What makes these story lines "ideological" is that storytellers and their audiences share a representational world that makes these stories seem factual. Hence, by telling and retelling these story lines, members of a social group (in this case, the dominant race) strengthen their collective understanding about how and why the world is the way it is; indeed these stories tell and retell a moral story agreed upon by participants. These racial narratives, therefore, do more than assist dominant (and subordinate) groups to make sense of the world in particular ways; they also justify and defend (or challenge, in the case of oppositional stories)[7] current racial arrangements.

Testimonies, by contrast, *are accounts in which the narrator is a central participant in the story or is close to the characters in the story.*[8] Testimonies provide the aura of authenticity and emotionality that only "firsthand" narratives can furnish ("I know this for a fact since I have worked all my life with blacks"). Therefore, these stories help narrators in gaining sympathy from listeners or in persuading them about points they want to convey. Though *seemingly* involving more detail and personal investment than story lines (but see my analysis below), many of the testimonies whites tell still serve rhetorical functions with regard to racial issues, such as saving face, signifying nonracialism, or bolstering their arguments on controversial racial matters. Moreover, they are often tightly linked to the story lines above as personal experiences are understood and interpreted through the lens of more general racial narratives and understandings about the world.

THE MAJOR STORY LINES OF COLOR-BLIND RACISM

During the Jim Crow era the myth of the black rapist became a powerful story line that could be invoked to keep blacks "in their place."[9] In the era of the new racism (see chapter 1), new story lines have emerged that help keep blacks and other minorities in their (new, but still secondary) "place." The major racial story lines of the post–civil rights era are "The past is the past," "I did not own slaves," "If [other ethnic groups] have made it, how come blacks have not?," and "I did not get a (job or promotion) because of a black man." Although some of these story lines (e.g., "The past is the past" and "I didn't own any slaves") were often interjected together by respondents, I present my discussion of each separately.

"The Past Is the Past"

"The past is the past" story line is central to color-blind racism since it fits well with the minimization of discrimination frame. Thus more than 50 percent (twenty-one of forty-one) of the college students and most DAS respondents used the story line most often when discussing affirmative action or government programs targeted for blacks. The core of this story line is that we must put the past behind us and that programs such as affirmative action do exactly the opposite by keeping the racial flame alive. A perfect example of how students inserted this story line was provided by Andy, a student at WU. Andy's answer to the question, "Do you believe that the history of oppression endured by minorities merits the intervention of the government on their behalf?" was,

> I almost—I think that the past is kind of the past and so, history of oppression?[10] I don't know if anyone [is] owed anything because of the, like, past [is] really past history, but to look at things, the way things are right at this moment and to try to move forward from there. Then I support some things, maybe affirmative action, so long as it wasn't a runaway sort of. . . .

Emily, a student at SU, used the story line in an exchange with the interviewer on the meaning of affirmative action:

> I have, I just have a problem with the discrimination, you're gonna discriminate against a group and what happened in the past is horrible and it should

never happen again, but I also think that to move forward you have to let go of the past and let go of what happened, you know? And it should really start equaling out 'cause I feel that some of, some of it will go too far and it'll swing the other way. One group is going to be discriminated against, I don't, I don't believe in that. I don't think one group should have an advantage over another regardless of what happened in the past.

Very few DAS respondents who expressed their displeasure with programs they believe benefit blacks solely because of their racial background did not use a version of this story line. For instance, Jennifer, a school-district personnel director in her forties, expressed her opposition to affirmative action in a straightforward manner: "In general I am against it. I think it had its place. It was necessary." She later reaffirmed her position using a version of the story line in response to a hypothetical case dealing with a company that decides to hire a black over a white applicant because of past discrimination:

Again, I don't think that we can make retribution for things that happened in the past. I don't think it serves any purpose today to try to fix something that happened a long time ago that doesn't affect anyone today. All it does is bring up to the surface that there was a problem.

Jennifer's last statement ("All it does is bring up to the surface that there was a problem") is the central ideological component of this story line. For whites, remedial policies are inherently divisive, hence whites' insistence on forgetting the past.

Kate, a salesperson and part-time college student in her twenties, used the story line to explain her opposition to government programs for blacks. Kate first stated, "To make up for what we did in the past, I'd say no. I mean, we can't still punish the Germans for what happened to the Jews so if that is to make up for what they did, then I'd say no." Since her answer left open the possibility there may be cases in which compensatory assistance was reasonable, the interviewer asked for clarification. After the interviewer read the question to Kate again, she answered,

Am I not elaborating enough? [*Interviewer: Oh, no, no, no, no, we're just . . .*] No, I don't think that the government should because I think that's saying "OK, we made a mistake a hundred of years ago so now we're gonna try to make up for it." But yet, you know, I think that is the past and you have to move along; I mean, should they admit that they made a mistake? Yes! But should there be programs for blacks that aren't for whites if they're in the same position, you know? If they're hurting or they're battered or they're starving should it be any different because they're not black? No!

Some respondents used the story line while venting lots of anger at the idea of affirmative action or reparations. John II, for instance, a retired architect and homebuilder in his late sixties, vented anger in his response to the question on reparations:

> Not a nickel, not a nickel! I think that's ridiculous. I think that's a great way to go for the black vote. But I think that's a ridiculous assumption because those that say we should pay them because they were slaves back in the past and yet, how often do you hear about the people who were whites that were slaves and ah, the whites that were ah? Boy, we should get reparations, the Irish should get reparations from the English. . . .

But what is ideological about this story? Is it not true that "the past is the past"? First, whites interpreted the past as slavery, even when in some questions we left it open (e.g., questions regarding the "history of oppression") or specified we were referring to "slavery *and* Jim Crow." Since Jim Crow died slowly in the country (1960s to 1970s), their constant reference to a remote past distorts the fact about how recent overt forms of racial oppression impeded black progress. This also means that most whites are still connected to parents and grandparents who participated in Jim Crow in some fashion. Second, the effects of historic discrimination have limited blacks' capacity to accumulate wealth at the same rate as whites. According to Melvin L. Oliver and Thomas M. Shapiro, the "accumulation of disadvantages" has "sedimented" blacks economically so that, even if all forms of economic discrimination blacks face ended today, they would not catch up with whites for several hundred years![11] Third, believing discrimination is a thing of the past helps whites reinforce their staunch opposition to all race-based compensatory programs. This story line, then, is used to deny the enduring effects of historic discrimination as well as to deny the significance of contemporary discrimination. Thus, when one considers the combined effects of historic and contemporary discrimination, the anchor holding minorities in place weighs a ton and cannot be easily dismissed.

"I Didn't Own Any Slaves"

The essence of the "I didn't own any slaves" story line is that present generations are not responsible for the ills of slavery. This story line was used frequently in conjunction with the story line of "The past is the past," but it was inserted less often (nine students and a third of DAS respondents). As with the previous story line, this one was usually invoked in discussions about affirmative action. For instance, Carol, a student at SU, said in response to the question on government intervention: "I mean, I almost kind of have the 'what happened, happened' attitude. You know, I mean, my generation certainly didn't inflict any of this onto your generation, I mean, if anyone should pay it's the generation that did the inflicting." Because the generation who "did the inflicting" is long gone, her suggestion would not have any impact on blacks today.

Lynn, an MU student, used the story line to explain her opposition to a hypothetical company hiring a black candidate over a white candidate because of past discrimination:

> I think I would, I would, I'd disagree, I think. I mean, yeah, I think I'd dis-
> agree because, I mean, even though it's kinda what affirmative action—well,
> it's not really because I don't think like my generation should have to—I
> mean, in a way, we should, but we shouldn't be punished real harshly for the
> things that our ancestors did, on the one hand, but on the other hand, I think
> that now we should try and change the way we do things so that we aren't
> doing the same things that our ancestors did.

Using the story line here gave credence to Lynn's stance on this case because she had stated before she supported affirmative action and she realized that this case was "kinda what affirmative action" is. It also helped Lynn to regain her composure after a serious bout of rhetorical incoherence ("I think I would, I would, I'd disagree, I think. I mean, yeah, I think I'd disagree because, I mean").

Finally, Sara, a student at SU, used the story line to state her view on government intervention on blacks' behalf:

> Hmm [*long exhalation*], maybe just—Well, I don't know 'cause it seems like
> people are always wondering if, you know, do we, like do we as white peo-
> ple owe people as black something their ancestors were, you know, treated
> so badly. But then, I mean, it wasn't really us that did that, so I don't know.
> I mean, I think that the race or that culture should, you know, be paid back
> for something in some way. But I don't think that . . . I don't know [*laughs*].

DAS respondents used this story line in ways similar to students. For example, Dina, an employment manager for an advertising agency in her early thirties, used the story line to answer the question on government compensation to blacks for past discrimination:

> No, and I, you know, I have to say that I'm pretty supportive of anything
> to help people, but I don't know why that slavery thing has a—I've got a
> chip on my shoulder about that. It's like it happened so long ago and you've
> got these sixteen-year-old kids saying, "Well, I deserve because great, great
> granddaddy was a slave." Well, you know what, it doesn't affect you. Me,
> as white person, I had nothing to do with slavery. You, as a black person, you

never experienced it. It was so long ago I just don't see how that pertains to what's happening to the race today so, you know, that's one thing that I'm just like, "God, shut up!"

Roland, an electrical engineer in his forties, also used the story line to oppose the idea of reparations:

I think they've gotten enough. I don't think we need to pay them anything or I think as long as they are afforded opportunities and avail themselves to the opportunities like everybody else, I, I don't know why we should give them any reparation for something that happened, you know. . . . I can't, I *can't* help what happened in the 1400s, the 1500s, or the 1600s, when the blacks were brought over here and put into slavery. I mean, I had no control over that, neither did you, so I don't think we should do anything as far as reparations are concerned.

Although most Detroit-area whites used this story line as part of their argumentative repertoire to explain their opposition to or doubts about affirmative action, occasionally they used them in odd places. For instance, Monica, a medical transcriber in her fifties with a strong commitment to the Jehovah's Witnesses religious viewpoint, used the story line while discussing discrimination. After a long statement arguing that because of past discrimination, blacks developed a cultural outlook based on the idea that they can't succeed because of discrimination, Monica then proceeded to argue, "It's, it's become such a mess and it's perpetuated again by media and by these special interest groups. You and I aren't responsible for what our ancestors did in slavery, that we didn't initiate that slavery."

As can be seen, these two story lines served whites as instruments to object to blacks' demands for compensatory policies. Furthermore, they helped whites stand on a high moral ground while objecting to these policies. But, again, what is ideological about this particular story line? It is a fact that most whites did not participate directly[12] in slavery or came to the country years after slavery had ended.[13] However, this story line ignores the fact that pro-white policies ("preferential treatment") in jobs, housing, elections, and access to social space ("No blacks and Mexicans allowed here!") have had (and continue to have) a positive multiplier effect for all those deemed "white." Thus, not surprisingly, "suspect" racial groups such as the Irish, Italians, and Jews,[14] among others, struggled to become "white" because by doing so, they could receive the manifold "wages of whiteness" (see chapter 1). Hence, the "It wasn't me"[15] approach of this story line does not fit the reality of how racial privilege operated and still operates in America. Although specific whites may not have participated directly in the overt discriminatory practices that injured blacks and other minorities in the past, they all have received unearned privileges[16] by virtue of being regarded as "white" and have benefited from the various incarnations of white supremacy in the United States.

"If Jews, Italians, and Irish Have Made It, How Come Blacks Have Not?"

Another story line that has become quite popular is "If (ethnic groups such as Japanese, Chinese, Jews, and Irish) have made it, how come blacks have not?" This story line is used by whites to suggest blacks' status in America is their own doing, because other groups who experienced discrimination in the past are doing quite well today. Few college students, but ten DAS respondents, used this story line. However, it is important to point out that 35 percent of the students agreed with the premise of this story line when it was asked in the survey.

One example of a student who used this story line is Kim, a student at SU. She inserted a version of the story line in combination with the "the past is the past" story line to explain why she does not favor government intervention on behalf of minorities:

> Um no. I think that, you know, a lot of bad things happened to a lot of people, but you can't sit there and dwell on that. I mean, like the Jewish people, look what happened to them. You know, do you hear them sitting around complaining about it, you know, and attributing, you know, anything bad that happens to them? I've never heard anyone say, "Oh, it's because I'm Jewish." You know, and I know it's a little different because, you know, a black, I mean, you can't really, a lot of, you can't really tell on the outside a lot of times, but, I mean, they don't wallow in what happened to them a long time ago. I mean, it was a horrible thing, I admit, but I think that you need to move on and try to put that behind, you know, put that behind you.

Although DAS respondents were more likely than students to use this story line, they did not use it as frequently as they did the previous two. An example of how they used this story line was provided by Henrietta, a transvestite school teacher in his fifties. Henrietta used the story line in his answer to the question on government spending on blacks' behalf:

> [*Five-second pause*] As a person who was once reversed discriminated against, I would have to say no. Because the government does not need programs if they, if people would be motivated to bring themselves out of the poverty level. When we talk about certain programs, when the Irish came over, when the Italians, the Polish, and the East European Jews, they all were immigrants who lived in terrible conditions, who worked in terrible conditions, too. But they had one thing in common: they all knew that education was the way out of that poverty. And they did it. I'm not saying the blacks were brought

over here maybe not willingly, but if they realize education's the key, that's it. And that's based on individuality.

Mandy, a registered nurse in her forties, used the story line to address the issue of whether or not blacks' standing in this country is due to of their values and laziness:

> *Mandy*: Generally, I think that's probably true. Now are you talking about *all minorities*? [*Interviewer*: Umhumm.] 'Cause I don't—when you look at the people coming from Asia, Japan, and China . . . they're making the honor roll. When you look at the honor [roll] here in Rochester, they're all foreign names. You know, some of those kids from minority families figured out that they had to work and strive and work harder if they were going to make it all the way to the top.
> *Interviewer*: Okay. So you're saying that you would classify minorities by race and go from there?
> *Mandy*: Not all minorities are lazy and lay on the couch all the time.

This story line equates the experiences of immigrant groups with that of involuntary "immigrants" (such as enslaved Africans). But as Stephen Steinberg has perceptively pointed out in his *The Ethnic Myth*, most immigrant groups were able to get a foothold on certain economic niches or used resources such as an education or small amounts of capital to achieve social mobility. "In contrast, racial minorities were for the most part relegated to the preindustrial sectors of the national economy and, until the flow of immigration was cut off by the First World War, were denied access to the industrial jobs that lured tens of millions of immigrants. All groups started at the bottom, but as Blauner points out, 'the bottom' has by no means been the same for all groups."[17] Thus, comparing these groups, as this story line does, is comparing apples and pears as a way to "blame the victims" (many minority groups).

"I Did Not Get a Job (or a Promotion), or Was Not Admitted to a College, Because of a Minority"

This story line is extremely useful to whites rhetorically and psychologically. When whites do not get a job or promotion, it must be because of a minority. If they are not admitted into a college, it must be because of a minority. This story line allows whites to never consider the possibility that they are not qualified for a job, promotion, or college. Curiously, the number of actual cases filed on reverse discrimination before the Equal Employment Opportunity Commission is quite small and the immense majority of them are dismissed as lacking any foundation.[18] Furthermore, as I will show, most versions of this story line lack substance, are based on limited data, and rely on less-than-credible information.[19] This lack of specificity, however, does not detract from the usefulness of this story line, since its sense of veracity is not based on facts, but on commonly held beliefs by whites. Hence, when whites use this story line, precise information need not be included. And because this story line is built upon a personal moral tale, many whites vent personal frustrations or resentment toward minorities while using it.

Almost a quarter of the students (ten of forty-one) and more than a third of the DAS respondents used this story line. For instance, Bob, the SU student cited above, opposed providing unique opportunities to minorities to be admitted into universities. After anchoring his view in the abstract liberalism frame ("you should be judged on your qualifications, your experience, your education, your background, not of your race"), Bob added,

> I had a friend, he wasn't—I don't like him that much, I think it's my brother's friend, a good friend of my brother's, who didn't get into law school here and he knows for a fact that other students less qualified than him *did*. And that really, and he was considering a lawsuit against the school. But for some reason, he didn't. He had better grades, better LSAT, better everything, and he—other people got in up above him, I don't care who it is, if it's Eskimo, or Australian, or what it is, you should have the best person there.

This is a classic example of this story line. Bob "had a friend" (who was not his friend, but his brother's friend and whom he did not "like that much") who claimed to know "for a fact" (facts he never documents) that minority students who were less qualified than his brother[20] were admitted into SU Law School. Bob uses the story line here to reinforce his view that admission to colleges ought to be strictly based on merits.

Kara, a student from MU, inserted the story line when she was asked if she had been a victim of "reverse discrimination":

> I think applying to schools. I know a couple of people, like, schools like Notre Dame that are, you know, very, like, competitive to get into. Like, I was put on the wait list where this kid in my school who was black was admitted and, like, for me, you know, like, I almost had a four point, you know, I did well on my SATs, and he was kind of a slacker, grade-point wise, and I always thought it *could* have been something else, but it didn't make sense to me and that was the only thing I could put it to.

When asked if she knew of other cases of "reverse discrimination," Kara added, "Yeah, especially my friends that applied to the Ivy League schools." They really felt that they were discriminated against.

Kara claims that while she was not admitted to Notre Dame, a black "kid" in her school who was "kind of a slacker" was. She believes the only logical explanation for this is "reverse discrimination" and that many of her friends experienced it, too. But we do not get any data on how she did on her SAT (she reports doing "well," but does not indicate her score) and, more significantly, we get absolutely no information on how well the black student did on the SAT. Regarding her friends' claims, Kara provides even less information.

This story line was also important for white DAS respondents, since more than a third of them used it. One example is Ann, a young, unemployed woman. She used the story line in her answer to the question, "Do you think that being white is an advantage or a disadvantage in contemporary America?":

No. It's, I don't know. [*Interviewer: Why do you think that?*] I don't know, it's [*laughs*], it's weird because my friend that is there, she went for a job interview with two of her white girlfriends. It was her and those three white females and the rest were black. Well, when they were done with the testing they took their scores and they all had the same scores, the three white girls. And they come out and they hire, they said that the two white girls didn't pass their math test, but they said that she passed hers and then they hired her.

Ann claims that a black friend of hers experienced preferential treatment in a job search. As usual in the iterations of this story line, the story is very fuzzy and refers to third parties. In Ann's narrative it is very difficult to assess any of the particularities of the case. How many people went for the job? How many tests did they take? What scores did all the applicants get? Were the applicants interviewed after they were tested? What kind of job were they applying for? The answers to all these questions are uncertain.

Marie, a homemaker in her late thirties, used the story line to explain her position on affirmative action:

Ah, I'm puzzled a little bit by that. I'm for making sure everybody gets equal opportunity. I think that there are points, though, where it is inappropriate. Just as an example, my sister has a good student that applied for a teaching position at a university and was told that she was one of three final candidates for the position, but the other two candidates, one was a Mexican American and the other was a black female. Unless she could prove she had some active minority in her background, she could not be considered for the position because they had to hire a minority.

Although Marie's story seems more robust than usual, the details do not square with what we know of the academic job market. First, based on the peculiar list of final candidates (peculiar because it is very unusual to have two minority scholars as finalists in a job search), it seems this job required expertise on racial matters. This does not disqualify the white applicant, but it adds some complexity to the story. Second, the argument that she had to prove some minority background to qualify for this position (after she made the final cut) is not credible. Had that been the case, this applicant could have successfully sued this university for discrimination. An alternative reading of the events is that this white applicant lost out to a minority candidate and explained this to herself, her professor, and her peers as many whites do, as a case of reverse discrimination.

Many of the workers in the sample vented lots of anger against what they regarded as "preferential treatment" for minorities, although few knew what affirmative action was. Not surprisingly, many used the story line in its most generic sense. The following two cases illustrate my point. First is Darren, a bus driver in his late forties. He opposed affirmative action by stating that "two wrongs don't make a right" and used the story line to supply evidence on which to base his opinion:

> Ah no, other than I have applied at jobs and been turned down because I was white. *Now, I have nothing* against the black person [if he] was qualified better than I was. But when the guy comes into the interview and I'm off on the side and I can hear them talking and he can't even speak good English, he doesn't know how to read a map, and they're gonna make him a bus driver and hire him over me. I've been doing bus driving off and on since 1973 and I know the guy well enough that [I know] he's a lousy driver. I know why he got the job, and I don't think that's fair.

Darren believed he was turned down for a job as a bus driver because he was white. Furthermore, he claimed that he overheard the interview and that his black competitor could not "even speak good English." But his story is as loose as the others. Both applicants now work in the same company, which suggests Darren got the job there at some point in time. And Darren failed to mention two other factors that may account—besides driving skills, which we cannot ascertain based on the information he provided—for why this other driver may have gotten the job before Darren did. First, this company is located in Detroit and it makes business sense to hire black bus drivers. Second, and more important, Darren has moved a lot in his life and has had more than twelve jobs. Hence, any rational manager must look at his record with some trepidation and wonder why this person has moved so much and whether he would be a reliable worker.

Tony, a carpet installer in his twenties, used a very unusual version of the story line to explain why he believes being white is no longer an advantage in America: "Oh yeah. Like when my girlfriend went to get on aid, the lady told her if she was black, she could have got help, but she wasn't black and she wasn't getting no help." Tony's account can be translated as "I did not get welfare because of blacks."

TESTIMONIES AND COLOR BLINDNESS

The role of testimonies in the color-blind drama cannot be underestimated. Almost every respondent in the two studies interpolated them for rhetorical purposes such as saving face, signifying nonracialism, or bolstering an argument. Notwithstanding that testimonies were more random than story lines, I classified them into three categories: stories of interactions with blacks (negative and positive), stories of disclosure of knowledge of someone close who is racist, and a residual category of *sui generis* testimonies. The purpose of this discussion is examining the similarities in the narrative form of these stories as well as assessing their rhetorical function. I discuss each story category separately below.

Stories of Interactions with Blacks

Most of the stories of interactions with blacks that whites told in these interviews were of two kinds. One type of story portrayed a negative incident with blacks usually used to justify a position taken on some issue (e.g., "Blacks are aggressive. A year ago I was called a racist by . . ."). The other type of story involved a positive incident or relationship with a black person as a way to signify the narrator's good relationships with or views toward blacks. About a third of the students and DAS respondents narrated one of these testimonies at some point in the interview.

Negative Interactions with Blacks

Mickey, a student at MU, acknowledged that his family talks about racial matters often and blamed it on the area they lived in. He said his family lived near Benton Harbor—a formerly white area that has become predominantly black, a neighborhood that has "one of the highest crime rates in, like, the country" and that "now [is] a really dirtiest place." The interviewer asked him whether or not people in his community worried about violence and crime spreading to their community. Mickey acknowledged that he thought "about that a lot" and added,

> But, I mean, nothing really happened horribly. Actually, a neighbor of mine [*laughs*]—kind of a grim story—I have a younger brother who's friends with one of my neighbors just down the street who hangs out with him sometimes. And he was drivin' downtown in Benton Harbor about a couple of

months ago, and I think he was trying to get some marijuana or somethin'
stupid like that, and he got beat over the head with a baseball bat. Got some
black eyes and he had brain damage. He's okay now, but he was in a coma
for a little bit. And he's like, I think he's got minor brain damage, irreversible.
But nothing that's affecting him, like, too bad but, I mean, that was just one
incident that happened a couple of months [ago] that made me think about
stuff like this.

This testimony helped Mickey to safely state later in the interview his
belief that blacks are "more aggressive" than whites and to suggest the
problems of Benton Harbor are moral ones.

Leslie, a student at WU, supported "proposing liberal values" and
"having people value the cultural diversity in our country" as a government strategy to increase school integration in America. Nevertheless, she
had reservations about busing and narrated the following story to bolster
her viewpoint:

There was a time when one of the black kids actually punched out the principal. And there was a time when I was in the P.E. locker room and I set my
bag down just to go to the bathroom and then come back out and everything
in my locker. I was gone maybe, you know, a minute and I come back and I
see a really big woman [with other students] stealing money out of my bag.
And I confronted them and they were like, "No, we're not doing anything,"
and so I went to the principal because they stole $60 [*laughs*]. And the only
reason I had that much money on me was that I was going shopping after
school and I con—confronted like the principal and he confronted them.
And they threatened to beat me up, and they were like, "You almost got us
suspended." And they like, surrounded me during lunch [*laughs*].

It is hard to determine if Leslie was picked on because she looked different (she was dressing hippie style) in this mixed school, a school that
nonetheless was majority white. The important matter, however, is that
she believes this is what happened and that her interpretation of this
experience informs her stand on busing. Leslie opposes busing and this
testimony gives her a convenient rationale for opposing it.

The last example of these stories from college students comes from
Rick, a Mormon student at WU. When asked about blacks' claims of experiencing discrimination, Rick suggested, "Some people read too much
into what other people say." He mentioned that he himself was accused
of being racist by a black man in a discussion about affirmative action:

I, I can't remember. It was—I think it was talking about affirmative action
or something, and he called me that I was being a racist or something and I
said, "I am sorry. I did not mean that in that way, if it was taken that way." I
totally apologized because I, my belief system doesn't incorporate racism, according to me. But maybe I wasn't being as sensitive or maybe he was being

oversensitive—I don't know which way it went—but from my experience I kind of developed the attitude that I think too many—Too often we are too easily offended and it goes both ways, not just blacks but whites, you know.

Although Rick stated that his hypersensitivity thesis works both ways, his story was narrated in response to a question about blacks and discrimination. When he was asked again if he believed blacks experienced lots of discrimination, he pointed out, "It depends on the part of country." This answer was used by many respondents to suggest that racism happens "elsewhere." Thus his testimony served him to bolster his belief that blacks falsely accuse whites of discrimination and, therefore, to minimize the significance of racism.

DAS respondents told negative stories of interaction with blacks, too. Bill, a retired school teacher in his eighties, narrated a story to explain why he thinks blacks and whites are different. After pointing out that blacks "seem to be very *religious*" and mentioning that they bought a church in his neighborhood, Bill claimed they forced a restaurant out of business:

> They did have a Sweden House on the corner and all the neighbors were happy about it because they could [go] to the Sweden House and have dinner. Well, before long the blacks took over. They are only one mile away and on Sunday afternoon, they come in droves, *in buses* from the churches, *bus loads of 'em*, and they all fill the restaurant and the white people come and see that and turn around and *go*. They burnt it down, the Sweden House. We don't have a Sweden House anymore.

The interviewer asked Bill why they closed the restaurant. Bill said that it closed because "they were not making any money on 'em." He explained this as follows:

> They like to eat. They *pile their* dishes just loaded with that stuff and I actually didn't see it, but I saw one lady come in with a full plate of chicken. I didn't pay much attention, but the next thing I know, they are leaving. Now I know she didn't eat all that chicken. She probably put it in her purse and walked out with it. I didn't see that. Lot of them are doing that, how can they make any money? And seeing that they are all *heavy people,* it seems like they do a lot of eating. *So* I don't know what to say about something like that.

Although most of this story is based on Bill's racist interpretation of events, the fact remains that he uses it to validate his belief that blacks "like to eat," are cheap, and steal.

The second example is Joan, a video store employee in her late thirties. She told a story about a black woman who unfairly accused her of being racist:

Like black people, they use their excuse that they're black and that's the reason why white people won't be accepting me. I've seen it, too. I had this black person, for instance, who chewed me out at Videobuster. Yelled at me a year ago. Started calling me a white honky and every racist slur that you could think of happened. My uncle showed up, you know, he works for the government and I get to see him often. He came in and I was in tears 'cause I was not brought up that way. This woman was totally flabbergasted because my uncle asked her if she had a problem and told her I was his niece. I just gave him a hug. This woman was calling me names that were totally uncalled for. She did not have a receipt. I wouldn't—I do it with everybody. You do not have a receipt, you don't get an exchange. She tried to return our products, our store rentals without store code on it as a gift from someone else. She said I was accusing her of stealing it from the store. I could not refund the money. She called me racial names.

Joan's story and case is very interesting, because she considered herself white, even though she claimed to have black, Native American, and Jewish in her background. She was coded as white (and apparently looked the part) because in the original survey she had stated that she was white. The "uncle" she referred to in this story was a black man, but in truth he was just her godfather. The rhetorical goal of this particular story was to punctuate her belief that blacks use race as an excuse, a belief that she repeated often in the interview.

Positive Interactions with Blacks

The number of whites narrating positive testimonies of interactions with blacks was similar to the number of those narrating negative testimonies. These stories had a positive self-presentation rhetorical goal. For instance, Mary, a student at SU, said, in response to the question on whether blacks self-segregate or are not made to feel welcome by whites, that her family is racist. In this context, Mary narrated her testimony of positive interactions with her black roommate:

My floor actually, the year I had a black roommate, happened to be predominantly African American and so those became some of my best friends, the people I was around. And we would actually sit around and talk about stereotypes and prejudices and I learned so much just about the hair texture, you know? What it means for a black person to get a perm versus me, you know. I learned *a lot.* And it really, I think, for me, broke down a lot of barriers and ended a lot of stereotypes I may still [have] had. Because like I said, I mean, those really became some of my best friends. And even still we don't really keep in touch, but if I see any of 'em on campus, still, you know, we always talk with each other and everything.

Mary's story rings of self-presentation from start to finish. Yet, because Mary was not too refined in her delivery, the story hurt her more than it helped her. For instance, she used the term "those" people twice and pointed out twice that they became "some of my best friends." Furthermore, her claim that she learned a lot from this interaction seems superficial, since she only talked about hair texture and perms. Finally, these nameless "best friends" later became only casual acquaintances after a year of sharing a floor with Mary.

Another example of how students used these positive stories was provided by John, a forty-year-old WU student. In response to the question, "Do you talk about race or racial issues now?" John inserted a story about his cousin marrying a black man:

> Yes I do, there was a cousin of mine—she married a black man. They came to visit me and I had to really look at this really close and consider the fact that he's actually a pretty neat person that she married and I considered it unfair that she should be made to feel saddened and I don't.

John's story helped him project an image of maturity and racial sensitivity. However, based on his answers throughout the entire interview, it is clear that John had some racist views about minorities. For example, John claimed that people from South India smelled differently because "they eat a lot of spices." He also pointed out that blacks exuded a strong body odor that has an "effect on people's psyche, how they react to the racial issue, a subliminal type of thing."

DAS respondents used these positive stories of interaction with blacks for the same purposes. However, because these respondents were older, their stories included a wider range of matters. John II, a semiretired house designer in his sixties, inserted a World War II story of positive interaction with blacks in response to the question on whether blacks are hard to approach or are not made to feel welcome by whites. After stating that he had no experiences upon which to base an opinion on this matter, John II narrated the following story:

> Three Filipino scouts and I were waiting, trying to catch a load south. We had one, probably a 200–300 watt bulb hanging over the intersection to put some light there, and there was an alley that went off on one of the roads that we could hear some shouting. We could see in the dark of that alley, see the light from a door and some three fellows ran out and saw us, the Filipino scouts and I, and thought we [were] the ones that had apparently done something outrageous and he opened up on us with an automatic carbine. So the Filipino scouts stood farther away from me and they got the cover and I got behind the curb. It wasn't quite enough curb to hide me and the fellow was shooting a full automatic. A jeep came in out of one of the roads and slid to

a stop and about the time he said, "Get in!" They said, "Let's go!" because I was in laying across the back seat and he took off. When we got down the road, I climbed out of the back seat into the front seat and it was a colored captain. He wouldn't give me his name or anything. He said, "That's all right," but I've always remembered that. He put himself at risk under fire to pick up a man and take him out of a line of fire.

John's testimony served him as a vehicle to state his view that blacks and whites can act civilized toward each other. His story resembles those that so many veterans tell of interracial solidarity during war. However, for John, as for many white veterans, these stories became just stories without much effect on their behavior or attitudes toward blacks after they returned to America.[21] For example, John II, who used the term "colored" to refer to the black man who saved his life, opposed inter-racial marriage and acknowledged that he is "more comfortable around whites because I've grown up with them" and, thus, had no qualms about neighborhoods or schools being almost completely white. Hence, John II's stand amounts to a modern version of the separate-but-equal policy of the past; blacks and whites can be civil toward each other, but they should not live near each other or marry each other.

Stories of Disclosure of Knowledge of Someone Close Who Is Racist

Twelve students and eight DAS respondents disclosed information about someone close being racist (usually a parent or grandparent). The narrative form used to disclose this information resembles confession in church, because respondents insert these testimonies as if they were expecting absolution from listeners from the possibility of being regarded as racist. These stories are structured around a trinity formula: confession, example, and self-absolution. The religious motif in these stories is further enhanced by the fact that it is usually through the influence of a woman (mother Mary) that the storyteller hopes to receive absolution. For example, Bob, the SU student previously cited, acknowledged that his father was racist in response to a question on whether his family talked about race while he was growing up:

Um [*clears throat*], you can tell my parents' background by the way they talk about things. They're both born in New York, a small town in New York. My mom is very open to things, but like my dad, he, he still uses terms like "them" and "those people" and stuff like that which I don't like at all, which I just don't even talk about and stuff like that with him. We get along, but only there's some things we don't agree with and that's something you can't change. That is, I've tried for twelve years. I remember one time, I think it was my dad asked me something like how come I didn't have any more white friends? And I said, "Well, why don't you go live in a white neighborhood and put me in a white school?" [*laughs*] So that was the end of that conversation.

Bob's story fits perfectly the trinity formula. First, he confesses that his father "uses terms like 'them' and 'those people.'" He then provides an exculpatory example of how he challenged his father's racist leanings. And throughout the narration, Bob inserts elements ("my mother is very open to things") or comments ("stuff like that which I don't like at all") to indicate he is not like his father, probably because of his mother, who "is very open to things."

Emily, the SU student cited above, in response to the same question Bob answered, admitted that her father was racist:

> Um, I don't know if it necessarily was a conversation, but my mom, I mean, she never was racist against people, you know. She always looked at them as people and stuff and I think my sister and I get a lot of that from her. And my dad is racist, but I didn't live with him growing up. My parents were divorced, but she would talk about, you know, that it's not good. And I remember one time, actually, I was a little girl, and I had my best friend was black, and I once said something that was—I don't know if it was racist, it just wasn't a very nice remark, I don't think. And my mom sat me down and said, "How do you think she would feel if she heard you say that?" you know. So she really she would call attention to things so we would pay attention to what was going on.

Emily uses all the elements of the trinity formula: confession ("my dad is racist"), self-absolution ("my sister and I get a lot of that from her"), and example (how her mother corrected her racist comment about her friend). Emily's rhetorical use of the story is clearer than Bob's, given that she focuses on proving that she takes from her mother's rather than from her father's side.

The last example of how college students used this story is from Mike, an MU student. In response to the question, "Do you ever talk about racial issues at home?" Mike said,

> Yeah we do. I mean, my dad came from a pretty racist background, I mean, not, you know, like—well, actually, his grandfather, I think, was in the Ku Klux Klan, um, until he got married. And my great grandmother, who I knew—she died, but I knew her—was completely the opposite. And basically when they got married, she said "no way." So *that* ended, but I mean, there was still a certain, you know, racism that pervaded. In his family they were pretty racist, so you'll still hear, you know, racial slurs slip out every once in a while, but I think he makes a conscious effort not to, I mean, he certainly didn't ever try to teach me things like that, you know. For one thing,

my dad was in the navy for a long time, so I grew up with my mom for the first five years or so, and then he worked and my mom stayed at home with me. So my dad's influence was not nearly as much as my mom's to begin with, and even when it was, I wouldn't say that influenced me a lot, but there were definitely, I mean, racist ideas in his family. And I see that with my grandparents, you know, his parents.

Mike confesses that his dad comes from a "pretty racist background." Then he mentions that his father's grandfather was in the KKK. Finally, he concludes the story by suggesting he was immune to this background, because his father "didn't try to teach me things like that" and because he was raised mainly by his mother.

Since we did not pose the question on whether respondents talked about race while growing up to DAS respondents, few (eight of sixty-six) used this personal story; and when they did, their delivery of the story was somewhat more disorganized than that of students. Yet, when DAS respondents inserted the story, it was also organized around the trinity formula. Scott, a twenty-three-year-old drafter, while explaining his view on whether blacks self-segregate or are not made to feel welcome by whites, revealed that his father was racist. In response to the specific question, "Do you think that (white workers) are apprehensive about approaching their black colleagues or the same?" Scott stated,

> The same way just reversed, you know, just 'cause you know. I mean, my dad grew up in Detroit in a real bad neighborhood and he was brought on that way, I mean, he is real prejudice. I brought one of my buddies home one time and he was like, "No, I don't want you hanging out with him," you know, he don't trust them.

Scott immediately added, "That's my dad though, but that's not me. I take, you know, I take people for what they are and I don't judge people by word of mouth, you know, just treat you the way you treat me." The interviewer then asked Scott why he did not develop the same attitudes toward blacks as his dad. Scott stated that it was due to his mom because "she went to Catholic school all the way up until high school. So, she's got a lot of Catholic values so, can't really be prejudice if you're, you're religious. So my mom always shunned on being prejudice." Scott's story is clearly framed by the trinity formula. First, he confesses his father is "real prejudice." Then, he uses the example of his father's racist views about his friend. Finally, Scott suggests he is not like his dad because of his mother's Catholic influence. However, among young DAS respondents, Scott had some of the most highly racialized views on a number of issues (see his views on interracial marriage in chapter 7).

The last example of a DAS respondent using this story is Jenny, a public-school administrator in her fifties. In response to the question on how she felt about the neighborhood where she grew up, Jenny stated that many of her neighbors were closed-minded and she labeled them as "Archie Bunkers." After narrating an incident in which one black kid was refused as a dance partner by a girl in her school, Jenny said,

> My grand, my grandmother, who was—she was Scandinavian. But she used to make fun of blacks. And when we would drive through a black neighborhood she would say things like, "Look at all the little chocolate drops." And I can remember being a young child—maybe five, six, or seven years old—and being offended by her remarks. My parents never, ever said anything like that. My parents were very open-minded and broad-minded.

Again, Jenny uses the same formula. First, she provides the confession about her grandmother harboring racist views. Then, she supplies the example of her grandmother making denigrating remarks about black children. Finally, Jenny distances herself from this relative by pointing out that she was "offended by her (grandmothers') remarks" as well as by saying that her parents were "very open-minded."

Am I making these stories seem racial? Is it not possible for whites to tell stories of family members who are racist without these stories being connected to color-blind racism? Is it not true that sometimes a story is just a story? If these testimonies were just random stories that people tell without any ideological content, one would not be able to find a similar structure in them and would have difficulty assigning any rhetorical function. Furthermore, the fact they were told at similar points in the interviews suggests they are part of what John Dollard labeled almost seventy years ago as "defensive beliefs."[22] In contrast, when white racial progressives mentioned having racist family members or growing up in racist neighborhoods, they did not use the trinity formula typical of this testimony (see chapter 7). From an analytical perspective, then, these testimonies cannot be seen as expressions of "facts" or just plain stories.

Other Personal Stories

The final group of personal testimonies is a residual category of race-related stories. These stories were even more sui generis and even less prevalent among respondents. Furthermore, they seemed to be of the last-resort variety and were not helpful all the time to respondents' attempts to save face. The two that appeared most often were stories about someone close being involved with a minority person and stories about having had good black friends in the distant past.

Someone Close to Me Married or Dated a Minority

These stories are kindred to the rhetorical move of "Some of my best friends are . . . ," discussed in chapter 4. Their purpose is mostly positive self-presentation. Because I do not think generalizations can be extrapolated from these stories, I just present one example of each. The example of the first testimony came from Trudy, a salesperson in her late twenties. When asked if she had ever dated a black man, she said, "No, no. No nev—There was this one guy I kind of liked. He was Oriental." When asked her view on interracial marriage, Trudy replied,

> I don't really know how I feel about that. I don't think there's anything wrong with it. I don't know if I had a child and they wanted to marry a black person, I don't know how I would feel. I think it might be kind of odd for the children. And in fact, my husband has this real good friend at work, her name is Laverne. She's black and her husband's white and, you know, they'll have us for dinner. I mean, real *nice couple*! I mean, I don't see anything wrong, you know, if that's what they want to do, I don't have a problem. Me, personally, I don't know if I would feel comfortable, you know.

The purpose of the story about her husband's "real good friend" seems obvious. By including this story, Trudy is able to express her personal concerns about interracial marriage as if they are nonracial because, after all, her husband has a black friend who is married to a white guy and they seem like a "real *nice couple*" and invite them for dinner. However, the oddity of the story and the fact she referred to her Asian date as "Oriental" does not make this an ideologically useful testimony.

I Used to Have Very Good Black Friends

White respondents who did not have any associations with blacks could not use the "Some of my best friends are blacks" move to signify color blindness. Thus, some of the respondents in this predicament claimed they *had* very good black friends in the past. As with the testimony above, I provide just one example. Lucy, a part-time cook for a vending company in her late sixties, had very few interactions with blacks throughout her life. However, when asked to describe the racial composition of her workplace, she said, "We used to have three colored girls, but since then, they have quit." Later on, in response to a question on her interaction with her coworkers, Lucy said the "commissary kitchen (people) were good friends," that she would "go out to dinner with people that used to work there and (the) ones that still do," and that they even "have a barbecue once a year and a picnic in the summer." Nevertheless, when asked if blacks participated in these activities, she said, "Uh, no, no." Because this answer did not fit very well the color-blind outlook that Lucy wanted to portray, she tried to amend it in her answer to the next question, dealing with the subject of so-called black self-segregation:

> Well, like I told you, we had some of 'em and Kathleen, she'd go out to dinner with us. You know and so, the individuals I think—her other girlfriend, she, she moved out of town and she came in, she came in to see us. And you know, we're real happy for her and in fact another one was just in not too long ago. She has—we told her, you know, well, she has made some mistakes, a couple of children and didn't get married. And we says, you know, "Deanna, go back to school." Well, she came back to tell us she listened to us and she's doing real well and a good job, you know. I suppose, you know, they're still friends of ours, you know. We don't see 'em that much anymore, but they did come back and say that they were happy they listened to us.

By resuscitating black acquaintances from the past and making them her friends (see chapter 6), Lucy attempted to rebuild her investment in color blindness. However, this rhetorical attempt was not very successful because Lucy is still trapped in the language of the past ("colored" and "some of 'em") and narrated a story pregnant with Jim Crow paternalism.

CONCLUSION

At the outset of this chapter I stated that we make stories and that these stories, in turn, make us. I described two types of racial stories, story lines and testimonies. These racial stories "make" whites, but also help them navigate the turbulent waters of contemporary public discussions on race. The four story lines I analyzed, "The past is the past," "I did not own slaves," "If (other ethnic groups such as Italians or Jews) have made it, how come blacks have not?" and "I did not get a (job or promotion) because of a black man," help whites discursively since they provide "evidence" to solidify their viewpoints. For example, if whites object to the idea of affirmative action or reparations, they can insert "The past is the past" or "I did not own any slaves" story lines to strengthen the apparent reasonableness of their argument. If the issue at hand is explaining blacks' status in America, the story line of "If (other ethnic groups such as Italians or Jews) have made it, how come blacks have not?" is very appropriate. Finally, because the story line of "I did not get a (job or promotion) because of a black man" seems personal (in truth, the facts included in this story line tend to be secondhand or based on racialized impressions of social outcomes), it has become a powerful rhetorical weapon to win arguments ("I know for a *fact* that . . .").

In addition to the rhetorical role filled by story lines, they also serve whites as vehicles to vent deep-seated emotions[23] about racial matters. In case after case, whether students or whites from the Detroit area, respondents vented anger about what they interpreted as blacks' whining ("I didn't own any slaves and I do not understand why they keep asking for things when slavery ended two hundred *God-damned* years ago!") or about not getting into certain jobs or universities because of minorities ("A friend of mine was not admitted into SU Law School, but many *unqualified* black students were and that's *wrong*"). The story lines then serve whites as legitimate conduits for expressing anger, animosity, and resentment toward racial minorities.

Although testimonies are more loose and unstructured than story lines, they are as important in whites' rhetorical arsenal. Almost every respondent used them at some point or another in the interviews. Even though these stories were more random, compared to story lines, I organized them into three categories, namely, stories of interactions with blacks (negative and positive), stories of disclosure of someone close who is racist, and other stories. The testimonies of disclosure of someone close who is racist serve clear self-presentational purposes ("I am not a racist like my dad, uncle, or friend"). Stories of positive interactions with blacks were also used for self-presentational purposes. For example, if a respondent had a "good experience" in the past with a black person, that experience could be used to cover up for a present that blacks are not part of, that is, for a totally white life—an apparent blemish in the color-blind fable. Testimonies of "bad experiences" with blacks were mostly used to give credence to respondents' negative views about blacks. For example, if respondents believe blacks are aggressive, narrating a story of a black person behaving in an aggressive manner helps them make the point.

Although the last category of personal stories is a residual one, I highlighted two that appeared more often in the interviews and seemed more structured, namely, "Someone close to me married or dated a minority" and "I used to have very good black friends." Respondents who used these stories usually had a positive self-presentational concern, even though these stories were largely ineffectual and extremely odd ("I am not a racist because my sister dated a black guy some time ago"). However, these stories were probably the *only* vehicles for signaling nonracialism for respondents who lived totally submerged in whiteness. Likewise, respondents who used the personal stories of "I used to have very good black friends" navigated completely white environments and hence depended on these recollections to validate their claim to color blindness.

A final point on story lines and testimonies: because these story lines are *social* products, the media play an important role in reinforcing them.[24] News reports on affirmative action seldom address the whiteness of academia or the workplace and its implications;[25] sensational reports on welfare cheats never address the reality of welfare, that people on welfare live below the poverty line;[26] stories of "bad" behavior by black and Latino youths are presented as "normal," whereas stories depicting "bad" behavior by white youths are not.[27] News reports on minorities thus tend to be presented as morality tales that support the various racial stories of the color-blind era. These reports are then recycled by the white audience as absolute truths ("Didn't you hear about that black guy who couldn't read and was admitted into Harvard? It was in the news."). Therefore, the media uses the racial stories we create and makes them as if they were independent creations that validate our racial angst.[28]

One of the things I have shown indirectly in this and previous chapters is that whites tend to interact mostly with whites. This fact, and its implications, has not been adequately examined by social scientists. Few have asked questions such as, What are the sociological and social-psychological consequences of whites living in primarily white environments? How can whites develop empathy and gain an understanding of blacks if so few of them develop meaningful interactions with them? I turn my attention to these and related matters in the next chapter.

NOTES

1. For an interesting discussion of stories and a superb story on how affirmative action is being undercut from within in academia, see Adalberto Aguirre Jr., "Academic Storytelling: A Critical Race Theory Story of Affirmative Action," *Sociological Perspectives* 43, no. 2 (2000): 319–39.

2. On this issue, see Margaret Somers, "The Narrative Constitution of Identity: A Relational and Network Approach," *Theory and Society* 23, no. 3 (1994): 605–49.

3. Aguirre, "Academic Storytelling," 320.

4. Stuart Hall, "The Narrative Construction of Reality," *Southern Review* 17, no. 2 (1984): 8.

5. Hall, "Narrative Construction," 8.

6. See most notably Ruth Frankenberg, *White Women, Race Matters* (Minneapolis: University of Minnesota Press, 1993). For an attempt at examining the ideological role of modern racial storytelling in America, see James Fraser and Edward Kick, "The Interpretive Repertoires of Whites on Race-Targeted Policies: Claims Making of Reverse Discrimination," *Sociological Perspectives* 43, no. 1 (2000): 13–28. See also Nina Eliasoph, "'Everyday Racism' in a Culture of Political Avoidance: Civil Society, Speech, and Taboo," *Social Problems* 46, no. 4 (1997): 479–502.

7. In this chapter, I focus on the *dominant* racial stories. The questions included in these projects did not elicit oppositional racial stories from blacks.

8. See Norman K. Denzin, *The Research Act* (Englewood Cliffs, N.J.: Prentice Hall, 1989).

9. Patricia Hill-Collins, *Black Feminist Thought* (New York: Routledge, 1990); Catherine Clinton, *The Plantation Mistress* (New York: Pantheon, 1982).

10. As in the previous chapter, I set off the pertinent phrase with a different font not to signify emphasis from the respondents, but to help readers identify the racial story.

11. Melvin L. Oliver and Thomas Shapiro, *Black Wealth/White Wealth* (New York: Routledge, 1995); Thomas M. Shapiro, *The Hidden Cost of Being African American: How Wealth Perpetuates Inequality* (London: Oxford University Press, 2004). For an estimate of how much America owes blacks, see Richard F. America, *Paying the Social Debt: What White America Owes Black America* (Westport, Conn.: Praeger, 1993). See also William A. Darity Jr., "Stratification Economics: The Role of Intergroup Inequality," *Journal of Economics and Finance* 29, no. 2 (2005): 144–53.

12. Most of the white population in the South participated in slavery as a social institution in, for example by participating in the patrol system, which sought to catch runaway slaves. See George P. Rawick, *From Sundown to Sunup: The Making of the Black Community* (Westport, Conn.: Greenwood, 1972).

13. Jim Goad, in his *The Redneck Manifesto* (New York: Touchstone, 1998), states that at the peak of slavery (1860), only one out of every fifteen whites was a slaveholder. However, Goad, whose manifesto includes a number of interesting ideas, fails to analyze how slavery formed a social system in which all whites participated (in patrols, in the war effort, in catching fugitives).

14. See David Roediger, *The Wages of Whiteness* (London: Verso, 1994); Noel Ignatiev, *How the Irish Became White* (New York: Routledge, 1995); and Karen Brodkin, *How Jews Became White Folks and What That Says about Race in America* (New Brunswick, N.J.: Rutgers University Press, 1998).

15. Eduardo Bonilla-Silva, Tyrone A. Forman, Amanda E. Lewis, and David G. Embrick, "'It Wasn't Me': How Will Race and Racism Work in 21st Century America," *Research in Political Sociology* 12 (2003).

16. On this point, see Joe R. Feagin, *Racist America: Roots, Realities, and Future Reparations* (New York: Routledge, 2000).

17. Stephen Steinberg, *The Ethnic Myth* (Boston: Beacon, 1989).

18. See Tom Wicker, *Tragic Failure* (New York: Morrow, 1996).

19. For a similar finding based on data from the Los Angeles Study of Urban Inequality (part of the Multi City Study of Urban Inequality), see chapter 14 in Lawrence Bobo and Susan Suh, "Surveying Racial Discrimination: Analyses from a Multiethnic Labor Market," in *Prismatic Metropolis: Inequality in Los Angeles,* edited by Laurence Bobo et al., 523–60 (New York: Russell Sage Foundation, 2000).

20. As Beverly Daniel Tatum points out, "When these stories are told, I wonder how the speaker knows so much about the person of color's resume." Tatum, *"Why Are All the Black Kids Sitting Together in the Cafeteria?": And Other Conversations about Race* (New York: Basic, 1997), 115.

21. S. A. Stouffer, *The American Soldier,* vols. 1 and 2 (Princeton, N.J.: Princeton University Press, 1949). See also Gordon W. Allport, *The Nature of Prejudice* (New York: Doubleday, 1954).

22. John Dollard, *Caste and Class in a Southern Town* (New York: Doubleday/ Anchor, 1957).

23. In his recent *Racist America,* Feagin has forcefully argued that emotions are a central part of "systemic racism."

24. The classic study on racism and the media is Paul Hartmann, *Racism and the Mass Media: A Study of the Role of the Mass Media in the Formation of White Beliefs and Attitudes in Britain* (Totowa, N.J.: Rowman & Littlefield, 1974). See also the important contributions of Teun van Dijk, in *News as Discourse* (Hillsdale, N.J.: Erlbaum, 1988) and *Racism and the Press* (London: Routledge, 1991), and by Darnell Hunt, in *Screening the Los Angeles "Riots": Race, Seeing, and Resistance* (New York: Cambridge University Press, 1996) and *O. J. Simpson Facts and Fictions: News Rituals in the Construction of Reality* (Cambridge: Cambridge University Press, 1999).

25. On this point, see Joe R. Feagin, Hernán Vera, and Nikitah Imani, *The Agony of Education: Black Students at White Colleges and Universities* (New York: Routledge, 1996).

26. On the realities of how women survive on welfare, see Kathryn Edin, *Making Ends Meet: How Single Mothers Survive Welfare and Long-Wage Work* (New York: Russell Sage Foundation, 1997). For a discussion on the limited supply of good jobs and its implications, see Gordon Lafer, *The Job Training Charade* (Ithaca, N.Y.: Cornell University Press, 2002).

27. For example, whereas gang-related activity in urban areas is naturalized, gang-like activity in the suburbs (such as drug selling and drug use, the many recent mass murders in schools, prostitution) is presented as exceptional behavior that we need to think long and hard about to prevent. For an example of the latter, see "Born to Be Bad," *Dateline NBC,* April 27, 1999.

28. Here I am borrowing Marx's idea of "commodity fetishism" to explain how these media stories operate.

6

~

Peeking Inside the (White) House of Color Blindness

The Significance of Whites' Segregation

In every racial ghetto there are particular "racial problems" unique to the lives and conditions of the people in that ghetto. [In] our white society, although we are not accustomed to thinking of ourselves as ghettoized people, we have a "white life style" and "white racial problems" which have emerged as a result of our confinement in a prison built by racism. . . . The language we speak, the food we eat, the people we marry, the songs we sing, and the organizations we belong to are unique because of our separate residential and cultural life.

—Joseph Barndt, *Liberating Our White Ghetto*

Social scientists in various fields have amply shown the serious repercussions of social and spatial isolation for blacks. For example, in the 1960s, observers of black ghetto life argued vigorously that the segregation experienced by blacks had led them to live in a "culture of poverty."[1] In the late 1970s and 1980s, this idea resurfaced in the work of conservative commentators such as Charles Murray and Lawrence Mead, liberal commentators such as William Julius Wilson and Ken Auletta, and even radical commentators such as Cornel West.[2] All these authors have argued that blacks segregated in ghettos have developed a cultural outlook that does not foster a sense of personal responsibility (Murray and Mead), produces pathological behavior (Wilson and Auletta), or that creates a profound sense of despair and nihilism (West). Other commentators have argued that segregation and isolation have led blacks in ghettos to develop a unique style ("cool pose"), an anti-intellectual strategy embodied in an "oppositional identity" to deal with educational barriers and to protect their self-esteem (Ogbu), and even a "code of the street" to conduct public interactions (Anderson).[3] Scholars have made analogous arguments about Latinos in similar circumstances.[4] (For critiques of these arguments that tend to "blame the victims," see Amanda E. Lewis, *Race in the Schoolyard: Negotiating the Colorline in Classrooms and Communities* [New Jersey: Rutgers University Press, 2003], and Judith Blau, *"Race in the Schools": Perpetuating White Dominance* [Boulder, Colo.: Lynne Rienner Publishers, 2003].)

One of the most lucid examples of this type of analysis is Massey and Denton's *American Apartheid.* In this book the authors clearly show the incredibly high levels of residential segregation and isolation experienced by blacks and speculate, based on the work of others, that these realities foment in blacks what they label "the culture of segregation" or "a set of behaviors, attitudes, and values that are increasingly at variance with those held in the wider society."[5] According to these authors, some of the major characteristics of this culture are little concern with marriage, a drug-related lifestyle, and even a "language of segregation."

Despite the serious limitations of this subcultural approach to the lifestyle of poor blacks,[6] no one should doubt that, in general, the social and spatial isolation of one group from others leads to differentiation of those groups as well as the development of group cohesion and identity in the segregated group. If this idea applies to racial minorities, it must apply to whites, too, and because whites experience even *higher* levels of social and spatial isolation than blacks, the "racial problems" related to their "confinement in the prison built by racism" must be as consequential as those produced by black and Latino ghettoization. Therefore, in this chapter I explore how whites' high levels of social and spatial segregation and isolation from minorities creates what I label as a "white *habitus,"*[7] a racialized, uninterrupted socialization process that *conditions* and *creates* whites' racial taste, perceptions, feelings, and emotions and their views on racial matters.

One of the central consequences of the white habitus is that it promotes a sense of group belonging (a white culture of solidarity) and negative views about nonwhites.[8] The analysis focuses on blacks in particular because of the data I have (see chapter 1), but also because blacks are still the racial antithesis of whites in the racial spectrum. I first examine whites' levels of residential segregation and personal association with blacks. Second, I explore how they interpret their racial segregation and isolation from blacks. Third, I present data that suggest some of the potential consequences of whites' limited level of interaction with blacks.

WHITES' RACIAL SEGREGATION AND ISOLATION

In surveys, whites express openness to and, in many cases, even preference for an interracial lifestyle.[9] The answers of both college students and DAS respondents to questions about residential and school integration as well as others indicating support for the principle of integration bear this out (see table 6.1).[10] Similarly, on traditional "social distance"[11]questions, such as whether respondents object to a family member inviting a black friend for dinner or whether they approve of marriage between blacks and whites, a large number of whites agreed with the racially tolerant response. Thus, 92 percent of the students (and 87.2 percent of the DAS respondents) indicated they had "no objection" to the former; 80.4 percent of students (and 57.7 percent of DAS respondents) approved of the latter.

However, based on their answers to questions dealing with their own behavior, whites seemed less committed to an interracial life. For example, when students were asked about the five people with whom they interacted most on a daily basis, 67.7 percent stated that none of these five people were black. Similarly, to the social-distance question, "Have you invited a black person for lunch or dinner recently?" 68.5 percent said "no" (see nontraditional items in table 6.1 below). In line with these findings, 87 percent of white DAS respondents admitted that none of their three closest friends were black, 89 percent that they had never had a romantic relationship with a black person, and 94.5 percent[12] had a white spouse at the time of the interview. Of the 323 white respondents in the DAS survey, only one was married to a black person at the time of the interview! In this section I begin to deconstruct the apparent "paradox"[13] between whites' commitment to the principle of interracialism and their mostly white pattern of association based on their answers to a series of questions about their past and present lives.

"It Was a White Neighborhood": Facts of Whites' Segregation and Isolation

If the survey results suggest that few whites live an integrated life, the interview data confirm it. For example, only four of the forty-one white students interviewed for this project reported having resided in neighborhoods with a significant black or other minority presence (i.e., where minorities made up at least 20 percent of their neighbors). Similarly, only eight of the sixty-six whites interviewed for DAS grew up in racially mixed neighborhoods. These findings are consistent with research on residential segregation.[14]

As perplexing as these numbers are, the facts of "whiteness" (levels of racial isolation and segregation from blacks) get more disturbing yet. For

Table 6.1.

Social Distance Questions	Survey Sample (N = 451)	Interview Sample (N = 41)	DAS Sample 9N = 323)
Traditional Items			
B2. If a black family with about the same income and education as you moved next door, would you mind it a lot, a little, or not at all?			
1. Not at all[a]	92.4%	95.1%	90.9%
B12. Do you approve or disapprove of marriage between whites and blacks?			
1. Approve	80.4	90.2	57.5
2. Not Sure[b]	12.9	4.9	—
3. Disapprove	6.7	4.9	42.5
B7. How strongly would you object if a member of your family had a friendship with a black person?			
1. No objection[a]	92.4	92.7	87.2
Nontraditional Items			
A13. Think of the five people with whom you interact the most on an almost daily basis. Of these five, how many of them are black?			
1. None	67.7	68.3	NA
2. One	20.0	24.4	
3. Two or more	12.2	7.3	
A15. Have you invited a black person for lunch or dinner recently?			
1. No	68.5	75.0	NA
2. Yes	31.5	25.0	
A6. Think of your three closest friends, other than relatives. How often do you engage in social activities with them:			
1. More than once a week			21.7
2. Once a week			29.5
3. Once a month	NA	NA	28.9
4. Less than once a month			17.1
5. Never			2.8
A7. How many of these (three) friends are (white/black)?			
0. None			87.0
1. One			11.2
2. Two	NA	NA	11.2
3. Three			0.6
H10. Does your spouse consider (himself/herself), primarily white or Caucasian, black or African American, American Indian or Alaska Native, Asian or Pacific Islander, or something else?			
1. White			94.5
2. Black			0.5
3. Native	NA	NA	0.5
4. Asian			1.5
7. Other			3.0
Have you ever had a romantic relationship with a (black/white) person?			
1. Yes	NA	NA	10.3
2. No			89.7

Sources: 1997 Survey of Social Attitudes of College Students and 1998 Detroit Area Study.

[a] Percentages in other categories were insignificant and thus are not reported here.

[b] The option of "not sure" was not included in the survey.

instance, two of the four college students who grew up in racially mixed neighborhoods did not associate with minorities and another one related to minorities in a racialized way.[15] Of the eight DAS respondents who grew up in mixed neighborhoods, two had no meaningful interactions with blacks and four had very limited interactions.

Not surprisingly, given whites' racial isolation, few reported having close minority or black friends. Although "friendship" is a hard concept to operationalize given its historically and culturally contingent nature and unclear boundaries, most researchers agree that close friends exhibit a high degree of *interaction, interdependence,* and *closeness.*[16] In fact, when researchers ask people about good friends, they have found that the most common metaphor for describing closeness is kinship. Thus, good friends are like family members.[17]

Based on these criteria and on respondents' self-reports on interracial "friendship," thirty-four of the forty-one college students did not have black friends while growing up (schools and neighborhoods). After cross-validating[18] the answers of those who reported friendship with blacks, *only* three of the remaining seven students had black friends while growing up. Among DAS respondents, sixty of the sixty-six reported not having close black friends in their neighborhoods. And, as with college students, after carefully examining the answers of the six respondents who claimed to have had black friends, only three could be regarded as having had a close black friend.

Since my claim that many whites inflate their reports on friendship with blacks is controversial, I provide two examples to illustrate how this process works. The first case is Sally, a student at MU. She grew up in Novi, Michigan, a neighborhood she described as "a hundred percent white and upper middle class." Consequently, all her neighborhood friends were white. Yet, Sally attended mostly "integrated" schools while growing up. When asked, "Who did you hang out with in school?" she responded,

> It wasn't bad. Everyone hung with everyone. In particularly, I'd have to say my three best friends were white girls, but I definitely had an excellent girl-friend that was African American and I had several acquaintances that were Asian. That's about it, never really any.

Sally's "excellent African American friend" did not participate in any of the activities she enjoyed with her "three best friends" on the weekends, such as playing tennis, going shopping, or just hanging out. Neither did Sally point to anything that indicated closeness nor interdependence between her and her black friend.

The second case is Pauline, a retired woman in her seventies. She grew up in Hamtramic, Michigan, a neighborhood where "there were a few (black families), but not many." When asked who her close friends were while growing up, Pauline said, "The majority were white." The interviewer followed up this answer with the question, "Do you remember having any black friends growing up?" Pauline's reply was, "I always had black friends, even when I worked[19] I had black friends. In fact, I had a couple of my best friends." Pauline also claimed having had black friends in schools because "I had *lots* of friends" and "I was popular at school." In both cases, Pauline seems to be referring to being "friendly" toward blacks rather than developing a meaningful personal interaction with blacks. This follows from her claim that she was trained to "respect everybody."

These findings are consistent with research on interracial friendship, which usually finds that fewer than 10 percent of whites have black friends.[20] Furthermore, the promotion of black associates into friends is consistent with research by survey expert Tom W. Smith. He shows that when whites are asked directly whether or not they have black friends, a large proportion (about 20 percent) say they do. When the question is filtered by asking first whether or not the respondent has friends, the proportion of respondents then claiming to have black friends declines significantly. Finally, when the respondents are asked first whether or not they have friends, then what their names are, and, finally, whether or not any of these friends are black, the proportion of whites claiming to have black friends declines precipitously.[21]

Can the low proportion of whites who befriend blacks be attributed to *hypersegregation,* as some researchers suggest?[22] Alternatively, if whites had the demographic chance of interacting with blacks of similar status, would they do so? Based on the data from my two studies, neither students nor Detroiters who had the demographic chance of interacting with blacks did so. For example, of the twenty-one students who attended "integrated" schools, only two developed meaningful associations with blacks. A higher proportion of DAS respondents (fifty of sixty-six) attended predominantly white schools, but of the sixteen who attended integrated schools, five had black acquaintances, five had no black associates, and only six had black friends.

Why is it that integrated schools have not provided a meaningful platform for interracial contacts? First, the structure of "desegregated" schools is such that interracial interactions do not lead to significant cross-racial relationships.[23] For instance, even when whites are bused to predominantly minority schools, tracking guarantees they have a mostly white experience in their schools.[24] Case in point: almost all of our respondents described their classes (academic track) as "mostly white," even in cases where the schools were described as 40 percent or more minority. Our respondents also rarely remembered being in classes or clubs in which students of color were the majority. Second, school integration typically occurs late in the lives of whites (usually in high school). By that time, they have already developed emotional attachments to whites as their primary social group, learned a number of stereotypes about minorities, and bypassed the development of the skills necessary to navigate multicultural situations. Ray, a student at MU, explained aptly this last point:

> *Interviewer*: Uh, so what about middle school or high school? Did it change much (compared to his previously all-white educational experiences)?[25]
> *Ray*: Yeah, middle school, things began to change a little bit. Because there were more areas being included. And things did become a little bit more diversified, but mostly, it was pretty much the same, the same song and dance, you know what I mean? Because, I don't know if this was the way they had it set up, but it was almost like they didn't want the sort of lower areas to assimilate with the upper areas until high school. And so that meant that it wasn't a whole new ball game in high school; the people that were friends before were pretty much stayed friends through there. And that's not a hundred percent true, but it seemed to me that things were pretty segmented in high school.

Another possible place for meaningful cross-racial interaction is college; because of "the emphasis on individual achievement and universalism in higher education, the college educated may be less likely to identify themselves with their social and cultural roots."[26] Yet, based on both survey and interview results of the two studies, the precollege pattern of limited and superficial interaction with blacks is maintained in college. As I stated earlier, nearly 70 percent of college students reported they neither have a black person among "the five people with whom they interact the most on an almost daily basis" nor have "invited a black person for lunch or dinner recently."[27] This finding was confirmed in the interviews. Of the thirty-eight students who did not have black friends before college, only two developed friendships with blacks in college. Among the three subjects who had black friends before going to college, only one befriended a black in college (her boyfriend, who was also from her hometown). Altogether, only three of the forty-one college students had a black friend at the time of the interview. This finding is also consistent with previous research about the limited extent of white-black interaction in college settings.[28]

In the case of DAS respondents, since all of them were eighteen years or older, the question that led us to assess their current level of interaction or association with blacks was "Are you currently in college, employed, searching for a job, or something else?" By far most white DAS respondents (forty-four) were working at the time of the interview, followed by retirees (ten), homemakers (six), people working part time (three), and unemployed (three). Of the whites in these various situations, forty-one found themselves in virtually all-white environments, but twenty-five were not. Of these twenty-five whites, eight did not associate with blacks at all, ten had superficial relationships with blacks, and only seven had black friends.

Once again, I found that a high proportion of the respondents promoted black acquaintances to "good friends" or even "best friends." Among college students, nearly 50 percent (nineteen of forty-one) stated they had black "friends" or that they "hung out" with blacks. After their claims were analyzed, however, it was clear that only three truly had black friends by the criteria discussed above. And among DAS respondents, a little more than a third (twenty-four of sixty-six) made such claims, even though only ten interacted with blacks in a serious fashion.[29] The following two cases exemplify respondents who promoted black acquaintances to friends in the college or work setting. The first case is Emily, a student at MU, who in response to a question about her college friends said, "almost, well, mostly white." Yet, almost immediately she added, "I have a few black friends." Since I instructed my interviewers to follow up whites' claims of friendship with blacks (I also asked them to do the same when blacks claimed friendship with whites, see chapter 8) to assess the degree of closeness of these relationships, the interviewer inquired about Emily's friends:

> *Interviewer*: Okay, and so, other than Jessica [her best white friend], who else? Are there other people that you really spend a lot of time with? Or . . .
> *Emily*: No. Just here and there, but I am really busy . . .
> *Interviewer*: So who, if you can give me a rundown of some of these other people that you mentioned, like a bigger crowd of people that you might hang out with? Maybe your roommate[30] is one of them. Um, who are those people? So, it sounds like Jessica is the person that you spend the most time with.
> *Emily*: Well, my roommate is—I'm friends with some girls in my hall. And they are all black and they are really nice. And I hang out with them and my roommate, sometimes we do stuff together like go to the mall or—it's not like I'm really good friends with them, but we do stuff together.

At the end, Emily recognized that "it's not like I'm really good friends with them," but the claim of friendship with blacks helped her maintain a pluralistic, color-blind outlook.

Jannis, a manager of human resources for a manufacturing firm she described as "55 percent black," when asked if she had friends in her job said, she had with "a certain amount of them." The interviewer then asked the racial background of her job friends and Jannis responded, "It really makes no difference" and that "staff members who are both black and white, we have shared meals with." But Jannis did not associate with any of these black friends outside her job or demonstrate having ever confided in them. Furthermore, Jannis believes self-segregation is natural because "no matter what racial group you are, you do, um, sort of *gather with* those people that are alike." This may explain why she described interracial marriage as "salmons swimming upstream."

Three things are noteworthy about these self-reports of friendship with blacks. First, blacks tend to be "otherized" ("these people," "them," and so forth) denoting the respondents' social distance from blacks. For example, black "friends" are hardly ever identified by their first names. Second, superficial contacts (for college students, sports, music,[31] and the occasional friendly talk with a black student and, for Detroit residents, the occasional lunch or talk at work with blacks) are used as self-evident facts of friendship. Missing from these reports of friendship with blacks is evidence of trust, of the capacity of confiding, and of interactions with these friends beyond the place or situation of formal contact (classroom, assigned roommates, or job). Finally, these "friendships" with blacks always disappear after the reason for the formal interaction ends—taking a class, rooming, playing in a band or in a sports team, or working in the same company.

"IT'S JUST THE WAY THINGS WERE": WHITES' INTERPRETATION OF THEIR OWN RACIAL SEGREGATION

Thus far I have shown that whites have very little contact with blacks in neighborhoods, schools, colleges, and jobs. But how do whites interpret their segregation and isolation from blacks? How do they feel about this racial reality that seems to contradict their endorsement of color blindness? The most significant finding in this section is that whites do not interpret their hypersegregation from blacks as a problem, because they do not interpret this as a *racial* phenomenon. Instead, they normalize this crucial aspect of their lives by either not regarding it as an issue or interpreting is as "normal," as "just the way things are." For instance, most respondents who lived in segregated neighborhoods described them as "all white," "predominantly white," or "primarily white," but when asked how they felt about this fact, few stopped to think this was problematic at all. Among college students, only five thought that the racial composition of their neighborhood was a problem and, among DAS respondents, only eight made such comments. Among the eight DAS respondents who commented negatively on the whiteness of the racial composition of their neighborhoods, one was a Jewish woman who complained about anti-Semitism, another was a Dutch person who complained about feeling isolated as a foreigner, and two others were whites who lived in minority neighborhoods while growing up. Therefore, only four DAS respondents recognized their racial isolation from minorities as a problem.

The typical college students described their feelings about their neighborhoods' racial makeups with statements such as "I liked it, it was fine to me" (Kim, SU); "When I was growing up, I didn't think about it much. I mean, it was fine for me, it doesn't really bother me that much" (Brian, SU); "I really didn't think about it" (Mary, MU); "Yeah, really comfortable" (Kara, MU); "I didn't care, which is pretty standard, I think, for the kids. It's taken for granted" (Bill, WU). The interpretation of hypersegregation as a normal, matter-of-fact affair was expressed by students with statements such as "It's like the perfect American neighborhood" and "The sort of white upper-middle-class, *Leave It to Beaver*'s what I think of" (Ray, MU) and "It was a middle-class normal neighborhood" (Rick, WU). DAS respondents' answers to a similar question produced responses such as "I loved it! Everybody was one big happy family" (Jill); "Well, it's a very comfortable town because if anybody had a problem, then the rest of the town was there to help you" (Monica); "Oh, it was great. They were all basically the same kind of people" (Don); and "They were good people. *It was a good neighborhood*" (Pat).

This lack of reflexivity is not surprising since, as psychologist Beverly Tatum argues, dominant identities tend to remain inarticulate precisely because they are seen as the "norm" and, therefore, "whites can easily reach adulthood without thinking much about their racial group."[32] Thus, whereas whiteness is not perceived as a racial category, other categories are; whereas a white neighborhood is a "normal" neighborhood, a black neighborhood is "racially segregated." Nevertheless, besides white racial progressives (see chapter 7) who recognized racial segregation and isolation as a problem, a few other respondents realized in the interview that the racial composition of their neighborhoods or networks of friends *could* be regarded as problematic. For these respondents, however, the issue was explaining these matters as not involving prejudice on their part. For instance, Carol, an SU student, said about the racial mix of her neighborhood, "Never, never entered my mind, it was just my neighborhood," and she stressed that her community was thoroughly mixed. However, when asked who her friends were, she pointed out that they were almost all white (she had one "Hispanic" friend). At this point Carol seemed to realize the contradiction between claiming that she lived in a mixed neighborhood and having virtually all-white friends. Hence, Carol remarked in a rather indignant tone, "I mean, I don't think it, like me being friends with them had anything to do with them being I guess white, it's just they lived like next door and across the street from me." Carol added that her friends' race was just the result of "location."

Sonny, an MU student, explained the limited interaction among blacks and whites in her school as a product of demography:

I don't think we had any black friends. I don't know why. It kind of stuck together and, I don't know, it wasn't that we, it wasn't that we wouldn't be, like allowing to black people, it's just that there was never, like, an opportunity. There's no population like around where I lived.

Ray, the MU student cited above, addressed the same issue in a rather defensive way:

I don't think there was any type of prejudice involved, I just think that we really didn't know these kids. You know what I mean? They lived in different neighborhoods, they went to different schools. And there was never any effort made to exclude, and if anything, there was effort made to cultivate these kids. Any type of discrimination in terms of anything was really just taboo at East Lansing. It wasn't like people were trying to exclude them, it's just that they didn't know them. It's just the way things were.

Naturalizing whites' racial isolation ("It's just the way things were"; see chapter 2) was a strategy adopted by most college students to rationalize their limited contact with blacks. For example, Daniel, a WU student and a recent immigrant to this country, stated about segregation, "I guess in American society it seems sort of, it sort of comes natural, it appears to be the way of things." Andy, another WU student, said about segregation, "I would agree that we don't, or Caucasian people, or the majority does not make things necessarily comfortable for them, but not like intentionally, so I think it just sort of comes up that way [*laughs*]." Sue, a student at SU, commented about the whiteness of her neighborhood, "I lived there since I was two, I don't really have much of an opinion on it. I just sort of, that's how it was."

The few DAS respondents who realized their limited interaction with blacks could be interpreted as "racist" were also keen in pointing out that race had no bearing in their lives. As college students, many used the demographic excuse to explain why they did not interact with minorities. For example, Kim, a housewife in her late twenties, had a racial life typical of DAS respondents. Kim grew up in various cities in Michigan with few blacks around and had no interactions with them. At the time of the interview she lived in a neighborhood she described as "mostly white." When asked if she had black friends in school, Kim said, "I never had close black friends." Kim then inserted a personal story about her father being racist (for a discussion on these stories, see chapter 4). Later on, when discussing with whom she interacted as a homemaker, Kim said,

Yep, yep, my husband has some black friends in, you know. You just don't see 'em [*respondent is referring to blacks here*]. They move or whatever, we don't see 'em. It's just—I wished I did so I could just say, you know, "I do" [have black friends]. They are just not around, they don't live in our area.

Trudy, a salesperson at a large retail store in her late twenties, also had the typical white life. She grew up in Warren, Michigan, an area she described as "pretty much white." She attended both private and public schools that she also described as "mostly white." In neither her neighborhoods nor the schools she attended did Trudy develop friendships with blacks. However, 20 percent of her coworkers are black. Yet, when asked about friends in her job, she reported they are "mostly white." When asked if she had any black friends in her job, Trudy said, "Yeah, mostly like acquaintances, not like real good friends." Asked about this situation, Trudy said she "didn't do a whole lot" with her black acquaintances because "I mean, I don't get a lot of opportunity because there are not a whole lot of black people that I work with."

Lastly, Rita, an underemployed worker at a cookie company in her twenties, explained her lack of black friends while attending racially mixed schools in Detroit: "No, but it wasn't because I didn't want to. It's not, it's not because—I didn't have a problem with them. It just, I never socialized with them. Yeah more like they actually never socialized with me."

Like Rita, whites' lack of reflexivity about how race fractures their own lives is evident in their racial projections on a variety of issues (for a discussion on the role of projection, see chapter 3). For example, Kara, an MU student, commented on so-called black self-segregation: "They just kind of clique with those people and at first I was like, I guess you are always kind of taken aback by it when you see, like, a whole table of minorities, it's harder to go up to people and talk to them when there's a whole group of them." Mickey, another MU student, said on the same issue, "I've definitely seen that. I think the one thing that sticks out the most, the one example, is just like, like dining facilities. Like it's never, it's never integrated. It's always, they always they have their own place to eat." The interviewer asked Mickey if he thought this practice was exclusive to blacks and he answered, "That's mainly just African American people, yeah." Finally, Dan, another student from WU, noted that the fact that blacks have "their own dorms, activities, clubs, and such might be a contributing factor because it kind of encourages them to spend more time with each other and not worry [about] interact[ing] with other people." Kara does not see white cliquing, Mickey does not see white tables, and Dan does not see white anything!

Many DAS respondents also projected racial motivations onto blacks. For example, Ian, a manager of information security for an automotive company in his fifties, addressed this issue as follows:

> I think they're hard to approach at times. At least the ones I have dealt with and deal with on a day-to-day basis. If you question 'em, they take it person-

ally, very defensive. And I try not to, not to make race an issue because I do have to deal with, you know, Indians and Chinese and everything and, as long as, you know, they can do the job, I have no problem with it. But when you constantly go to somebody and say—just follow up with 'em, "Did you do this? Did you do that? Did you make sure of this?" and they take it personally, I have a problem with that. You know, 'cause it's not, you know, we're not bothering to check anybody's integrity. It's just, "Did you get the job done?" and, at times they don't like to be questioned.

When asked if he thought this was "more a problem of self-segregating or a problem of not feeling welcomed" by whites, Ian answered without any hesitation: "Self-segregating."

Matt, a city worker in his twenties, provided a similar one-sided explanation:

Yeah right. I don't know about hard to approach but from ah, where I've worked in the past and presently, it seems they're not open to any information or ideas from white folks. That they're, you know, set in their own way or maybe their way is a better way, which may or may not be true. But they're, they're not hard to approach. I have no problem approaching them, but when I do, it's like it goes in one ear and out of the other. They don't really, you know, take what you have to say as either encouragement or support or help. And, you know, just view a white guy talking for no reason.

Finally, various respondents made direct statements that signify they regard whiteness as "normal" and, therefore, nonracial. For example, Rick, a WU student, said that blacks are into the "me syndrome," which he thinks is "so stupid," and added that in his dealings with people from other ethnic groups the question of segregation "wasn't even approached, we were just friends and because I grew up in a white neighborhood, I really didn't see race." What allows Rick to say that because he "grew up in a white neighborhood" he "didn't see race" is that he interprets "race" as something that only racial minorities have.

Lee, another WU student, complained about the monotony of his neighborhood because it was "all white people, but we lived pretty close to Washington, D.C., and there was a lot of culture there, I mean." Therefore for Lee,[33] culture, which he defines narrowly as music, food, and arts, was the prerogative of D.C., an area that was more than two-thirds black at the time of the interview. For Lee, then, blacks and Latinos have "culture," but whites (who are not regarded as a race) do not.

Many DAS respondents also saw blacks and other minorities as the only actors who could be regarded as racial. Although this can be inferred from the way they answered many questions, a few used expressions that showed this directly. For example, Susie, a social worker in her late forties, said about the racial mix in her school, "I don't think there was *any* racial children in my, you know, public schools." Susie repeated the expression (racial children) when describing the racial makeup of her workplace:

> Oh, jeez, I just had an employee with that. Umhum [*raises voice*] I think it's probably 52/48 [percent], 52 being Caucasian, 48 being black, close to 50/50. But she indicated [*referring to a black "friend" at work*] there's a few blacks missing [*lowers voice*], one of my racial friends.

The data presented in this section indicates that whites do not see or interpret their own racial segregation and isolation as a racial issue at all. This blindness is central for understanding their views on a host of racial matters. Recognizing whites' lack of realization that race matters in their lives, combined with their limited interracial socialization, helps decipher the apparent contradiction between their stated preference for a color-blind approach to life (which corresponds to their perception of how they live their own lives) and the white reality of their lives. I examine this apparent contradiction by focusing on their views on the sensitive matter of interracial relations.

"IF TWO PEOPLE ARE IN LOVE . . .":
WHITES' VIEWS ON INTERRACIAL MARRIAGE

Despite whites' stake in color blindness, in surveys they are more likely to oppose interracial marriage than any other form of interracial association.[34] For example, only 57.5 percent of white DAS respondents approved of interracial marriage in the survey. Although the approval rate was higher among college students—80 percent for white-black unions and 86 percent for white-Mexican unions—it was still lower among students than was support for other social-distance questions (see table 6.1). This latter finding about college students fits research that suggests educated people are more likely to express approval for the principles of integration.[35]

Nevertheless, most DAS respondents and even the few college students who admitted they had problems with interracial marriage in the interviews brandished a laissez-fare or color-blind view on love. Love was described as a matter of personal choice between two people and, thus, as no one else's business because "love conquers all obstacles" (see my discussion of abstract liberalism in chapter 2).[36] Yet, this endorsement of color blindness in romantic relationships cannot be interpreted in a straightforward manner. Most respondents *qualified* their support in such a way or live such segregated lifestyles that their laissez-faire positions on this subject seem empty. Furthermore, too many whites express an aversion for blackness ("negrophobia") that casts doubt on their professed color blindness.

In table 6.2, I map respondents' answers to the interracial marriage question. The classifications are not mutually exclusive (e.g., some respondents I classified as 2s could have been classified as 4s) and cannot be read as an ordinal scale, that is, as moving from racial progressives to racial reactionaries (e.g., some respondents I classified as 3s or 4s were in fact more racially progressive than some who were 2s). The purpose of this taxonomy is just to organize answers to this question rather than provide the ultimate analysis of which respondents are truly "for" or "against" these unions.

In the case of college students, the typical response was category 4, respondents who qualified their support with expressions of concern for the children, family reactions, or location, or with rhetorical maneuvers indicative of little personal commitment to these unions (*"They* can have all the fun *they* want, it doesn't bother *me* at all"). Eight students supported interracial marriage but had all-white associations[37] and two admitted directly that they would not do it themselves. Among DAS respondents, the typical response was also category 4 (32 percent), followed closely by respondents who opposed interracial marriage (22 percent). A similar proportion of DAS respondents and college students stated their support for interracial marriage in the interviews (32.5 percent to 33 percent).

Since the responses to this sensitive question are complex, I present various examples from each category. First I provide examples of respondents' answers in category 1—those who approved of interracial marriage and had an interracial lifestyle.[38] Kay, a student at MU, answered the interracial question in the following manner: "I don't see anything wrong with it [*laughs*]." Kay laughed because before this question was posed to

Table 6.2.   Respondents' Answers to the Interracial Marriage Question

	Respondents	
DAS Students Respondents' Views on Interracial Marriage	*(%)*	*(%)*
1. Support marriage/Interracial life	5 (12.5)	7 (11.0)
2. Support marriage/Primary white networks	8 (20.0)	14 (22.0)
3. Reservations toward intermarriage/Interracial life	4 (10.0)	2 (3.0)
4. Reservations toward intermarriage/Primary white networks	21 (52.5)	21 (32.0)
5. Opposes intermarriage/Interracial life	0 (0.0)	7 (11.0)
6. Opposes intermarriage/Primary white networks	2 (5.0)	14 (22.0)
Total number of respondents	40 [a]	65 [a]

[a] The question was not asked to one of the students and one of the DAS respondents.

her she had said that her boyfriend was black (she was the only white dating or married to a black among the 107 whites interviewed in these two projects). Franci, a homemaker in her twenties, answered the question similarly: "As long as they're happy, go for it!" Although many other whites used expressions such as this one, they immediately added long-winded statements qualifying their support. In contrast, respondents in this category answered without hesitation and had an interracial lifestyle that included in some cases having dated across the color line. Franci, for example, had dated *four* minority men, one of whom was black.

But even in this category, which was the most internally consistent, there was some variance. For instance, Scott, a mechanical drafter in his twenties, answered the interracial question as follows: "If you are comfortable with it, do it. You know, I mean, I'm looking for a Vietnamese—half-Vietnamese, half-Chinese right now. That's my dream woman right there. I love Asian women." Scott, who had dated Asian (half-Vietnamese), Latino, and Arab women in the past, seems like a clear example of respondents in category 1. Yet, Scott's fascination for Asian women was highly racialized (he stated he liked them because their food "is awesome," they are "just so attractive to me," and he "just love[s] the Asian race, it's mystical to me in a way") and in tune with the way that many white men think of Asian women today.[39] Even more problematic was Scott's response in a follow-up to the interracial marriage question. After Scott stated he would have "no problem" marrying someone of a different race, the interviewer asked him, "So what do you think about people who are absolutely against it, you know, who want to keep the races pure or whatever?" His answer was,

> I mean, I kind of, I feel that way also because I kind of, I don't know, I kinda wanna stay with my nationality in a way, you know. I think once, once you start breaking away, you start losing your own like deep home family values and in a way, you get mixed emotions, you know. But then again, it's just like the old times are gone, you know it's all modern-day now. So really you[r] nationality really don't, shouldn't count. But then again some people don't want to have so much blood within their family, within their name, you know. I know people that will not marry unless they're a hundred percent Italian. I got a couple of people who will not date anyone unless they're hundred percent Italian, so. . . .

Based on this response and the fact that Scott was classified as having an interracial lifestyle because he had *one* black friend while growing up, he could have been classified as someone who opposes interracial marriage.

Respondents in category 2—those who approved of interracial marriage but associated primarily with whites—had more diverse responses.

Some were respondents on the "racial progressive" side (see chapter 7) such as Sam, a warehouse laborer in his twenties. His response to the intermarriage question was, "I have no problems with it. I just did it." Sam was married to a Mexican American woman and stated he had been "attracted [to black women] but I've really never dated anyone like that." Others were supportive of interracial marriage, but had a racial preference for white mates. For example, Ray, an MU student cited above, answered the interracial marriage question as follows:

> I think that there's, I think that interracial marriage is totally legitimate. I think if two people love each other and they want to spend the rest of their lives together, I think they should definitely get married. And race should in no way be an inhibitive factor.

Although Ray seems supportive of interracial marriage (despite using some indirectness), his life before college and in college was centered exclusively around whites. He grew up in a midsize city in the Midwest in an upper-middle-class neighborhood that he characterized as "all white" and described his friends as "what the average suburban kid is like nowadays." More significantly, Ray, who was extremely articulate in the interview, stuttered remarkably over the question (asked before the one on intermarriage) dealing with whether or not he had ever been attracted to blacks (see chapter 3 for Ray's answer). Ray's hesitation was due to the fact he is not attracted to black women, something that clashes with his self-proclaimed color-blind approach to love and his apparent support for interracial marriages.

The third and fourth categories include respondents who had reservations about interracial marriage. I discuss them together because there are no meaningful variations in these two categories and I provide many examples, as a large number of respondents (nearly 50 percent) were in one of these two kindred categories. Most of the respondents in categories 3 and 4 stated they had no problem with interracial marriage but proceeded to cite reasons why these marriages are more difficult. A typical example is Olga, a software salesperson for an insurance company in her forties:

> Well, I guess my only concern is always if there's children and how those children will be accepted or not accepted. And it would be nice to think that the world would be lovely and wonderful but, you know, I think people should be allowed to do whatever they want to do. I don't think you should look at people's skin color or their origin or anything to determine what it is you want to do. However, what are you putting those kids through when they're a mixed that *neither* culture would accept because the cultures are sometimes just as bad about sticking together as they are about claiming that no one will let them in and out of each other's areas. So sometimes that really

affects the kids and neither culture will accept the child as being their culture or the other. So that concerns me, but in general, I don't have any problem with any of that.

Joann, a clerk in a department store in her early sixties, stated, "Except for someone that might be extremely young, I think that [if] they want to marry outside their race and put up with what they [will face], that's their problem." But Joann acknowledged that interracial marriage could not have happened in her own family because,

> I, that I never [*very loud*] even though—because my husband was "whites marry whites, blacks marry blacks," he was very prejudice about it. He grew up with that made up [in] his mind and that was it. Any white could marry any whites but blacks marry blacks and that is the way it was.

Ian, the manager of information security cited above, said in typical fashion about interracial marriage, "I don't have a problem with it at all," but added,

> There's gonna be problems. White and Chinese, white and even Italian, there's gonna be problems, white and black. I have no problems with it, but they better face the facts of life, they're gonna have a lot of problems. And they're not gonna be accepted, I don't, at least, I don't think very well by either side.

College students in these categories answered in similar fashion. For instance, Sally, an MU student, stated her view on interracial marriage as follows:

> I certainly don't oppose the marriage, not at all, depending on where I am, if I had to have a concern, yes, it would be for the children. You know, it can be nasty and then other kids wouldn't even notice. I think I could care less what anyone else does with their lives, as long as they are really happy. And if the parents can set a really strong foundation at home, it can be conquered, but I'm sure, in some places, it could cause a problem.

Sally's apprehension matched the nature of her life and her specific views on blacks. Sally's network of relationships was, in terms of interactions, relationships, and residence, an almost entirely white one. When asked about her romantic life, Sally said that she had never dated a person of color and recognized that "I've never been attracted to a black person" and that "I never look at what they look like, it just hasn't occurred in my life."

Some respondents in these two categories could have been classified as people who opposed interracial marriage, even though they did not say so. For example, Mandi, a nurse working in a nursing home in her thirties, answered the question on intermarriage by saying, "I wouldn't do it." When asked for her general position, she said, "I don't think I could tell people what to do. I think it's hard on people when they marry outside their race. The children." Thus Mandi relies on abstract liberalism for her general position on interracial marriage, but is clear that interracial marriage is not for her.

Another example is Dina, an employment manager for an advertising agency in her twenties. Her answer to the interracial marriage question was,

> I don't have an issue with it at all. You know, I personally, I don't [date people] of another race so it's very difficult for me to say, but I don't think [*sighs*] I can't see myself ever doing that, marrying someone of another race. But we have friends in interrational—interracial relationships and. . . .

Interestingly, Dina had dated a black man for a week in high school. Yet, she pointed out that "he was kinda like a white person, you know, he acted white, he talked white" and that she did it to "kinda just to tick off my grandpa." In general, Dina said, "The guys I dated were white jocks kinda guys."

Finally, I present respondents answers in categories 5 and 6, those who opposed interracial marriage. The first example is Janet, a married student at SU. Janet, like a number of respondents, accused people in interracial relationships of being selfish:

> I would feel that in most situations they're not really thinking of, of the child. I mean, they might not really think anything of it, *but* in reality I think most of the time the child is growing up, he's going to be picked on because he has parents from different races, and it's gonna, and it's gonna ultimately affect the child and, and the end result is they're only thinking of them—of their own happiness, not the happiness of the kid.

The interviewer followed up by asking, "How do you think your family would deal with it if you or someone else in your family became involved with someone of another race?" Janet's answer was, "They would *not* like it *at all* [*laughs*]!"

Most older respondents expressed their disapproval of interracial marriage without hesitation and relied on Jim Crow tenets to justify their position. For example, Jim, a retired man in his seventies, stated,

> Well, I'm against it. I think scripture says that we should be very careful how we should choose our mates. I may love the girl I want to marry and she's black, but I just can't look at that situation. I have to look at what's going to

happen afterwards, what's going to happen to our kids. They're the ones
who take a beating. You're not white, you're not black.

However, some older respondents expressed their opposition in a more
refined manner. For instance, Rhonda, a part-time salesperson in a golf
store and of Jewish background, used the movie *Fiddler in the Roof* to state
her view on this matter: "A bird and a fish can fall in love but where
do they go to nest?" After saying this, Rhonda narrated a testimony
(see chapter 4) to suggest blacks and whites should not marry because
it causes many problems for the children. She then commented, "The
children are the ones that are—they're the ones that are not going to be,
they're the ones that don't [know] where they belong. They don't know if
they are white, they don't know if they're black."

As the previous examples illustrate, the argument of the children (or
concerns for family) are not much different than those of respondents in
categories 3 and 4. More significantly, a few respondents in these categories (those who opposed interracial marriage) used the jargon of color
blindness in their responses. For example, Henrietta, a transsexual school
teacher in his fifties, answered the question on intermarriage as follows:
"[*Five-second pause*] If two people . . . are [in love] . . . I see nothing wrong
with it. It's their business." Henrietta seems to have a laissez-faire view
on interracial marriage. However, after stating his view, Henrietta proceeded to discuss the problems he has seen among biracial children in his
school. In this discussion, Henrietta seemed to change his mind and said,
"I would say I would have to be against it." The interviewer then asked
him, "So then it sounds like you yourself would not consider marrying
someone of another race or . . . ?" Henrietta responded, "It depends. It
depends on how I feel about the person due to my upbringing, could I, if
you're asking me could I marry a black man? No. If you are asking me if I
could marry an Asiatic man or an American, Native American man? Yes."

There are three things clear from the answers of the respondents in
these studies to the question on interracial marriage. First, although most
use the language of color blindness ("I have no problem with it" or "If
two people are in love"), their answers reveal a deep level of reservation
if not outright opposition toward these unions. Second, a large number
of whites express a clear preference for whites as mates that seems to
violate their professed color blindness. Third, even though whites do not
have much contact with blacks or with people in interracial marriages,
they reject these unions because of presumed "problems" that transpire
in these marriages.

I suggest whites' answers to the interracial marriage question are prima
facie evidence of one of the consequences of the white habitus. Whites'
answers signify they have serious difficulties in thinking about these re-

lationships as normal. From a social-psychological perspective, this is not a mystery. How can whites fall in love with people whom they never see, whom they regard as "different," and with whom they hardly associate? Hence, what their answers to the interracial question betray is that whiteness as a lifestyle fosters whiteness as a choice for friends and partners. Their answers also reveal concerns for not sounding "racist," concerns that fit well what I have discussed about color-blind racism so far.

CONCLUSION

At the outset of this chapter I argued that whites live a white habitus that creates and conditions their views, cognitions, and even sense of beauty and, more importantly, fosters a sense of racial solidarity. This postulate fits the arguments and findings of the status construction and social identity theories. Whereas work in the social identity tradition has amply demonstrated how little it takes to create antagonistic groups, work in the status construction tradition has shown that once there are two or more status groups in a social system, those at the top tend to adjudicate the status differences to nominal characteristics such as race and gender.[40] Research in these traditions has also uncovered that when status differences between groups exist, as in the case between whites and blacks, the advantaged group develops its own "groupthink," values, and norms to account for and rationalize these differences.

In this chapter I documented three things related to the white habitus. First, I showed that whites experience tremendous levels of racial segregation and isolation while growing up. That isolation continues in college and in the workplace, even when blacks are present in these environments. Second, I documented how whites, for the most part, do not interpret their racial isolation and segregation from blacks as racial. Instead, they either do not see any need to explain this or explain it as a nonracial matter ("Race has nothing to do with it" or "That's the way things are"). Lastly, I examined their answers to the interracial marriage question and suggested that they are an example of what the white habitus produces, as they signify, despite the color-blind rhetoric, that whites are not very likely to engage in interracial unions with blacks.

The social psychology produced by the white habitus leads to the creation of positive self-views ("We are nice, normal people") and negative other views ("They are lazy").[41] The more distant the group in question is from the white "norm," other things being equal, the more negative whites will view the group. Because blacks are the group farthest from whites residentially and socially in this country[42]—although not necessarily culturally[43]—they are the most likely candidates for debasement.[44]

In previous chapters I documented how whites see blacks in a negative light. For example, they regard blacks as lazy, as welfare-dependent, and as receiving preferential treatment. They also believe blacks complain too much about racism and discrimination. This negative view on blacks extends to the most personal realm: close interracial associations as friends and significant others. Although most whites rely on color blindness ("race doesn't matter"), a free-market logic on human relationships ("if two people are in love"), and liberal individualism ("I don't think that anyone should have the right to tell anyone else whether or not they should marry") to articulate their views on interracial marriage, few seem to support these relationships and, more significantly, to be in a position to ever engage in one or even to be neutral in case a close family member enters into one.

Whites' lack of true empathy for or interest in interracial marriage with blacks should not be a shock or a mystery to readers. People cannot like or love people they don't see or interact with. This truism has been corroborated by social psychologists, who for years have maintained that friendship and love emerge when people share activities, proximity, familiarity, and status.[45] Thus, whites' extreme racial isolation from blacks does not provide fertile soil upon which primary interracial associations can flourish, regardless of blacks' level of assimilation. Therefore, whites' theoretical support for interracial associations with blacks is not likely to lead to significant increases in their personal associations with blacks.

The social and political implications of the white habitus are very significant. The universe of whiteness navigated on an everyday basis by most whites fosters a high degree of homogeneity of racial views and even of the manners in which whites express these views. Despite the civil rights revolution, whites, young and old, live a fundamentally segregated life that has attitudinal, emotional, and political implications. Yet it is important to underscore the existence of racial progressives in these samples. Their existence suggests that although the white habitus conditions whites' lives, whites can, as Marx said, "make their own history."[46] I found a number of respondents who lived interracial lifestyles, understood the significance of contemporary discrimination, and did not rely on color blindness to articulate their racial views. I turn my attention to this group of racial progressives in the next chapter.

NOTES

1. The premier author in this tradition was Oscar Lewis, *La Vida: A Puerto Rican Family in the Culture of Poverty* (New York: Random House, 1966). For a radical version of this theory at the time, see Michael Harrington, *The Other America: Poverty in the United States* (New York: Macmillan, 1962).

2. Charles A. Murray, *Losing Ground: American Social Policy, 1950–1980* (New York: Basic, 1984); Lawrence M. Mead, *Beyond Entitlement: The Social Obligations of Citizenship* (New York: Free Press, 1986); William Julius Wilson, *The Truly Disadvantaged: The Inner City, the Underclass, and Public Policy* (Chicago: University of Chicago Press, 1987); Ken Auletta, *The Underclass,* updated and revised (Woodstock, N.Y.: Overlook, 1999); and Cornel West, *Race Matters* (Boston: Beacon, 1993).

3. John Ogbu, *Minority Education and Caste: The American System in Cross-Cultural Perspective* (New York: Academic, 1978), and Elijah Anderson, *Streetwise* (Chicago: University of Chicago Press, 1990).

4. Hints of this stand can be seen in James Diego Vigil, *Barrio Gangs: Street Life and Identity in Southern California* (Austin: University of Texas Press, 1988), but more clearly in Philippe Bourgeois, *In Search of Respect: Selling Crack in El Barrio* (New York: Cambridge University Press, 1995).

5. Douglas Massey and Nancy Denton, *American Apartheid* (Chicago: University of Chicago Press, 1993), 165–66.

6. See the introduction to my *White Supremacy and Racism in the Post–Civil Rights Era* (Boulder, Colo.: Rienner, 2001).

7. Bourdieu defines habitus as "not only a structuring structure, which organizes practices and the perception of practices, but also a structured structure: the principles of division into logical classes which organizes the perception of the social world is itself the product of internalization of the division into social classes." The most important contribution of this concept, however, is that it shapes an actor's "perception, appreciation and action" through routinization, without express calculation, and with little need for external constraints. I extend his class-inspired notion of habitus to the field of race. Pierre Bourdieu, *Distinction* (Cambridge, Mass.: Harvard University Press, 1984), 170, and *Pascalian Meditations* (Stanford, Calif.: Stanford University Press, 1997), 138.

8. On this point, see Matthhijs Kalmijn, "Intermarriage and Homogamy: Causes, Patterns, Trends," *Annual Review of Sociology* 24 (1998): 395–421.

9. Howard Schuman et al., *Racial Attitudes in America: Trends and Interpretations* (Cambridge, Mass.: Harvard University Press, 1997).

10. Recent surveys, however, have found that whites and blacks are growing increasingly comfortable with the idea of segregation, so long as it is not enforced through violent means, that is, so long as it is by "choice." See Peter Grier and James N. Thurman, "Youth's Shifting Attitudes on Race," *Christian Science Monitor,* August, 18, 1999.

11. Gordon Allport, *The Nature of Prejudice* (New York: Doubleday, 1954).

12. This proportion is in line with the general population, as 93 percent of whites do not intermarry. See Rachel Moran, *Interracial Intimacy: The Regulation of Race and Romance* (London: University of Chicago Press, 2001).

13. Schuman et al., in their *Racial Attitudes in America,* label the gap between the number of whites who approve of the principle of integration and the policies to implement integration a "paradox." I suggest this is just an apparent paradox the mystery behind which becomes clear when it is viewed within an ideological framework. Whites adopt an *abstract* notion of liberalism that has little import to their life, relations, and attitudes about a variety of *real* and *concrete* racial matters.

14. Massey and Denton, *American Apartheid*; Reynolds Farley, *The New American Reality* (New York: Russell Sage Foundation, 1996); and Kalmijn, "Intermarriage and Homogamy."

15. Kara, the respondent in question, referred to her Asian friend as "Oriental" and had very stereotypical views on blacks. In the survey, however, she claimed that she interacted almost daily with a black person. This person was her black maid.

16. Michael Argyle and Monika Henderson, *The Anatomy of Relationships* (London: Routledge, 1985), and Beverly Fehr, *Friendship Process* (Newbury Park, Calif.: Sage, 1996).

17. On this point, see Lillian B. Rubin, *Just Friends: The Role of Friendship in Our Lives* (New York: HarperCollins, 1985).

18. We cross-examined whites about their self-reports of friendship with blacks because (1) previous research suggested that race is among the most salient similarity factors upon which friendships are based (Helen Gouldner and Mary Strong, *Speaking of Friendship: Middle-Class Women and Their Friends* [New York: Greenwood, 1987]); (2) survey research has found that few whites (7 to 10 percent) have black friends (Mary R. Jackman and Marie Crane, "'Some of My Best Friends Are Black . . .': Interracial Friendship and Whites' Racial Attitudes," *Public Opinion Quarterly* 50 [Winter 1986]: 459–86); and (3) self-reports by whites on friendship with blacks are highly unreliable (Benjamin DeMott, *The Trouble with Friendship: Why Americans Can't Think Straight about Race* [New York: Atlantic Monthly, 1995]). Thus, we followed up every respondent's self-report of friendship with blacks with questions such as "What kind of things do you do with your black friend?" and "How often?" We did the same with black respondents.

19. I did not find any reference to these black friends at work in any part of the interview.

20. Jackman and Crane, "Some of My Best Friends"; Maureen Hallinan and Richard A. Williams, "The Stability of Students' Interracial Friendships," *American Sociological Review* 52, no. 2 (October 1987): 653–64. See also Bonilla-Silva, Embrick, Ketchum, and Saenz, "Where Is the Love? Why Whites Have Limited Interaction with Blacks," *Journal of Intergroup Relations* 32, no. 1 (2004): 24–38; Bonilla-Silva and Embrick, "'Every Place Has a Ghetto . . .': The Significance of Whites' Social and Residential Segregation," *Journal of Symbolic Interaction* 30, no. 3 (Summer 2007): 323–45.

21. Tom W. Smith. "Measuring Inter-Racial Friendships: Experimental Comparisons," paper presented at the annual meeting of the American Sociological Association, August 6, 1999, in Chicago.

22. Massey and Denton, *American Apartheid*; Farley, *New American Reality.*

23. Clairette P. Armstrong and A. James Gregor, "Integrated Schools and Negro Character," in *White Racism and Black Americans*, edited by David G. Bromley et al., 101–49 (Cambridge, Mass.: Schenkman, 1972); P. Rosenbaum, "Five Perspectives on Desegregation in Schools: A Summary," in *When Schools Are Desegregated: Problems and Possibilities for Students, Educators, Parents, and the Community*, edited by M. L. Wax (Washington, D.C.: National Institute of Education, 1979). For a recent estimate of the high levels of racial isolation of all racial/ethnic groups in schools, see Kara Joyner and Grace Kao, "School Racial Composition and Racial Homophily," *Social Science Quarterly* 81 (2000): 810–25. For recent studies on how race is

reproduced in schools, see Amanda E. Lewis, *Race in the Schoolyard: Negotiating the Colorline in Classrooms and Communities* (New Brunswick, N.J.: Rutgers University Press, 2003); Judith Blau, *"Race in the Schools": Perpetuating White Dominance* (Boulder, Colo.: Lynne Rienner Publishers, 2003).

24. J. L. Epstein, "After the Bus Arrives: Resegregation in Desegregated Schools," *Journal of Social Issues* 41, no. 3 (1985): 23–43; Gary Orfield and Susan Eaton, *Dismantling Desegregation* (New York: New York Press, 1996).

25. First, the names of all the respondents are fictitious. Second, the responses were transcribed as close as possible to the spoken utterances, because lapses, self-corrections, and pauses were relevant data. Third, all the italics in the quotes were added to emphasize important material.

26. Kalmijn, "Intermarriage and Homogamy," 401; Sean-Shong Hwang, Rogelio Saenz, and Benigno E. Aguirre, "Structural and Individual Determinants of Outmarriage among Chinese-, Filipino-, and Japanese-Americans in California," *Sociological Inquiry* 64, no. 4 (1994): 396–414.

27. The Bogardus social distance scale has seven items, ranging from would "admit to close kinship by marriage" to would "exclude from my country." See Gordon Allport, *The Nature of Prejudice* (New York: Doubleday, 1954). For examples of traditional survey questions on social distance, see Schuman et al., *Racial Attitudes in America.*

28. Joe R. Feagin, Hernán Vera, and Nikitah Imani, *The Agony of Education: Black Students at White Colleges and Universities* (New York: Routledge, 1996).

29. I counted as friends those who interacted with blacks outside their jobs. This was a more flexible criterion for DAS respondents than it was for college students. For example, it included two respondents who just bowled or played basketball with blacks.

30. Emily had said that her roommate was "Korean . . . from Hawaii," that she was "really nice," and that they "got along really well." However, Sally never mentioned her roommate's name and said that she had "her own friends, I have mine."

31. Although sports and music are central to the repertoire of social activities of youth, the fact that most of these reports on friendship with blacks were around these two activities suggests (1) that the associations involve a small degree of emotional commitment and (2) that whites may still think that blacks only care about sports and music. For a historical explanation of the latter, see John Hoberman, *Darwin's Athletes* (Boston: Houghton Mifflin, 1997).

32. Beverly Daniel Tatum, *"Why Are All the Black Kids Sitting Together in the Cafeteria?": And Other Conversations about Race* (New York: Basic, 1997), 93. See also Ashley W. Doane, "White Identity and Race Relations in the 1990s," in *Perspectives on Current Social Problems*, edited by Gregg Lee Carter, 151–59 (Boston: Allyn and Bacon, 1997).

33. Lee had mentioned in the interview he is majoring in music and that he is totally into black music.

34. Schuman et al., *Racial Attitudes in America*; Eduardo Bonilla-Silva, DAS 1998.

35. Schuman et al., *Racial Attitudes in America.*

36. Yanick St. Jean, "Let People Speak for Themselves: Interracial Unions and the General Social Survey," *Journal of Black Studies* 28, no. 3 (1998): 398–414.

37. I am not suggesting that people who have an entirely white network of associations are "racist." Conceptually, I argue that racism ought to be studied

in a *structural* manner. In my work, I use the term "racism" exclusively to designate the racial ideology of a *racialized social system* and, thus, labeling someone as "racist" represents a regression to an individualist and subjectivist reading of racial matters. The issue here is assessing the real degree of support for interracial relationships among whites. Thus, it is necessary to have a larger picture in view to clearly demarcate the *meaning* and *implications* of respondents' self-reported approval of interracial relationships. By including elements from the respondents' lives (such as lack of meaningful interracial interaction or fear of blacks), I am able to interpret their positions on interracial marriages in terms of a larger context.

38. We were flexible in the classification of respondents as having an interracial lifestyle. Hence respondents who had one black friend at *any* point in time were regarded as having an interracial lifestyle.

39. Asian women are viewed by many white men as highly "desirable" because they are supposed to be subservient and sensual, as "China Dolls," the label given to this stereotype by the Media Action Network for Asian Americans. See Media Action Network for Asian Americans, *A Memo from MANAA to Hollywood: Asian Stereotypes* (www.manaa.org/asian_stereotypes.html).

40. This literature has also uncovered that when status differences between groups exist, as in the case between whites and blacks, the advantaged group develops its own "groupthink," values, and norms to account for and rationalize these differences. See Cecilia Ridgeway and James Balkwell, "Group Processes and the Diffusion of Status Beliefs," *Social Psychology Quarterly* 60, no. 1 (1997): 14–31; Cecilia Ridgeway, Elizabeth Heger Boyle, Kathy J. Kuipers, and Dawn T. Robinson, "How Do Status Beliefs Develop? The Role of Resources and Interactional Experience," *American Sociological Review* 63 (June 1998): 331–50.

41. Interestingly, a recent review of the past thirty years of work in the area of social psychology labels the area "color blind" and concludes that "social psychologists . . . have given race and ethnicity less attention than it warrants." Hence, we still lack serious social-psychological analyses of the various ways in which race affects multiple social processes. Matthew O. Hunt, Pamela Braboy Jackson, Brian Powell, and Lala Carr Steelman, "Color Blind: The Treatment of Race and Ethnicity in Social Psychology," *Social Psychology Quarterly* 63, no. 4 (2000): 360–61. See also Carla Goar's article, "Even the Rats Are White: White Supremacy in Experimental Methodology," in *White Logic, White Methods: Racism and Methodology*, edited by Eduardo Bonilla-Silva and Tukufu Zuberi (Lanham, Md.: Rowman & Littlefield, 2008).

42. For data on segregation by groups, see Douglas S. Massey and Nancy A. Denton, "Trends in the Residential Segregation of Blacks, Hispanics, and Asians: 1970–1980," *American Sociological Review* 52, no. 6 (December 1987): 802–25. For data on interracial perceptions of social ranking of the races, see Lawrence D. Bobo and Devon Johnson, "Racial Attitudes in a Prismatic Metropolis: Mapping Identity, Competition, and Views on Affirmative Action," in *Prismatic Metropolis: Inequality in Los Angeles*, edited by Lawrence D. Bobo et al., 81–163 (New York: Russell Sage Foundation, 2000).

43. Greeks, Arabs, and Armenians, for instance, are, culturally speaking, farther from "whites" than blacks, yet they have been incorporated into whiteness.

44. As Joe R. Feagin points out in his *Racist America: Roots, Realities, and Future Reparations* (New York: Routledge, 2000, 132), because of the racial demography and ecology of everyday life, the majority of blacks spend much more time interacting with whites than the majority of whites spend interacting with blacks. Most blacks work, shop, or travel with large numbers of white Americans, whereas relatively few whites do the same with large numbers of black men and women. White views of blacks are not likely to be grounded in numerous equal-status contacts with blacks. The sense of white superiority is reinforced by the continuing process in which whites live separated from black Americans or other Americans of color. White isolation and lack of contact feeds negative stereotyping, and there is little chance to unlearn inherited antiblack attitudes. For a recent update, see Joe R. Feagin's latest book, *Systemic Racism: A Theory of Oppression* (New York: Routledge, 2006).

45. John Sabini, *Social Psychology* (New York: Norton, 1992).

46. The phrase is "Men make their own history, but they do not make it just as they please"; it appears in *The Eighteenth Brumaire of Louis Bonaparte*. David McLellan, *Karl Marx: Selected Writings* (New York: Oxford University Press, 1982).

7

❧

Are All Whites Refined Archie Bunkers?

An Examination of White Racial Progressives

Most whites in the United States rely on the ideology of color-blind racism to articulate their views (by relying on the frames of the ideology), present their ideas (by using the style of the ideology), and interpret interactions with people of color (by sharing the racial stories of the ideology). They believe blacks are culturally deficient, welfare-dependent, and lazy. They regard affirmative action and reparations as tantamount to "reverse discrimination." And because whites believe discrimination is a thing of the past, minorities' protestations about being racially profiled, experiencing discrimination in the housing and labor markets, and being discriminated against in restaurants, stores, and other social settings are interpreted as "excuses." Following the color-blind script, whites support almost all the goals of the civil rights movement in principle, but object in practice to almost all the policies that have been developed to make these goals a reality. Although they abhor what they regard as blacks' "self-segregation," they do not have any problem with their own racial segregation because they do not see it as a racial phenomenon. Finally, although they sing loudly the color-blind song, as I showed in the previous chapter, they live a white color-coded life.

Does this mean that all whites are refined Archie Bunkers? Does every single white subscribe to the frames, racial stories, and style associated with color-blind racism? The answer is obviously not. Historically, racial progress in America has always transpired because of the joint efforts of racial minorities and white progressives. No one can forget the courageous efforts of whites such as John Brown, Thaddeus Stevens, Charles Sumner, Lydia Maria Child, the Grimke sisters, and the many whites who joined the civil rights movement; no one should ever ignore white militants who struggled for racial equality and who risked their lives for this goal.[1] Therefore today, as yesterday, a portion of the white population is not singing the tune of color blindness. Who are these modern-day "white traitors"?[2] Are they middle-class, educated, racially enlightened whites, as most social scientists contend?[3] Are they more likely to be socialized outside the white habitus (see chapter 6)? Are racial progressives beyond racial contradictions? These are some of the questions I examine in this chapter.

THE SURPRISING DEMOGRAPHY OF RACIAL PROGRESSIVES

Interview data from the 1997 Survey on Social Attitudes of College Students and the 1998 Detroit Area Study suggest young, working-class women are the most likely candidates to be racial progressives.[4] This finding contradicts the claims of most of the media and scholars (from Theodor Adorno's *The Authoritarian Personality* onward), who contend "racists" are poor or working-class whites.[5] These commentators contend poor whites project their fears, their sense of losing out, and their concerns with demographic, civil, and political changes in America onto racial minorities. These opinion-shaping agents also propagate the view that most whites, whom they classify as "middle class," are racially tolerant. But if racism is systemic,[6] this view of "good" and "bad" whites distorts reality. Systems of privilege are defended by most of their beneficiaries in a variety of ways. Some actors defend systemic privilege through violence, but most do so by following the normal customs and practices that help keep the system in place. Hence, the analytical (and political) issue regarding "racism" (racial ideology) ought always to be, What segment of the dominant race does not subscribe to the dominant racial ideology and why not?

I classified as racial progressives respondents who support affirmative action and interracial marriage and who recognize the significance of discrimination in the United States. In cases in which respondents exhibited reservations on one of the issues, I made an effort to search for other elements disclosed in the interview to help me classify the respondents (e.g., whether they had meaningful relationships with minorities or the degree of racial progressiveness on other race-related issues discussed in the interviews). Based on these criteria, I classified 15 percent of college students (six of forty-one) and 12 percent of the DAS respondents (eight of sixty-six) as racial progressives.

PROFILES OF RACIAL PROGRESSIVES: COLLEGE STUDENTS

I classified two students at WU and three at MU as racial progressives. Common characteristics of these five respondents were their class background (four belonged to the working or lower-middle class), gender (all were women), and being in college. Other elements that affected their degree of racial progressiveness were having meaningful associations or friendships with people of color (three of these women had dated black or Latino men) and having a very liberal or radical political ideology. I profile three of these students in the following pages.

Beth: "Being a White Male I Guess You Don't Realize Shit Unless It's Shoved in Your Face."

Beth was a student at WU at the time of the interview. She grew up in southeast Portland in a lower-middle-class neighborhood and, although she classified herself as middle class, she acknowledged that while she was a child, her parents were not "making a whole lot." This element, the fact that her father was a supervisor in a factory and had only a high-school diploma, and the neighborhood where she grew up suggest Beth had a strong working-class influence in her formative years.

Beth was exposed early on in her life to people from many backgrounds. Of the four friends she mentioned from her childhood, one was half black, another was an adopted Thai, and another was Chinese. Among the four friends she mentioned having in middle school, one was a girl from Trinidad and another was from China. Although Beth had only dated white males in her life (one had some Native American ancestry but, as she pointed out, "he doesn't appear as stereotypical minority, he just looks white"), she acknowledged having had a "major crush on a black guy in middle school." When probed on this matter, Beth stated she did not make a move because she was "too shy." In addition, she mentioned that this black boy dated one of her white friends later on, which made her "so mad."

Beth described herself politically as "very liberal" and, based on what she said throughout the interview about a number of social issues, the label fit. For instance, she supported interracial marriage strongly. Beth's answer to the interracial question was different from those of most whites:

> I don't think that there is a problem with it at all. Yeah, it's going to be different when the races are not so able to clearly define anymore. I mean, it's going to be a whole new identity for us to label again, but I don't know, I think the labeling just after a while, it's going to become obsolete.

Her views on affirmative action were equally strong. For example, Beth said in reference to a white male in one of her classes who opposed affirmative action that "being a white male I guess you don't realize shit unless it's shoved in your face." Furthermore, Beth mentioned that she told this student the following in reference to his view on affirmative action:

> I said, "Well, if you think it's a quota system, well you're wrong" and that maybe it's hard to see what these people go through all their life and, I mean—me too, being female, what you go through, just the slight discrimination here and there, this like common slur, you don't understand that. You just think it's a harmless joke, but it's not. It builds up [*giggles*]. He was just not getting it.

Beth understood that discrimination affects the life chances of minorities and even supported programs compensating minorities for past discrimination, because "it's hard to start when you have hit rock bottom, it's hard to climb back up." Although three of the other progressive students had difficulty understanding the significance of school and neighborhood integration, Beth argued that "integration can change [people's] hearts" and that "if people learn to get along they can, but if they're kept apart from each other they won't know how to communicate."

Yet, as with all the progressives in the sample, Beth's radicalism had some limitations. For example, although Beth had an impressive level of interaction with minorities before she entered college, she acknowledged, "I don't have a lot of contact with minorities here." Beth also interprets affirmative action exclusively as a program to guarantee equal opportunity for minorities to compete fairly with whites or, in Beth's words, as a program that "just gives them the chance to at least try."[7] Despite this limited interpretation of affirmative action, Beth supported providing unique educational opportunities for minorities because "many won't get a chance otherwise in any way, shape, or form" and supported hiring the minority applicant in two of the hypothetical cases of the ABZ company. Also, when asked if the decisions of this hypothetical company could be regarded as reverse discrimination, she said, "Well, look at the workplace. It's 97 percent white and who is getting the preferential treatment?"

Mandy: "I Think That It Is People Who Oppose Interracial Relationships Based on the Problem They Would Have with Kids [That] Make the Problems for Their Kids."

The second case is Mandy, a half-Cherokee[8] student from WU. She was one of the few students who acknowledged in the survey as well as in the interview that she came from a working-class background. Mandy reported that she lived in "a section of town that was considered to be for all the white trash." Mandy, who is married, described her household as "poor" and stated that she and her husband earn less than $20,000 a year.

In the survey Mandy pointed out that she was "extremely liberal" on economic and social issues and said in the interview she had participated in feminist organizations as well as in groups defending the rights of gays and lesbians. Although she grew up in an area she described as "98 percent white," she indicated she had Native American, black, and Asian friends. She dated a black man and mentioned that he "is still a very good friend of mine." In line with this history, Mandy supported interracial unions in a strong fashion:

> I think that it is people who oppose interracial relationships based on the problem they would have with kids [that] make the problems for their kids [*laughs*]. I have a lot of friends who are in interracial marriages and they have children and those children are well loved, they are well socialized, they know who they are, where they come from. And I just think it's people who oppose it who create the most problems.

Mandy was very clear about the impact of discrimination on racial minorities and narrated two incidents she witnessed to illustrate her position. One of these incidents reveals how clearly she understands the new face of discrimination:

> I was in a country store and I had my backpack, which was empty. And I was trying to figure out something to take to a potluck for school, and I was in there forever, walking around, and the guy at the counter didn't care. And I could've stuck anything in my backpack if I wanted to. So I went up to pay for the item, "Well, how are you doing, ma'am?" and "Are you having a good day?" And all of sudden, I saw his face change and he was looking past me, and he just had this weird look on his face. So I turned around and there was a black man standing behind me. He went over to the guns, picking out a gun. And I'm standing there with money in my hand, and this guy goes, "Can I help you?" to the guy. He says, "Do you need something, sir? Is there anything you need?" And just kept looking at him. And so I said, you know, "Here's my money [*laughs*] if you want to take it." And he's all so sorry and he's taking my money, but he's still keeping an eye on this guy. And I looked at the guy and he had this look on his face that just broke my heart because you could tell that he has to deal with this and I have never had to deal with that.

Because Mandy understood that discrimination happens today, she was one of the few whites who supported providing some kind of financial compensation to minorities for past discrimination, either through government programs or direct payments.

Although Mandy hesitated in her support of affirmative action in the direct question, her answers to the specific ABZ company decisions were positive. For example, whereas most whites thought hiring a black job candidate who scored slightly less than a white on a test amounted to reverse discrimination, Mandy opined "the country had a history of hiring only white people over black people, then it's about damn time they hired a black person and, if it is discriminatory toward the white person, too bad." She was also one of the few who pointed out that "five percentage points wasn't enough of a difference in terms of score." When asked about the notion of reverse discrimination, Mandy said, "Discrimination in reverse? The minute you were born in this country white male you have so many more privileges than the rest of the people, it's unbelievable."

Of the forty-one college students, Mandy was the most consistently racially progressive respondent (see the beginning of this chapter for the discussion of the elements involved in classifying respondents as "progressives"). The only troublesome issues in her answers were a comment about her being "a little hesitant" if she had to sit at an all-black table, her overt concern with merits as the basis for affirmative action programs, and the fact that she described her extended family as "very racist." Although the story was not delivered as an ideological testimony (it did not use the trinity formula; see chapter 5), having family members who are "very racist" bears on anybody's life. My point is not to make her racist by association. Instead, I suggest that having family members who are "very racist" imprints some of her actions and views whether she wants it to or not. For example, she acknowledged her family had "a hard time" when she dated the black man. She also acknowledged that her brother believes he has been a victim of "reverse discrimination," although she disagrees adamantly with him on this issue. However, on the latter issue, she used arguments similar to those of her own brother to support affirmative action. Thus, Mandy's associations with her family will continue to be a part of her social milieu, as few people can dissociate themselves totally from the important people in their lives.[9]

Kay: "I've Been Going Out with the Same Guy Since My Sophomore Year in High School. He's Black."

Kay was a sophomore at MU when she was interviewed. As with most racial progressives, Kay is from a lower-class background. She grew up in Cassopolis, a small but very diverse community in Michigan. Kay stated that the community was "30 to 40 percent black" and "10 to 20 percent" Laotian. She had minority friends while growing up and attended the local public school, which was more than 50 percent minority.

While at MU, she was dating a young black man from Cassopolis with whom she had been since high school. Her association with this black man brought her into contact at MU with other people of color. Therefore, Kay's answer to the interracial marriage question was, "I don't see anything wrong with it." Kay appreciated racial diversity and stated,

> I think it's a very good thing, because I'm glad that I came from a diverse environment. Because the white friends that I do have here, like, came from Catholic schools that were all white and all girls, and it's just—they are *so* different from me, and they are *so* sheltered. And I'm really glad and, like, proud of where I came from.

She also supported affirmative action and connected it to her own admission to MU:

> Because I'm, like, compared to lots of other people, my grade point average isn't high and it's good they look at other, like, your activities and not just your grade point average, because that doesn't reflect, you know, how good of a student you are, just your grade point average. You know, they need to look at lots of other things.

Kay was one of the few respondents in the two studies who understood that affirmative action was not just about race and that many colleges admit a portion of their students based on criteria other than grade point average and SAT scores. Nevertheless, Kay was the most tenuous racial progressive among college students. For example, even though she supported affirmative action and claimed that diversity had been very important in her life, she objected to the hypothetical ABZ company hiring an equally qualified black over a white applicant for diversity concerns:

> Well, I guess if I was, like, put in the situation and, like, I think about if I was in that situation, if *I* was the applicant, *I* would be very upset. If I found out that was the reason, you know, I don't think that's a very good reason. Just because, you know, we have a lack of diversity. I mean, you need, I don't know [*laughs*] I'll just shut up [*laughs*].

All of Kay's answers to the questions about the hypothetical ABZ company were problematic and similar to those of most whites. This was also the only subject in the interview that made her hesitate to the point of becoming rhetorically incoherent (see chapter 4).

Kay also opposed busing and used the frame of abstract liberalism to explain her stance. When asked if the government should intervene to make sure school integration becomes a reality, she said, "I think people should be able to go to school where they want to go to school. I mean, not be forced to have so many, you know, so many black people at this school, so many Asian people at this school, you know, that's difficult." Kay's specific view on busing was, "I don't know if you've heard of Benton Harbor, Michigan. Like, they bus the black people *in* from there *to* their school because their community is, like, all white. I don't know exactly why they did it, but I just think it's kind of ridiculous."

Finally, as with most whites who dated or interacted heavily with blacks, Kay's parents objected to it. For instance, she explained, "My parents always told me that I could be friends with black people, but I couldn't date them." As in Mandy's case, this fact of Kay's life does not condemn her to racism for life; however, racialized considerations will affect her decision-making process in the future, so long as she interacts with her family.

PROFILES OF RACIAL PROGRESSIVES:
DETROIT AREA RESIDENTS

Although I classified eight DAS respondents as racial progressives, four were distinctly more progressive than the others. As with the college students, these respondents were mostly women (seven of eight), from working-class or lower-middle-class backgrounds (six of eight), and had an interracial lifestyle. I profile two of the most progressive whites from the 1998 DAS first, followed by two somewhat-less-progressive ones.

Sara: "Why [Was the Company 97 Percent White]?
Because That's, Well, the Fact There Is Racism."

Sara is an unemployed woman in her twenties who was born and raised in Detroit city in a low-income neighborhood. She characterized the diversity in her neighborhood as "just a bunch of different people." This description corresponds to the friends she had: one Arab, one black, one white, and one Mexican. Sara still lives in the neighborhood she grew up in, which she describes as "all low-income" and as very racially diverse. The schools she attended were also diverse and her best friend was a black girl named Bridget. She and Bridget hung out together in school and even skipped classes together.

Sara's interracial lifestyle included having "an affair with a black guy," whom she described as "real sweet." Although later on she clarified that this "affair" was "just a date," Sara seemed to truly have an interracial life. For example, her current boyfriend was "Hispanic" and her own sister was marrying a black man with whom she had had two children. Therefore, her answer to the interracial marriage question was a straight "I think if you love that person, it's your business; no one else has a right to say anything."

Her answers to the discrimination question were consistently progressive. She believes blacks experience daily discrimination and that they are not more lazy than whites, and even supports the idea of government spending on blacks' behalf to compensate for past discrimination. Sara, as many of the poor and uneducated whites in the sample, had very little knowledge about programs such as "busing" or "affirmative action" and could not provide sensible answers to questions about them. Yet, when affirmative action–type hiring situations were posed to her through the hypothetical ABZ company, she opposed the three decisions. Nevertheless, she was one of the few whites who, when asked to explain why this company was 97 percent white, said, "*Why?* Because that's, well, the fact there is racism." Furthermore, she expressed a strong view against whites who are angry about an almost-all-white company hiring blacks:

> I couldn't, I couldn't say that they should be angry about it. You know, but, you know, they should try to, they need more black people in there, yes they do. They have to have the fairness to because if they, if they can do that *job,* then let them have that job. Don't—I think that's so stupid about the discrimination bullshit [referring to whites who claim they experience discrimination].

Sara's answer to the last question of the interview, "If you were the president of the USA, what would you do to eliminate racial inequality and ease racial tensions?" was yet another example of her progressiveness:

> [*raises her voice*] I would put down that it should be equal to each and every person that's out there. Equal school, equal jobs, everything should be equal. I don't think one should get more than another. It should be right down the middle, equal. Equal to them both.

When asked if there was anything else she wanted to add, Sara said, "Um, I know a lot of people out there don't believe in whites and blacks mixing in marriages and stuff, but I think that's wrong. I think that if they love each other, then that's their business. I think people should leave them alone."

Sue: "I Suppose If You Keep Running Your Head into the Wall, after a While You Just Say, 'No More.'"

Sue's class background is confusing. Although she grew up in an upper-middle-class household, she seems to be in a different class today. Sue is a retired school teacher in her early fifties, but as with many older, single adults, has experienced a step back in her class status. She described her current job situation as follows: "I do real estate and estate cleanup on the side [*laughs*] to supplement my income so that's about where I'm at. Or for free rent or whatever, like, I'm here for free rent [indecipherable] paint it up, clean it, no bills. That'd be a good business for you [*addressing the interviewer*]."

Sue seems to have had a mostly white network of associates from childhood until adulthood, but she pointed out that she became (and still is) close to the "cleaning lady" that worked for her father and that "I had friends at college of color and I never had any problem with it." Later on, she referred to her "black acquaintances" and the "hard way to go" they have in the workplace. Although Sue's connections to blacks are tenuous, they are real. For example, she remained in contact with the "cleaning lady" who worked for her father after the employment situation ended.

Sue believes discrimination is an important factor explaining blacks' status and she acknowledged that "people have not given them the chances." She said she had seen this since early on in her life with the "Kentucky and hillbilly attitude." When asked if laziness had anything to do with blacks' contemporary situation, Sue answered,

> I don't think it's true. I think many of 'em work twice as hard as [*indecipherable*] because it's made so difficult for them. Others, I don't know if I agree with this or whatever, I suppose if you keep running your head into the wall after a while you just say, "No more."

Sue supports affirmative action, believes that being white is an advantage, and thinks that whites' anger about it stems from their fear of losing control:

> I think because they feel they're gonna lose control of what they assume is a weaker entity of society. And I don't think they want them to have the opportunities to become equals, because they don't want them sitting next to them in the country club or sitting next to them in the office place. They just like to keep 'em right where they are at, underneath their feet. You know, I think a lot of it is fear. Because I think anger is repressed fear, it's repressed. Fear, they are scared and I don't know why, you know, what its cause is; it's obviously their background, too.

But as all white racial progressives, Sue had some contradictions. First, her stance on interracial marriage was not very progressive. Although Sue stated, "I don't have a problem with it" and pointed out that there are several members of her family in interracial marriages, she also said, "I wonder about the children, if it's fair because society I don't think gives 'em a fair chance and sometimes I feel sorry for the kids. I have some empathy there, I don't know about—reserve my judgment on that."

Furthermore, Sue herself would not get involved in interracial marriages because of "a very bad experience with a [black] man that worked for my father in our home." Although she says that now she feels "very comfortable with men of color," she has not been able to "totally erase that."[10]

Sue also interpreted some of the differences between whites and blacks as biological. For example, although Sue believes the differences between whites and blacks are "cultivated," she said that "the fat, wider noses makes them, it's easier for them to [be] high altitude runners." Later on, she added, to accentuate her position, "I mean, I have no rhythm, I mean, black friends of mine [have it]." Fortuitously, she ended this problematic discussion by saying, "I think they do get a lot of practice."

Lastly, Sue's mostly white network of interaction and the fact that her boyfriend and some of her friends are prejudiced must affect her cognitions and views. For instance, why would a racial progressive date (and remain with) someone who is "prejudiced"? Do the views of her prejudiced boyfriend and friends affect her own views? Can associating with color-blind or outright Jim Crow–prejudiced whites muffle Sue's racial progressiveness? Susan admitted that "my boyfriend, he's prejudiced" and, as part of her answer to the question on white advantage, said that her boyfriend says that "he wishes he was a black woman, you know, 'cause [*laughing*] he'd be up many levels." Sue stated she supports affirmative action, but used the frame of abstract liberalism to oppose *all* the hiring decisions of the hypothetical ABZ company. Once again, I am not suggesting she is guilty of racism by association. However, my point again is to underscore that networks of social interaction matter whether actors are aware of it or not.

Staci: "Probably Because of Racism"

Staci was a school custodian in her fifties. She grew up in Troy, Michigan, in a middle-class community (her parents even owned a small cottage in northern Michigan). The majority of her networks until she began her life as a worker were completely white. However, Staci has worked as a hair stylist and now works as a custodian, which has brought her to a high level of interaction with blacks over the past twenty-five years of her life. Although Staci has never dated across the color line, she has no objections to interracial marriage. In her answer to the question on this matter Staci included just a minor qualification:

> I think it's just fine. You know, if you find someone that, you know, is your soul mate, I see nothing wrong with it whatsoever. It's a—I think it's probably difficult because of the way other people will, you know, view you but if they're a strong enough person to handle that, then I think it's just fine.

Staci believes discrimination against blacks is daily and pointed out how she thinks it happens:

> Probably in a million different ways: from buying something at, you know, waiting in line just to buy—not waiting in line but at a counter to buy something at a store and maybe you're the first [to] buy [and] you don't get waited on, you know, in proper sequence or. . . . You know, I hadn't experienced it myself, so it's hard to say but I'm sure there's many ways for that to occur.

When asked why blacks are worse off than whites, Staci answered point blank, "Probably because of racism." She also believes being white is an advantage and described white-skin privilege as follows:

> Things are more accessible to you, you know. You don't walk into somewhere and you're not automatically judged by your skin color. You know, you're just more or less accepted until, you know, people find out whether or not they like you and if they're going to give you the benefit of the doubt, you know, second chances like that. That would be an advantage.

Nevertheless, color-blind racism has affected racial progressives too. Thus, Staci believes blacks do not deserve any special government assistance and used the "the past is the past" story line to punctuate her view: "People have to let go of the past." To explain her stance on reparations, she used yet another story line: "You've got the Irish, your Italians, all kinds of people that came over here to this country that weren't treated nicely when they first arrived and, you know, you can't give reparations to everyone that has been mistreated." Staci also opposed busing and believed residential segregation is "more a matter of economics than anything" (this is the "anything but racism" semantic move). When pressed in a follow-up question on this subject, she used the abstract liberalism frame and said that "the government can't start telling people where to live" and that residential choice was "one of the things you strive for in life to be able to, you know, live in a neighborhood where you want, to go to schools that you feel would be right for your children and I don't think that's any of the government's business where people live." Finally, Staci also opposed affirmative action and two of the three ABZ company hiring decisions.

Judy: "I'm for It [Affirmative Action] a Little Bit, Not Real Dramatically."

Judy is a college professor of nursing in her forties. She grew up between Kalamazoo and Royal Oak, Michigan, areas she described as "mainly Caucasian." Her neighborhood as well as school friends while growing up were all white, but that changed in college as she developed friend-ships with black women. She meets once a month with one of her black friends to have dinner, share life stories, and "trade poems." In her current job, most of the staff and 30 percent of the professors are black. When asked if she interacts with her black peers, she said, "Oh yeah! I interact pretty heavily with the minority faculty because I chair the cultural relations committee in our college, so I've done that for the last couple of years so I *deliberately* engage them in conversation and interaction."

Judy realizes discrimination is still important and described various examples of old- and new-style discrimination. For example, Judy said that a black man told her that he was not served "at Henry Ford Hospital" because he was black. Judy also said that many blacks are used as guinea pigs because they are black and poor. Finally, she mentioned that a black woman told her that when she shops in the suburbs "she notices that people won't give her change in her hand" because they are "fearful of her and that bugs her to death." As with many racial progressives, Judy's experience as a woman helped her empathize with blacks' plight. For instance, while explaining how the few blacks that move up in society "feel always on display," she connected it to her experiences as a woman:

> It's kind of like women, you know. I have to be that much better just because of various conditions and practices that occur. So in that way I can understand it because it's difficult being a woman in this society. It is planned, it's organized by men. It's set up for them and we've had to struggle to become equal. It's just that way for people of color.

Although I classified Judy as a racial progressive, almost all her answers to crucial racial questions were not completely progressive and, on occasion, they were not different from those of most whites. For example, her answer to the interracial marriage question was typical:

> Oh, I have—I think it's acceptable. Naturally, it's [*lowers voice*]—the [*raises her voice*] problems with it I think only occur as it surrounds the kids and growing up in a culture that does not support, you know, such a—it doesn't really support interracial marriage, our culture. So I think that the couple is—are adults when they take this on and it's a choice and they know what they are doing and [I] think they have more struggles because they don't really have a culture that says, "OK, great, whoever you are is fine!" So that's kind of a problem; that's the biggest problem I see.

When asked if she would have considered interracial marriage herself, she said, "I don't think at the time I married I would [have], which would have been, you know, twenty-five years ago." However, she added immediately, "Currently I would."

Similarly, on the crucial question of affirmative action, Judy said that, "I'm a little bit for it, not real dramatically." She then proceeded to state that it is a "temporary solution," that "it's bad" when "it's used for quotas," that it should not be used for "real jobs," and that it is not "consistent with the rest of the marketplace values." Therefore, when asked if she thought affirmative action was unfair to whites, Judy said that "it can be unfair to whites" when it is used in the workplace. She also had lots of difficulties accepting any of the hiring decisions of the hypothetical ABZ company.

Finally, she could see almost no role for the government in dealing with racial inequality or residential and school segregation. Throughout the interview, when asked to specify a solution to these problems, Judy suggested education and dialogues as the solutions. For example, Judy's solution to residential segregation is "town meetings." The government intervention she favors is "day-care centers and schools and I think maybe more education programs would be best." Judy also stated that she liked Bill Clinton's racial dialogues because "we need to dialogue about this rather than trying to fix it through these, like affirmative action program[s], after the fact." And when asked what she would do to eliminate racial inequality and ease racial tension if she were the president of the United States, Judy said, "Start with educational programs" and "Keep the education coming and spend money on it."

CONCLUSION

In this chapter I profiled white racial progressives. Contrary to those who hold the "commonsense" view on racial matters, racial progressives are more likely to come from working-class backgrounds. Specifically, I found that young, working-class women are more likely than any other segment of the white community to be racially progressive. They were more likely to support affirmative action and interracial marriage, have close personal relations with minorities in general and blacks in particular, and understand that discrimination is a central factor shaping the life chances of minorities in this country. Most also admitted that being white is an advantage in this country.

Although these respondents were substantially different in their views from most whites in these two studies, many of their views denoted the influence of color-blind racism. For example, all these respondents, though to various degrees, have been influenced by the frames of color blindness and, hence, on some issues had *exactly* the same views as most whites. Many had problems with affirmative action programs and policies; a few had serious problems with them. Others pondered the "problems" children of interracial couples would face. Yet others thought residential and school decisions ought to be left to "people's choices" and, thus, saw no reason for governmental intervention on these matters.

Elsewhere I have argued that whiteness is *"embodied racial power"* because "all actors socially regarded as 'white' . . . receive systemic privileges just by virtue of wearing the white outfit whereas those regarded as nonwhite are denied those privileges."[11] However, the wages of whiteness are not equally distributed. Poor and working-class whites receive a better deal than their minority brethren, but their material share of the benefits of whiteness is low, as they remain too close to the economic abyss.[12] Hence, white workers have a powerful reason to exhibit more solidarity toward minorities than whites in other classes.

But if this is so, why have most workers in the United States been historically antiblack, antiminority, and anti-immigrant?[13] I believe the answer has to do with the interaction between race and gender. It has been white *male* workers who have historically supported the racial order. Why? Because whether in periods of economic security or insecurity, white masculinity has provided white men with economic and noneconomic benefits.[14] During good times, working-class men have been "the kings of the castle" (the home) and, during bad times (when "their" women have had to work in the paid labor force), they have been able to maintain a sense of control by demanding a traditional patriarchal organization of the home and by "patrolling neighborhoods" and the family from racial "pollution" (see reference on Fine and Weis in note 14).[15] The white male bond[16] thus has prevented working-class white men from joining progressive racial movements en masse.

In line with this argument, one can also understand why white women are the most likely segment to express solidarity with racial minorities. Since systems of domination are always "articulated,"[17] actors who experience multiple oppressions are more likely to share literally a "social space" as well as a set of experiences that tend to develop a sense of "commonality."[18] Since the 1960s, the percentages of racial minorities and white women in the working class have increased. According to Yates (2005) the majority of minimum wage workers and workers making no more than a dollar above the minimum wage are women (nearly 60 percent in either case). Furthermore, research by Mitra Toossi (2002) illustrates that by 2050 the share of white non-Hispanics in the U.S. labor force will decrease from 73 to 53 percent. In contrast, blacks are expected to increase their numbers in the workforce from 12 percent to 14 percent and Hispanics and Asians are expected to more than double their numbers in the labor force (from 11 to 24 percent for the former and from 5 to 11 percent for the latter).[19] The complex workings of contemporary racialized capitalism have created a situation in which white women and racial minorities increasingly share similar class conditions in the workplace[20] as well as social debasement, a situation that already is producing high levels of joint political action in a variety of areas.[21]

In my two projects, racially progressive women, one after the other, used their own experiences of discrimination as women as a lens through which to comprehend minorities' racial oppression. It was also clear that their shared class vulnerability with minorities (such as bad jobs and low wages) was involved in their racial progressiveness and it may even be the reason why they were the most likely subgroup of all the whites in these samples to have dated across the color line. As Gordon Allport argues, race contacts among *equals* lead to better race relations.[22]

Besides the class/gender background of this group of whites, what other attributes do they share that may explain their high propensity for racial progressiveness? First, most of these respondents grew up in racially mixed neighborhoods. Although growing up in "integrated" neighborhoods does not necessarily lead to racial progressiveness (e.g., Bob, a respondent from SU, grew up in an integrated neighborhood), it increases the likelihood of equal-status contacts between whites and people of color, which may in turn increase the likelihood of whites appreciating minorities as their equals. Second, and maybe related to the first attribute, almost all these respondents had minority friends while growing up. As I pointed out in chapter 6, whites' own racial segregation and isolation leads them to a white habitus that impedes the development of empathy toward people of color and fosters a sense (and the views that accompany this sense) of "us versus them." This "(white) racial solidarity" is less likely to develop among whites who have real friendships with minorities, because race "can be a function of experiences and ties";[23] the more positive experiences and ties whites have with people of color, the more likely they are to see them in their full humanity. Third, many of these respondents were, in general terms, either politically progressive or radical. Hence, they were able to make connections that few whites are able to make (e.g., connecting patriarchal, class, and racial oppression). Fourth, many of these respondents had dated across the color line. Although dating or marrying someone of a different race does not translate into beliefs of racial equality (e.g., Scott, a twenty-three-year-old mechanic, had dated Asian and Arab women but regarded them as racialized and sexualized objects), the work most people in these relations do *before* and *during* the interaction requires dealing with many of the central racial aspects of American society.[24]

These findings can be used for research and politics. Other researchers must examine systematically whether or not my findings can be replicated. They may lead us away from the idea that racial tolerance is increased through mere education and into more specific formulations on what education does and does not do and for whom. We should also examine whether or not the four additional variables I mention above (growing up in mixed neighborhoods, having black friends, being politically progressive, and dating across the color line) do in fact increase, separately or together (what social scientists call "the interaction effect"), the likelihood of being racially progressive. Politically, my findings point to the need of a new kind of working-class politics in America (see chapter 9). If working-class women are more likely to be racially progressive, organizations seeking progressive social change must rethink their politics. It may be that, after all, class will be the uniting factor in progressive politics, but it will be class solidarity through race and gender prisms.[25]

If racial progressives are influenced by color-blind racism, are blacks influenced too? That is, are blacks as color blind as whites—progressive or not? Do they use the frames of color-blind racism as much as whites? Do they resort to the style of color blindness when expressing their racial views? Do blacks use the racial stories of color blindness to punctuate their racial positions? I examine these matters in the next chapter.

NOTES

1. On antiracist whites from 1619 until the Civil War, see Herbert Aptheker, *Anti-Racism in U.S. History: The First Two Hundred Years* (New York: Greenwood, 1992). On white women in the struggle for racial equality, see Gerda Lerner, *The Grimké Sisters from South Carolina: Pioneers for Woman's Rights and Abolition* (New York: Schocken, 1967). On whites in the struggle for equality in the twentieth century, see Manning Marable, *Race, Reform, and Rebellion: The Second Reconstruction in Black America, 1945–1990* (Jackson: University Press of Mississippi, 1991).

2. I borrow the phrase "white traitors" from the journal *Race Traitors*.

3. Lawrence Bobo and Fred Licari Bobo, "Education and Political Tolerance: Testing the Effects of Cognitive Sophistication and Target Group Affect," *Public Opinion Quarterly* 53, no. 5 (1989): 547–59; Lincoln Quillian, "Group Threat and Regional Change in Attitudes toward African-Americans," *American Journal of Sociology* 102, no. 3 (1996): 816–60.

4. My finding corresponds to the recent findings of two social psychologists who studied high-school seniors from 1976 to 1992. They point out that these young women were "more willing to be friends with people of other races, to live near them and work with them, and to have their future children associate with them." Monica Kirkpatrick Johnson and Margaret Mooney Marini, "Bridging the Racial Divide in the United States: The Effect of Gender," *Social Psychology Quarterly* 61, no. 3 (1998): 247–58. See also Emily W. Kane, "Racial and Ethnic Variations in Gender-Related Attitudes," *Annual Review of Sociology* 26 (2000): 419–39.

5. Jack Levin and Jack McDevitt, in their 1993 *Hate Crimes*, suggest, "Hate crimes are more often committed under ordinary circumstances by otherwise unremarkable types—neighbors, a coworker at the next desk, or groups of young-

sters looking for a thrill" (5). The authors also report an increase in racist attitudes and violence among white students across America. See *Hate Crimes: The Rising Tide of Bigotry and Bloodshed* (New York: Plenum, 1993). For a scathing critique of white middle-class liberals who blame the problem of racism on poor whites, see chapter 10 in Jim Goad, *The Redneck Manifesto* (New York: Touchstone, 1997).

6. See Eduardo Bonilla-Silva, "Rethinking Racism," *American Sociological Review* 62, no. 3 (1997): 465–80. For a more accessible formulation, see Joe R. Feagin, *Racist America: Roots, Realities, and Future Reparations* (New York: Routledge, 2000).

7. If affirmative action programs do not include goals, concerns about how race affects the scores of minorities in examinations, and a true interest for diversity, affirmative action is no more than window dressing and it does not make a significant dent in narrowing the gap between minorities and the majority. See Edward Dorn, *Rules and Racial Equality* (New Haven, Conn.: Yale University Press, 1979).

8. Mandy was in our sample because on the survey question on racial identity she identified herself as "white." She also added that she "looks white."

9. We noted in the interviews that when people said that their family was "racist," "conservative," or "very racist," this had a bearing on their own racial views. For example, on many occasions the respondents even quoted some of the racist members of their families as sources of authority on an issue.

10. This is a racialized interpretation of the sexual incident. Although most white women experience terrible things with white men, it is when they have such encounters with blacks that they develop "negrophobia." That is, when white men molest them, they do not develop "whitephobia." On this point, see Alexander Thomas and Samuel Sillen, *Racism and Psychiatry* (New York: Brunner/ Mazel, 1972).

11. Eduardo Bonilla-Silva and Ashley Doane Jr. (eds.), "New Racism, Color-Blind Racism, and the Future of Whiteness in America," in *Whiteout: The Continuing Significance of Racism* (New York: Routledge, 2003).

12. I agree with David Roediger that white workers receive a psychological wage from whiteness, but I insist that they receive other important material incentives too (better jobs and more job security, slightly higher wages, better access to good schools and neighborhoods). If the "wages of whiteness" were just psychological, one would expect more whites to become "white traitors." See David Roediger, *The Wages of Whiteness* (London: Verso, 1994).

13. See David Goldberg, *The Color of Politics: Race and the Mainsprings of American Politics* (New York: New York Press, 1997).

14. See Michelle Fine and Lois Weis, *The Unknown City: Lives of Poor and Working-Class Young Adults* (Boston: Beacon, 1998); Lillian B. Rubin, *Families on the Fault Lines: America's Working Class Speaks about the Family, the Economy, Race, and Ethnicity* (New York: HarperCollins, 1994); and Dana D. Nelson, *National Manhood: Capitalist Citizenship and the Imagined Fraternity of White Men* (Durham, N.C.: Duke University Press, 1998).

15. This is not a novel argument. See Catherine Clinton, *The Plantation Mistress* (New York: Pantheon, 1982).

16. I owe this concept to David G. Embrick, who studied the various forms of exclusion of minorities and women in a bread company while he was a graduate student in sociology at Texas A&M University.

17. For a discussion on the notion of articulation, see Jennifer Daryl Slack, "The Theory and Method of Articulation in Cultural Studies," in *Stuart Hall: Critical Dialogues in Cultural Studies,* edited by David Morley and Kuan-Hsing Chen, 112–27 (London: Routledge, 1996).

18. Pierre Bordieau, "Social Space and Symbolic Power," *Sociological Theory* 7 (Spring 1980): 12–25.

19. Data from Mitra Toossi, "A Century of Change: The U.S. Labor Force, 1950–2050," *Monthly Labor Review* 125, no. 5 (May 2002) and David Roediger, "What If Labor Were Not White and Male?" For a similar claim, see pages 179–92 in David R. Roediger, *Colored White: Transcending the Racial Past* (Berkeley: University of California Press, 2000; London: Verso, 2002).

20. See Barbara Reskin and Irene Padavic, *Women and Men at Work* (Thousand Oaks, Calif.: Pine Forge, 2002).

21. David Roediger, *Colored White.* See also Robin R. Kelley, *Yo' Mama's Disfunktional: Fighting the Culture Wars in Urban America* (Boston: Beacon, 1997). For a similar argument, see Joe R. Feagin and Hernán Vera, *White Racism: The Basics* (New York: Routledge, 1995).

22. Gordon Allport, *The Nature of Prejudice* (New York: Doubleday, 1954).

23. Rachel F. Moran, *Interracial Intimacy: The Regulation of Race and Romance* (Chicago: University of Chicago Press, 2001), 81.

24. On this point, see Beverly Daniel Tatum, *"Why Are All the Black Kids Sitting Together in the Cafeteria?": And Other Conversations about Race* (New York: Basic, 1997), 96.

25. "Class is not a unified group, and people similarly situated in this social space will not necessarily form specific groups or organizations. Yet the complex historical workings of capitalism create changing conditions, physical spaces, and opportunities for people to engage in a range of possibilities of resistance in a variety of different kinds of collectivities. Class as serial structure constrains and enables action, but does not determine it." Sonya O. Rose, "Class Formation and the Quintessential Worker," in *Reworking Class,* edited by John R. Hall, 133–66 (Ithaca, N.Y.: Cornell University Press, 1997), 151.

8

Are Blacks Color Blind, Too?

Survey researchers are mostly in agreement about blacks' racial attitudes. Although they all underscore that blacks share basic elements of "Americanism" or the "American Creed," such as the belief that those who work hard will be compensated in life, they also point out that blacks have vastly different positions than whites on central racial issues.[1] For example, in surveys blacks and whites consistently have polar views on issues such as the significance of discrimination in America, the merits of affirmative action, support for certain government programs, and busing. Surveys even find significant differences in the level of support for interracial social interaction (twenty percentage points on some items).[2]

The survey results of the 1998 DAS are in line with these findings too. For instance, whereas 53 percent of whites stated their preference for neighborhoods that are "all" or "mostly" white, only 22 percent of blacks preferred neighborhoods described as "all" or "mostly" black. In fact, 62 percent of blacks preferred neighborhoods described as "half and half." Regarding the policy of busing, 69 percent of whites opposed it, compared to 26 percent of blacks. On the hot issue of affirmative action, 50 percent of whites stated they would support a proposal similar to that passed in California in 1996 to eliminate affirmative action, if such a proposal were put on the ballot in the state of Michigan. In stark contrast, only 6 percent of blacks said they would support such a proposal. Finally, whereas 56 percent of whites agreed that this country has experienced a lot of racial progress, only 29 percent of blacks agreed with this position.

Have these observed attitudinal differences between blacks and whites been corroborated in qualitative studies? The answer to this question is not clear, because qualitative studies of blacks' attitudes are sparse, single-issue driven, and based on segments of the black community, and they usually do not cover a wide range of racial issues. Most qualitative data on blacks' views are part of larger studies on the woes of the black upper or middle class, the working class, the working poor, or the black underclass.[3] Other qualitative research on blacks addresses specific aspects of their lives, such as their experiences in historically white colleges or with interracial friendship.[4]

Given the limited number of systematic, qualitative studies of blacks' views, in this chapter, using interview data I gathered as part of the 1998 DAS, I examine black Detroiters' racial views. My specific goal is to assess the extent to which blacks rely on the frames, style, and racial stories of color blindness to articulate their positions. I recognize, however, that the relatively small size of the sample (N 17) limits the possibility of generalizing from this study. Yet, because the cases were randomly selected from a randomly chosen larger sample (see chapter 1), I believe the results are robust and will be corroborated in studies with larger samples of blacks.

I proceed as follows: first, I assess the influence of the frames of color blindness on blacks; second, I examine the extent to which blacks rely on the style of color-blind racism; finally, I explore whether or not blacks have adopted the racial stories of color-blind racism.

SLIGHTLY COLOR BLIND:
COLOR-BLIND RACISM'S FRAMES AND BLACKS

Do blacks endorse the frames of color-blind racism? Do they use its frames as the foundation upon which to articulate their views on racial matters? Content analysis of the interviews with black and white DAS respondents suggests blacks are significantly less likely than whites to use the frames of color blindness directly. As table 8.1 shows, whereas all these frames are essential to whites' explanations of racial matters, only three (abstract liberalism, cultural racism, and naturalization of racial matters) have impacted blacks' consciousness.

Because the direct effect of the frames of color-blind racism on blacks is minimal, it is plausible to argue that blacks and whites navigate two totally different ideological worlds and thus that color-blind racism is partially ineffective. However, an ideology is not dominant because it affects all actors in a social system in the *same* way and to the *same* degree. Instead, an ideology is dominant if *most* members (dominant and subordinate) of a social system have to accommodate their views vis-à-vis that ideology.[5] If an ideology dominates the space of what people think is feasible and thinkable, and even provides the parameters to oppose the status quo, then that ideology is dominant. In this section I analyze how the different frames of color-blind racism have affected blacks. My main contention is that color-blind racism has affected blacks *indirectly* and that this has consequences for the likelihood of blacks developing an all-out oppositional ideology to color-blind racism.

Abstract Liberalism and Blacks

Abstract liberalism is the explanatory well from which whites gather ideas to account for residential and school segregation, limited levels of interracial marriage, and a host of other racial issues. Slightly more than a third of the blacks in this study used this frame directly in their answers.[6] I will illustrate in this section how this frame has affected blacks' views on two issues, namely, affirmative action and school and residential segregation.

Affirmative Action

Affirmative action has become emblematic of racial tensions in contemporary America. Not surprisingly, the frames of color blindness had very little direct and indirect influence on blacks on this important subject. Blacks overwhelmingly expressed support for affirmative action and other race-targeted programs and rebuked white opposition to them. A typical response to the question "Are you for or against affirmative action?" was that of Edward, an unemployed man in his fifties:

> I'd say that I would have to be for affirmative action simply because you still have ignorant people. Some of these ignorant people are in control and have a little more power than I'd like to think they should have in regards to what they can do to prevent other people from having opportunities that means that they can't have growth and development. Affirmative action is a means and method. Then it's like a key when you got a locked door. You've got to have it.

When asked, "What would you say to those who say affirmative action is unfair to whites?" Edward responded, "I tell them that 'What do you call fair?' If you got everything, it's kind of like saying you are upset because you got ice cream and you don't have a cone. Then put it in a bowl, you already got everything. Don't worry about it."

Regina, a poor homemaker in her early fifties with little formal education, expressed her support for affirmative action in clear terms. Her answer to the affirmative action question was, "I'm for it." In the follow-up question about whether affirmative action could be regarded as unfair to whites, Regina stated, "Well, I say the colored race have had a *hard time*

Table 8.1. Deployment of Color-Blind Frames by White and Black Respondents, DAS 1998

Frames	Whites	Blacks
Abstract Liberalism	64/67 (96%)	6/17 (35%)
On Affirmative Action	59/67 (88%)	1/17 (6%)
Cultural Racism	59/67 (88%)	4/17 (24%)
Naturalization	27/67 (43%)	4/17 (24%)
Denial of Discrimination's Systemic Nature	56/67 (84%)	1/17 (6%)

all they lives and the whites, it's been easy for them. I think they should give them [blacks] a break."

Finally, Joe, an electronic technician in his thirties, echoed the views of the previous respondents on whites' concerns about the unfairness of affirmative action: *"They need to wake up and smell the roses."*

Only one black respondent, Irma, an accounting clerk in her early thirties, opposed affirmative action. She explained her opposition to affirmative action in a way that resonates with how whites explain their opposition to this program: "Affirmative action [*draws out the words*], I guess I would say I'm against because I believe you should have the equal opportunity not just be given something just because of your race. I think it's just for equal opportunity." However, Irma's stand on affirmative action was more complex than this answer suggests. For instance, Irma believes discrimination is an everyday matter and she provided personal examples. When asked, "Have you yourself experienced that type of discrimination," she said, "[*answers immediately*] Oh yeah, umhum." At the interviewer's request, Irma elaborated about her personal encounters with discrimination: "Um, we've experienced discrimination in our neighborhoods growing up as kids walking down the street. Police officers were, you know, call you names, you know, the white race would call you names, throw chocolate milk at you." Consistent with this answer, Irma supported the decision of the hypothetical ABZ company, described as 97 percent white, to hire a black over a white candidate to redress past discrimination. And when she was asked, "What do you say to those who think that this is preferential treatment?" Irma replied,

> We say some blacks take so much discrimination that sometimes, I guess, we deserve a break. But I still think that given, put on the same playing field and same rules and same kind of scores and everything like that, whoever gets the highest scores should be able to fill that position.

Irma realizes that "blacks take so much discrimination," but hopes to live in a society where race does not matter in hiring decisions. Yet, since

Irma realizes that employers are not color blind; when asked why she thought the hypothetical company in the question was 97 percent white, she suggested, "Probably 'cause they wanted to keep it like that."

School and Residential Segregation

In contrast to the issue of affirmative action, abstract liberalism had a profound influence on how blacks interpreted segregation. Although a large number of blacks blamed the government, whites, or racism for residential segregation (seven of seventeen) and a majority blamed them for school segregation (twelve of seventeen) and demanded school equality (in funding and otherwise), blacks' views were not monolithic. Four blacks believed school or residential segregation was "natural," three that blacks had something to do with residential segregation or that it was "no one's fault," and two that racial segregation was not a problem. More significantly, six blacks used the abstract liberalism frame directly to account for school or residential segregation. (Note that the numbers do not add up here because some respondents blamed whites for segregation and still used the abstract liberalism frame or claimed that blacks had something to do with it too.)

First, let me provide one example of how *most* blacks answered the questions on residential and school segregation. Latasha, a self-employed nail polisher in her late twenties, blamed government for the lack of school integration. She pointed out that whereas schools in the suburbs "might get $2,500 per child," public schools in Detroit city "only get $1,000 per child." She asserted in her discussion on busing that "the problem you come about education, it's the money, that's what the main thing is, is the money with the kids." Latasha's concern with the limited funding received by inner-city schools was echoed by most blacks.

Latasha aspires to live in a society where race does not affect people's residential choices, or in her words, "You shouldn't have to single yourself to this area or single yourself to that area because you're [of a] different race." However, because Latasha realizes discrimination has not disappeared in America, her color-blind dream is not like that of whites. After stating her hope for a race-neutral housing market, for example, Latasha acknowledged of race that *"sometimes it is"* a factor. More specifically, Latasha commented she has experienced discrimination herself while shopping in downtown Detroit. Therefore, she supported government intervention to guarantee blacks access to all neighborhoods and programs to improve the neighborhoods where most blacks live.

Although most blacks blame whites or the government for the high level of segregation in the United States, their views are more mixed and contradictory. For example, Tyrone, an unemployed man in his early forties, supported school and residential integration. Tyrone stated his support for residential integration, a choice supported by 62 percent of blacks in the survey, as follows: "I think all the neighborhoods should be mixed. Then every—then there wouldn't be no concept of how different people are. They would know how each race would be." However, Tyrone opposed government intervention to guarantee residential integration: "Well, you can't tell people where [to] live. They got to pay for their own house, so people are going to live where they want to live. So you can't do that." Tyrone used the abstract liberalism frame ("You can't tell people where to live" and "They got to pay for their own house") to oppose doing anything about one of the central factors behind blacks' contemporary plight in America.[7] Interestingly, Tyrone, as I will show below, was a strong supporter of government intervention on many other racial matters.

Tyrone's contradictory position on this issue was not unique. For example, Mark, a bus driver in his thirties, recognized the role of white violence in the maintenance of school segregation. Yet he opposed government intervention to increase residential integration:

No more than if blacks or whites attempt to integrate an area and are faced with, are faced with . . . [*Mark whispers to himself: "I can't think of the word"*] aggression when attempting to do so. And I can't say necessarily the federal government, but on a local level, they should be afforded every protection or opportunity that they deserve and that is their right.

Mark's answer, particularly his insistence on governmental intervention to guarantee individuals' access to housing markets, is almost verbatim the standard answer offered by most whites to this question.

One good example of how abstract liberalism has blurred blacks' views on some issues was provided by Nel, a retired janitor in her early seventies who thought racism was an important force behind neighborhood segregation. However, Nel believed blacks were partly responsible for this situation:

Well, [the] only thing I can say is, I believe the whites don't want to live around blacks and some of the blacks don't want to live around the whites. It is because they have, well, they have a chip on their shoulder. I think a neighborhood is much better when it's mixed, you know. We got the little thing that's racism. That's what causes a lot of this, too, between black and white.

The consequence of interpreting neighborhood segregation as the outcome of people's choices ("some blacks don't want to live around the whites") is that Nel did not see any role for government to help remedy this situation.[8] Hence Nel stated in a pessimistic manner the following about the prospects of the government redressing residential segregation in America: "They go [*laughs*] ah, if they were right it would be good if they could do something about it, but I don't see much [they can do]."

Finally, one extreme example of blacks' reliance on abstract liberalism to explain segregation is Carla, an executive secretary in her forties. She believed that school segregation was a matter of choice:

> I think it's everybody's fault except for the government. White people and black people choose to put their children in [the] school that they wanted them to be into and a lot of time you go into a school and they say, "There's a lot of black people enrolled and I'm going to send you to this one," or, "It's more white people here than black so I'm going to send you to this one." So it's more so the parents' fault.

For Carla, neighborhood segregation is the product of people's choices. Therefore, she does not believe anything can be done about it. She says of the prospects of changing the situation, "Nothing, I mean, nothing as far as showing anybody anything or telling anyone anything. They will only do what they want to do so you can tell them and stress it but if they choose not to, they won't."

Cultural Racism and Blacks

Whites' cultural explanation of blacks' standing in America affected directly only a few blacks (three of seventeen). The typical black respondent argued this is a ruse used by whites to hide their role in blacks' contemporary situation. For example, Jimmy, a social worker in his forties, explained blacks' lower standing compared to whites as follows:

> Because the whites are in the majority and all and they're in a position of power. They got the wealth, they do the hiring, they [are] the employers opposed to the employees. They—we have the last hired, the first fired, and we get the lowest jobs and those [are] the things that perpetuate those situations and all.

Another example of blacks' typical responses to this question is Trisha, a homemaker in her early forties: "I wouldn't say they lazy. I think they just say you lazy 'cause you black. But I don't think they is. They just don't want to give them a chance to prove themselves that they can achieve more."

Despite the fact that few blacks bought completely this cultural explanation, this *bounded* the way many blacks discuss issues such as discrimination or the specific charge that they are lazy. The direct and indirect influence of this cultural frame in the interviews did not come as a total surprise, since in the survey a significant proportion of blacks agreed with many stereotypes about blacks. For instance, 32 percent of blacks agreed with the proposition that blacks are "violent," 32 percent with the idea that blacks are "lazy," and 30 percent with the notion that blacks are "welfare-dependent" (50 percent, 20 percent, and 53 percent of whites agreed with these stereotypes, respectively).

The two examples below illustrate how this frame has bounded blacks' views. First is Vonda, a homemaker in her late fifties with very little education. She explained blacks' lower standing compared to whites in the following way: "Ah. [*Eight-second pause*] I don't know, I don't know how to answer that one. Maybe if they get off their butts and get an education like white, I don't know. Maybe that's it."

When asked specifically if she believes blacks are worse off than whites because they are lazy, Vonda stated, *"Yeah, I think they probably more and more lazy than white are."* Although Vonda's answer sounds much like those of whites on this issue, it is important to point out that she agreed with the majority of blacks on most of the other issues.

Next is Regina, a homemaker in her early fifties who shared most positions on race issues with the majority of blacks in the sample. Yet, the cultural theme framed the way she explained why blacks are worse off than whites in this country:

> Well, I don't think they [lack] the proper, you know, things to succeed, but the ones that wants to have, they can have. But it's just some don't want to have anything. They can't blame it on other person, *which I don't.* I don't blame it on anyone 'cause I don't have anything. I blame it on myself 'cause I think I should have did better when I was coming up and got a better education.

Nevertheless, Regina, as most blacks, believes discrimination is important and stated without hesitation and with emphasis that being white is still an *"Advantage!"* When she was asked, "Why?" Regina replied, "Because of they *color.*" In her responses to the questions on discrimination, Regina said blacks experience "a lot of discrimination" and that the reason why blacks have a lower standing than whites is because "they don't have the education that they should have."

There are two significant things to underscore about Vonda's and Regina's answers. First, both accept the cultural premise to explain blacks' status in America (laziness is a central reason why blacks are behind whites in this country) although Regina limits it to some blacks. The second point is that, as most blacks, both of these respondents believe discrimination is a central factor behind blacks' current standing in America. Their puzzling stance (believing that blacks are lazy but that discrimination is central) exemplifies how color-blind racism has affected some blacks on central racial matters.

Naturalization of Racial Matters and Blacks

Although blacks do not have a cohesive view on segregation, their explanations of why segregation exists are different from those of whites. Most blacks point out that whites have something to do with segregation or that whites do not want to live or share resources with blacks. For example, Jimmy, the social worker cited above, said about school segregation:

> Yeah, I think the mixing of the races in the school, to me, is probably the whites' fault, to me. And, if it's a better school, and blacks try to go there and all, I think they are not really welcome and given an opportunity to [develop] and then they don't get the—In the inner city and all, it's not—the schooling the funding or whatever is not the same. If it was equal here in the black and white areas and all, they might not even want to go there. But I think this, if they, [when] they try to go to better schooling, I think they're prohibited from going there more so by whites and the government and all.

Yet, some blacks (three of seventeen) relied on the naturalization frame mixed with abstract liberalism to explain segregation. For instance, although Jimmy underscored the role of discrimination in school segregation, he attributed neighborhood segregation to natural tendencies in people:

> Well, I'm sure that people clique by choice and all. I mean whites tend to stay with whites because they're comfortable. But given, you know—I'd say if we tried to mix a little more, we might tend to get together more and all, integrate more and all, but as it stands now and all, we tend to be comfortable [with] our race and that's the way it generally goes.

Natasha, a licensed practical nurse in her early thirties, blamed the government for the low level of school integration in this country "because they make the laws." She also supported busing because it is "a good thing because you get to know about other peoples' cultures and their way of living." However, Natasha believes neighborhood segregation is the product of peoples' natural choices or, in her own words,

> I really don't [think about this situation] 'cause I move basically [*giggles*] where I can afford it. I don't think that any one race shouldn't be allowed anywhere in this world. It's a free country, so. I think they just choose to be with *their* kind. Blacks choose to live around blacks and whites choose to live around whites.

Therefore, when asked if she believes the government can play a role in remedying residential segregation, Natasha said,

> No, but I think that [there] shouldn't be any limitations on that one man, one black woman moving into an all-white neighborhood. He shouldn't get treated any different. But I know that [*lowers voice*] [I am] fantasizing [*very loudly and giggles*]. I mean, you never know, it may work out. I really don't think the government should get into it because I don't think they'd say, "OK, this is a white [*raises voice*] neighborhood," you know what I'm saying? Like I said, people tend to segregate together."

The third respondent who used the naturalization frame was Mark, the bus driver cited above. Mark believes school segregation is maintained by whites—often through violent means—to the detriment of "many bright African American students in urban areas [who do] not have the means to get to predominantly white schools to be afforded greater learning experiences." However, Mark explained neighborhood segregation as the outcome of natural tendencies in people:

> It's something that's gonna naturally occur. And both because of economic and social grievances, there are gonna be some whites that are economically better off than other whites and other blacks and they are gonna want to be along with other races. And that holds true with both blacks also.

Minimization of Racism and Blacks

Notwithstanding how color-blind racism affects blacks' understandings of various racial issues, the reality of discrimination is such that few blacks believe discrimination is no longer very significant. An overwhelming majority of blacks stated that antiblack discrimination is still central in America. In the survey questions regarding this issue, blacks' answers confirming discrimination were twenty to thirty percentage points higher than those of whites. More significantly, 61 percent of blacks, compared with only 33 percent of whites, agreed with the statement "Blacks are in the position that they are as a group because of present day discrimination."

Blacks' answers to the questions about discrimination in the in-depth interview were as strong, if not stronger, than their answers in the survey. For example, Tyrone, the unemployed man cited above, said about blacks facing discrimination,

> I think sometimes you do. 'Cause I used to work in Sterling Heights [a neighborhood in Detroit]. I used to be out their waiting on the bus, somebody

would drive by and call me a "black-ass nigger" at least three times out of the week [*laughs*] and I'm just trying to work and come home [*Interviewer: Wow!*].

Likewise, when he was asked why he thinks blacks have a lower standing than whites in America, he cited racial discrimination as a factor:

Well, 'cause who is the boss? He want to give you the worse job 'cause of the color of your skin. I been through that up in Sterling Heights. Me and Dwayne was the only two blacks in the maintenance department. Me and Dwayne got the nastiest jobs they was. They go, "Go get them they'll do it!" And they'd come get me and Dwayne. Me and Dwayne got the nastiest jobs.

Accordingly, Tyrone was a strong supporter of affirmative action, government programs for blacks, and even of reparations. He stated his support for reparations as follows:

They should get something [*raises his voice*], they should get something. They was suppose to give the black man forty acres and a mule. Where's my forty acres of land at or my money that you going to pay me for these forty acres I *was supposed to get?* You know, give me a tractor, give me some money, give me something!

Natalie, a data entry clerk in her twenties, said about whether or not blacks experience lots of discrimination, "I think some blacks do experience it." When asked to give examples, Natalie, as most blacks,[9] narrated a personal experience.

Yes, I agree with that because I have had, store [*stutters slightly*] people that work in stores follow me around [*raises her voice*] "*May I help you?*" you know, they do it in a way that you, if you weren't paying attention, you wouldn't think that they were following you but they are, and they tend to follow black people more than they do other people.

Consistent with her view on discrimination, Natalie believes blacks are worse off than whites because of "racism" and thus supported government intervention on blacks' behalf. Her response to the question on whether government should intervene on blacks' behalf was,

Yes, because they tend to have, they [*raises her voice*] have *programs* for other people who suffered past discrimination. They help like Japanese people and stuff, so why can't they help us? I mean, basically, the reason that we were discriminated against and people from Japan were discriminated against their own people by their own people, but we helped them out. Why they can't help some black people like they do them?

Other respondents narrated incidents typical of post–civil rights discrimination.[10] For example, Jimmy, the social worker cited above, said of discrimination:

> Well, I think it's real and it's true and all and if you really—it's just hard to get the evidence and put it on the table and expose it and all. But examples are like when you see a black and a white go out together to apply for an apartment and the white get told one thing and given the better break and the black being told the opposite thing and a worse break. It's just one way to expose it and all. But it is real and it does exist and it's just hard to uncover and all.

Latasha, the self-employed nail polisher cited before, answered the question about the significance of discrimination for blacks in a personal way:

> You do, you do, you really do because you have some people that just won't let it go. You know, they put on a lot of front and a lot of air and you have some people that just won't let go and some people just won't hide it. They'll slap it right in your face and do it right in front of you.

When asked if she could provide any examples, she narrated how her own supervisor avoids dealing with her directly and relegates this task to some of her white coworkers.

Thelma, a widow in her late sixties, answered the discrimination question by saying, "By whites? [*Interviewer: Or by whomever, yeah anyone.*] Yeah!" When prompted to say more on this subject, Thelma said, "Because it's like me or you go to a job and apply for a job, right. They turn us down and this white man or white female walks up there and they hire her like this. So that's discrimination right there!"

One of the scariest incidents of overt discrimination was narrated by Edward, the unemployed forty-one-year-old man cited above. As part of his explanation about the interactions he used to have with whites in jobs, he narrated the following incident:

> I even had an argument when I was hired at Cross Company, and guess what it was about? They said how violent we were and I was commenting about "Well, look, man, y'all ain't no different." And guess what? I had somebody jump up behind me—and we are in an engineering office—and he called me. And who I thought was a fairly decent person, I thought who I was on good terms with. And they started this conversation about racism, about the difference between black and white people. It wasn't me. I'm the only black person in the office. I'd exchanged my viewpoint with people in the office. He jumps up and he wasn't necessarily being insulted. He jumps us and calls me an African Nigger. He comes around the drafting board and

I coaxing him along because I'm thinking that he's not gonna do anything. But the guy swings at me and clips me in the jaw.

So far I have shown that blacks believe discrimination is salient, that it affects them personally, and that it operates in crude and subtle ways. Yet, the minimization of racism frame has affected how *some* blacks think about discrimination. For example, most whites regard discrimination *exclusively* as old-fashioned, one-on-one racist behavior by whites against minorities and, therefore, think discrimination is declining in significance. Some blacks agree with this view and do not think discrimination is important. For instance, Carla, the executive secretary mentioned above, answered the discrimination question by stating, "I don't experience ah, did you say racial discrimination? I don't experience discrimination in daily life, maybe on one or two occasions but not every day."

Other blacks who regarded discrimination as overtly racist behavior believed that only blacks who work with whites experience lots of discrimination. For example, Alma, a homemaker and part-time worker, answered the discrimination question as follows:

Well, if they are [*giggles*], I mean, that's kind of hard to say for everybody because on the average most people don't be around another race every day in order to consider discrimination. But probably a person that works on [a] mixed, you know, with whites and blacks, it's well, yeah those I've heard have the discrimination.

Yet other blacks qualified their answers ("some blacks experience discrimination, but . . .") and used the cultural and abstract liberalism frames to explain the status of blacks. For instance, Natasha, the practical nurse cited above, answered the discrimination question as follows: "I'd say [*high-pitched voice*] some probably do, they probably do. It depends on what plan in their life, where they are, besides their job, what type of job, they would get some discrimination." When pressed by the interviewer with the question, "How much do you think it affects, you know, black people, this discrimination, in their daily lives?" Natasha stated,

It don't—it [doesn't stop] anything as far as that goes, you know. You know what I am saying? You might have to deal with it, but you have to keep going. I don't think it really puts an impact on it, on your day, or inhibits anybody from doing what they want to do or being what they want to be. That's up to the individuals.

Vonda, the homemaker cited above, could not even assess whether or not discrimination affects blacks a lot: "[*Eight-second pause*] I don't know how to, you know, I don't know how to answer that one."

THE STYLE OF COLOR-BLIND RACISM AND BLACKS

I suggested in chapter 4 that the style of color blindness is oblique, indirect, subtle, and full of apparent ambivalence and even flat-out contradictions. My main finding in this section is that blacks have not been affected in any meaningful way by the style of color-blind racism. Because the influence of the style of this ideology on blacks is virtually nonexistent in some areas (racist terminology, racial projections, and diminutives), here I examine only its impact in the areas of semantic moves and rhetorical incoherence.

Semantic Moves and Blacks

Whites use a number of verbal pirouettes to avoid appearing "racist." Specifically, I argue that color blindness has a peculiar *race talk* that includes semantic moves in situations in which whites feel they may sound racist. Although some analysts might expect blacks to be as conscious of not being perceived as antiwhite as whites are of being perceived as antiblack, or that they might be as conscious as whites of being seen as having strong racial views, my findings suggest otherwise—a finding that is consistent with previous work.[11] In general, blacks call it as they see it. If they oppose interracial marriage, they are significantly less likely than whites to beat around the bush. If they do not have white friends or do not associate with whites, they say so without promoting a white acquaintance to the friend status.[12] If blacks agree or disagree with a policy, they usually state their opinion clearly. I suggest this straightforwardness reflects the fact that blacks have very little to hide—or very little to lose—in the contemporary racial order.[13] Whereas in slavery or Jim Crow, blacks had to be "stage Negroes"[14] if they wanted to survive, as a consequence of new norms, whites now have to be "stage whites." Therefore, being at the bottom of the racial order in post–civil rights America gives blacks at least the freedom to speak their minds.

An area that potentially could have made blacks defensive and brought out some rhetorical hesitation was the issue of "reverse discrimination." Nevertheless, blacks were clear in their beliefs that this idea is nonsense. Jimmy, the social worker cited above, said that whites who talk about "reverse discrimination" are "just hollerin'." Jimmy's response to a question about whether or not the decision of a hypothetical company hiring a black over a white job candidate was discriminatory against whites[15] was as follows:

> Yeah it's discriminating against whites, but in the sense that you already got
> all the power of a position and all. And it's like you're a hundred percent

and all and if I say go down to 97 percent you'll holla' you're discriminating against me and all. But, you know what I mean, you need some discrimination [*laughs*].

Although Jimmy interprets affirmative action as "discriminatory," he believes it is necessary to improve blacks' status. Malcolm, a construction worker in his forties, expressed views similar to Jimmy's and in a straightforward manner as well. For instance, when asked about his view on affirmative action, he answered "I'm for it." His response to a follow-up question asking if he thought this program was unfair to whites was, "Well, racism affects all blacks but affirmative action affects a certain percentage of whites. So you really can't compare. You know, like this, they call it anti-[*lowers his voice*] discrimination or, you know, you can't compare the two."

Although most blacks answered the questions without filtering them through the rhetorical maze of color blindness, a few answered questions using phrases similar to those of color blindness. However, I suggest these respondents, unlike whites, were not trying to buffer polemical or racist views. Instead, they were usually pointing out contradictions between the way things *ought to be* and the way things *are*. For example, Tyrone, the unemployed worker I cited before, used what could be seen as the "yes and no" move to explain his view on affirmative action.

Well one way I'm for it, one way I'm against it. Now, if everybody had equal chance, there's nothing against the color of your skin or nothing, we wouldn't need affirmative action. But by the way not giving people chances, we need it. You gotta have something, you know, to help.

Although his answer seems to include the "yes and no" move ("one way I'm for it, one way I'm against it"), Tyrone does not hesitate at all in stating that because America is not color blind, we need affirmative action ("You gotta have something to help"). By contrast, when whites used the "Yes and no, but" move, they added other phrases to signify ambivalence and insecurity (e.g., "I am not sure" or "I don't know"), even when they were making a strong case one way or the other (see chapter 3). Tyrone did not do that. Further evidence that Tyrone was not ambivalent or trying to hide his views on affirmative action discursively comes from his answer to the question about whether or not the decisions of the hypothetical company were discriminatory against whites. His answer was, "How can they discriminate against whites when the employment is 97 percent white? That's no discrimination! You got 97 percent white people and 3 percent of a different race."

In the same vein, when he was asked to explain why so many whites seem to be angry about affirmative action, Tyrone replied in a way that is consistent with his strong support for affirmative action:

> Well some of them figure out that they are not getting a fair chance. Some of them don't like it just because it's helping the blacks. But to me, you know, like I said, if we all had a fair chance, we wouldn't need affirmative action. They ought to know. See, they not black and how can they say this is what they go through? They ain't never been black. They ain't never been through what we go through.

Another semantic move that has become quite popular among whites is "Some of my best friends are black." I did not find a single black respondent who used the analogous phrase "Some of my best friends are white." Whereas whites used this phrase to inflate their associations with blacks and, occasionally, to be able to say something very negative about blacks, blacks did not resort to similar phrases to state their views about whites. For example, blacks who did not have white friends had no problem stating it. The following examples illustrate how blacks who did not have white friends described this situation. Mark, the bus driver previously cited, when questioned about whether or not he had close white friends in school, responded, "At Renaissance I didn't have any close white friends. I had some that I interacted with that were associates and acquaintances." Later in the interview, when asked if he had white friends on his current job, Mark said, "I can't say I have any friends. I have those whites that I associate with basically on the job." Natasha, the young practical nurse cited above, when asked, "Did you have any close white friends in school," replied, "Ah no, I didn't have any." Regina, the homemaker cited above, stated in no uncertain terms that she did not have white friends while growing up: "No, not down [*raises her voice*], not in Louisiana. No."

Rhetorical Incoherence and Blacks

Most whites in these studies were incoherent at some point in the interviews because of the racially sensitive nature of the subject of discussion. In contrast, when blacks were incoherent, it was because either that was their usual speech pattern or they lacked knowledge of the issue at hand. For example, whereas the topic of intermarriage led many whites to virtual muteness, blacks stated their views on this matter without much hesitation. Their behavior on this subject corresponds to the survey results. Fifty-eight percent of whites and 88 percent of blacks in the DAS survey approved of interracial marriage. However, when the question was "Suppose your own child married (a white/a black) person. Would you mind it a lot, a little, or not at all," 58 percent of whites said they would mind it "a lot" while 32 percent said they would mind it "a little," whereas 84 percent of blacks said that they would not mind it at all, a number that almost matches the 88 percent who approved of interracial unions. This suggests blacks have more consistent views on this sensitive matter and, therefore, may be less likely than whites to try to provide socially desirable answers.

Whether blacks approved of interracial marriage and would do it themselves (eight of seventeen), approved of it but would never do it themselves (seven of seventeen), approved of it but pointed out problems the couples might face (two of seventeen), or were opposed to these relationships (one of seventeen), they stated their answers in a clearer manner than white respondents (numbers add up to eighteen rather than seventeen, because the answer of one respondent fit two categories). Before proceeding with my analysis, I need to add two caveats. First, I am interested in highlighting the *form* or *style* of their answers rather than examining the ultimate meaning of their answers. Second, I must point out the asymmetric interpretation of these questions for black and white respondents.[16] Whereas for whites the question of interracial marriage seems to evoke visceral reactions based on racialized readings of black bodies, for blacks—particularly for older blacks—the question evokes a history of rejection, exclusion, and even the not well-studied social and family training among blacks of avoiding these relationships to stay out of trouble. This means that blacks' and whites' disapproval of interracial marriage means different things because the issue evokes different historical and personal circumstances and reactions.

An example of a black respondent who had no problems with interracial marriage but would not do it herself was Nel, the retired janitor cited above:

> *Interviewer*: OK, thank you. Now can you tell me, I guess the, you know, [who] were the people that you dated and married, were they—what race were they?
> *Nel*: Black [*laughs*].
> *Interviewer*: They were all black?
> *Nel*: Yeah.
> *Interviewer*: All right, thank you. Let's see, now, did you ever have any romantic interest in a white person?
> *Nel*: I never even dreamed, you know, thought of it.
> *Interviewer*: Now why is that?
> *Nel*: I don't know. You're talking 'bout like romance, no? [*unintelligible*] I really can't answer that question.

Nel's answers in this series of questions were, for the most part, very straightforward. Only on the last question, dealing with why she did not have any romantic interest in whites, did Nel not provide a satisfactory answer. However, the demeanor, tone, and rhetoric used by Nel and the other respondents to questions in this category suggest they were not trying to hide or distort their feelings and opinions on this sensitive matter.

Nel's straightforward style, for example, surfaced even when she was asked her opinion on interracial marriage. Nel's answer was a simple "I don't think there's anything wrong with it." When the interviewer asked Nel to explain this answer, she stated, "I don't see anything, really, I don't see any difference no more than the skin tone." Although this answer *could* be interpreted as a baseless one similar to that of most whites, Nel did not qualify her support for these marriages, as most whites did. Moreover, Nel added the following piece of information that bolstered the credibility of her answer: "But now I have a brother who's still [alive] and his [white] wife. And they was just so nice, you know. They lived up in Minnesota but they were nice, you know. Maybe that's why I don't think anything about it, you know."

Eight black respondents approved of interracial marriage and said they would do it themselves. Their answers to the interracial questions were similar to that of Irma, the young conservative accounting clerk previously cited:

> *Irma*: I, it doesn't matter to me. If, if the persons [are] in love, then it don't matter.
> *Interviewer*: Would you yourself have considered marrying someone from a different race?
> *Irma*: Yeah if I had, if the opportunity were, yeah I guess.

An extreme example of blacks who subscribed to this view is Carla, the executive secretary previously cited. She is also an example of how straight blacks were in answering the interracial marriage question. Her answer was, "If you like it, I love it." Asked if she would consider marrying outside her race, she said, "Yes." These answers were unusual for blacks but fit Carla's answers on this and other subjects. For example, when Carla was asked if she had ever had any romantic interest in people of other races, she said, "[I] always wanted to." And when she was asked if she had ever been interested in whites, she said, "Yes."

Black respondents who opposed interracial marriage said so without much hesitation. For instance, Joe, an electronic mechanic in his forties, opposed interracial relationships without hesitation:

> *Interviewer*: Did you ever have any white relationships?
> *Joe*: No.
> *Interviewer*: Did you ever have any romantic interest in a white person?
> *Joe*: No.
> *Interviewer*: And why would you think that is so?
> *Joe*: My preference.

Interviewer: Is your spouse the same racial background as you are?
Joe: Yes.
Interviewer: People have mixed feelings about marrying outside their race. What is your view on this delicate matter?
Joe: [*clears throat*] I feel people of the same race should stay together instead of interacting.
Interviewer: So you yourself would not consider marrying someone or would not have considered marrying someone of a different race?
Joe: I would say that. I would say that.

Joe answered all these difficult questions the same way he answered all the questions throughout the interview: in a short and precise manner.

Of all the blacks in this sample, I found only two who hesitated in a notable way on the interracial marriage question. The hesitation of one of these respondents came when the interviewer asked him a question that was not part of the interview protocol. Malcolm, the construction worker cited above, hesitated somewhat in his answer to the question "Did you think you could see yourself having a romantic interest in another black person here?" Malcolm's answer to this question was, "I probably would. I, I, if it happened like that, then I'd say either way." The interviewer posed this rather unusual question to Malcolm, a man in his forties, because he described himself as a "solitary person" but said he had dated a few women while he was in the "service" in Germany and *all of them* were white. His hesitation, then, could be attributed to the interviewer addressing a sensitive issue but on a different front: a forty-something man not involved with *any woman* (was he concerned that the interviewer was checking his sexual orientation?) or his exclusive interest in *white* women (was he concerned that the interviewer thought he was a negrophobic black?).

RACIAL STORIES OF COLOR BLINDNESS AND BLACKS

In chapter 5, I documented the salience of four color-blind story lines, namely, "The past is the past," "I didn't own any slaves," "I did not get a (job/promotion) because of a black man," and "If (ethnic groups such as Jews and Italians) have made it, how come blacks have not?" I also discussed the role that testimonies or personal stories have in the color-blind ideology. I argued that racial stories help whites seal tightly their larger color-blind fable by providing gut-level, emotional arguments to validate some important myths about race relations in America. Notwithstanding that color blindness has tainted the way blacks formulate many issues, based on my analysis of the seventeen interviews it seems that blacks are not buying into these stories in any significant way. I could not detect any influence of the latter two story lines, even among conservative black respondents, and I could detect none whatsoever of testimonies. Nevertheless, the story lines "The past is the past" and "I never owned any slaves" affected one black respondent directly and four indirectly.

The first two stories, which tend to appear together, were used directly by Carla, the conservative executive secretary. She answered the question on reparations as most whites did:

> That became [a] topic in school. I don't remember what I said but right now I feel that was so long ago that the people who are here now didn't have anything to do with it. So I don't feel it would, I mean, you can say you're sorry but it's not, it's not going to take back what happened. Therefore, I don't think it's necessary.

Although these stories and their logic affected very few blacks directly, they affected four blacks indirectly. For example, Natasha, the young practical nurse, answered the question on reparations as follows: "Yeah, I think so. But are there any of those people around? Would it go to that, to those surviving family members?"

Although Natasha supports reparations, she seems influenced by the idea that only people who were *directly* affected by slavery can demand compensation. This idea, mentioned by many white respondents, operates under the assumption that discrimination is a matter of a distant past that does not affect blacks' life chances today. If discrimination ended in the 1860s, then blacks who were affected by it are long gone and reparations and other forms of government intervention on blacks' behalf are unnecessary.

Another example of the indirect influence of these stories is Edward, the unemployed forty-one-year-old man. His answer on reparations was, "Oh bullshit, no, no! I think that America needs to think about its people now and the American people are all kind of folks." Edward exhibits the same emotion as many whites when answering this question ("Oh bullshit, no, no!") and thinks, like most whites, that the issue is helping all Americans now rather than dwelling on the past.

CONCLUSION

In this chapter I examined the extent and ways in which color-blind racism affects blacks. First, I showed that blacks, for the most part, do not subscribe wholeheartedly to the frames of color blindness. Furthermore, I pointed out that blacks have oppositional views on many important issues. For example, they believe discrimination is a central factor shaping their life chances in this country, firmly support affirmative action, and are very clear about whites' advantageous position in this society. However, I also documented that some of the frames and ideas of color blindness have had a significant *indirect* effect on blacks. For example, the frame of abstract liberalism has shaped the way many blacks explain school and residential segregation. Second, I documented that the style of color-blind racism has had a very limited impact on blacks. Whereas whites hesitate and use double-talk to state their views on racial matters, blacks state their views clearly and without much hesitation, even when the topic of discussion is interracial marriage. Finally, I suggested that only two of the four story lines of color blindness have had some impact on blacks. Although most of the impact of these stories was indirect, the fact that five of the seventeen blacks were directly or indirectly affected by these stories suggests the ideological transmission belt is working well. Thus, I regard the ideology of color blindness as the current *dominant* racial ideology because it binds whites together and blurs, shapes, and provides many of the terms of the debate for blacks.

For students of ideology my findings should not be surprising. Dominant actors (men, capitalists, whites), by virtue of their centrality in the social system and their superior resources, are able to frame the terrain of debates and influence the views of subordinated groups. Therefore, as I argued above, a dominant ideology is effective not by establishing ideological uniformity, but by providing the frames to organize difference.[17] As Nicos Poulantzas wrote about dominant class ideology,

> The dominance of [an ideology] is shown by the fact that the dominated classes live their conditions of political existence through the forms of dominant political discourse: this means that often they live *even their revolt* against domination of the system within the frame of reference of the dominant legitimacy.[18]

Women and workers, for example, may have views that are different from those of men and capitalists, but they share enough of their views and ideas, and more important, the *terrain* of political discourse, so that even their challenges to patriarchy and capitalism fall within the limits of what is "legitimate" for men and capitalists. Women and workers may demand "equal opportunity"—a demand that does not subvert the parameters of gender or class rule—but they are less likely to struggle for proportional representation and rewards in all social networks and institutions or for wealth redistribution.

What is the significance of my findings? On the one hand, my findings reveal in some detail the precise way in which blacks disagree with whites on central racial issues of our time. For example, unlike whites, blacks realize that racism is structural and that lack of power and differential access to rewards is at the heart of America's racial situation. Therefore, they strongly support programs such as affirmative action, despite the relentless ideological campaign against this program. On this, I concur with those[19] who claim that blacks and whites have different views on most racial issues. On the other hand, my findings reveal quite clearly that blacks are influenced *directly* (e.g., the cultural rationale and naturalization of racial matters) and *indirectly* (e.g., the free-market rationale and laissez-faire racism) by the frames of color blindness. For example, although one would expect blacks to have a strong tendency against the "culture of poverty" concept, I found that too many buy into substantial parts of this argument. This ideological infiltration of the frames of color blindness into blacks' political consciousness hinders the development of an all-out oppositional ideology or "utopia"[20] to fight contemporary white supremacy. Thus, because so many blacks are swayed by elements of color blindness, the struggle against color-blind racism will have to be waged not only against color-blind whites, who cannot see the centrality of race in America, but also against the many *slightly* color-blind blacks.

One burning question that many readers may have is whether blacks are as "racist" as whites. To properly answer this question, I need to go back to the theoretical framework that anchors this book: the racialized social-system framework (see chapter 1). My concern has been describing the dominant racial ideology of the post–civil rights era in detail and exploring how it affects whites and blacks. In this process, I have avoided moralizing the analysis (attempting to identify "good" and "bad" people). My overall findings are that *most* whites believe this new ideology wholeheartedly and rely on its various elements to articulate their views on racial matters and that a significant number of blacks are indirectly affected by this ideology and use some elements of it, too.

But I do not want to avoid what may be the real question for some readers: are blacks as "racist" (meaning antiwhite) as whites (meaning antiblack)? This question, which was formulated by some white respondents in my studies, has received some legitimacy in liberal and radical circles by the position articulated by Michael Omi and Howard Winant in the 1994 edition of their important book, *Racial Formation in the United States.*[21] In this book, Omi and Winant argue racism amounts to any practice that *"creates or reproduces structures of domination based on essentialist categories of race."*[22] Based on this criterion, they conclude blacks can be "racist," too, and that, in fact, some are. From the racialized social system framework vantage point I have developed, the answer to this question is different. First, the question needs to be rephrased from "are blacks as 'racist' as whites?" to "are blacks as 'prejudiced' as whites." I do so because the concept of "racism," as used by most social scientists and commentators, is grounded on methodological individualism (the separation of "racist" and "nonracist" individuals) and psychologism (assuming "racist" individuals are pathological, whereas those who are not "racist" are normal). In contrast, I have attempted to conceptualize racism as a sociopolitical concept that refers exclusively to racial ideology that glues a particular racial order. Thus, I have suggested that color-blind racism is the ideology of the "new racism" era. My answer, then, to this rephrased question is that any race (or ethnic group) can be "prejudiced" against any other race or races (e.g., blacks can be anti-Jewish and Jews can be antiblack). Regarding the matter of the degree to which blacks are antiwhite, most research suggests they are *less likely* to be antiwhite than whites are to be antiblack. In fact, the most interesting finding on prejudice research is that blacks are almost as likely as whites to believe many of the antiblack stereotypes.[23]

If the question is, "Are blacks *likely* to develop a racialized social system in the United States with blacks as the dominant race?" the answer is absolutely not. Blacks lack the power[24] (organizational capacity and resources) to carry out a nationalist program[25] to create a pro-black racial state. Blacks also lack the demographic capacity (numbers) needed to mount a revolution like blacks did in Haiti in the eighteenth century. In fact, given current changes in the racial demography of the nation (blacks are no longer the largest minority group in the nation), the most likely scenario for the future is that race relations will become Latin America–like, that is, that a new, triracial order will emerge with a pigmentocratic component to it.[26] As a Latin America–like society, any form of race-based contestation will become increasingly more difficult, which, as in Latin America, will allow white supremacy to reign supreme, hidden from public debate.

In the next chapter, I hypothesize what the future of racial stratification in the United States might look like in the future.

NOTES

1. Jennifer Hochschild, *Facing Up to the American Dream* (Princeton, N.J.: Princeton University Press, 1995).

2. Michael Dawson, *Behind the Mule: Race and Class in African American Politics* (Princeton, N.J.: Princeton University Press, 1994); Hochschild, *Facing Up*; Lee Sigelman and Susan Welch, *Black Americans' View of Racial Inequality: The Dream Deferred* (Cambridge: Cambridge University Press, 1991); Howard Schuman et al., *Racial Attitudes in America* (Cambridge, Mass.: Harvard University Press, 1997).

3. On the black upper middle class, see Sharon Collins, *Black Corporate Executives: The Making and Breaking of a Black Middle Class* (Philadelphia: Temple University Press, 1997). On the black middle class, see Joe R. Feagin and Melvin Sikes, *Living with Racism: The Black Middle-Class Experience* (Boston: Beacon, 1994).

An example of work on the black working class is Lillian Rubin, *Families on the Fault Line: America's Working Class Speaks about the Family, the Economy, Race, and Ethnicity* (New York: HarperCollins, 1994). On the black working poor, see Michelle Fine and Lois Weis, *The Unknown City: Lives of Poor and Working-Class Young Adults* (Boston: Beacon, 1998). Finally, on the black underclass, see Elijah Anderson, *Streetwise* (Chicago: University of Chicago Press, 1990).

4. Examples are Joe R. Feagin, Hernán Vera, and Nikitah Imani, *The Agony of Education: Black Students at White Colleges and Universities* (New York: Routledge, 1996), or, on interracial friendship, Mary W. McCullough, *Black and White as Friends: Building Cross-Race Friendships* (Cresskill, N.J.: Hampton, 1998). Two exceptions to this trend are Robert Blauner's *Black Lives, White Lives* (Berkeley: University of California Press, 1989), and Studs Terkel's *Race: How Blacks and Whites Feel and Think about the American Obsession* (New York: Doubleday, 1993). Although these two books are exceptional examples of interview-based research with blacks, both are based on *unsystematic* samples and lack a rigorous analytical strategy.

5. Mary R. Jackman, *The Velvet Glove: Paternalism and Conflict in Gender, Class, and Race Relations* (Berkeley: University of California Press, 1994).

6. It is worthwhile to point out that blacks subscribed to traditional laissez-faire views (not race related) in the survey at rates similar to those of whites. For example, 94 percent of blacks and 95 percent of whites agreed with the statement, "Any person who is willing to work hard has a good chance of succeeding." Similarly, 59 percent of blacks and 71 percent of whites agreed with the statement, "Most people who don't get ahead should not blame the system; they have only themselves to blame." For similar findings, see Lawrence Bobo and James Kluegel, "Opposition to Race-Targeting: Self-Interest, Stratification Ideology, or Racial Attitudes?" *American Sociological Review* 58, no. 4 (1993): 443–64.

7. Douglas Massey and Nancy Denton, *American Apartheid* (Chicago: University of Chicago Press, 1993).

8. It is important to point out that blacks were significantly more likely than whites to report having friends from the other group (39 percent of blacks reported having one or more white friends, whereas only 13 percent of whites reported having one or more black friends) and to have a preference for living in integrated neighborhoods.

9. Most blacks reported personal examples of old-fashioned discrimination in stores, with coworkers, supervisors, or police, and in encounters with regular white folks.

10. See chapter 3 in Eduardo Bonilla-Silva, *White Supremacy and Racism in the Post–Civil Rights Era* (Boulder, Colo.: Rienner, 2001).

11. Blacks' straight talk on racial matters can be seen in Blauner, *Black Lives, White Lives*; Rubin, *Families on the Fault Line*; and Fine and Wise, *The Unknown City*.

12. See chapter 5. See also Tom W. Smith, "Measuring Inter-Racial Friendships: Experimental Comparisons," paper presented at the annual meeting of the American Sociological Association, August 6, 1999, in Chicago, in which he documents through survey experiments how whites inflate the number of black friends they have.

13. Based on 1998 research by Public Agenda—a nonpartisan and nonprofit public opinion research organization—with 1,600 white and black parents, the organization concluded that,

Conventional wisdom in research circles says an African American moderator is necessary to ensure forthright focus group conversations with African Americans. But one of
the earliest observations in this project was that it was far easier for a white moderator
to talk with an all-black group about race and schools than for a white moderator to
discuss these issues with an all-white group.

In the same report, the organization suggested the following about the implications of whites' silence about their true views:

But the reticence of white parents to talk explicitly means their fears and anxieties
remain beneath the surface. One consequence is that while the views of African-American parents are resolved and focused, the views of whites about race and the schools
often seem murky and ambivalent, replete with twists and turns in attitudes that are
difficult to unravel because they are sometimes hidden—sometimes not worked-
through—and rarely discussed.

See www.publicagenda.org/specials/moveon/moveon8.htm.

14. David R. Goldfield, *Black, White, and Southern: Race Relations and Southern
Culture, 1940 to the Present* (Baton Rouge: Louisiana State University Press, 1990).

15. The scenarios were varied (equal qualifications, white slightly more qualified, and decision based on past discrimination by the company) to allow examination of the strength and consistency of respondents' views on this sensitive
issue.

16. This is an interpretative problem that plagues survey research. The interpretation of the survey questions and the meaning of the answers often hinge on
the respondents' race. Thus, for example, when whites and blacks both agree that
discrimination is still important in America, they mean totally different things
(see chapter 4).

17. See William H. Sewell Jr., "The Concepts(s) of Culture," in *Beyond the Cultural Turn,* edited by Victoria E. Bonnell and Lynn Hunt, 35–61 (Berkeley: University of California Press, 1999).

18. My emphasis. Nicos Poulantzas, *Political Power and Social Classes* (London:
Verso, 1984), 223.

19. Dawson, *Behind the Mule*; Donald Kinder and Lynn Sanders, *Divided by
Color* (Chicago: University of Chicago Press, 1996).

20. Teun van Dijk, *Ideology: A Multidisciplinary Approach* (London: Sage, 1998),
182.

21. Michael Omi and Howard Winant, *Racial Formation in the United States*
(New York: Routledge, 1994). For disclosure purposes, I argue in my *White Supremacy and Racism in the Post–Civil Rights Era* that "most radical writing on race
in the 1990s has been inspired by Omi and Winant" and that "my own theory
owes heavily to their work." However, I also point out some of the serious limitations of their "racial formation" perspective. I also wish to acknowledge that
Omi and Winant are extraordinarily collegial and generous comrades and that I
am indebted to them in many ways. Yet, I disagree profoundly with them on the
matter of "black racism."

22. Omi and Winant, *Racial Formation,* 71.

23. See Lawrence Bobo and Devon Johnson, "Racial Attitudes in a Prismatic Metropolis." For a discussion of the historical roots of why whites are more likely to be antiblack than blacks are to be antiwhite, see Mia Bay, *The White Image in the Black Mind: African-American Ideas about White People, 1830–1925* (New York: Oxford University Press, 2000).

24. I also disagree with Omi and Winant's assertion that blacks have "power." If by power they mean the capacity to enact their racial interest into concrete policies and crystallize it into institutions, blacks have very little power and seem to be losing the little they have by the day. As a matter of fact, given the new racial demography of the nation, blacks are likely to continue losing power in the future. On the concept of power, see Keith Dowding, *Power* (Minneapolis: University of Minnesota Press, 1996), and the always-indispensable Nicos Poulantzas, *Political Power and Social Classes*.

25. However, and as one would expect from any oppressed people, blacks have had nationalist tendencies from slavery until today. For a historical analysis of black nationalist forces and programs in the twentieth century, see Roderick Bush, *We Are Not What We Seem: Black Nationalism and Class Struggle in the American Century* (New York: New York University Press, 1999). For a recent analysis of nationalism among blacks, see Michael C. Dawson, *Black Visions: The Roots of Contemporary African-American Political Ideologies* (Chicago: University of Chicago Press, 2001).

26. Eduardo Bonilla-Silva and Karen Glover, "'We Are All Americans': The Latin Americanization of Race Relations in the USA," in *The Changing Terrain of Race and Ethnicity: Theory, Methods and Public Policy,* edited by Amanda E. Lewis and Maria Krysan (New York: Russell Sage Foundation, 2004).

9

⤳

E Pluribus Unum, or the Same Old Perfume in a New Bottle?

On the Future of Racial Stratification in the United States

WHAT DOES ALL THE RACIAL NOISE MEAN?
A SKETCH OF THINGS TO COME

Latinos are now officially the largest minority group in the nation. According to the Census Bureau, while blacks comprise 13 percent of the U.S. population, Latinos are 16.3 percent.[1] This Latino population explosion, generated by immigration, has already created a number of visible fractures in the United States that seem to be shifting the racial terrain. In academic circles, for instance, conservative scholars have begun attacking the new racial demography as devastating for the future of the country. An example of these scholars is Harvard's political scientist, Samuel Huntington, who in his recent book, *Who Are We? The Challenges to America's National Identity,* argued that Latino immigration threatens Anglo-Saxon American culture as well as the political integrity of the country.[2] And politicians in both parties as well as prominent newscasters such as Lou Dobbs—since 2003 or so, he has addressed every night the topic of illegal immigration in his show *Lou Dobbs Tonight* in his nightly segment "Broken Borders"[3] and almost all *Fox News* commentators (e.g., Brit Hume, Tony Snow, Sean Hannity, John Gibson, and Fox's most vitriolic newscaster, Bill O'Reilly) articulate and inflame the anti-immigrant fears for the wider public.

In addition to the Latino population explosion, other trends have emerged that challenge our traditional biracial divide (white vs. non-white) and, more specifically, our black-white understanding of racial politics in the United States. For example, another group that has gained visibility in our racial discussions is Asian Americans, partly because of their demographic gains (they are now 5 percent of the population), partly because as a group, they are perceived as doing very well economically and educationally, and, more importantly, partly because they are still viewed by most Americans through the lenses of developments in South East Asia.[4] On this last point, the commercial rise of Japan and, particularly, of China, has generated a fear of the East that can be seen in movies (e.g., *Red Corner* [1997], *Mulan* [1998], etc.), political scandals, and in the way China is discussed almost every night in the news.[5]

Yet another illustration of the changing racial terrain in the United States is our recent national discussion on the status of "multiracial" and "biracial" people.[6] Two events shaped our collective engagement on these matters over the last ten years. First, phenom golfer Tiger Woods, son of a black father and a Tai mother, made a public statement suggesting he was not black but rather "Cablanasian" (a mixture of Caucasian, black, and Asian). This led to a furious public debate on what it means to be "black" or "mixed" and whether or not people could claim a racial identity other than those already inscribed in our racial pentagram. (Who had ever heard of such a thing as a Cablanasian?) Second, the struggle by people in the multiracial movement[7] to force changes in the way the Census Bureau gathered racial data—specifically, to include a multiracial category, which coincided with efforts by Republican politicians to end the collection of racial data altogether—ended with the addition of the "More than one race" item in the 2000 Census schedule.

Finally, and related to some of the developments mentioned above, the rate of interracial dating and marriage between Latinos and whites and Asians and whites has skyrocketed.[8] In general, interracial marriage, which accounted for less than 1 percent of all marriages in the country, accounts today for 5.4 percent. Many demographers and a few public intellectuals have heralded this development as signifying the erosion of racial boundaries and maybe pointing the way out of our national racial quagmire.[9]

Thus, as I write this revised edition, we all ponder about what will be the future of race in America. How will the Latino population explosion affect the three-hundred-year-old racial drama of the country? Will Latinos replace blacks as the racial boogeyman[10] or will they become white, as some analysts have suggested?[11] And how will Asians fit in the emerging racial totem pole? Will they be treated as white or vilified as the enemies within, as happened to Japanese Americans during World War II? Or do all these trends signify that I have wasted my time (and your money) writing this book because, as some public commentators have argued, we live in the time of "the end of racism" or, at least, of "the declining significance of race"?[12]

These are the kinds of issues that prompted me to write this chapter. My basic claim, unlike the romantic predictions of assimilationists[13] or the racialized pessimism of Anglo-Saxonists such as Huntington, is that all this reshuffling denotes that the biracial order typical of the United States, which was the exception in the world racial system,[14] is evolving into a complex and loosely organized triracial stratification system similar to that of many Latin American and Caribbean nations. Specifically, I contend that the emerging triracial system will be comprised of "whites" at the top, an intermediary group of "honorary whites"—similar to the coloreds in South Africa during formal apartheid, and a nonwhite group or the "collective black" at the bottom. I sketch in figure 9.1 what these three groups may look like. I hypothesize that the white group will include "traditional" whites, new "white" immigrants and, in the near future, totally assimilated white Latinos (e.g., former secretary of education Lauro Cabazos, the football coach of the University of Wisconsin Barry Alvarez, and actors such as Martin Sheen), lighter-skinned multiracials, and other subgroups; the intermediate racial group or honorary whites will comprise most light-skinned Latinos (e.g., most Cubans and segments of the Mexican and Puerto Rican communities), Japanese Americans, Korean Americans, Asian Indians, Chinese Americans, and most Middle Eastern Americans; and, finally, that the collective black group will include blacks, dark-skinned Latinos, Vietnamese, Cambodians, Filipinos, and Laotians.

As a triracial system (or Latin- or Caribbean-like racial order), race conflict will be buffered by the intermediate group, much like class conflict is when the class structure includes a large middle class. Furthermore, color gradations, which have always been important matters of within-group differentiation, will become more salient factors of stratification. Lastly, Americans, like people in complex racial stratification orders, will begin making nationalists appeals ("We are all Americans"), decry their racial past, and claim they are "beyond race."

This new order, I argue, will be apparently more pluralistic and exhibit more racial fluidity than the order it is replacing. However, this new system will serve as a formidable fortress for white supremacy. Its "we are beyond race" lyrics and color-blind music will drown the voices of those fighting for racial equality ("Why continue talking about race and racism when we are all Americans?") and may even eclipse the space for talking about race altogether. Hence, in this emerging Latin America–like America, racial inequality will remain—and may even increase—yet there will be a restricted space to fight it.

I must state a few important caveats before I proceed any further. First, figure 9.1 is heuristic rather than definitive and thus is included here just as a guide of how I think the various ethnic groups will line up in the

"Whites"
Whites
  New whites (Russians, Albanians, etc.)
  Assimilated white Latinos
  Some multiracials
  Assimilated (urban) Native Americans
  A few Asian-origin people

"Honorary Whites"
  Light-skinned Latinos
  Japanese Americans
  Korean Americans
  Asian Indians
  Chinese Americans
  Middle Eastern Americans
  Most multiracials

"Collective Black"
  Vietnamese Americans
  Filipino Americans
  Hmong Americans
  Laotian Americans
  Dark-skinned Latinos
  Blacks
  New West Indian and African immigrants
  Reservation-bound Native Americans

Figure 9.1.   Preliminary Map of Triracial Order in the USA

emerging racial order. I acknowledge, however, that the position of some groups may change (e.g., Chinese Americans, Asian Indians, and, particularly, Arab Americans—on this, please see my comments at the end of the chapter), that the map is not inclusive of all the groups in the United States (for instance, Samoans, Micronesians, and Eskimos, among others, are not in the map), that it is *possible* that more than three racial strata emerge, and that at this early stage of this project and given some serious data limitations, some groups may end up in a different racial strata altogether (for example, Filipinos may become "honorary whites" rather than another group in the "collective black" strata). More significantly, if my Latin Americanization thesis is accurate, there will be categorical porosity as well as "pigmentocracy" making the map useful for group- rather than individual-level predictions. The former refers to individual members of a racial strata moving up (or down) the stratification system (e.g., a light-skin middle-class black person marrying a white woman and moving to the "honorary white" strata) and the latter refers to the rank ordering of groups and members of groups according to phenotype and cultural characteristics (e.g., Filipinos being at the top of the "collective black" given their high level of education and income as well as high rate of interracial marriage with whites). Lastly, since I am predicting the future, I truly hope that we can prevent the crystallization of this racial order altogether or at least derail it partially.

In this chapter I proceed as follows. First, since I am suggesting the United States is becoming Latin America–like, I enumerate succinctly a few of the major features of racial stratification in Latin America. Second, I explain why I contend a triracial system is emerging. Third, I examine a few available objective (e.g., data on income and education), subjective (e.g., racial attitudes and racial self-classification), and social interaction indicators (intermarriage and residential choices) to see if they fit the expectations of my Latin Americanization thesis. Lastly, I discuss the implications of this new order for the racial politics of the future.

HOW RACIAL STRATIFICATION WORKS IN THE AMERICAS

Despite claims of nonracialism ("We don't have racism here. That is an American problem."), racial minorities in Latin American countries tend to be worse off, comparatively speaking, than racial minorities in Western nations. Yet, few revolts in the twentieth and twenty-first centuries in Latin America have had a clear racial component (important exceptions such as the Zapatista movement notwithstanding). This apparent contradiction is explained by the fact that race has very limited "discursive space" in Latin America and, in order for people to struggle along an axis of social division, that axis must be visible and real to them. "Prejudice"— Latin Americans do not talk about "racism"—is regarded as a legacy from slavery and colonialism and "racial" inequality (again, Latin Americans and Caribbeans do not believe race is part of their social reality) is regarded as the product of class dynamics.

Since examining the long history that produced this state of affairs is beyond the scope of this chapter, I just sketch[15] six central features of Latin American (and Caribbean) racial stratification.

1. Miscegenation or "Mestizaje"

Latin American nation-states, with a few exceptions, are thoroughly racially mixed. Racial mixing, however, in no way challenged white supremacy in colonial or postcolonial Latin America since (1) the mixing was between white men and Indian or black women, maintaining the race/gender order in place; (2) the men were fundamentally poor and/or working class, which helped maintain the race/class order in place; (3) the mixing followed a racially hierarchical pattern with "whitening" as a goal; and (4) marriages among people in the three main racial groups were (and still are) mostly homogamous (among people from the same racial strata).

2. Plural Racial Stratification Systems

Although Portuguese and Spanish colonial states wanted to create "two societies," the demographic realities of colonial life superseded their wishes. Because most colonial outposts attracted very few Europeans, these societies developed intermediate groups of "browns," "pardos," or "mestizos" that buffered sociopolitical conflicts. Even though these groups did not achieve the status of "white" anywhere, they nonetheless had a better status than the Indian or black masses and, therefore, developed their own distinct interest.

3. Colorism or Pigmentocracy

There is yet another layer of complexity in Latin American racial stratification systems. The plural racial strata are also internally stratified by "color" (in quotation marks because in addition to skin tone, phenotype, hair texture, eye color, culture and education, and class matter in the racial classification of individuals in Latin America), a phenomenon known in the literature as pigmentocracy or colorism.

4. *"Blanqueamiento"*: Whitening as Ideology and Practice

"Blanqueamiento" (whitening) has been treated in the Latin American literature as an ideology. However, *blanqueamiento* was and is a real economic, political, and personal process. At the personal level, families can be colored or even racially divided and exhibit differential treatment toward dark-skinned members. Thus, rather than showing Latin American racial flexibility, racial mixing oriented by the goal of whitening shows the effectiveness of the logic of white supremacy.

5. National Ideology of "Mestizaje"

National independence in Latin America meant, among other things, silencing any discussion about race and forging the myth of national unity. After years of attempting to unite Latin American nations under the banner of *Hispanidad*, a more formidable ideology crystallized: the ideology of *mestizaje* (racial mixing). Although Latin American writers and politicians have praised the virtues of *mestizaje*, this notion has worked as an ideology to help keep race below the social radar and better safeguard white power.

6. "We Are All 'Latinoamericanos'": Race as Nationality/Culture

Most Latin Americans refuse to identify themselves in racial terms. Instead, they prefer to use national (or cultural) descriptors such as "I am Puerto Rican or Brazilian." This behavior is cited as an example of the fluidity of race in Latin America. However, defining the nation and the "people" as the "fusion of cultures" (even though the fusion is viewed in a Eurocentric manner), is the logical outcome of all of the factors mentioned above. Nationalist statements such as "We are all Puerto Ricans" are not evidence of nonracialism, but the direct manifestation of the racial stratification peculiar to Latin America.

WHY LATIN AMERICANIZATION NOW?

What are the reasons behind racial stratification becoming Latin America–like at this point in our history? The reasons, in my estimation, are multiple. First, as I discussed above, the demography of the nation is changing. Racial minorities are now about 30 percent of the population and, as population projections suggest, may become the numeric majority by the year 2050. This rapid darkening of America is creating a situation similar to that of Puerto Rico, Cuba, or Venezuela in the sixteenth and seventeenth centuries, or Argentina, Chile, and Uruguay in the late eighteenth and early nineteenth centuries. In both historical periods, the elites realized their countries were becoming majority "black" (or "nonwhite") and devised a number of strategies (unsuccessful in the former and successful in the latter) to whiten their population.[16] Although whitening the population through immigration or by classifying many newcomers as white is a possible solution to the new American demography, for reasons discussed below, I do not think this is likely.[17] Hence, a more plausible accommodation to the new racial reality is to (1) create an intermediate racial group to buffer racial conflict,[18] (2) allow some newcomers into the white racial strata, and (3) incorporate most immigrants into the collective black strata.

Second, as part of the tremendous reorganization that transpired in America in the post–civil rights era, a new kinder and gentler white supremacy emerged, which I labeled elsewhere as the "new racism" (for a quick summary of my argument, see chapter 1 in this book or chapter 4 in my 2001 book *White Supremacy and Racism in the Post–Civil Rights Era*). In post–civil rights America the maintenance of systemic white privilege is accomplished socially, economically, and politically through institutional, covert, and apparently nonracial practices. Whether in banks or universities, in stores or housing markets, smiling discrimination tends to be the order of the day. This "softer" kind of discrimination is in line with the way discrimination operates in Latin America and will ease the transition to a discourse of "racism is declining in significance here."

This new white supremacy has also produced an accompanying ideology that rings Latin America all over: the ideology of color-blind racism. This ideology, as it is the norm all over Latin America, denies the salience of race, scorns those who talk about race, and increasingly proclaims that "We are all Americans." (This is the main subject of this book and thus needs little discussion here.)

Third, race relations have become globalized. The once almost all-white Western nations have now "interiorized the other."[19] The new world systemic need for capital accumulation has led to the incorporation of "dark" foreigners as "guest workers" and even as permanent workers. Thus today European nations have racial minorities in their midst who are progressively becoming an underclass,[20] have developed an internal "racial structure" (see chapter 1) to maintain white power, and have a curious racial ideology that combines ethnonationalism with a race-blind ideology similar to the color-blind racism of the United States today.[21]

This new global racial reality, I believe, will reinforce the Latin Americanization trend in the United States as versions of color-blind racism will become prevalent in most Western nations. Furthermore, as many formerly almost-all-white Western countries (e.g., Germany, France, England, etc.) become more and more diverse, the Latin American model of racial stratification may surface in these societies too.

Fourth, the convergence of the political and ideological actions of the Republican Party, conservative commentators and activists, and the so-called multiracial movement has created the space for the radical transformation of the way we gather racial data in America. One possible outcome of the Census Bureau categorical back-and-forth on racial and ethnic classifications is either the dilution of racial data or the elimination of race as an official category. At this point, Ward Connerly and his cronies lost the first round in their California Racial Privacy, but I believe they may be successful in other states and, given the changes in the Supreme Court, their efforts may bear fruit in the near future.

If race disappears as a category of official division, as it has in most of the world, this will facilitate the emergence of a plural racial order where the groups exist in *practice* but are not officially recognized—and anyone trying to address racial divisions is likely to be chided for racializing the population. This is, as I have argued elsewhere, the secret of race in Latin America.[22]

Lastly, the attack on affirmative action, which is part of what Stephen Steinberg (1995) has labeled as the "racial retreat,"[23] is the clarion call signaling the end of race-based social policy in the United States. The recent Supreme Court *Grutter v. Bollinger* decision, hailed by some observers as a victory, is at best a weak victory because it allows for a "narrowly tailored" employment of race in college admissions, imposes an artificial twenty-five-year deadline for the program, and encourages a monumental case-by-case analysis for admitting students that is likely to create chaos and push institutions into making admissions decisions based on test scores. Again, this trend reinforces the trend toward Latin Americanization because the elimination of race-based social policy is, among other things, predicated on the notion that race no longer affects the life chances of Americans. Nevertheless, as in Latin America, we may eliminate race by decree and maintain—or even see an increase in—the degree of racial inequality.

A LOOK AT THE DATA

To recapitulate, I contend that because of a number of important demographic, sociopolitical, and international changes, the United States is developing a more complex system of racial stratification that resembles those typical of Latin American societies. I suggest three racial strata will develop, namely, whites, honorary whites, and the collective black and that "phenotype" will be a central factor determining where groups and members of racial and ethnic groups will fit—lighter people at the top, medium in the middle, and dark at the bottom.[24] Although I posit that Latin Americanization will not fully materialize for several more decades, in the following sections I provide a cursory analysis of various objective, subjective, and social interaction indicators to see if the trends support my thesis.

A. Objective Standing of "Whites," "Honorary Whites," and "Blacks"

If Latin Americanization is happening in the United States, gaps in income, poverty rates, education, and occupational standing between whites, honorary whites, and the collective black should be developing. The available data suggests this is the case. In terms of income, as table 9.1 shows, "white" Latinos (Argentines, Chileans, Costa Ricans, and Cubans) are doing much better than dark-skinned Latinos (Mexicans, Puerto Ricans, etc.). The apparent exceptions in table 9.1 (Bolivians and Panamanians) are examples of self-selection among these immigrant groups. For example, four of the largest ten concentrations of Bolivians in the United States are in Virginia, a state with just 7.2 percent Latinos (Census Bureau 2000).[25]

Table 9.1 also shows that Asians exhibit a pattern similar to that of Latinos. Hence, a severe income gap is emerging between groups I label as honorary white Asians (Japanese, Koreans, Filipinos, and Chinese) and those I suggest belong to the collective black (Vietnamese, Cambodian, Hmong, and Laotians).

The analysis of data on education, occupations, and unemployment reveals similar patterns (for tables on these matters, see the chapter referred to in footnote 15). That is, light-skinned Latinos and elite Asians do significantly better than their darker brethren in all these areas.

B. Subjective Standing of Racial Strata

Social psychologists have amply demonstrated that it takes very little for groups to form, develop a common view, and adjudicate status positions to nominal characteristics.[26] Thus, it should not be surprising if gaps in income, occupational status, education, and employment among these various strata are leading to early stages of group formation. For example, members of the groups I label as likely to become honorary white may be classifying themselves as "white" and believing they are different (better) than those I argue likely to comprise the collective black category. If this is happening, members of these groups should also be in the process of

Table 9.1. Mean Per Capita Income[1] ($) of Selected Asian and Latino Ethnic Groups, 2000

Latinos	Mean Income	Asian Americans	Mean Income
Mexicans	9,467.30	Chinese	20,728.54
Puerto Ricans	11,314.95	Japanese	23,786.13
Cubans	16,741.89	Koreans	16,976.19
Guatemalans	11,178.60	Asian Indians	25,682.15
Salvadorans	11,371.92	Filipinos	19,051.53
Costa Ricans	14,226.92	Taiwanese	22,998.05
Panamanians	16,181.20	Hmong	5,175.34
Argentines	23,589.99	Vietnamese	14,306.74
Chileans	18,272.04	Cambodians	8,680.48
Bolivians	16,322.53	Laotians	10,375.57
Whites	17, 968.87	Blacks	11,366.74

Source: 2000 PUMS 5% Sample.

[1] I use per capita income because family income distorts the status of some groups as some groups have more individuals contributing toward the family income than other groups (e.g., the case of most Asian families).

developing white-like racial attitudes befitting of their new social position and differentiating (distancing) themselves from the members of the group I believe will comprise the collective black.

In line with my thesis, I expect whites to be making distinctions between honorary whites and the collective black, specifically, exhibiting a more positive outlook toward honorary whites than toward members of the collective black. Finally, if Latin Americanization is happening, I speculate that members of the collective black should exhibit a diffused and contradictory racial consciousness as blacks and Indians do throughout Latin America and the Caribbean.[27] I examine some of these matters in the following subsections.

SOCIAL IDENTITY OF HONORARY WHITES

1. Self-Reports on Race: The Case of Latinos

Historically, most Latinos have classified themselves as "white" but the proportion of Latinos who self-classify as such varies tremendously by group. Hence, as table 9.2 shows, whereas 60 percent or more of the members of the Latino groups I regard as honorary white self-classify as white, 50 percent or fewer of the members of the groups I regard as belonging to the collective black do so. As a case in point, whereas Mexicans, Dominicans, and Central Americans are very likely to report "Other" as their preferred "racial" classification, most Costa Ricans, Cubans, Chileans,

Table 9.2   Racial Self-Classification by Selected
Latin America–Origin Latino Ethnic Groups, 2000

	White	Black	Other	Native American	Asian
Dominicans	28.21	10.93	59.21	1.07	0.57
Salvadorans	41.01	0.82	56.95	0.81	0.41
Guatemalans	42.95	1.24	53.43	2.09	0.28
Hondurans	48.51	6.56	43.41	1.24	0.29
Mexicans	50.47	0.92	46.73	1.42	0.45
Puerto Ricans	52.42	7.32	38.85	0.64	0.77
Costa Ricans	64.83	5.91	28.18	0.56	0.53
Bolivians	65.52	0.32	32.79	1.32	0.05
Colombians	69.01	1.53	28.54	0.49	0.44
Venezuelans	75.89	2.58	20.56	0.36	0.60
Chileans	77.04	0.68	21.27	0.44	0.56
Cubans	88.26	4.02	7.26	0.17	0.29
Argentines	88.70	0.33	10.54	0.08	0.35

Source: 2000 PUMS 5% Sample.

and Argentines choose the "white" descriptor.[28] Hence, the data in this table seems to fit my thesis.

2. "Racial" Distinctions among Asians

Although for political matters, Asians tend to vote panethnically,[29] distinctions between native-born and foreign-born (e.g., American-born Chinese and foreign-born Chinese) and between economically successful and unsuccessful Asians are developing. In fact, according to various analysts, given the tremendous diversity of experiences among Asian Americans "all talk of Asian panethnicity should now be abandoned as useless speculation."[30] Leland Saito (1998), in his *Race and Politics*, points out that many Asians have reacted to the "Asian flack" they are experiencing with the rise in Asian immigration by fleeing the cities of immigration, disidentifying from new Asians, and invoking the image of the "good immigrant." In some communities, this has led to older, assimilated segments of a community to dissociate from recent migrants. For example, a Nisei returning to his community after years of overseas military service, told his dad the following about the city's new demography: "Goddamn dad, where the hell did all these Chinese come from? Shit, this isn't even our town anymore."[31]

To be clear, my point is not that Asian Americans have not engaged in coalition politics and, in various locations, participated in concerted efforts to elect Asian American candidates. My point instead is that the group labeled "Asian Americans" is profoundly divided along many axes and thus I forecast that many of those already existing divisions will be racialized by whites (e.g., sexploitation of Asian women by lonely white men in the "Oriental bride" market) as well as by Asian Americans themselves (e.g., intra-Asian preferences seem to follow a racialized hierarchy of desire).[32]

RACIAL ATTITUDES OF VARIOUS RACIAL STRATA

1. Latinos' Racial Attitudes

Although researchers have shown that Latinos tend to hold negative views of blacks and positive views of whites,[33] the picture is more complex. Immigrant Latinos tend to have more negative views about blacks than native-born Latinos. For instance, a study of Latinos in Houston, Texas, found that 38 percent of native-born Latinos compared to 47 percent of foreign-born held negative stereotypes of blacks. This may explain why 63 percent of native-born Latinos versus 34 percent of foreign-born report frequent contact with blacks.[34]

But the incorporation of the majority of Latinos as "colonial subjects" (Puerto Ricans), refugees from wars (Central Americans), or illegal migrant workers (Mexicans) has foreshadowed subsequent patterns of integration into the racial order. In a similar vein, the incorporation of a minority of Latinos as "political refugees" (Cubans, Chileans, and Argentines) or as "neutral" immigrants trying to better their economic situation (Costa Rica, Colombia) has allowed them a more comfortable ride in America's racial boat. Therefore, whereas the incorporation of most Latinos in the United States has meant becoming "nonwhite," for a few it has meant becoming almost white.

Nevertheless, given that most Latinos experience discrimination in labor and housing markets as well as in schools, they quickly realize their "nonwhite" status. This leads them, as Nilda Flores-Gonzales (1999) and Suzanne Oboler (1995) have shown, to adopt a plurality of identities that signify "otherness."[35] Thus, dark-skinned Latinos are even calling themselves "black" or "Afro-Dominicans" or "Afro-Puerto Rican."[36] For example, José Ali, a Latino interviewed by Clara Rodriguez (2000) in her book *Changing Race,* stated, "By inheritance I am Hispanic. However, I identify more with blacks because to white America, if you are my color, you are a nigger. I can't change my color, and I do not wish to do so."

When asked, "Why do you see yourself as black?" he said, "Because when I was jumped by whites, I was not called 'spic,' but I was called a 'nigger.'"[37]

The identification of most Latinos as "racial others" has led them to be more likely to be pro-black than pro-white. For example, data on Latinos' racial affects toward various groups indicates that the proportion of Mexicans and Puerto Ricans who feel very warm toward blacks is much higher (about 12 percentage points for Mexicans and 14 percentage points for Puerto Ricans) than toward Asians (the readings in the "thermometer" range from 0 to 100 and the higher the "temperature" is, the more positive are the feelings toward the group in question). In contrast, the proportion of Cubans who feel very warm toward blacks is 10 to 14 percentage points *lower* than Mexicans and Puerto Ricans. Cubans are also more likely to feel very warm toward Asians than toward blacks. More fitting of my thesis, analysis of the same data in table 9.3 shows that Latinos who identify as "white" express similar empathy toward blacks and Asians, those who identify as "black" express the most positive affect toward blacks—about 20 degrees warmer toward black than toward Asians (data now shown here). Again, this finding is fitting of my thesis.

Table 9.3.   Proportion of Latinos Who Express High Affect toward Blacks and Asians

Degrees-of-Feeling Thermometer	Blacks	Asians
Mexicans		
51–74	11.9	11.8
75–100	34.3	22.2
Puerto Ricans		
51–74	11.8	9.0
75–100	39.5	25.3
Cubans		
51–74	14.5	9.9
75–100	25.1	29.9

Source: Forman, Martinez, and Bonilla-Silva, "Latinos' Perceptions of Blacks and Asians: Testing the Immigrant Hypothesis" (unpublished manuscript).

2. Asians' Racial Attitudes

Various studies have documented that Asians tend to hold antiblack and anti-Latino attitudes. For instance, a study found that Chinese residents of Los Angeles expressed negative racial attitudes toward blacks.[38] One Chinese resident stated, "Blacks in general seem to be overly lazy" and another asserted, "Blacks have a definite attitude problem."[39] Studies on Korean shopkeepers in various locales have found that over 70 percent of them hold anti-black attitudes.[40]

These general findings are confirmed in table 9.4. This table has data on the degree (in a scale running from 1 to 7) to which various racial groups subscribe to stereotypes about the intelligence and welfare dependency of other groups. The table clearly shows that Asians (in this study, Koreans, Chinese, and Japanese) are more likely than even whites to hold anti-black and anti-Latino views (for example, whereas whites score 3.79 and 3.96 for blacks and Latinos, Asians score 4.39 and 4.46). In line with this finding, they hold, comparatively speaking, more positive views about whites than Latinos and blacks.[41] Thus, as in many Latin American and Caribbean societies, members of the intermediate racial strata buffer racial matters by holding more pro-white attitudes than whites themselves.

3. The Collective Black and Whites' Racial Attitudes

After a protracted conflict over the meaning of whites' racial attitudes (for a discussion, see Bonilla-Silva and Lewis 1999), survey researchers seem to have reached an agreement: "a hierarchical racial order continues to shape all aspects of American life" (Dawson 2000, 344). Whites express/defend their social position on issues such as affirmative action and reparations, school integration and busing, neighborhood integra-

Table 9.4.   Relationship between Race/Ethnicity and Racial Stereotypes on Intelligence and Welfare Dependency of Blacks, Latinos, Asians, and Whites in Los Angeles, 1993–1994

| | Group Stereotyped | | | |
	Blacks	Latinos	Asians	Whites
Group Stereotyping				
Unintelligent?				
White	3.79	3.96	2.90	3.09
Asians	4.39	4.46	2.90	3.25
Latinos	3.93	3.57	2.74	2.87
Blacks	3.31	3.96	3.21	3.32
F-ratio	***	***	***	***
Prefer Welfare?				
White	4.22	4.08	2.30	2.48
Asians	5.10	5.08	2.52	2.93
Latinos	5.57	4.49	2.77	2.77
Blacks	4.12	4.29	2.67	2.77
F-ratio	***	***	***	***

Source: Los Angeles Study of Urban Inequality, 1993–1994.

tion, welfare reform, and even the death penalty (see Sears, Sidanius, and Bobo 2000; Tuch and Martin 1997; Bonilla-Silva 2001). Regarding how whites think about Latinos and Asians, not many researchers have separated the groups that comprise "Latinos" and "Asians" to assess if whites are making distinctions amongst them. However, the available evidence suggests whites regard Asians highly and are significantly less likely to hold Latinos in high regard.[42] Thus, when judged on a host of racial stereotypes, whites rate themselves and Asians almost identically (favorable stereotype rating) and rate negatively (at an almost equal level) both blacks and Latinos.

Bobo and Johnson also show that Latinos tend to rate blacks negatively and that blacks tend to do the same regarding Latinos. They also find that Latinos, irrespective of national ancestry, self-rate lower than whites and Asians (blacks, however, self-rate at the same level with whites and as better than Asians). This pattern seems to confirm Latin Americanization as those at the bottom in Latin America tend to exhibit a diffused rather than clear racial consciousness. My contention seems to be also bolstered by their findings that "blacks give themselves ratings that tilt in an unfavorable dimension on the traits of welfare dependency and involvement with gangs" and that "for Latinos three of the dimensions tilt in the direction of negative in-group ratings."[43]

SOCIAL INTERACTION AMONG
MEMBERS OF THE THREE RACIAL STRATA

If Latin Americanization is happening, one would expect more social (e.g., friendship, associations as neighbors, etc.) and intimate (e.g., marriage) contact between whites and members of the groups I label honorary white than between whites (and honorary whites) and members of the collective black. A cursory analysis of the available data suggests this is in fact the case.

1. Interracial Marriage

Although most marriages in America are still intraracial, the rates vary substantially by group. Whereas 93 percent of whites and blacks marry within-group, 70 percent of Latinos and Asians do so, and only 33 percent Native Americans marry Native Americans.[44] More significantly, when one disentangles the generic terms "Asians" and "Latinos," the data fits even more closely the Latin Americanization thesis. For example, among Latinos, Cuban, Mexican, Central American, and South Americans have higher rates of outmarriage than Puerto Ricans and Dominicans.[45] Although interpreting the Asian American outmarriage patterns is very complex (groups such as Filipinos and Vietnamese have higher than expected rates in part due to the Vietnam War and the military bases in the Philippines), it is worth pointing out that the highest rate belongs to Japanese Americans and Chinese and the lowest to Southeast Asians, a pattern that seems to fit the contours of my Latin Americanization argument.[46]

Furthermore, racial assimilation through marriage ("whitening") is significantly more likely for the children of Asian-white and Latino-white unions than for those of black-white unions, a fact that bolsters my Latin Americanization thesis. Hence, whereas only 22 percent of the children of black fathers and white mothers are classified as white, the children of similar unions among Asians are twice as likely to be classified as white.[47] For Latinos, the data fits even closer my thesis as Latinos of Cuban, Mexican, and South American origin have high rates of exogamy compared to Puerto Ricans and Dominicans.[48] We concur with Moran's (2001)[49] speculation that this may reflect the fact that because Puerto Ricans and Dominicans have far more dark-skinned members, they have restricted chances for outmarriage to whites in a highly racialized marriage market.

2. Residential Segregation among Racial Strata

An imperfect measure of interracial interaction is the level of neighborhood "integration."[50] Nevertheless, the various indices devised by demographers to assess the level of residential segregation allow us to gauge in broad strokes the level of interracial contact in various cities. In this section, I focus on the segregation of Latinos and Asians as the high segregation experienced by blacks is very well known.[51]

RESIDENTIAL SEGREGATION AMONG LATINOS

Researchers have shown that Latinos are less segregated from and are more exposed to whites than blacks.[52] Yet, they have also documented that dark-skinned Latinos experience black-like rates of residential segregation from whites. Early research on Latino immigrant settlement patterns in Chicago, for example, showed that Mexicans and Puerto Ricans were relegated to spaces largely occupied by blacks, in part because of skin color discrimination.[53] More recent studies find also this race effect on Latino residential segregation patterns. Latinos who identify as white, primarily Cubans and South Americans, are considerably more likely to reside in areas with non-Latino whites than are Latinos who identity as black, mainly Dominicans and Puerto Ricans.[54]

RESIDENTIAL SEGREGATION AMONG ASIANS

Of all minority groups, Asian Americans are the least segregated from whites. However, they have experienced an increase in residential segregation in recent years.[55] In a recent review Zubrinsky Charles (2003) found that from 1980 to 2000, the index of dissimilarity for Asians had increased three points (from thirty-seven to forty) while the index of exposure to whites had declined sixteen points (from eighty-eight to sixty-two).[56] Part of the increase in segregation (and the concomitant decrease in exposure) may be the result of the arrival of newer and poorer immigrants from Southeast Asia.[57] For example, the Vietnamese—a group I predict will be part of the collective black—almost doubled its size between 1990 and 2000. While the majority of residential segregation studies are based on black, Latino, and Asian proximity to whites, which limits an examination of intragroup differences among Asians and Latinos, the fact that Asians have much lower dissimilarity indexes and higher exposure indexes vis-à-vis Latinos and blacks, fits my overall claim that the majority of Asians will belong to the honorary white category.

DISCUSSION

I have presented a broad and bold thesis about the future of racial stratification in the United States.[58] However, at this early stage of the analysis and given the serious limitations of the data on "Latinos" and "Asians" (most of the data is not parceled out by subgroups and hardly anything is provided by skin tone), it is hard to make a conclusive case. I acknowledge that factors such as nativity or socioeconomic characteristics may explain some of the patterns I documented.[59] Nevertheless, the fact that almost all the objective, subjective, and social interaction indicators I reviewed were in the direction I predicted, supports my Latin Americanization thesis. For example, the objective data clearly shows substantive gaps between the groups I labeled "white," "honorary whites," and the "collective black." In terms of income and education, whites tend to be slightly better off than honorary whites who tend to be significantly better off than the collective black. Not surprisingly, a variety of subjective indicators signal the emergence of *internal* stratification among racial minorities. For example, whereas some Latinos (e.g., Cubans, Argentines, Chileans, etc.) are very likely to self-classify as whites, others are not (e.g., Dominicans and Puerto Ricans living in the United States). This has led them to develop a racial attitudinal profile, at least in terms of subscription to stereotypical views about groups, similar to that of whites. Finally, the objective and subjective indicators had a correlate at the level of social interaction. Data on interracial marriage and residential segregation shows that whites are significantly more likely to live nearby honorary whites and to intermarry them than members of the collective black.

I also acknowledge that my racial map and arguments can be debated and, since I have already heard some critiques, I wish to take the opportunity to defend my case. The three criticisms of my work I hear most often are the following: (1) Why do I classify Arab Americans as "honorary white" at a time when all Arabs, and folks who look like them, are being labeled terrorists? (2) How can I predict that color blindness will become even more salient when there seems to be a resurgence of old-fashioned racism? (3) Why do I suggest a triracial order will emerge when many Latinos and whites fight to become white?

The first person with whom I debated some of these points was my wife, who happens to be a Palestinian woman. And I will state here exactly what I told her in the privacy of our home. Regarding the first point, I used a semantic move and told her "I love you baby, but . . ." and proceeded to explain to her that this map is heuristic and, thus, that it is not definitive. Groups may move up or down and I am willing to contemplate this possibility *if the data warrants it*. However, because the data in this chapter—and in forthcoming work—does not show that Arab Americans or Asian Indians (a group that is, for many reasons, in a similar location in whites' imaginary to Arab Americans) have changed their racial politics, I am not inclined to move them to the "collective black" category. In fact, I suggest their historical position is analogous to that of Japanese Americans during World War II. (In their case, the record shows that despite suffering from the horrible ignominy of internment, Japanese Americans returned rather quickly to an in-between status in the racial order and as the favored minorities for whites. Furthermore, they did not shift their political lenses and join in the struggle with other minorities in the sixties and seventies. In contrast to Latinos, blacks, and Native Americans, Japanese Americans hardly participated in the civil rights movement.) Thus, Arab Americans may be suffering from a sort of collective punishment from whites by being regarded as terrorists, as fundamentalist, as uncivilized or differently civilized, but I do not see systematic evidence suggesting they are developing an oppositional identity such as that exhibited by other minorities. But, as I also told my wife, if I see data suggesting that "Arab Americans"[60] are in fact becoming members of the "collective black" and behaving as such in terms of their patterns of interaction, I am willing to revise my map.

Regarding the second point, I still maintain that color blindness will become the glue that will bind the triracial order. This does not mean that Jim Crow racism is totally dead or that it may not temporarily gain space—making Amerika feel more like Amerikkka. However, we must understand that because color blindness is about maintaining white power, this ideology, as all ideologies, can bend in many ways to help in this task. Even the material I included in the main text of the book showed that it is possible for whites to claim they are color blind and still talk about race in crude ways. Examples of this phenomenon abound. For instance, every night you can watch Lou Dobbs on CNN attack so-called illegal aliens, talk about China and India as if they were the real economic threat for America, trash Arab nations, and make fun of so-called political correctness in a color-blind way. And "in point of fact," to use one of Lou Dobbs's favorite verbal mannerisms, whenever anyone calls him "racist" or claims he is "being racist," he gets indignant and claims to be above the racial fray. Similarly, the way President Bush and his cabinet have attempted to thread the needle in this "War on Terror" fits the logic of color blindness. Their rhetorical plan seems to be, "Say a lot about the 'enemy,' but use disclaimers so that you can never be pinned down as intolerant or racist."

Lastly, on the matter of whether Asians and Latinos will join the ranks of whites, I simply state almost verbatim what I stated in a debate on this matter in an edited book with my colleague George Yancey, author of *Who Is White? Latinos, Asians, and the New Black/Nonblack Divide.*[61] Although Yancey's claim is meritorious—he claims that because most Asians and Latinos self-identify as white in the Census, they should therefore be considered as such—and I have many coincidences with him (I too argue that many Latinos and Asians will become white), I believe his overall claim is unlikely. There are four reasons why I think his general prediction is unlikely. First, Latinos and Asians are not "new immigrants." They have been in the United States since at least the nineteenth century. Therefore, if they were going to become white, that process should have started in the 1830s (for Mexican Americans) and 1840s for (Chinese Americans). The fact that this has not happened in mass (I acknowledge that some Asians and Latinos, like light-skinned blacks in the past, became white through passing) suggest that the racialization of these groups is different from that of people of European descent.

Second, all racial categories are historico-political constructions and, therefore, always exhibit malleability and porosity. However, the incorporation of groups into the U.S. white category has shown, so far, to have some epidermic boundaries, that is, groups and individuals added to the category have been European-looking. Hence, *groups* lacking epidermic capital, such as Latinos and Asians, will have more trouble getting admission into whiteness (but I point out that individual members of these groups can use their individual racial capital, such as light skin color, eye color, etc., to move up the racial ladder).

Third, the kind of assimilation process experienced by many of the groups that are presumed to become white (e.g., Mexican Americans, Dominicans, Puerto Ricans, Filipinos, etc.) seems different from that of European immigrants in the early part of the twentieth century. Thus, analysts now talk about "segmented assimilation" to refer to the variety of outcomes of these groups.[62]

And fourth, the class and cultural distance between the masses of Mexican, Central American, and some Asian immigrants and whites is such that it is unlikely that most of them will be able to become white. The Mexican, Puerto Rican, Dominican barrios and the Chinese, Korean, Vietnamese towns across the nation are not like the temporary ethnic ghettos of the past. Some of these neighborhoods have more than one hundred years of existence, a very long time to be regarded as "transition neighborhoods."

I restate for the record that I acknowledge that many of these new immigrants as well as many of the old minority citizens will either become white or near-white (honorary white). My big difference with Yancey and others is that I believe that most of these people will not become white and will accompany blacks in the large loosely organized racial strata at the bottom of the racial order.

Race Struggle in a Latin America–like United States

If my predictions are right, what will the consequences of Latin Americans be for race relations in the United States? First, racial politics will change dramatically. The "us versus them" racial dynamic will lessen as "honorary whites" grow in size and social importance. They are likely to buffer racial conflict—or derail it altogether—as intermediate groups do in many Latin American and Caribbean countries.

Second, the ideology of color-blind racism that I examined in this book is likely to become even more salient in the United States. Color-blind racism is in fact an ideology similar to that prevailing in Latin American and Caribbean societies and like there, it will help glue the emerging racial order and buffer racial conflict.

Third, if the state decides to stop gathering racial statistics, the struggle to document the impact of race in a variety of social venues will become monumental. More significantly, because state actions always impact civil society, if the state decides to erase race from above, the *social* recognition of "races" in the polity may become harder. We may develop a Latin American–like "disgust" for even mentioning anything that is race-related.

Fourth, the deep history of black-white divisions in the United States has been such that the centrality of the black identity will not dissipate. For instance, research on the "black elite" shows that it exhibits racial attitudes in line with their racial group.[63] That identity, as I suggested in this chapter, may be even taken up by dark-skinned Latinos as it is being rapidly taken up by most West Indians. For example, Al, a fifty-three-year-old Jamaican engineer interviewed by Milton Vickerman (1999), stated,

> I have nothing against Haitians; I have nothing against black Americans. . . . If you're a nigger, you're a nigger, regardless of whether you are from Timbuktu. . . . There isn't the unity that one would like to see. . . . Blacks have to appreciate blacks, no matter where they are from. Just look at it the way I look at it: That you're the same. [64]

However, I expect some important changes to take place even among the black population. Their racial consciousness, I argue, will become more diffused. For example, blacks will be more likely to accept many stereotypes about themselves (e.g., "We are lazier than whites") and exhibit what I label here as a "blunted oppositional consciousness" (see chapter 8). Furthermore, the external pressure of "multiracials" in white contexts[65] and the internal pressure of "ethnic" blacks may change the notion of "blackness" and even the position of some "blacks" in the system. Colorism may become an even more important factor as a way of making social distinctions among "blacks."[66]

Fifth, the new racial stratification system will be more effective in maintaining white supremacy. Whites will still be at the top of the social structure but will face fewer race-based challenges. And, to avoid confusion about my claim regarding "honorary whites," let me clarify that I believe their standing and status will be ultimately dependent upon whites' wishes and practices.[67] "Honorary" means that they will remain secondary, will still face discrimination, and will not receive equal treatment in society. For example, although Arab Americans should be regarded as "honorary whites," their treatment in the post–September 11 era suggests their status as "white" and as "Americans" is tenuous at best. Although some analysts and commentators may welcome Latin Americanization as a positive trend in American race relations,[68] those at the bottom of the racial hierarchy will soon discover that behind the statement "We are all Americans" hides a deeper, hegemonic way of maintaining white supremacy. As a Latin America–like society,[69] the United States will become a society with more rather than less racial inequality but with a reduced forum for racial contestation. The apparent blessing of "not seeing race" will become a curse for those struggling for racial justice in years to come. We may become "All Americans," as commercials in recent times suggest, but paraphrasing George Orwell, "some will be more American than others."

In the next chapter of this book, I will tackle the meaning of the election of President Obama. Although many commentators and analysts believe his election signifies "the end of racism" or a monumental change in our long racial history, I will argue that it is in line with color-blind racism.

NOTES

1. Data from,"2010 Census Shows America's Diversity" a report sponsored by the U.S. Census Bureau which can be found at the following address: www.census.gov/newsroom/releases/archives/2010_census/cb11-cn125.html.

2. The reference for Huntington's book is *Who Are We?* (New York: Simon & Schuster, 2004). As a quick refutation, the United States has never had an "Anglo-Saxon" because the culture of the country has always reflected waves of incorporation of peoples as colonial subjects (e.g., Mexicans and Indians), as immigrants (e.g., Italians, Scandinavians, etc.), and slaves (e.g., Africans).

3. For a critique of the way Lou Dobbs frames the immigration debate, skews his list of invitees, and distorts the data on immigration he presents in his show, see Peter Hart's article, "Dobbs' Choice: CNN Host Picks Immigration as His Ax to Grind," February 2004 in the website of FAIR (Fairness and Accuracy in Reporting).

4. Asian Americans were, from the first time they set foot in this country, a very small group (about 1 percent of the population) very regionally concentrated (mostly on the West Coast). But since the enactment of the 1965 Immigration Act, this group has grown in size exponentially and is now represented in most states. And this group, perceived as a success story, has in fact the highest proportion

of college graduates (50 percent) and a high level of income. For recent data on this group, see the U.S. Census Bureau release, "Asian/Pacific American Heritage Month, May 2005," located in www.census.gov/Press-Release/www/releases/archives/facts--for--features--special--editions/004522.html. For critiques of the "model minority" myth and explanations of the success story of Asian Americans, see Frank H. Wu, *Yellow: Race in America Beyond Black and White* (New York: Basic Books, 2003).

5. On the political scandals, one just need to remember how easy it was for the Republican Party to accuse the Democratic Party of selling the nation's sovereignty to China in the 2000 election because they allegedly accepted contributions from Chinese citizens. (For a critique, see Wu, *Yellow.*) For examples on the anti-Chinese views expressed in the news, tune in to almost any channel every night and see how they frame trade issues ("They are taking us for a ride!"), energy issues ("They are using too much energy!"), or intellectual property right issues ("They are stealing our intellectual property!"). On the latter point, we must always remember that if we super-exploit nations all over the world, we have no moral ground to defend intellectual property rights. It is simply another case of the rooster coming back home to roost.

6. I place these two concepts in quotation marks for two reasons. First, since we are all one species, the notions such as "multiracial" or "biracial" reify biological interpretation of race. Second, all humans are "multiracial" (in the sociological sense of the notion of race) since we are the product of 2 million years of mixing, migrating from place to place, and mixing some more. What has allowed people to signify their multiracialism in the United States nowadays is the transition from the Jim Crow era—when all people were either white or nonwhite—to the post–civil rights racial era in which there is seemingly more space and fluidity for individuals to choose their identity, racial or otherwise.

7. I have said elsewhere that there is no multiracial movement per se, if by that one means a social movement. What we have is many organizations, without much coherence, articulating the views and angst of either parents (usually white mothers) of biracial children or the organizations of biracial children in colleges and professional circles.

8. For a perceptive examination of interracial marriage and now race still ordains our mate selection, see Rachel Moran, *Interracial Intimacy: The Regulation of Race and Romance* (Chicago and London: University of Chicago Press, 2001).

9. The comments on demographers, and the data on rates of interracial marriage, refer to Sharon Lee and Barry Edmonston, "New Marriages, New Families: U.S. Racial and Hispanic Intermarriage," *Population Bulletin,* June 2005. An example of a public intellectual heralding interracial marriage as the solution to America's racial problems is Randal Kennedy, *Interracial Intimacies* (New York: Pantheon, 2003).

10. Jennifer Wilbanks's story of the Georgia woman who disappeared the day before her wedding in the summer of 2005, shows that Latinos may be moving into a position in our culture analogous to that of blacks. Wilbanks claimed she was kidnapped by a Hispanic man and a white woman. Initially, the story was believed, but soon after, the police realized the story was fabricated. But of interest in this case is that Wilbanks did not rely on the traditional "black man story"

and used what seems to be the new game in town: "The Hispanic man did it." Also, the fact that we believed her story until we were told it was not true suggests there is a new racial sensitivity or fear emerging in the country.

11. See, for example, George Yancey, *Who Is White?: Latinos, Asians, and the New Black/Nonblack Divide* (Boulder, Colo.: Lynne Rienner Publishers, 2003).

12. Denish D'Souza, *The End of Racism* (New York: Free Press, 1995); William J. Wilson, *The Declining Significance of Race* (Chicago: University of Chicago Press, 1978).

13. See, for example, Richard Alba and Victor Nee, *Remaking the American Mainstream: Assimilation and Contemporary Immigration* (Boston and London: Harvard University Press, 2004).

14. The arguments and data for this chapter come from my ongoing project titled, "'We Are All Americans!': The Latin Americanization of Racial Stratification in the United States." For a discussion on the racialization of the world system, see Etienne Balibar and Immanuel Wallerstein, *Race, Nation, and Class: Ambiguous Identities* (London: Verso, 1991).

15. Experts interested in the references on this section should consult my chapter, "'We Are All Americans!': The Latin Americanization of Racial Stratification in the United States," in *The Changing Terrain of Race and Ethnicity*, edited by Maria Krysan and Amanda E. Lewis, 149–83 (New York: Russell Sage Foundation, 2004).

16. Aline Helg, "Race in Argentina and Cuba, 1880–1930: Theory, Policies, and Popular Reaction," in *The Idea of Race in Latin America, 1870–1940*, edited by Richard Graham (Austin: University of Texas Press, 1990).

17. Two example of this posture are Herbert J. Gans, "The Possibility of a New Racial Hierarchy in the Twenty-first Century United States," in *The Cultural Territories of Race: Black and White Boundaries*, edited by Michele Lamont (Chicago: University of Chicago Press, 1999), and Jonathan W. Warren and France Winddance Twine, "White Americans, the New Minority? Non-Blacks and the Ever-Expanding Boundaries of Whiteness," *Journal of Black Studies* 28, no. 2 (1997): 200–218. A quick rebuttal of their view is that Latinos and Asians have been here for a long time and have not become white en masse. Thus, I expect that the bulk of the Latino and Asian immigrants coming to America (increasingly poor and many in a tenuous legal status in the country) will not join the ranks of the white group as these analysts predict.

18. Any social stratification order that does not have intermediate strata is more likely to be fraught with conflict of the "'We' versus 'Them'" kind and require a more heavy investment in coercion as a way of keeping social order. On this point, see Gerhard E. Lenski, *Power and Privilege: A Theory of Social Stratification* (Chapel Hill: University of North Carolina Press, 1984). Hence, my claim here is that the development of this intermediate group will act as a "buffer" for social conflict. The white-nonwhite dynamic typical of the American racial order will be blurred by more complex racial lines of contestation.

19. See Robert Miles, *Racism after Race Relations* (London and New York: Routledge, 1993) and Robin Cohen, *Global Diasporas: An Introduction* (Seattle: University of Washington Press, 1997).

20. See Stephen Castles and Mark Miller, *The Age of Migration: International Population Movements in the Modern World* (Hong Kong: Macmillan, 1993).

21. For more on this argument, see my "'This Is a White Country': The Racial Ideology of the Western Nations of the World-System," *Sociological Inquiry* 70, no. 3 (2000): 188–214.

22. See, Eduardo Bonilla-Silva, "The Essential Social Fact of Race: A Reply to Loveman," *American Sociological Review* 64 (2000): 899–906.

23. Stephen Steinberg, *Turning Back: The Retreat from Racial Justice in American Thought and Policy* (Boston: Beacon Press, 1995).

24. However, phenotype in Latin America can be perceptually and socially "lightened" (or "darkened") by nonphenotypical characteristics such as education, language, culture, class, and occupational background. A black-looking person with a Ph.D. from Harvard who makes lots of money may not be regarded as black in Puerto Rico or Brazil. Similarly, I believe that although most Asian Indians range in color from dark to quite dark, they are likely to be regarded as honorary whites because of their mastery of the English language, high levels of education, and other nonphenotypical factors.

25. Whereas the Bolivian Census of 2001 reports that 71 percent of the Bolivians self-identify as Indian, less than 20 percent have more than a high school diploma, and 58.6 percent live below the poverty line, 66 percent of Bolivians in the United States self-identify as white, 64 percent have twelve or more years of education, and have a per capita income comparable to that of whites. Thus, this seems like a case of self-selection, that is, Bolivians in the United States do not represent Bolivians in Bolivia. The information on Bolivia comes from Censo Nacional de Población y Vivienda, *Bolivia: CaraterÀ1Àsticas de la Población*, Serie Resultados, vol. 4 (La Paz: Ministerio de Hacienda, 2002).

26. On this see the classic work of Henri Tajfel, "Experiments in Intergroup Discrimination," *Scientific American* 223 (1970): 96–102. See also the contributions of Cecilia Ridgeway. For an example, see her "The Social Construction of Status Value: Gender and Other Nominal Characteristics," *Social Forces* 70, no. 2 (1991): 367–86.

27. Michael G. Hanchard, *Orpheus and Power: The Morimiento Negro of Rio de Janeiro and São Paulo, Brazil, 1945–1988* (Princeton, N.J.: Princeton University Press, 1994).

28. Survey experiments have shown that if the question on Hispanic origin is asked first, the proportion of Latinos who report to be "white" increases from 25 to 39 percent (Martin, Demaio, and Campanelli 1990). The same research also shows that when Latinos report to belong to the "Other" category, they are not mistaken, that is, they do want to signify they are neither black nor white. Unfortunately, we do not have results by national groups. Are Cubans more likely to claim to be white if the order of the questions is changed? Or is the finding symmetrical for all groups? Regardless we think this finding does not alter the direction of the overall findings on the self-identification of various Latino groups.

29. See Yen Le Espiritu Espiritu, *Asian American Panethnicity: Bridging Institutions and Identities* (Philadelphia: Temple University Press, 1992).

30. E. San Juan Jr., "The Limits of Ethnicity and the Horizon of Historical Materialism," in *Asian American Studies: Identity, Images, Issues Past and Present*, edited by Esther Mikyung Ghymn (New York: Peter Lang, 2000), 10.

31. Leland T. Saito, *Race and Politics: Asian Americans, Latinos, and Whites in a Los Angeles Suburb* (Urbana: University of Illinois Press, 1998), 59.

32. My comments on Asian Americans, in case some readers have doubts, apply to Latinos, too. Latinos, as I have argued so far, are not a monolithic group and have serious divisions that mimic elements of the divisions seen among Asian Americans. For instance, a study on Latino attitudes toward immigration released in June 2005 reported, "Although an overwhelming majority of Hispanics expresses positive attitudes toward immigrants . . . a significant minority, concentrated among native-born Latinos, is concerned that unauthorized migrants are hurting the economy." The study estimates the size of this group as 30 percent of the native-born population, but does not go further in attempting to identify the characteristics of this segment. Perhaps they are the light-skinned, well-educated, Hispanics that I label here honorary white. See Robert Suro, "Attitudes towards Immigrants and Immigration Policies: Surveys among Latinos in the U.S. and Mexico," *Pew Hispanic Center*, August 16, 2005.

33. On the racial attitudes of Latinos, see Wallace Lambert and Donald Taylor, *Coping with Cultural and Racial Diversity in Urban America* (Westport, Conn.: Praeger, 1990), and, particularly, Tatcho Mindiola Jr., Yolanda Flores Niemann, and Nestor Rodriguez, *Black-Brown Relations and Stereotypes* (Austin: University of Texas Press, 2002).

34. Mindiola, Niemann, and Rodriguez, *Black-Brown Relations and Stereotypes*.

35. See Nilda Flores-Gonzales, "The Racialization of Latinos: The Meaning of Latino Identity for the Second Generation," *Latino Studies Journal* 10, no. 3 (1999): 3–31, and Suzanne Oboler, *Ethnic Labels, Latino Lives: Identity and the Politics of (Re)Presentation in the United States* (Minneapolis: University of Minnesota Press, 1995).

36. On Dominicans and their racial history, see David Howard, *Coloring the Nation: Race and Ethnicity in the Dominican Republic* (Boulder, Colo.: Lynne Rienner Publishers, 2001).

37. Clara Rodriguez, *Changing Race: Latinos, the Census, and the History of Ethnicity in the United States* (New York: New York University Press, 2000) 56.

38. Lawrence Bobo, Camille Zubrinksy, James Johnson Jr., and Melvin Oliver, "Work Orientation, Job Discrimination, and Ethnicity," *Research in the Sociology of Work* 5 (1995): 45–85.

39. Bobo, Zubrinsky, Johnson, and Oliver, "Work Orientation," 78. See also Lawrence Bobo and Devon Johnson, "Racial Attitudes in Prismatic Metropolis: Mapping Identity, Stereotypes, Competition, and Views on Affirmative Action," in *Prismatic Metropolis*, edited by Lawrence Bobo, Melvin Oliver, James Johnson, and Abel Valenzuela (New York: Russell Sage Foundation, 2000).

40. On the views of Asian Americans, see Ronald Weitzer, "Racial Prejudice among Korean Merchants in African American Neighborhoods," *Sociological Quarterly* 38, no. 4 (1997): 587–606; In-jin Yoon, *On My Own: Korean Businesses and Race Relations in America* (Chicago: University of Chicago Press, 1997); and Pyong Gap Min, *Caught in the Middle: Korean Communities in New York and Los Angeles* (Berkeley: University of California Press, 1996).

41. For a more thorough analysis, see Bobo and Johnson, "Racial Attitudes in Prismatic Metropolis."

42. Bobo and Johnson, "Racial Attitudes in Prismatic Metropolis."

43. Bobo and Johnson, "Racial Attitudes in Prismatic Metropolis," 103.

44. Moran, *Interracial Intimacy*, 103.

45. Greta A. Gilbertson, Joseph P. Fitzpatrick, and Lijun Yang, "Hispanic Out-Marriage in New York City—New Evidence from 1991," *International Immigration Review* 30 (1996).

46. See Harry L. Kitano and Roger Daniels, *Asian Americans: Emerging Minorities* (Englewood Cliffs, NJ: Prentice Hall, 2000).

47. House Committee on Reform and Oversight, Subcommittee on Government, Management, Informational Technology, *Hearings on Federal Measures of Race and Ethnicity*, May 22, 1997 (prepared testimony of Professor Mary C. Waters, Department of Sociology, Harvard University).

48. Gilbertson, Fitzpatrick, and Yang, "Hispanic Out-Marriage in New York City."

49. Moran, *Interracial Intimacy*.

50. For some of the limitations of this index, see Eduardo Bonilla-Silva and Gianpaolo Baiocchi, "Anything but Racism: How Sociologists Limit the Significance of Racism," *Race and Society* 4 (2001): 117–31.

51. See, for example, Douglass S. Massey and Nancy A. Denton, *American Apartheid* (Cambridge, Mass.: Harvard University Press, 1993), and Milton Yinger, *Closed Doors, Opportunities Lost: The Continuing Costs of Housing Discrimination* (New York: Russell Sage Foundation, 1995).

52. See Douglass S. Massey and Nancy A. Denton, "Trends in the Residential Segregation of Blacks, Hispanics, and Asians: 1970–1980," *American Sociological Review* 52, no. 6 (1987): 802–25. For a recent review of the overall trends, see Camille Zubrinsky Charles, "The Dynamics of Racial Residential Segregation," *Annual Review of Sociology* 29 (2003): 167–207.

53. See John J. Betancur, "The Settlement Experience of Latinos in Chicago: Segregation, Speculation, and the Ecology Model," *Social Forces* 74 (1996): 1299–1324.

54. See John R. Logan, "How Race Counts for Hispanic Americans," Lewis Mumford Center, University of Albany, 2003. Retrieved from http://mumford1.dyndns.org/cen2000/BlackLatinoReport/BlackLatino01.htm.

55. On this point, see William H. Frey and Reynolds Farley, "Latino, Asian, and Black Segregation in U.S. Metropolitan Areas: Are Multi-ethnic Metros Different?" *Demography* 33, no. 1 (1996): 35–50, and Michael J. White, Ann E. Biddlecom, and Shenyang Guo, "Immigration, Naturalization, and Residential Assimilation among Asian Americans in 1980," *Social Forces* 72, no. 1 (1993).

56. The dissimilarity index expresses the percentage of a minority population that would have to move to result in a perfectly even distribution of the population across census tracts. This index runs from 0 (no segregation) to 100 (total segregation) and it is symmetrical (not affected by population size). The exposure index measures the degree of potential contact between two populations (majority and minority) and expresses the probability of a member of a minority group meeting a member of the majority group. Like the dissimilarity index, it runs from 0 to 100, but unlike it, it is asymmetrical (it is affected by population size). See Zubrinsky Charles, "The Dynamics of Racial Residential Segregation."

57. See Frey and Farley, "Latino, Asian, and Black Segregation in U.S. Metropolitan Areas."

58. I am not alone in making this kind of prediction. Scholars such as Arthur K. Spears, Suzanne Oboler, Gary Okihiro, and Mari Matsuda have made similar claims recently. See Arthur K. Spears contribution in his edited book, *Race and Ideology: Language, Symbolism, and Popular Culture* (Detroit: Wayne State University Press, 1999); Suzanne Oboler, "'It Must Be a Fake!': Racial Ideologies, Identities, and the Question of Rights in Hispanics/Latinos," in *The United States: Ethnicity, Race, and Rights,* edited by Jorge J. E. Garcia and Pablo De Greiff (New York: Routledge, 2000); Gary Okihiro, *Margins and Mainstreams: Asians in American History and Culture* (Seattle: University of Washington Press, 1994); and Mary J. Matsuda, *Where Is Your Body? And Other Essays on Race, Gender and the Law* (Boston: Beacon Press, 1996).

59. An important matter to disentangle empirically is whether it is color or nativity, education, or class that determines where groups fit in our scheme. A powerful alternative explanation to many of my preliminary findings is that the groups I label "honorary whites" come with high levels of human capital *before* they achieve honorary white status in the United States; that is, they fit this intermediate position because of neither their color nor their race, but rather because of their class background. Although this is a plausible alternative explanation that we hope examine in the future, some of the available data suggests that race/color has something to do with the success of immigrants in the United States. For example, the case of West Indians—who come to the United States with class advantages (e.g., educational and otherwise) and yet "fade to black" in a few generations—suggests that the "racial" status of the group has an independent effect in this process. It is also important to point out that even when some of these groups may do "well" objectively, when one checks their returns to their characteristics is when one realizes how little they get for what they bring to the fore. And, as Waters and Eschbach stated in a review of the literature on immigration, "The evidence indicates that direct discrimination is still an important factor for all minority subgroups except very highly educated Asians." Mary C. Waters, Mary C. Eschbach, and Karl Eschbach, "Immigration and Ethnic and Racial Inequality in the United States," *Annual Review of Sociology* 21 (1995): 442. However, even highly educated and acculturated Asians, such as Filipinos, report high levels of racial discrimination in the labor market. Not surprisingly, second- and third-generation Filipinos self-identity as Filipino American rather than as white or "American." For references on all these matters and a slightly more elaborate discussion, see Eduardo Bonilla-Silva, *Anything but Racism* (New York: Routledge, 2004).

60. The term "Arab Americans" may in fact be too wide to hide multiple realities. My wife, Mary Hovsepian, a sociologist at Duke, has suggested to me that maybe Christian Arabs will become white-like and Muslim Arabs will become black-like. Although I still have not seen data suggestive of this trend, I remain observant of this possibility.

61. George Yancey, *Who Is White? Latinos, Asians, and the New Black/Nonblack Divide* (Boulder, Colo.: Lynne Rienner Publishers, 2003).

62. Alejandro Portes and Ruben G. Rumbaut, *Legacies: The Story of the Immigrant Second Generation* (Berkeley and Los Angeles: University of California Press, 2002).

63. See Michael Dawson, *Behind the Mule: Race and Class in African American Politics* (Princeton, N.J.: Princeton University Press, 1994).

64. Milton Vickerman, *Crosscurrents: West Indian Immigrants and Race* (New York: Oxford University Press, 1999), 199.

65. Kerry Ann Rockquemore, Kerry Ann Brunsma, and David L. Brunsma, *Beyond Black: Biracial Identity in America* (Thousand Oaks, Calif.: Sage, 2002).

66. For a recent discussion and analysis on this matter, see Cedric Herring, Verna M. Keith, and Hayward D. Horton, *Skin Deep: How Race and Complexion Matter in the "Color-Blind" Era* (Urbana: University of Illinois Press, 2003).

67. The work of Claire Jean Kim on "triangulation" seems appropriate here. She argues that Asian Americans have been triangulated vis-à-vis blacks and whites. On the one hand, whites value Asian Americans as a model minority worthy of praise, but at the same time, they ostracize them civically as unworthy of assimilation. Albeit my data on marital assimilation and neighborhood segregation suggests that the second pole is more complex than Kim suggests, her point is well-taken. See Claire Jean Kim, "The Racial Triangulation of Asian Americans," *Politics and Society* 27, no. 1 (March 1999): 105–38. For a similar point with tons of examples, please see Frank H. Wu, *Yellow*.

68. In the last few years, Harvard political scientist Jennifer Hochschild has been working on a project dealing with the significance of color for Americans. Although her project is similar to mine and we have shared platforms a few times, she believes that this development may be progressive as it will lessen racial boundaries. I, as a black-looking man who lived for twenty-one years in a so-called racial democracy, know that colorism is no solution to racialization but is in fact a different version of it.

69. "Latin America–like" does not mean exactly like Latin America. The four-hundred-year history of the American racial formation has stained the racial stratification order forever. Thus I expect some important differences in this new American racial stratification system compared to that "typical" of Latin American societies. First, phenotype-based discrimination will not work perfectly. Hence, for example, although Asian Indians are dark-skinned, they will still be higher as a group in the stratification system than, for example, Mexican American *mestizos*. Second, Arabs, Asian Indians, and other non-Christian groups are unlikely to be allowed complete upward mobility unless they engage in passing. The events of September 11, 2001, and our intervention in Afghanistan and Iraq—both of which may force the U.S. military to remain in the area for a long time—are reinforcing the traditional view of whiteness as a Christian-only identity. Third, because of the three hundred years of dramatic racialization and group formation, most members of the historically nonwhite groups will maintain "ethnic" (Puerto Ricans) or racial claims (e.g., blacks) and demand group-based rights.

10

≈

Race Matters in Obamerica[1]

The Sweet (but Deadly) Enchantment of Color Blindness in Black Face

Madness is rare in individuals—but in groups, parties, nations, and ages it is the rule.

—Friedrich Nietzsche, *Beyond Good and Evil*

Four years ago, when I wrote the first draft of this chapter, many Americans (mostly white but also some confused people of color) believed that the election of Barack Obama as the forty-fourth president of the nation was truly a foundational event. My critical views on Obama, on his centrism, and particularly on his color blindness were not appreciated by most. I was accused of all sorts of things; I still am, albeit with less emphasis given that we have four years of data on Obama. But I maintained my stand that we needed to explain why, in a country where race matters at all levels, a black man was elected president. It was not enough to postulate that Obama could not be elected, as many race commentators did, or to suggest his election meant we were close to the end of racism (I remind readers that only 43 percent of whites voted for Obama in 2008 and 39 percent in 2012, and not all who did were "beyond race"). Hence, now that Obama was reelected so narrowly, we must revisit how he was elected president in the first place, what he did as president, and what is the meaning of eight years of *Obamerica*. This chapter is my effort to remain engaged in the politics of race in the so-called post-racial moment we live in.

"WE ARE ALL MAD HERE":
ON MADNESS IN THE AMERICAN WONDERLAND

In this chapter, I explain the "miracle" that happened in 2008 and its continuation in 2012: the election (and now, reelection) of a black man as president of the United States. My explanation runs counter to those who believe his victories represent the "end of racism" and the beginning of the era of "no more excuses"[2] for people of color. I contend Obama's ascendancy to the presidency is part and parcel of the "new racism" in the United States since the early 1970s. We have seen the rise of a few, carefully chosen minorities who are willing to propound a happy version of the American story, and the elevation of these minority politicians as "evidence" that America has overcome. This fairy tale is the most popular way to explain American racial politics, despite the depressing statistics telling a different story about what it means to be a minority in America in 2011.

This chapter is also a call to progressives and liberals who believed in Obama's message of hope and change to get serious. In 2013, we now have four years of Obama's presidential record to scrutinize, as we have done with all prior presidents. As I was involved in debates about Obama leading up to the 2008 election, I revisit my predictions to evaluate whether the president has delivered on his promises, or whether, as I predicted, he has been far more moderate (centrist) than progressives were willing to admit in 2008.

But before I begin, several clarifications are needed to avoid unnecessary confusion. First, my criticism of Obama is neither of all he stands for nor of all of his actions in office. Second, although I will criticize President Obama's image, politics, and policies, I want to be absolutely clear on one important point: in comparison to the president he replaced in 2008 and the Republican candidates he has faced, Obama seems like pure gold. Third, since Obama emerged as a viable candidate, the bulk of the American intelligentsia ceased its critical mission. Being critical is part of the job of intellectuals in any society, and when they are not critical, they abdicate their responsibility.

"DOWN THE RABBIT HOLE":
THE REAL QUESTION POSED BY OBAMA'S VICTORY

George Orwell stated a long time ago that "to see what is in front of one's nose needs constant struggle."[3] In the 2008 election cycle, Americans did not see what was in front of their noses; they saw what they wanted and longed to see. Whereas blacks and other people of color saw in Obama the impossible dream come true, whites saw the confirmation of their belief that America is indeed a color-blind nation. But facts are, as John Adams said, "stubborn things,"[4] and astute social analysts know that since the late 1970s, racial progress in the United States has stagnated and, in many areas, regressed. The evidence of such a state of affairs is, as the title of a report of the early 1990s put it, "clear and convincing."[5] All socioeconomic indicators reveal severe racial gaps in income, wealth, housing, and educational and occupational standing. Since I have addressed these inequalities in previous work,[6] I will review here some economic disparities as documented for 2008—the year Obama was elected president. All the statistics I cite, unless otherwise specified, come from the report "State of the Dream 2009: The Silent Depression,"[7] a very useful compendium of information from sources such as the Census Bureau and the Bureau of Labor Statistics.

- The black unemployment rate in 2008 was 11.9 percent. Among young black males aged sixteen to nineteen, unemployment was 32.8 percent (v). (Unemployment for whites in 2008 was 5.8 percent.) The median household incomes of blacks and Latinos were $38,269 and $40,000, respectively, while the median household income of whites was $61,280 (v).
- Blacks and Latinos had poverty rates of 24 percent and 21 percent, respectively, compared to a 10 percent poverty rate for whites (v).
- People of color were more likely to be poor (24.5 percent), remain poor (54 percent), and move back into poverty from any income class status than their white counterparts (vi).
- Nearly 30 percent of blacks had zero or negative worth, versus 15 percent of whites (vi).

Citing data from the "State of Black America 2009" report by the Urban League, Earl Graves Jr., from *Black Enterprise*, said the following on the wealth disparity:

- Nationally, the typical African American family in 2008 possessed less than 10 percent of the net worth of the average white family. Almost 30 percent of black families had zero or negative net worth. And far fewer blacks than whites benefit from inherited wealth or assets.
- Only 18 percent of people of color had retirement accounts, compared to 43.4 percent of their white counterparts.
- On *average*, people of color had 8 cents for every dollar of white wealth.[8]

When we look at the most recent available statistics, blacks and Latinos have not made up for the gap in employment, income, and wealth. In fact, they have actually fallen further behind whites under Obama. In the month before the 2012 election, according to data from the Bureau of Labor Statistics, the overall unemployment rate was at 7.9 percent. While whites' unemployment was at 6.6 percent, Latinos experienced higher unemployment (11 percent), and blacks were more than twice as likely as whites to be unemployed (14.3 percent).[9] And 40.9 percent of uninstitutionalized (i.e., not incarcerated) black men and women between ages sixteen and nineteen were unemployed.[10]

This growing racial disparity is also starkly visible in statistics on poverty. Although the media and Wall Street reported an early recovery from the recession, in 2010 the Census reported the poverty rate had increased to 15.1 percent, a fifty-two-year high.[11] While 12.8 percent of whites were poor (an increase of 2.8 percent), 27.6 percent of blacks and 25.3 percent of Latinos were poor in 2011, a respective increase of 3.6 percent and 4.2 percent in only three years.[12] In other words, the already-substantial racial poverty gap increased after the recession. Black average income decreased to $32,229 in 2011, a loss of $6,000 or *18 percent of income* from 2008. While whites' incomes also decreased by a significant amount, they still earned $20,000 more than blacks, on average.[13]

These statistics are frightening indicators of the worsening economic well-being of blacks, but they do not tell the true extent of the story—as we have seen, the racial wealth disparity can be even more important than income differences.[14] Perhaps most sobering is the doubling of the wealth gap between blacks and whites in only four years, between 2005 and 2009. Where the gap used to be ten-to-one, whites now possess on average *twenty* times the wealth of blacks and *eighteen* times that of Latinos.[15] Much of this huge jump in wealth disparity comes from the racialized effects of the housing market crash. The Center for Responsible Lending reported that by the end of the crash, almost a quarter of black homeowners would lose their homes due to foreclosure, although whites experienced more foreclosures.[16] Several major banks (Wells Fargo, Bank of America, and SunTrust) have already agreed to settlements for their targeting of black and Latino customers and communities for subprime mortgages and higher rates,[17] but it is not clear that these practices will be stopped.

The racial inequality that persists today is not the product of "impersonal market forces"[18] or due to the presumed cultural, moral, ethical, intellectual, or family "deficiencies" of people of color, as conservative commentators have argued. Racial inequality today is due to the "continuing significance" of racial discrimination.[19] The scholarly community has documented the persistence of discrimination in the labor and housing markets and has uncovered the coexistence of old-fashioned as well as subtle "smiling discrimination."[20]

But racial discrimination is not just about jobs and housing: discrimination affects almost every aspect of the lives of people of color. It affects them in hospitals,[21] restaurants,[22] trying to buy cars or hail a cab,[23] driving,[24] flying,[25] or doing almost anything in America. Indeed, "living while black [or brown]"[26] is quite hard and affects the health (physical and mental) of people of color tremendously, as they seem to always be in "fight or flight" mode.[27]

Despite the continuing significance of racism in minorities' lives, whites' racial policy attitudes in 2008 had not changed significantly since the 1980s.[28] Instead, most[29] contemporary researchers believe that since the 1970s, whites have developed new ways of justifying the racial status quo distinct from the "in your face" prejudice of the past. Analysts have labeled whites' post–civil rights racial attitudes as "modern racism," "subtle racism," "aversive racism," "social dominance," "competitive racism," or the term I prefer, "color-blind racism." But regardless of the name given to whites' new way of framing race matters, their switch from Jim Crow racism to color-blind racism did not change the basics, as the new version is as good as the old one, if not better, in safeguarding the racial order.

Misrecognizing the nature of the current racial regime, too many liberal and progressive commentators dug a deep hole for themselves in the 2008 election, as they either went with the flow and assumed Obama was truly about social and racial change, or they took the stand that white racism would prevent Obama from getting elected.[30] But there is a more fitting, historically accurate, and sociologically viable explanation. The "miracle"—the fact that race matters in America tremendously, yet we elected a black man as our president—is but an apparent one. Obama, his campaign, and his "success" are the outcome of forty years of racial transition from the Jim Crow racial order to the racial regime I have referred to as the "new racism." In the new America that presumably began on November 4, 2008, and was extended in 2012, racism has remained firmly in place and, even worse, is becoming a more daunting obstacle. The apparent blessing of having a black man in the White House is likely to become a curse for black and brown folks.

In the remainder of this chapter I do three things. First, I describe the context that made it possible for someone like Obama to be elected president. Second, I discuss what Obama did in order to be elected president. Finally, I review Obama's policies in the first half of his presidency, to show how we have been delivered the same old politics in a new package.

FROM JIM CROW TO THE NEW RACISM REGIME

The Obama phenomenon is the product of the fundamental racial transformation that transpired in America in the 1960s and 1970s. Unlike Jim Crow, the new racial order that emerged—the "new racism"—reproduces racial domination mostly through subtle and covert practices that are often institutionalized, defended with coded language (*"those* urban people"), and bonded by the racial ideology of color-blind racism. Compared to Jim Crow, this new system seems genteel, but it is extremely effective in preserving systemic advantages for whites. The new regime is, in the immortal lyrics of Roberta Flack's song, of the "killing me softly" variety.

In chapter 2, I have described in detail how the new racial practices for maintaining white privilege operate ideologically, socially, and economically. Given the focus of this chapter, I will just briefly present my analysis of political developments. These days, several major factors limit the advancement of people of color in the political arena. There are multiple structural barriers to the election of black and minority politicians including racial gerrymandering, multimember legislative districts, and the like. Despite some progress in the 1970s, people of color are still severely underrepresented among elected (whites still show a preference to vote for white candidates) and appointed officials. And because most minority politicians must either "compromise" to get elected or are dependent upon local white elites, their capacity to enact policies that benefit the minority masses is quite limited.

More significantly, in my early analysis on these matters I mentioned the emergence of a new type of minority politician. By the early 1990s it was clear that both major political parties (but the Democratic Party in particular) had learned from the perils of trying to incorporate veteran civil rights leaders such as Jesse Jackson. Regardless of the limitations of Jackson as a leader and of his "rainbow coalition" strategy of the 1980s, he and his coalition proved to be too much of a challenge to the "powers that be."[31] Hence, both parties and their corporate masters developed a new process for selecting and vetting minority politicians. After the Democratic Party co-opted civil rights leaders such as John Lewis, Andrew Young, and the like, they began manufacturing a new kind of minority politician (the Republican Party followed suit later). Today's electorally oriented minority politician is not the product of social movements, usually joins the party of choice while in college, moves up quickly through the party ranks, and, most importantly, is not a race rebel.[32] The new minority politicians, unlike their predecessors, are not radicals talking about "the revolution" and "uprooting systemic racism." If Republican, they are antiminority conservatives such as Michael Steele (the former chairman of the Republican National Committee), Allen West (former U.S.

representative from Florida), Marco Rubio (senator from Florida), Susana Martinez (governor of New Mexico), Bobby Jindal (governor of Louisiana), and Nikki Haley (governor of South Carolina). If a Democrat, they are post-racial leaders with center to center-right politics such as Harold Ford (former congressman from Tennessee and former head of the now-defunct conservative Democratic Leadership Council and an MSNBC commentator), Cory Booker (Newark's mayor since 2006), Deval Patrick (governor of Massachusetts since 2006), Adrian Fenty (D.C.'s mayor from 2006 to 2010) and, of course, Barack Obama. Plutocrats love these kinds of minority politicians because, whether Republican or Democrat, neither represents a threat to the "power structure of America,"[33] instead representing Booker T. Washington–style accomodationism.

Obama's case is illustrative. Although during his carefully orchestrated presidential campaign he and his team touted his credentials as a "community organizer," Obama's real story at the moment of his political conception is quite different. During the campaign Obama said "community organizing is 'something I carry with me when I think about politics today—obviously at a different level and in a different place, but the same principle still applies.'"[34] His wife, Michelle Obama, added, "Barack is not a politician first and foremost" and that "he's a community activist exploring the viability of politics to make change."[35] But the historical record is quite different. First, Obama accomplished quite little in his two years as a *paid*[36] community organizer: all reports, including Obama's own account in *The Audacity of Hope*, reveal he was very disappointed with the pace of change. Second, by 1987 he had all but abandoned Saul Alinsky's ideal of the community organizer and was dreaming of getting elected to office. Hence, in the same article, which is sympathetic to Obama, the author states that "Obama . . . has become exactly the kind of politician his mentors might have warned against."[37]

The record also shows that by the time Obama ran for office in 1996, he had already acquired many of the typical characteristics of post–civil rights minority politicians. After he won the Illinois state race in 1996, Adolph Reed, a black political science professor and contributor to various progressive magazines, said the following about Obama:

> In Chicago, for instance, we've gotten a foretaste of the new breed of foundation-hatched black communitarian voices; one of them, a smooth Harvard lawyer with impeccable do-good credentials and vacuous-to-repressive neo-liberal politics, has won a state senate seat on a base mainly in the liberal foundation and development worlds. His fundamentally bootstrap line was softened by a patina of the rhetoric of authentic community, talk about meeting in kitchens, small-scale solutions to social problems, and the predictable elevation of process over program—the point where identity politics converges with old-fashioned middle-class reform in favoring form

over substance. I suspect that his ilk is the wave of the future in U.S. black politics, as in Haiti and wherever else the *International Monetary Fund* has sway. So far the black activist response hasn't been up to the challenge. We have to do better.[38]

Obama negotiated Chicago Democratic politics quickly and successfully, and by 2002, he had become the darling of the city's black elite, and soon, the white elite. Christopher Drew and Mike McIntire, in a 2007 article in the *New York Times*, state that Obama "improbably" raised fifteen million dollars for his senate campaign.[39] But their characterization of this quick turnaround (from having problems settling his campaign debt from his loss to Congressman Bobby Rush in 2000 to the success of his campaign in 2004) as "improbable" is inaccurate, because by 2003 Obama had already received the blessing from the Democratic Party elders and financiers, beginning with a fundraiser held at the home of Vernon Jordan, according to Paul Street. Street states that "Obama passed this preliminary trial with *flying colors*."[40] The people in the meeting liked his academic background, suave and cool style, and political outlook. Attendees such as Gregory Craig (big-time attorney and former special counsel to Bill Clinton), Mike Williams (legislative director of the Bond Market Association), and other big wheelers appreciated that Obama was not a "racial polarizer" (that is, that he was not Jesse Jackson–like) and that he was not "anti-business." This explains the seemingly "improbable" victory of Obama in the 2004 senate race and the 700 million dollars he was able to raise in the 2008 presidential campaign. According to an investigative report by Ken Silverstein[41] and a book by David Mendell,[42] Obama rose quickly beyond the confines of Illinois because the American elite resolutely loved his "reasonable tone."

Therefore, post–civil rights minority politicians like Obama are not truly about deep change, but about compromise. If they were about fundamental changes to the American social order, they would not be the darlings of the two mainstream parties. Although some post–civil rights minority politicians may, from time to time, "talk the talk," their talk is rather abstract almost to the point of being meaningless, and they seldom if ever "walk the walk." For instance, Obama talked during the campaign about corporate lobbyists, but said nothing about *corporate power*; complained about "big money" in politics yet raised more money than *any* politician in American history; subscribed to the Republican lie about a crisis in Social Security and is likely to follow through with policies to "save" a program that is solvent;[43] and talked about alternative energy sources and clean energy yet was in bed with folks in the "clean coal" and "safe nuclear energy" camp.[44]

Based on all the information at hand, there is no question that politicians like Obama are "accomodationist"[45] *par excellence* and teach the "wretched of the earth" the wrong political lesson: that electoral, rather than social-movement, politics[46] is *the* vehicle for achieving social justice. In the next section we show that Obama's political road to the (still) White House perfectly fits the practices and tone of post–civil rights minority politicians.

"'WHO ARE YOU?' SAID THE CATERPILLAR": ON THE MEANING OF OBAMA'S POLITICS

When questions arose during the campaign about Obama's progressiveness due to his support of the Foreign Intelligence Surveillance Act (FISA)[47] and other reactionary positions he held, Obama said in an interview with the *New York Times* that "I am someone who is no doubt progressive."[48] However, true to the style of post–civil rights minority politicians, he insisted he did not like to be "labeled" as right or left and preferred to be regarded as a "nonideological" and "pragmatic" politician. As the campaign advanced, Obama's nonideological stand betrayed a conservative bent, and some commentators questioned his commitment to "progressiveness." For instance, in harsh yet prophetic words, *Huffington Post* blogger Taylor Marsh labeled Obama's brand of progressiveness as "progressive cannibalism." He was referring to Obama's willingness "to do whatever he can to get elected, cannibalizing his own and our ideals as he goes; bringing as many people along as he can, including conservatives who will have no allegiance to what progressives have worked for over decades to achieve."[49] And indeed, as Glen Ford has argued, far from representing the "lesser of two evils," Obama in 2012 is actually "the more effective evil,"[50] because the left is not prepared to fight his policies.

In this section I restate doubts I raised about Obama during the 2008 campaign and argue that his politics and tone were not, as so many liberals and progressives believed, *tactical* maneuvers to get elected, but represented who Obama truly was and how he has governed. Because the concerns I expressed about the Obama phenomenon during the 2008 and 2012 campaigns were borne out by subsequent events in his first term, I reproduce them here almost verbatim. I maintain the present tense used in the original, but the statements are formatted as extracts to distinguish them from the brief (and contemporary) discussion that appears after each one.

> The first concern I have is that Obama does not represent a true social movement, but an undercurrent of various actors and contradictory forces that did not necessarily agree on fundamental issues. Lacking a social movement with a common agenda, I believe his presidency will

become problematic as we have no way of predicting his actions and will not have people "in the streets" to curb them if needed.

When I wrote this, some commentators thought Obama had a "grass-roots" approach to politics.[51] However, all his political praxis during the campaign was in line with mainstream party politics (in fact, all he did was *through* the Democratic Party) and did not emanate from or create a social movement. The massive rallies and the 700 million-plus dollars he raised in the campaign did not emanate from the organized (or unor-ganized, as many social movements follow a more spontaneous path[52]) movements created by the efforts of activists with a common agenda. The mantra of his campaign, "Change we can believe in," was so ab-stract that almost anything and anyone could have fit in. The most sig-nificant matter, however, was that Obama supporters lacked a common agenda and belief system. What I argued during the campaign—that white support was not indicative of post-racialism—has now been cor-roborated in post-election studies. Noted survey researchers Professor Tom Pettigrew from UC–Santa Cruz and Professor Vincent Hutchings from the University of Michigan found that Obama's white voters were just slightly less prejudiced than McCain's white voters. And because Obama's white voters were younger than McCain's, as they age and face real-life issues (e.g., getting a job, getting married, selecting a neighbor-hood and schools for their kids, etc.), they are likely to regress to their racial mean—that is, will develop views similar to those of older whites today.[53]

> Second, none of the policies Obama has offered on the crucial issues of our time (health care, NAFTA, the economy, immigration, racism, the Wars, etc.) are truly radical and likely to accomplish the empty yet savvy slogan he adopted as the core of his campaign: change.

Few of Obama's ardent supporters had a clue about his policy propos-als and even about his positions on crucial issues. As Ashley Doane has pointed out, this phenomenon among otherwise well-informed people resembles Goffman's phenomenon of "studied nonobservance," where everyone pretends not to notice a violation of norms for the sake of get-ting along. For instance, while on vacation in the summer of 2008, I had a discussion with several minority professors about Obama in which they told me I was "too harsh" on Obama. As the discussion proceeded, I said, "I cannot not believe you are all for Obama so blindly given his support for the death penalty." One of them laughed and told me that Obama was not for the death penalty. I urged the colleague to check the matter on the Internet, and, a minute later, the person said, "Well, but Obama has a *nu-*

anced position," to which I replied, "When one is *dead* there is no *nuance*." Later, I will discuss some of these policies and how they do not represent change, but more of the same.

> Third, Obama has reached the level of success he has in large mea-
> sure because he has made a strategic move toward racelessness and
> adopted a post-racial persona and political stance. He has distanced
> himself from most leaders of the civil rights movement, from his own
> reverend, from his church, and from anything or anyone who made
> him look "too black" or "too political." Heck, Obama and his cam-
> paign even retooled Michelle Obama[54] to make her seem less black,
> less strong, and more white-lady-like for the white electorate!

Throughout Obama's first term, Obama has always tried to avoid seeming *too* black. (For instance, press aides apparently refused to put the Obamas on BET for the first six months of Obama's presidency.[55]) Such careful dancing around reminding the electorate of his blackness has also limited Obama's responses to racist events, sometimes farcically (as in the infamous "beer summit" with Skip Gates and the white police officer who arrested him in his home). But this also has important ramifications for Obama's policy, as I will show below. Indeed, political scientist Daniel Gillion has found that in the first half of Obama's term, the president has said less about race than *any* president since 1961.[56]

President Obama's "race lite" stand was vital during the campaign and remains so. He has avoided any serious discussion on race and, when forced to talk about it, has remained frustratingly vague. For instance, in a 2008 interview with ABC's George Stephanopoulos, he took seemingly all sides on affirmative action. He talked about the importance of *how* affirmative action is carried out, mentioned that race still matters, said his daughters probably will not need affirmative action, and hinted at a class-based program.[57] In a comment on Obama's performance in the interview, Peter S. Canellos observed in the *Boston Globe* that Obama rarely deals with the substance of the policies, but focuses on the values, a tactic that seems to go well with his supporters.[58]

Obama's post-racial stand during the campaign was not a new thing. Those who have read his books *Dreams of My Father* and *The Audacity of Hope* are familiar with his long-standing attempt to be if not *beyond* race at least *above* the racial fray. Hence, it was not the least surprising when President Obama answered the only question he was asked about race in his first press conference by suggesting race was a factor in life but that he was dealing with America's "real" problems.[59] It was also not surprising when in his second press conference he answered a question by Andre Showell, a black journalist, about what specific policies he had enacted to benefit minority communities, with ideas reminiscent of how conservatives frame race matters.

> So my general approach is that if the economy is strong, that will lift all boats as long as it is also supported by, for example, strategies around college affordability and job training, tax cuts for working families as opposed to the wealthiest that level the playing field and ensure bottom-up economic growth. And I'm confident that that will help the African-American community live out the American dream at the same time that it's helping communities all across the country.[60]

As part of his post-racialism, Obama avoided the term "racism" in his campaign until he was forced to talk about race. And in that "race speech" that so many commentators heralded and compared to speeches by MLK (a truly heretical view), he said Reverend Wright's statements "expressed a profoundly distorted view of this country—a view that sees white racism as endemic" and classified them as "divisive." This should be surprising to race scholars across the nation who regard racism as indeed "endemic" and know that race has been a "divisive" matter in America since the seventeenth century!

For readers who are familiar with my work,[61] it should not be surprising to learn that I agree with Reverend Wright about his claim that racism is endemic to America. Thus, I do not believe his statements were "divisive." Our nation has been deeply divided by race (and class and gender as well) since colonial times! Obama's speech was clearly a *political* speech intended to appease the concerns of his white supporters riled by the media-driven frenzy in March of 2008 based on a snippet of a sermon given by Reverend Wright.[62]

Obama's speech had three serious problems. First, Obama assumed racism is a moral problem (he called it a "sin") that can be overcome through goodwill. In contrast, I have argued that racism forms a structure and, accordingly, the struggle against racism must be fundamentally geared toward the removal of the practices, mechanisms, and institutions that maintain systemic white privilege. Second, Obama conceived "racism" (in his view, prejudice) as a two-way street. In the speech he stated that *both* blacks and whites have legitimate claims against one another, that is, that blacks have a real beef against whites because of the continuing existence of discrimination and whites against blacks because of the "excesses" of programs such as affirmative action. Obama was wrong on this point because blacks do not have the institutional power to implement a pro-black agenda, whereas whites have had this kind of power from the moment this country was born.[63] He was also wrong because whites' claims of "reverse discrimination" do not hold much water empirically.[64] And when he hints at the "excesses" of the 1960s, which he did

.

in this speech, he is truly talking nonsense! The data show that affirmative action has been at best a Band-Aid approach to deal with the hemorrhage of racial inequality. Third, Obama's post-racial call for everyone to "just get along"[65] so that we can deal with America's real problems shows the Achilles heel of his stand: he truly does not believe racism is a serious structural problem in America. Otherwise he would not insist—and he has continued this line of argument—that we must get on with America's *real* problems such as the economy, health care, the wars, and the like. Yet the speech accomplished its mission: it placated his white supporters who, from then on, hardly showed more concerns about Obama's racial views.[66] The speech, accordingly, can be classified as a "neoslave narrative," as sociologist Tamara K. Nopper has aptly suggested:[67] an accounting of America's progress through the iniquities of slavery to the bright days of emancipation.

> Fourth, as Glen Ford, executive editor of the *Black Agenda Report*; Adolph Reed; Angela Davis; Paul Street; and a few other analysts suggested, Obamania was (and still somewhat is) a "craze."[68] His supporters refused (and many still refuse) to even listen to facts or acknowledge some very problematic positions Obama has, such as his support for the death penalty. Although there is a larger space today than in 2008 to criticize Obama from the left, that space is still very limited, particularly in the black community. I was severely stung by the nationalist bee in presentations before minority audiences in 2008 and again in 2012.

Obama's liberal and progressive supporters wanted to believe, in ahistorical fashion, that Obama was a stealth progressive who once elected would turn left.[69] But, paraphrasing Martin Luther King Jr., "leaders should not be judged by the color of their skin but by the *content of their politics*" and the content of Obama's politics was (and is) center to center-right. Black and progressive America, unfortunately, seems destined to learn this lesson after this "neo-mulatto"[70] rents the White House for a short while and does not do any meaningful renovation.

Anyone who lived in the United States during the 2008 presidential campaign knows that the entire country was captivated by Obama, who, despite my criticisms, is a truly outstanding orator, astute politician, and remarkably charismatic man. The problem, however, remains. If Obama's charisma and charming smile prevent us from asking the hard questions, probing his record, and acknowledging his actual positions on issues, then we risk endorsing style over substance and flowery rhetoric over truly progressive positions. As Conor Friedersdorf recently put it, "Obama soothes with rhetoric and kills people in secret."[71]

Lastly, perhaps the most important factor behind Obama's success, and my biggest concern, is that he and his campaign mean and evoke different things and feelings for his white and nonwhite supporters. For his white supporters, he is the first "black" leader they feel comfortable supporting because he does not talk about racism; because he reminds them every time he has a chance he is half-white; because he is so "articulate" or, in Senator (now Vice-President) Biden's words, echoed later by Karl Rove, Obama was "the first mainstream African-American who is articulate and bright and clean and a nice-looking guy"[72] because Obama keeps talking about national unity; and because he, unlike black leaders hated by whites such as Jesse Jackson and Al Sharpton, does not make them feel guilty about the state of racial affairs in the country.[73]

Since very early on in Obama's campaign, his white supporters were *not* on the same page as his minority supporters. He quickly became for whites an Oprah- or Tiger Woods–like figure, that is, a black person who has "transcended" his blackness and become a symbol.[74] For instance, Katie Lang, a white woman profiled in a *Washington Post* article, stated that "'Obama speaks to everyone. He doesn't just speak to one race, one group,' and added, 'He is what is good about this nation.'"[75] And many whites, like Joyce Heran in the article I cite above, said without much hesitation that if Obama were like Jesse Jackson or Al Sharpton, they "probably wouldn't like him as much."[76]

In sharp contrast, for many nonwhites, and blacks particularly, Obama became a symbol of their possibilities. He was indeed, as Obama said of himself, their Joshua[77]—the leader they hoped would take them to the Promised Land of milk and honey. They read between the lines and thought Obama had a strong stance on race matters. For the old generation desperate to see change before they die,[78] and for many post–Reagan generation blacks and minorities who have seen very little racial progress during their lifetimes, Obama became the new messiah of the civil rights movement.

In a country with a racial history such as ours and where successful black leaders end up killed (Martin Luther King Jr. and Malcolm X), vilified (Malcolm X, Minister Farrakhan, and Reverend Al Sharpton), or ridiculed (almost all black politicians), one understands why the possibility of a having a black president became a symbol of the aspirations of the entire black community. In interviews with dozens of blacks from across the nation after the Iowa victory, the *New York Times* reported they "voiced pride and amazement over his victory [in the caucus] and the message it sent."[79]

The love fest between blacks and Obama that began in January 2009 after an initial period of doubt has not ended. A Pew poll conducted in late 2009 showed that blacks' perceptions of racial progress had dramatically improved in the past few years, a jump attributable to Obama's election.[80] Two years further into Obama's presidency, 85 percent of blacks said they were optimistic about their future, and 65 percent were happy with their financial situation.[81] Given the stark economic disparities I laid out earlier in this chapter, these are unexpected findings, to say the least. Although blacks' nationalist moment has a *raison d'être*, people ultimately do not eat pride, cannot find a job by feeling good about themselves, or fight discrimination by telling white folks, "We have a black president so you better behave" (would this have helped Harvard professor Henry Louis Gates?).[82] The recently deceased Professor Ronald Walters, a black political scientist at Maryland, wisely said immediately after Obama was elected president that *"one should not let the honeymoon that President Obama is enjoying among blacks and their leaders extend too far into the future."*[83]

Since I first wrote this chapter, there are some hints that this honeymoon is souring in some quarters. While only a few black commentators and public figures who had supported Obama had turned to critique in the first few years of his presidency,[84] by the last months of the 2012 election there was a thread of more nuanced debate about what Obama offers black voters. A former Obama supporter, Tavis Smiley, recently told the *Times* that "African-Americans will have lost ground in the Obama era." And Fredrick Harris wrote about blacks' declining fortunes under Obama in the *New York Times* just before the 2012 election. He found it to be a "tragedy" that "black elites—from intellectuals and civil rights leaders to politicians and clergy members—have acquiesced to this decline, seeing it as the necessary price for the pride and satisfaction of having a black family in the White House."[85]

"'WELL! WHAT ARE YOU?' SAID THE PIGEON. 'I CAN SEE YOU'RE TRYING TO INVENT SOMETHING!'": MY PREDICTIONS DURING THE CAMPAIGN AND MY SCORECARD

Social scientists must always verify how their analyses hold up over time. In this section, I restate predictions I made during the presidential campaign and assess my "batting average." I made two large predictions. First, I predicted the voices of those who contend that race fractures America profoundly would be silenced. Obama's blackness, I suggested, would become an obstacle for people of color, as whites would throw it back at them—as well as his words and actions (and even Michelle's)[86] —as evidence that race was no longer a big deal in America.[87] Second, I argued Obama's election would bring the nation closer to my prediction about racial stratification in the United States becoming Latin America–*like* (see chapter 9 of this book). Obama's presidency, I claimed, would accelerate the pace toward *symbolic* unity without the nation enacting the social policies needed for all of us to be truly "*all* Americans." And like in Latin American countries, Obama's nationalist stance ("There's not a black America and white America and Latino America and Asian America; there's the United States of America"[88]) might shut the door for the recognition of race as a central factor of life. *Obamerica* may bring us closer than ever to a "multiracial white supremacy"[89] regime similar to those in Latin America and the Caribbean where "racially mixed" folks are elected to positions of power without that altering the racial order of things or how goods and services are distributed.

These are two broad predictions, and we will need to see how history plays out in assessing them. However, early studies have shown some support for my prediction that Obama's election would lead to the perception that racism is over, with potentially harmful consequences for people of color. For instance, Valentino and Brader[90] found that a good number of whites perceived less racial discrimination immediately after the election; importantly, these people also now had worse opinions of blacks and greater opposition to affirmative action and immigration. And Tesler[91] found that even the supposedly neutral issue of health care gained racial relevance when associated with Obama. Both studies indicate whites are experiencing racial resentment around Obama and his policies. Furthermore, there is some evidence that whites' resentment is translating into increased individual racism. A set of Associated Press surveys published in 2012 showed that whites demonstrated more racism than in 2008 when Obama was elected, whether measured through explicit views or implicit biases.[92]

All this should come as no surprise to those of us who have been following the events following Obama's election. Indeed, since 2009 we have seen the resurgence of old-fashioned, overt racism in response to the country's election of a black president. So many people rushed to racist forums immediately following Obama's election that the website Stormfront had to be temporarily shut down.[93] This was soon followed by the birth of the Tea Party Movement, whose white supporters frequently voiced racist opposition to Obama. He was challenged by the emergence of the "birther" movement, playing on Obama's "difference," which alleged Obama was not born in the United States and therefore ineligible to be president. Although he eventually produced his "long form" certificate proving he was born in Hawaii, one in four Americans (and more than half of all Republicans) still believe Obama was born outside the country.[94] And the absurdity continued: in October 2012, Donald Trump offered to donate $5 million to a charity of Obama's choice if he would release his passport history and college records.[95]

Obama's opponents have used a similar racializing tactic by developing the narrative that Obama is a Muslim. This story has been so successful that by the end of his first term, a third of Republicans thought Obama is a Muslim, double the number who thought so in 2008; and a third of *all* registered voters said they didn't know what religion he was, according to a Pew poll.[96]

These narratives of Obama as a foreigner or a Muslim were reinforced by racist imagery. The *New York Post* ran a cartoon of Obama as a chimpanzee shot dead by the NYPD.[97] This was just one of many popular racist images, many of which were altered to depict Barack or Michelle Obama with watermelon and KFC buckets. Just after Obama's inauguration, a California mayor e-mailed a picture to his friends showing the White House lawn turned into a watermelon patch. A Republican official in Orange County sent a picture depicting Obama as a chimpanzee with chimpanzee parents, captioned, "Now you know why—no birth certificate."[98]

In the lead-up to the 2012 election, several Romney supporters got attention for racist displays. One man, who lynched a chair in his yard after Clint Eastwood's infamous speech delivered to an empty chair representing Obama, said, "People say that I'm racist. Well, maybe I am a little toward this president. I'm not toward black people, I am toward the President of the United States."[99] Another man put an Obama mask on a monkey statue in his yard with a sign reading "NOBAMA." But even here, there's color blindness or racism denial: according to CBS, "Caldwell said the set-up had nothing to do with race."[100] In October, a man in New Jersey set up a storefront display with a picture of Obama as a "witch doctor" in loincloth and bone through his nose. He gave interviews where he said the following:

- "It always comes down to the race card."[101]
- "If you want to call me a racist then go ahead. I can assure you I am not a racist; I just really want to see Obama go. . . . This is a good example of where race relations are under this guy's administration. . . . This has absolutely nothing to do with race."[102]
- "I don't even see color."[103]

My point here, to be clear, is that within the overall development of the new racism regime and the new phase where minority politicians can be in power, it is possible for more crude forms of racism to reemerge and even to remain in place. Hence, new racism and old-fashioned racism may coexist somewhat happily in *Obamerica*.

I now review more targeted predictions I made during the election based on President Obama's first four years in office. First, based on promises and remarks Obama made during the campaign, I predicted he would increase the size of the military, wait longer than planned for withdrawing from Iraq, increase the scope of the military intervention in Afghanistan, and, more problematically, bomb Pakistan if he got "actionable intelligence." Here I was wrong only in failing to predict the true scope of the president's involvement in the Middle East and other regions. While millions of leftists mobilized to end Bush's invasion of Afghanistan and Iraq, there has been very little challenge, or even discussion, of Obama's imperial foreign policy. In past versions of this chapter, I discussed Obama's slow withdrawal from Iraq and Afghanistan and referred to the possibility of further military involvement in Pakistan. Since then, we have learned much more about the extent of the president's foreign involvement in a wide array of countries. In several respects, Obama has gone beyond his Republican predecessor, particularly in his redefinition of executive power to wage war, kill any person deemed an enemy (including Americans) without trial, use unmanned drones to terrorize populations in multiple countries, detain people indefinitely, and spy on American citizens.

We have entered a new era of the "War on Terror" in which our engagements have no defined beginning or end, nor are we clear on how many countries we are bombing (by September 2012, the count included Afghanistan, Iraq, Pakistan, Somalia, Yemen, Libya, and threats of strikes in Syria and Iran). Even in Iraq, where Obama finally removed all combat troops in December 2011, there is already discussion of sending some units back to that country.[104] Obama's "surge" (escalation) of the Afghanistan war tripled the number of troops in the country. Even now that he has sent thirty thousand troops back home, there are still sixty-six thousand American soldiers there, eleven years into our longest war ever. Obama plans to shift the war to a "support" mission by 2014, but this is not the same as ending the war and bringing all troops home. In fact, Obama and Afghan president Karzai quietly signed a deal in April 2012 agreeing to the United States' continued presence in the country until at least 2024[105] with as many as twenty-five thousand troops,[106] only eight thousand fewer than when Bush left office in 2009.[107] We must also note Obama's 2011 war in Libya, widely regarded as a success on the left, but which was waged without congressional approval (and Obama was threatening to renew drone strikes in October 2012).[108]

Progressives, who loudly decried hints of war with Iran in the Bush years, are also quiet as the media continues to breathlessly report Obama's and Netanyahu's threats against Iran. Obama set the stage for war, increasing Bush's cyber-attacks on Iran (the first time a country has waged this attack on another country),[109] building a missile-defense system in Qatar,[110] having his national security adviser brief Netanyahu on his contingency plans for an Iran strike,[111] allowing the DNC to call

Jerusalem the capital of Israel in its party platform,[112] and refusing to take a military strike off the table as he repeatedly expressed his support for Israel. In September 2012, the United States and Britain even sent warships into the Persian Gulf (in Iranian and Omanian waters) to practice breaking a potential Iran blockade.[113] As Glenn Greenwald has pointed out,[114] we should also be considering the impact of nonmilitary campaigns against Iranian citizens. According to reports,[115] the United States' economic sanctions on Iran, begun in 2010, are causing medicine and food shortages and leading to riots.

Any assessment of Obama's military policy must also take into account his dramatically stepped-up use of unmanned drones for "military strikes" wielded both by the military and the CIA.[116] While the administration has claimed that civilian losses are minimal, this is not the case. A reanalysis of casualty figures for twenty-four drone strikes in Pakistan based on interviews with victims' families and other information found a systematic underestimate of the number of civilian deaths when using media reports. This underestimating has grown even worse under Obama, who solved the problem of civilian deaths by redefining any strike victim as a "combatant" if male and over fourteen.[117] But beyond arguing over the number of deaths, we must also pay attention to the impact of the drones on the living. An NYU/Stanford report[118] details the costs to those living in the area of Pakistan most targeted by drones: beyond the property damage, the psychological costs are severe. Unsure when the next attack will strike, parents keep their children out of school. People fear to assist victims of drone strikes because a second strike has been known to target rescuers, a potential war crime.[119] Far from making us safer, Pakistan's foreign minister has attributed her country's anti-Americanism to these attacks.[120] As opposition Pakistan politician Imran Khan put it, "The war on terror has become a war of terror."[121]

Beyond his attacks on the Middle East, President Obama's drastic expansion of executive power in order to wage this undefined war is beyond frightening. FISA requests and an NSA whistleblower have shown that electronic surveillance has dramatically risen under Obama.[122] The administration is also resisting a judge's hold on its program of indefinite detention of terrorism suspects (defined as any person who "substantially supported al-Qaeda, the Taliban, or associated forces") without trial; this program was challenged by reporters who feared the law was broad enough to potentially include them. Most frightening was the *New York Times*'s 2012 disclosure of Obama's "kill list," where individuals, including U.S. citizens, are targeted for assassination, usually by drone strike, before any accusations of guilt were made.[123] In a recent article on how Obama's approach is setting us up for a "permanent war," Greg Miller writes, "Targeted killing is now so routine that the Obama Administration has spent much of the past year codifying and streamlining the processes that sustain it."[124] He notes that the CIA has requested more drones in its budget, turning it into a "paramilitary force."[125]

Put together, Obama's foreign policy is extremely concerning for its abuse of executive power to engage in unchecked military actions. If these policies were being implemented by a Republican president, the left would be in a continuous uproar.[126] But as I predicted, the resistance to these terrible policies has been anemic: no matter what he has done, Obama is still considered to be a "nice guy." Where they are not simply silent, some liberals either justify supporting Obama's actions against the alternative (as Rebecca Solnit did in a recent piece in *The Nation*), or actually celebrate them, as did a *Huffington Post* reporter, who claimed "Obama must be doing something really right" with foreign policy since the Republicans were avoiding the topic in their convention.[127]

And the international community, with few exceptions, has given Obama a pass no matter what. He received the Nobel Peace Prize in 2009 and has not been rebuked by the European leaders or by the European left on his foreign policy. For instance, during the Bush years (2000–2008), the European community was up in arms against his interventionism and militarism, and even in 2011 Bush had to cancel a planned trip to Switzerland over concerns about protests.[128] However, this same community has not said anything about Obama's Bush-Lite foreign policy, and Obama still enjoys sky-high approval ratings in many European countries.[129]

Second, I suggested Obama was going to put together a very conservative cabinet. As predicted, the conservative people who advised him during the campaign are now the core of his cabinet. His advisers have included Hillary Clinton, Robert Gates (kept on from the G. W. Bush administration), Larry Summers (a Clinton-era holdout infamous for his famous sexist speech at Harvard), Paul Volker (who served under Carter and Reagan), and Timothy Geithner (who has followed the interests of Wall Street). President Obama does not have a *single* radical voice on his team. And let's not forget that Obama's cabinet is not as diverse as one would expect,[130] and that the few people of color in his cabinet are in secondary positions.

Any turnover in staff would be an opportunity to move in a leftward direction, if Obama's progressive supporters were right that his early centrist talk was setting up a future turn to the left, but instead Obama reinforced ties to previous administrations and financial interests. Since Rahm Emanuel left as chief of staff in 2011 to run for mayor of Chicago, for instance, he has been succeeded by William Daley and Jack Lew, both Clinton advisors. All three men are former investment bankers, and Lew, the current chief, last worked in Citigroup's "proprietary trading" department, betting against the housing market just before the recession.[131] And

Obama's second-term cabinet nominations have been even more disappointing. Obama nominated a Republican, Chuck Hagel, to the position of secretary of defense. Perhaps his most offensive decision was to nominate John Brennan, who supported extraordinary rendition and torture under Bush, the "key architect" of Obama's drone wars,[132] to head up the CIA. Obama had to withdraw Brennan's name in his first term due to a (rare) uproar from the left over Brennan's history. His decision to choose Brennan again, now that Obama has been safely reelected, is a huge insult to his base (and should chasten those who told us that Obama just had to get elected, and then reelected, before he could bring out his hidden, progressive side).

Third, I suggested Obama was going to compromise on his promise of taxing the rich. In his first term, Obama unequivocally did so, extending the tax cuts for those making over $250,000 for another two years *and* revising the estate tax according to Republican demands, in a so-called compromise. The president claimed this compromise was necessary to insure unemployment benefits: in exchange, he won the extension of unemployment insurance benefits (for only one year), and other tax credits designed to stimulate the economy and return money to middle-class Americans. But the small-business benefits Obama has touted as making this "compromise" worthwhile are smokescreens. The *New York Times* cites government and nonpartisan analyses stating that "less than 3 percent of filers with small-business income pay at the top two income tax rates, and many of those are doctors and lawyers in partnerships."[133] When one considers only small businesses with actual employees, these businesses would have been responsible for only 12 percent of the new income taxes. Besides, not all these small businesses are actually small: 20,000 of the businesses filing in 2011 under this category made over $50 million.[134] In other words, even the liberal policies obtained as "concessions" primarily benefitted the wealthy. Delaying taxing the rich if the economy is not doing well indicates that President Obama's economic views are in line with the "Chicago School."[135]

At the beginning of Obama's second term, Obama doubled down on his poor tax "compromises." Rather inexplicably, as his opponents were in disarray and failed to produce a coherent alternative, Obama broke his oft-repeated promise to raise taxes on families earning more than $250,000 in annual income, moving the line to those making over $400,000 per year (only the richest 1.5 percent). When one combines this change with Obama's decision not to extend the payroll tax cut (which helped lower- and middle-income families), and the cuts in Social Security (no longer tying rate increases to inflation), it's clear that Obama is willing to bargain away most progressive values without gaining much in return. Jonathan Chait compared Obama's negotiation to the "tight-weak" style of poker playing, where the player loses weak hands and fails to take advantage of strong ones.[136] But such a criticism still presumes that Obama actually shared our progressive values in the first place.

Fourth, I suggested Obama's health care plan was weak and that his "pragmatism" was going to make it even weaker. Specifically, I argued that Obama's proposed reform was far off from what the country needed: a universal, single-payer health care plan.[137] This was a bone of contention during the campaign, as independent observers commented that Obama had the weakest health care plan of all the contenders for the Democratic Party's nomination. While Obama did pass a health-care reform bill in 2009 that included some fixes, the bill ultimately passed without the "public option" to buy insurance directly from the government. The debate left a bad taste in the mouths of progressives as Health and Human Services secretary Kathleen Sebelius, Max Baucus, and other Democrats emphasized that single-payer insurance was "not on the table."[138] Obama tried to exclude members of his own party such as Congressman John Conyers from Michigan, a leading proponent of a single-payer system, from meetings on health care reform. Conyers, after he threatened to picket outside the White House, was invited to the summit and, later on, in a presentation at Thomas Jefferson University described the attendees of the meeting as follows: "It was very heavy with corporate health care interests—Big Pharma, insurance companies—the people who don't want single payer."[139]

Instead of single-payer, Obama's plan institutes a mandate forcing everyone to purchase private insurance, and subsidizing plans for those who can't afford insurance but don't qualify for Medicaid (constituting a giant payout to the insurance industry). We should remember that, despite Republican opposition to Obama's health care reform, the mandate was originally a Republican idea. As John Cassidy writes,

> The problem is fundamental. Setting aside the expansion of Medicaid and some long-overdue restrictions on the egregious behavior of health insurers, this isn't really health-care "reform": it is a significant expansion of the current system of private insurance, with the taxpayer footing the bill. It is Mitt Romney's Massachusetts experiment writ large, a peculiar amalgam of egalitarian intent and corporate welfare: egalitarianism in the form of providing health care to those who can't afford it; corporate welfare in the form of paying corporations such as Aetna and Wellpoint generously to take on millions of new enrollees. If the average American doesn't realize this, people on Wall Street do. Since Obama's election, in November, 2008, Aetna's stock has gone from $20 to $35; Wellpoint's has gone from $30 to $63.[140]

Fifth, I predicted that because of Obama's weak stand on race and his post-racial persona and appeal, he was not going to enact any meaningful policies to ameliorate racial inequality. Obama's so-called middle-ground position on race can be examined in chapter 7 of his book, *The Audacity of Hope*. There he insists that although race still matters, "prejudice" is declining, and as proof he heralds the growth of the black elite, whose members do not "use race as a crutch or point to discrimination as an excuse for failure."[141] He acknowledges the existence of significant gaps between whites and minorities in income, wealth, and other areas and voices only tepid support for affirmative action, yet engages in a Bill Cosby–like critique of blacks and states they watch "too much television," engage in "too much consumption of poisons," lack an "emphasis on educational achievement," and do not have two-parent households.[142] So what is his solution to deal with racial inequality? "An emphasis on universal, as opposed to race-specific, programs," which he believes "isn't just good policy; it's also good politics."[143] He also discusses the problem of the black "underclass" and chastises those unwilling to accept the role of "values" in their predicament.[144] Although he mentions that "culture is shaped by circumstances,"[145] his emphasis is on behavior.[146]

Since taking office, Obama has maintained this universalist position. I believe the $789 billion stimulus package his administration passed in early 2009, which gave control to localities on how to use the funds, is a case in point. Giving money directly to localities without any controls is quite problematic, as localities have historically distributed funds in a way that preserves existing inequities.[147] Unless one adopts what john powell labels "targeted universalism"—a perspective that takes into consideration that people are differently situated in the social order and, thus, that some may need more resources than others—"universal" efforts such as this one will not reduce racial inequities.[148]

Obama's first term has indeed been notable for its lack of race-specific policies, even despite the staggering economic statistics I cited earlier. His inaction has been especially visible on the issue of black unemployment. Despite the severity of the problem, Obama said in 2009 he couldn't make policy specifically helping blacks find work: "I can't pass laws that say I'm just helping black folks. I'm president of the entire United States."[149] When the Congressional Black Caucus called him out for not doing enough for blacks in this area, Obama famously told the caucus to "take off your bedroom slippers. . . . Stop complaining, stop grumbling, stop crying."[150] To blacks who accuse him of not being aggressive on race, Mr. Obama has a reply: "I'm not the president of black America," he has said. "I'm the president of the United States of America."[151]

Obama's reticence on race has meant that he has avoided discussing even those issues that whites stereotypically associate with blacks. In the 2012 election debates, Romney and Ryan repeatedly talked about poverty and food stamps (in a racially pointed way), but Obama never mentioned either of these.[152] In 2011, he was the first president since 1948 who failed to acknowledge poverty or the poor in his State of the Union speech.[153] Amidst continued high unemployment and astronomical wealth inequality, our president seems unable to acknowledge, much less defend, the 46 million people living below the poverty line. Our "progressive" president's refusal to strongly defend antipoverty programs will have reverberating effects for poor people of all races.

Obama's refusal or inability to address race directly is also exacerbating the problem of voter suppression. In the lead-up to the 2012 election, as many states passed or introduced voter ID laws, people of color were purged from the polls, and vigilante groups further suppressed the vote with voter intimidation,[154] Obama was silent on the issue of voting rights. When Michelle Obama spoke to the CBC in September 2012, she said, "We cannot let anyone discourage us from casting our ballots"—but she did not directly address, much less criticize, states' new voter ID laws.[155] This was especially embarrassing as even former RNC chairman Michael Steele, who is far from a racial progressive, spoke out against "frivolous or harmful laws" undermining Republicans' attempts to woo voters of color.[156] When Jay Leno asked Obama directly about voter suppression two weeks before the election, he responded only that "it's a problem" before refusing to comment on the voter ID lawsuits, saying only that we "should be thinking about ways to make it easier for folks to vote," and then turned to praise early voting instead.[157]

Obama's single initiative directly targeted at blacks, conveniently announced in the summer before the 2012 election, is in the relatively uncontroversial area of education. While eliminating educational disparities is a laudable goal, the initiative seems cynically designed to allow Obama to point to the program as helping blacks, while announced with little fanfare and little funding so as to not attract attention from whites. But all in all, Obama has left us high and dry—and his campaign doesn't even try to hide it. In 2012, some black donors were disappointed at a campaign meeting when Obama officials "handed out cards with talking points on the Administration's achievements for various groups—women, Jews, gays and lesbians—and there was no card for African-Americans."[158]

In the 2012 election, Obama took support from blacks for granted, but he also seems to have been correct in assuming he could get away with it, enjoying both increased black voter turnout and 93 percent of black votes.[159] In September 2012, Representative Emanuel Cleaver of the Congressional Black Caucus acknowledged that black members of Congress had been holding Obama to a lower standard. Pointing to the historic level of African American unemployment, Cleaver said, "If we had a white president we'd be marching around the White House."[160] In his article, Butler compares blacks' easing up on Obama to the gay community's insistent pressure. When it looked like he was going to stall them early in his administration, they got him to overturn "Don't Ask, Don't Tell" and express support for gay marriage. Where is the black community exerting similar pressure on Obama?

Sixth, I criticized the progressive and liberal community in America for being in "silly season," to use Obama's terminology, regarding the amount of money he raised, how he raised it (bundling), and for ignoring the implications this money would have in his administration.[161] Are we not concerned that Wall Street and HMOs *support* Obama? Do we believe that 700 million dollars in donations did not affect his administration in 2008? I could not have predicted the Supreme Court's decision on *Citizens United* and its huge impact on political campaigns, primarily by permitting unlimited spending on campaigns and the creation of super PACs that repackage anonymized donations. But although Obama has denounced the decision, he has taken advantage of *Citizens* by sending his campaign manager Rahm Emanuel to head the super PAC Priorities USA. As a campaign finance lawyer observed, "The real scandal in the 2012 election is the activities that are perfectly legal."[162] And reports coming in just after the 2012 election suggest that both sides are already actively fundraising for the next campaign.[163]

A common argument on the left is that Obama is constrained in his policy efforts by a republican House (articulated recently by Michael Eric Dyson in his debate with Glen Ford in September 2012). But, as Ford replied, Obama is not a "victim of all these Republican forces, but in fact he is the initiator, from within the Democratic Party, of these austerity measures."[164] In fact, many of Obama's most dangerous policies—the expanded War on Terror or his doubling Bush's number of deportations, did not come from Republican pressure. Most likely, they were instead motivated, if indirectly, by corporations whose military-industrial infrastructure needs more bodies for private prisons and more targets for our bombs. At the very least, we should consider who profits from these policies.

These were my predictions and arguments about Obama and, sadly, many have become a reality and others seem very likely. Obama is clearly not a stealth progressive, but a centrist, pro-market, traditional politician with a *quasi*-color-blind view about race matters in America. By early in his presidency, Obama himself had accepted part of this characterization as when, in a meeting with centrist members of his party in April of 2009, he described himself as a "new Democrat" and as a "pro-growth Democrat,"[165] both clear signifiers of his pro-business stance.

To be clear, my characterization of President Obama is political and policy-based rather than moral or personal. Like so many Americans, I also believe President Obama is a more capable, dignified, and shining

representative of this country in the world platform than his predecessor. There is little doubt that Obama projects to the world community a
much better image of this nation and its possibilities. Even before he was
elected, international polls showed that up to three-fourths of people in
the world believed that "an Obama presidency would see improved U.S.
relations with the rest of the world."[166]

In past versions of this chapter, I cited several of Obama's policies I
found relatively admirable, to clarify that I did not believe all of his policies are wrongheaded. Unfortunately, at the end of his first term, many of
these have been weakened or undermined by other actions he has taken.
Below I will provide brief updates on the policies I once applauded, to
show that even where Obama has been good, he has rarely lived up to
the hype.

Lilly Ledbetter Fair Pay Act: While Obama deserves kudos for signing
this act on his first day in office, it does not mandate equal pay for women
(as he sometimes implies in campaign speeches)[167] but only facilitates
litigation. Also, under Obama, the EEOC has brought only six sex-based
pay lawsuits, as compared to eighteen under Bush at the same point in
his presidency, and charges of sex-based discrimination have actually
dropped slightly,[168] the reverse of what one would expect had the act
succeeded. Indeed, he may have oversold the impact of the legislation to
court women voters,[169] 55 percent of whom voted for him in 2012.[170]

Cessation of so-called enhanced interrogation techniques (torture): Soon after
his election, Obama reversed his promise of releasing pictures of prisoners who were tortured,[171] successfully pressured Spain in 2009 to drop
its indictments of top Bush officials for torture,[172] reinstated "military
tribunals,"[173] and, as I have noted above, defended his policy of indefinite
detention for terrorism suspects and affiliates. Conservative columnist
Charles Krauthammer argues that Obama's denunciation of torture
should be weighed against his preference to simply kill potential enemies
on his "kill list," without interrogation.[174] And as of late 2012, Guantanamo's prison remained open, despite Obama's repeated promises to close
it, with 169 detainees awaiting trial and another 87 prisoners who have
been exonerated, but not freed.[175]

*Public statements about wanting to extend a hand to leaders of "rival na-
tions"*: While Obama has received a lot of criticism for his supposed love
relationship with Chavez, his administration has been funding anti-
Chavez resistance movements.[176] Under Obama's administration, USAID
has continued to fund "pro-democracy" efforts against governments
deemed unfriendly to the United States, as in Cuba, where a USAID employee was discovered to be clandestinely bringing technological equipment into the country and sentenced for undermining the government.[177]

And Bolivia has just accused the U.S. embassy in that country of working to destabilize it.[178]

The achievement of reform of our health care system (even if it ends up not delivering a single-payer system, a reformed bad system will be better than the current one): See my concerns above. Some features of this plan will improve lives for many Americans, despite my concerns above. But on the other hand, what does it mean that Obama's administration cannot even advertise its own "success?" At the 2012 Democratic National Convention, not a single person mentioned Obamacare's greatest achievement: providing an additional 30 million people with Medicaid coverage. As with Obama's refusal to even say the word "poverty," Democrats feared arousing prejudice with the very word "Medicaid."[179]

Support of the "Employee Free Choice Act" which would facilitate workers' efforts to get unionized: Obama hesitated early in his first term on this policy and urged workers to find a "compromise" with the business community,[180] was absolutely quiet during the 2011 pro-union movement in Wisconsin and elsewhere, and surrounds himself with "education experts" (most notably Arne Duncan) who want to dismantle unions and increase charter schools.

New emission and mileage standards:[181] While Obama has also made some good investments in clean energy, this is too little, too late, as he pledges to pursue an "all of the above" approach that involves nuclear energy, dangerous natural gas drilling or "fracking," coal, and, likely, approving the construction of a tar sands oil pipeline across part of the United States.

Legislation to exert some control over the credit card industry:[182] While Obama's creation of the Consumer Financial Protection Bureau is admirable, his appointment of Richard Cordray, rather than the more progressive Elizabeth Warren (who conceived of the bureau and did much of the work to set it up), is less so.[183]

"'TUT, TUT, CHILD!' SAID THE DUCHESS. 'EVERYTHING'S GOT A MORAL, IF ONLY YOU CAN FIND IT'": LET SOCIAL JUSTICE NOT DIE AT THE ALTAR OF "PRAGMATISM" AND COLOR BLINDNESS

During the election, my overall claim was that the Obama phenomenon was not a "miracle" or an event that denotes how far we have come in the arena of "race relations,"[184] but the product of forty years of racial transition. As such, Obama's election as president may help bring to the fore a more powerful type of racial domination: a Latin America–like multiracial white supremacy order.[185] In *Obamerica* the space for talking about race matters may dwindle, as whites have gained the upper hand symbolically. Although little has changed in the fundamentals of the racial order, having a black man "in charge" gives the impression of monumental change and allows whites to tell those who research, write, talk, and organize against racial inequality that they must be crazy. Whites can now say, "How can racism be important in a country that just elected a black man as its president?"

I also argued that Obama's politics and stand on racial matters epitomize the character of America's racial regime, which, among other things, brought forth the post–civil rights minority politician. Although Obama is the most successful exemplar of this new kind of politician, the Democratic and Republican landscape is dotted with them, and I forecast many will emerge as central political figures in the near future. Let us not forget, for example, that before Obama, former secretary of state General Colin Powell could have run for president in 1996.[186] In that year an exit poll conducted the day of the election revealed that had Powell, rather than Bob Dole, been the candidate for the Republicans, he would have won the election.[187]

President Obama has emphasized his interest in "bipartisanship," on not being "ideological," and on his "pragmatic" approach to politics as policy.[188] But what does this mean and what does it imply? I argue that Obama's pragmatism and distaste for what he calls "ideology" betrays his center-right stand on most issues. This argument is not entirely original, as *New York Times* writer David Leonhardt dissected Obama's policy views in a piece titled "Obamanomics," where he described Obama as a "University of Chicago Democrat" and suggested that "Obama simply is more comfortable with the apparent successes of laissez-faire economics."[189] More tellingly, Leonhardt wrote that "invoking pragmatism doesn't help the average voter much; ideology, though it often gets a bad name, matters, because it offers insight into how a candidate might actually behave as president."[190]

Interestingly, like all Democratic presidents and presidential candidates since Lyndon B. Johnson, Obama depends on strong electoral support from minority communities. If at some point black and Latino supporters, who were crucial for Obama's victories in 2008 and 2012,[191] realize he is not enacting policies that have benefitted them, they may walk out of the Democratic Party's electoral coalition. But since there are no other electoral options at this juncture, what political options are there for people of color and progressives to make sure the change they were promised is delivered? In the concluding chapter of this book, I offer some advice to progressives who want to make "change you can believe in" more than a vacuous phrase.

NOTES

1. By Obamerica I mean the fact that Obama was elected without the backing of a social movement; hence, rather than a politician representing *change*, he represented *more of the same*.

2. Wornie L. Reed and Bertin M. Louis, "'No More Excuses': Problematic Responses to Barack Obama's Election," *Journal of African American Studies* 13, no. 1 (2009): 97–109. From Bill Cosby to Bill Bennett, from John Lewis to Will Smith, from the Obamas (both) to far too many black and white pundits, the profoundly conservative, outdated, and empirically wrong claim of "now blacks have no more excuses" has reemerged. For a refutation, see Reed and Louis, "'No More Excuses.'"

3. George Orwell, "In Front of Your Nose," in *The Collected Essays, Journalism, and Letters of George Orwell*, vol. 4, edited by S. Orwell and I. Angus (New York: Harcourt, Brace, and World, 1946).

4. The exact quote from the second president of the United States is "Facts are stubborn things; and whatever may be our wishes, our inclinations, or the dictates of our passion, they cannot alter the state of facts and evidence." The quote can be found in the website of Law Professor Douglas Linder, Famous American Trials, "Boston Massacre Trials, 1770," at www.law.umkc.edu/faculty/projects/ftrials/bostonmassacre/bostonmassacre.html.

5. Michael Fix and Raymond J. Struyk, *Clear and Convincing Evidence: Measurement of Discrimination in America* (Washington, D.C.: Urban Institute, 1993).

6. Particularly in chapter 4 of my book, *White Supremacy and Racism in the Post-Civil Rights Era* (Boulder, Colo.: Lynne Rienner Publishers, 2001).

7. Amaad Rivera, Jeannette Huezo, Christina Kasica, and Dedrick Muhammad, "State of the Dream 2009: The Silent Depression," United for a Fair Economy, January 15, 2009, retrieved from www.faireconomy.org/files/pdf/state_of_dream_2009.pdf (accessed March 31, 2013).

8. Earl Graves, "State of Black America," *Black Enterprise*, April 8, 2009, retrieved from www.blackenterprise.com/blogs/2009/04/08/state-of-black-america-wealth-for-life (accessed March 21, 2013).

9. U.S. Department of Labor, Bureau of Labor Statistics, *The Employment Situation—October 2012*, tables A2–A3, retrieved from www.bls.gov/news.release/archives/empsit_11022012.pdf (accessed January 16, 2013).

10. Bureau of Labor Statistics, *The Employment Situation*, table A4.

11. Carmen DeNavas-Walt, Bernadette D. Proctor, and Jessica C. Smith, "Income, Poverty, and Health Insurance Coverage in the United States: 2011," U.S. Census Bureau, September 2012, retrieved from www.census.gov/prod/2012pubs/p60-243.pdf (accessed March 31, 2013).

12. DeNavas-Walt, Proctor, and Smith, "Income, Poverty, and Health Insurance Coverage in the United States."

13. DeNavas-Walt, Proctor, and Smith, "Income, Poverty, and Health Insurance Coverage in the United States."

14. Melvin Oliver and Thomas Shapiro, *Black Wealth, White Wealth* (New York: Routledge, 1995).

15. Rakesh Kochhar, Richard Fry, and Paul Taylor, "Wealth Gaps Rise to Record Highs Between Whites, Blacks and Hispanics," Pew Research Center, July 26, 2011, retrieved from http://pewresearch.org/pubs/2069/housing-bubble-sub prime-mortgages-hispanics-blacks-household-wealth-disparity (accessed March 31, 2013).

16. Center for Responsible Lending, "Lost Ground, 2011: Disparities in Mortgage Lending and Foreclosures," November 17, 2011, retrieved from www .responsiblelending.org/mortgage-lending/policy-legislation/regulators/facing -the-foreclosure-crisis.html (accessed March 31, 2013).

17. Charlie Savage, "Wells Fargo Will Settle Mortgage Bias Charges," *New York Times,* July 12, 2012, retrieved from www.nytimes.com/2012/07/13/business/ wells-fargo-to-settle-mortgage-discrimination-charges.html (accessed March 31, 2013).

18. William Julius Wilson, *The Declining Significance of Race: Blacks and Changing American Institutions* (Chicago: University of Chicago Press, 1978); *The Truly Disadvantaged* (Chicago: University of Chicago Press, 1987).

19. Joe R. Feagin, "The Continuing Significance of Race: Antiblack Discrimination in Public Places," *American Sociological Review* 56, no. 1 (1991): 101–16.

20. Roy Brooks, *Integration or Separation? A Strategy for Racial Equality* (Cambridge, Mass.: Harvard University Press, 1996). For a great review of the contemporary landscape of discrimination, see Devah Pager and Hannah Sheppard, "The Sociology of Discrimination: Racial Discrimination in Employment, Housing, Credit, and Consumer Markets," *Annual Review of Sociology* 34 (2008): 181–209.

21. Janice Blanchard and Nicole Lurie, "R-e-s-p-e-c-t: Patient Reports of Disrespect in the Health Care Setting and Its Impact on Care," *Journal of Family Practice* 53 (2004): 721–31; Louis A. Penner, John H. Dovidio, Donald Edmondson, Rhonda K. Dailey, Tsveti Markova, Terrance L. Albrecht, and Samuel L. Gaertner, "The Experience of Discrimination and Black-White Health Disparities in Medical Care," *Journal of Black Psychology* 35 (2009): 180–203.

22. Sarah E. Rusche and Zachary W. Brewster, "'Because They Tip for Shit!': The Social Psychology of Everyday Racism in Restaurants," *Sociology Compass* 2, no. 6 (2008): 2008–29.

23. Ian Ayres, *Pervasive Prejudice?* (Chicago: University of Chicago Press, 2002); Serge Kovaleski and Sewell Chan, "D.C. Cabs Still Bypass Minorities, Study Finds: City Crackdown Called Sporadic, Inadequate," *Washington Post,* October 7, 2003, retrieved from www.highbeam.com/doc/1P2-313833.html (accessed March 31, 2013).

24. Albert Meehan and Michael Ponder, "Race and Place: The Ecology of Racial Profiling African American Motorists," *Justice Quarterly* 19 (2002): 399–430.

25. Cathy Harris, *Flying While Black: A Whistleblower's Story* (Los Angeles: Milligan, 2001).

26. In the 1960s, sociologist Paul M. Siegel wrote a very influential paper titled "On the Cost of Being a Negro" (*Sociological Inquiry* 35, no. 1 [1965]: 41–57) documenting the multiple and deleterious impact of racism on blacks. This idea was updated in the 1990s with the notion of "living while black," "driving while black," and so on. In a recent paper, Shaun Gabbidon and Steven A. Peterson updated the evidence: "Living While Black: A State-Level Analysis of the Influence

of Select Social Stressors on the Quality of Life Among Black Americans" *Journal of Black Studies* 37, no. 1 (2008): 83–102. I added "brown" to the text in the quote, as many scholars have performed similar analyses for Latinos and Asians and have documented that racism affects them adversely, too.

27. Professor William A. Smith has worked tirelessly to demonstrate that racism produces the syndrome he calls "racial battle fatigue." The constant thinking, preparing, expecting, and being concerned about the potential for racial discrimination creates an almost-constant state of "fight or flight" in people of color, with deleterious health consequences. See William A. Smith, Walter Allen, and Lynnette Danley, "'Assume the Position . . . You Fit the Description': Psychosocial Experiences and Racial Battle Fatigue among African American Male College Students," *American Behavioral Scientist* 51, no. 4 (2007): 551–78.

28. Steven Tuch and Michael Hughes, "Whites' Racial Policy Attitudes in the Twenty-First Century: The Continuing Significance of Racial Resentment," *The ANNALS of the American Academy of Political and Social Science* 634 (2011): 134.

29. Conservative race analysts, such as Hoover Institute senior fellow Paul Sniderman, have carried the academic torch for the white majority who insist that whites are mostly tolerant, that we still have a few bigots but they are few and far between, and that white views on crime, welfare, government intervention, and affirmative action are "principled" rather than race-based (see chapter 1). His latest book on race attitudes in the United States is *Black Pride and Black Prejudice* (Ewing, N.J.: Princeton University Press, 2002).

30. Most liberal and progressive commentators bought Obama's arguments, ideas, and even style. Noteworthy examples were black public intellectuals such as bell hooks, Michael Eric Dyson, Manning Marable, and Cornel West (after some initial hesitation), who supported Obama almost uncritically. An example of the analysts who thought Obama unlikely, or very difficult, to be elected is Joe R. Feagin. See his comments, as well as those of five other analysts including me, in "The Social Significance of Race," at www.contexts.org/obama (accessed March 31, 2013).

31. Manning Marable, "Jackson and the Rise of the Rainbow Coalition," *New Left Review* 1, no. 149 (1989), retrieved from http://newleftreview.org/I/149/manning-marable-jackson-and-the-rise-of-the-rainbow-coalition (accessed March 31, 2013).

32. Political scientists have been exploring this trend for a while and called it "deracialization." See, for example, Georgia Persons, *Dilemmas of Black Politics: Issues of Leadership and Strategy* (New York: HarperCollins, 2009).

33. Still one of the best books on the "power structure" of America and how the system works is the classic yet magnificently updated book by William G. Domhoff, *Who Rules America? Power, Politics, & Social Change*, 5th ed. (New York: McGraw-Hill, 2006).

34. John B. Judis, "Creation Myth," *The New Republic*, September 10, 2008, retrieved from www.newrepublic.com/article/creation-myth-0 (accessed March 31, 2013).

35. Judis, "Creation Myth."

36. One must be careful not to equate the work and politics of paid "activists" with the work and politics of grassroots organizers. Although both may be

motivated by similar principles, unpaid work produces a totally different kind of political experience and generates a deeper political experience.

37. Judis, "Creation Myth."

38. Adolph Reed, "The Curse of Community," *Village Voice*, January 16, 1996— reprinted in *Class Notes: Posing as Politics and Other Thoughts on the American Scene* (New York: New Press, 2000), 13.

39. Christopher Drew and Mike McIntire, "After 2000 Loss, Obama Built Donor Network from Roots Up," *New York Times*, April 3, 2007, retrieved from www .nytimes.com/2007/04/03/us/politics/03obama.html?_r1 (accessed March 31, 2013).

40. Paul Street, *Barack Obama and the Future of American Politics* (Boulder, Colo.; and London: Paradigm Publishers, 2009), xxiii, my emphasis.

41. Ken Silverstein, "Barack Obama, Inc.: The Birth of a Washington Machine," *Harper's*, November 2006, retrieved from www.harpers.org/archive/ 2006/11/0081275 (accessed March 21, 2013).

42. David Mendell, *Obama: From Promise to Power* (New York: HarperCollins, 2007).

43. On this matter, see Dean Baker and Mark Weisbrot, *Social Security: The Phony Crisis* (Chicago: The University of Chicago Press, 2001), and Paul Krugman, "Played for a Sucker," *New York Times*, November 16, 2007, retrieved from www .nytimes.com/2007/11/16/opinion/16krugman.html?_r=0 (accessed March 31, 2013).

44. See chapter 1 in Street, *Barack Obama and the Future of American Politics*.

45. Manning Marable, *Race, Reform and Rebellion: The Second Reconstruction and Beyond in Black America, 1945–1990* (Oxford: University Press of Mississippi, 1991).

46. Arguably the weight of the historical evidence shows that *fundamental* social change is the product of social protest. See Frances Fox Piven, *Challenging Authority: How Ordinary People Change America* (Lanham, Md.: Rowman & Littlefield, 2006).

47. FISA was originally enacted in 1978. This act became extremely problematic as President Bush reportedly used it in an abusive way in violation of the Fourth Amendment. In 2008, the act was going to be amended to make sure that those who provided information to the government (telecommunication giants) in violation of privacy rights could not be prosecuted, but Republicans derailed this by adding amendments to a bill sponsored by Senators Dodd and Feingold, which were supported by then-Senator Obama. For a blow-by-blow account, see Jack Tapper, "Obama's FISA Shift," ABC News, July 9, 2008, retrieved from http:// abcnews.go.com/blogs/politics/2008/07/obamas-fisa-shi (accessed March 31, 2013).

48. Michael Powell, "Obama Addresses Critics on 'Centrist' Moves," *New York Times*, July 8, 2008, retrieved from http://thecaucus.blogs.nytimes .com/2008/07/08/obama-addresses-critics-on-centrist-moves (accessed March 31, 2013).

49. Taylor Marsh, "Barack Obama's Progressive Cannibalism," *Huffington Post*, December 8, 2007, retrieved from www.huffingtonpost.com/taylor-marsh/ barack-obamas-progressiv_b_75933.html (accessed March 31, 2013).

50. Democracy Now, "'Effective Evil' or Progressives' Best Hope? Glen Ford vs. Michael Eric Dyson on Obama Presidency," September 7, 2012, retrieved from

www.democracynow.org/2012/9/7/effective_evil_or_progressives_best_hope (accessed March 31, 2013).

51. For an example of this view, see Amy Sullivan, "A Leader of Obama's Grassroots Army," *Time*, April 21, 2008, retrieved from www.time.com/time/magazine/article/0,9171,1834670,00.html (accessed March 31, 2013).

52. Frances Fox Piven and Richard Cloward, *Poor People's Movements* (New York: Vintage, 1978).

53. For research that shows that younger cohorts are not as racially "tolerant" as people believe, see Scott Blinder, "Dissonance Persists: Reproduction of Racial Attitudes among Post–Civil Rights Cohorts of White Americans," *American Politics Research* 35, no. 3 (2007): 299–335, and Tyrone A. Forman and Amanda E. Lewis, "Racial Apathy and Hurricane Katrina: The Social Anatomy of Prejudice in the Post–Civil Rights Era," *Du Bois Review* 3, no. 1 (2006): 175–202. We still need, however, systematic longitudinal studies on cohorts to assess how their attitudes vary throughout important milestones in the life course.

54. See AFP, "Michelle Obama Working Hard on New Image," *The Times*, June 24, 2008.

55. Jodi Kantor, "For President, a Complex Calculus of Race and Politics," *New York Times*, October 23, 2012, retrieved from www.nytimes.com/2012/10/21/us/politics/for-president-obama-a-complex-calculus-of-race-and-politics.html?pagewanted=2&_r=1&smid=fb-share (accessed March 31, 2013).

56. Cited in Ta-Nehisi Coates, "Fear of a Black President," *The Atlantic*, September 2012, retrieved from www.theatlantic.com/magazine/archive/2012/09/fear-of-a-black-president/309064 (accessed March 31, 2013).

57. Since taking office, Obama's administration has defended affirmative action to achieve increased diversity, but not to remedy past (or current) racial injustices.

58. Peter Canellos, "On Affirmative Action, Obama Intriguing but Vague," Boston.com, April 29, 2008, retrieved from www.boston.com/news/nation/articles/2008/04/29/on_affirmative_action_obama_intriguing_but_vague (accessed March 31, 2013).

59. Here is the exchange between President Obama and the journalist Ann Compton:

President Obama: Ann Compton? Hey, Ann. You sound surprised.
Ann Compton: I am surprised. Could I ask you about race?
President Obama: You may.
Ann Compton: Yours is a rather historic presidency. And I'm just wondering whether, in any of the policy debates that you've had within the White House, the issue of race has come up or whether it has in the way you feel you've been perceived by other leaders or by the American people? Or has the last 64 days before [*sic*] a relatively color-blind time?
President Obama: I—I think that the last 64 days has been dominated by me trying to figure out how we're going to fix the economy, and that affects black, brown and white. And, you know, obviously, at the inauguration, I think that there was justifiable pride on the part of the country that we had taken a step to move us beyond some of the searing legacies of racial

discrimination in this country, but that lasted about a day. And—and, you know, right now, the American people are judging me exactly the way I should be judged. And that is: Are we taking the steps to improve liquidity in the financial markets, create jobs, get businesses to re-open, keep America safe? And that's what I've been spending my time thinking about.

The transcript of the press conference can be found at www.washingtonpost .com/wp-dyn/content/article/2009/03/24/AR2009032403036.html (accessed March 31, 2013).

60. You can fi Y the transcript of the press conference at www.huffingtonpost .com/2009/04/29/obama-100-days-press-conf_n_193283.html (accessed March 31, 2013).

61. Particularly in Eduardo Bonilla-Silva, "Rethinking Racism," *American Sociological Review* 62, no. 3 (1997): 465–80, and *White Supremacy and Racism in the Post–Civil Rights Era.*

62. History was made based on a snippet of a sermon (or perhaps, as I allude below, pasting snippets from several sermons) from a reverend, a church, a congregation, and a religious tradition white America knew almost nothing about. On March 21, CNN's Anderson Cooper in his blog exculpated Reverend Wright from most of the charges. Cooper listened to the entire sermon and found that the "chickens coming home to roost" comment was a quote from Edward Peck, the former U.S. ambassador to Iraq, and he did not find the "God damn America" statement in this sermon, which suggests that someone did a job on this reverend to hurt Obama's presidential chances. See Anderson Cooper's blog, "The Full Story Behind Rev. Jeremiah Wright's 9/11 Sermon," *AC360*, March 21, 2008, retrieved from http://AC360.blogs.cnn.com/2008/03/21/the-full-story-behind -rev-jeremiah-wrights-911-sermon (accessed March 31, 2013).

63. A truly wonderful book outlining the role of race from the moment this country was born through today is Joe R. Feagin, *Racist America* (New York and London: Routledge, 2001).

64. See chapter 4 of this work, and Vincent J. Roscigno, *The Face of Discrimination: How Race and Gender Impact Work and Home Lives* (Lanham, Md.: Rowman & Littlefield, 2007).

65. Obama is cited in *Newsweek*, after the Wright controversy and the "race speech," saying the following:

Race is a central test of our belief that we're our brother's keeper, our sister's keeper. . . . There's a sense that if we are to get beyond our racial divides, that it should be neat and pretty, whereas part of my argument was that it's going to be hard and messy—and that's where faith comes in.

66. A few weeks after this speech, Obama threw Reverend Wright "under the bus" (this expression became very popular in this campaign) and, later on, renounced his affiliation to the Trinity United Church of Christ. And a few weeks after these actions by Obama, a poll by the Pew Research Center for the People and the Press indicated that most Americans believed he had handled the controversy well and 48 percent of whites agreed with this stand (although 45 percent disagreed). See www.people-press.org/files/legacy-pdf/407.pdf.

67. Tamara Nopper, "Barack Obama's Community Organizing as New Black Politics," special issue of *Political Power and Social Theory*, "Rethinking Obama," edited by Eduardo Bonilla-Silva and Louise Seamster, vol. 22 (2011): 51–73, retrieved from http://tamaranopper.com/wp-content/uploads/2012/01/barack-obamas-community-organizing-as-new-black-politics-nopper-2011.pdf (accessed March 31, 2013).

68. Collective behavior analysts define "crazes" as all-involving phenomena where participants seem fanatical and devoted to the craze whether it is in the religious, economic, aesthetic, or political realm. For a classic statement on this matter, see Neil J. Smelser, *Theory of Collective Behavior* (New York: Free Press, 1962).

69. On this point, Adolph Reed mockingly wrote in an article the following:

> A friend of mine characterizes this as the "we'll come back for you" politics, the claim that they can't champion anything you want because they have to conciliate your enemies right now to get elected, but that, once they win, they'll be able to attend to the progressive agenda they have to reject now in order to win. This worked out so well with the Clinton presidency, didn't it? Remember his argument that he had to sign the hideous 1996 welfare reform bill to be able to come back and "fid" it later? Or NAFTA? Or two repressive and racist crime bills that flooded the prisons? Or the privatizing of Sallie Mae, which set the stage for the student debt crisis? Or ending the federal government's commitment to direct provision of housing for the poor?

Adolph Reed, "Sitting This One Out," *The Progressive*, November 2007, retrieved from www.progressive.org/mag_reed1107 (accessed March 31, 2013).

70. Hayward Derrick Horton and Lori Latrice Sykes, "Toward a Critical Demography of Neo-Mulattoes: Structural," in *Skin Deep: How Race and Complexion Matter in the "Color-Blind" Era*, edited by Cedric Herring, Verna Keith, and Hayward Derrick Horton, 159–73 (Urbana: University of Illinois Press, 2004).

71. Conor Friedersdorf, "Why I Refuse to Vote for Obama," *The Atlantic*, September 26, 2012, retrieved from www.theatlantic.com/politics/archive/2012/09/why-i-refuse-to-vote-for-barack-obama/262861 (accessed March 31, 2013).

72. Xuan Thai and Ted Barrett, "Biden's Description of Obama Draws Scrutiny," CNN, January 31, 2007, retrieved from http://articles.cnn.com/2007-01-31/politics/biden.obama_1_braun-and-al-sharpton-african-american-presidential-candidates-delaware-democrat?_s=PM:POLITICS (accessed March 31, 2013).

73. Many of the arguments I stated early in the campaign were articulated by other commentators. See David Greenberg's article in the *Washington Post*, "Why Obamania? Because He Runs as the Great White Hope," January 13, 2008, retrieved from www.washingtonpost.com/wp-dyn/content/article/2008/01/11/AR2008011101414.html (accessed March 31, 2013).

74. Gary Kamiya, a writer for liberal journal *Salon*, wrote a provocative piece in February of 2008 titled "It's OK to Vote for Obama Because He's Black," retrieved from www.salon.com/opinion/kamiya/2009/04/29/race (accessed March 31, 2013). After he stipulated that his support for Obama was not exclusively based on his race, he bluntly stated,

> But if Obama were a white junior senator from Illinois with the same impressive personal and professional qualities—the same intelligence, empathy, speaking skills,

legislative tenure and life story—there'd be no way he'd have the name recognition to
mount a major campaign in the first place. And if he did manage to run, it's unlikely he
would have inspired such a passionate and widespread following. Obama's charisma,
which is his unique political strength, is real, but it cannot be separated from the fact
that he's black. When Obama speaks of change and hope and healing divisions, his
words carry an electric charge because of who he is: He *embodies his own message,* the
very definition of charisma. As a black man offering reconciliation, he is making a
deeply personal connection with whites, not merely a rhetorical one.

75. Lynne Duke, "How Big a Stretch? For Barack Obama, Winning the White
House would Mean Bridging the Biggest Gap of All," *Washington Post,* May
7, 2007, retrieved from www.washingtonpost.com/wp-dyn/content/article/
2007/05/06/AR2007050601255.html (accessed March 31, 2013).

76. Duke, "How Big a Stretch?"

77. In his speech in Selma, Alabama, Obama spoke of the Moses generation
(the civil rights generation) and thanked them for bringing them 90 percent on
the road to equality (this pleased some in the audience, even though it was factu-
ally wrong). There he laid claim to the mantel of the Joshua generation, who is
charged with bringing his people to the Promised Land. Although he talked of
generations, he clearly did not mind the implications of talking in the singular
about Joshua. The speech can be found at Lynn Sweet, "Obama's Selma Speech.
Text as Delivered," *Chicago Sun Times,* March 5, 2007, retrieved from http://blogs
.suntimes.com/sweet/2007/03/obamas_selma_speech_text_as_de.html (accessed March 31, 2013).

78. See the profile of Evelyn Glore Ashford, a ninety-three-year-old woman,
by Thomas C. Fox in his piece for the *National Catholic Reporter* on April 28, 2009.
There Mrs. Ashford said, like so many older African Americans, that "'I'm just
so glad I've lived to see this day. I've always had hope that blacks would be
recognized for their achievements and contributions. Now I see it's finally happening." The article can be read at ncronline.org/news/people/100-days-obama-
leadership-black- pride-runs-high (accessed March 31, 2013).

79. See Diane Cardwell, "Daring to Believe, Blacks Savor Obama Victory," *New
York Times,* January 5, 2008, retrieved from www.nytimes.com/2008/01/05/us/
politics/05race.html (accessed March 31, 2013).

80. Pew Research Center, "Blacks Upbeat about Racial Progress, Prospects a
Year after Obama's Election," January 12, 2010, retrieved from www.pewsocial
trends.org/2010/01/12/blacks-upbeat-about-black-progress-prospects (accessed
March 31, 2013).

81. Michelle Singletary, "In Rough Economic Times, Black Americans Hold
On to Their Optimism," *Washington Post,* February 19, 2011, retrieved from www
.washingtonpost.com/wpdyn/content/article/2011/02/19/AR2011021903265
.html (accessed November 5, 2012).

82. In late July of 2009, Professor Gates, a world-renowned writer, scholar,
and public figure, was racially profiled in his own house. For details on this
story, see Melissa Trujillo, "Henry Louis Gates Arrested, Police Accused of Racial
Profiling," *Huffington Post,* July 20, 2009, retrieved from www.huffingtonpost
.com/2009/07/20/henry-louis-gates-jr-arre_n_241407.html (March 31, 2013).

83. Ronald Walters, *White Nationalism, Black Interests: Conservative Public Policy and the Black Community* (Detroit: Wayne State University Press, 2003), my emphasis. In this article Professor Walters judged the first hundred days of Obama's presidency and gave him a B (and I think he was very generous). The article can be found at http://blackcommentator.com/322/322_aal_grading_obama_cover_printer_friendly.html (accessed March 31, 2013).

84. In earlier versions of this chapter, I mentioned Michael Eric Dyson, an early Obama supporter who began criticizing President Obama in 2009 and said, among many other things, that Obama "is willing to sacrifice the interests of African Americans in deference to a conception of universalism because it won't offend white people." His first critical engagement can be seen at www.youtube .com/watch?v=k0mEzQMQd5s&feature=player_embedded. (He did, however, support Obama for reelection in 2012. And he may have done so because he has become a regular commentator on MSNBC, a liberal, pro-Obama TV station that does not tolerate serious criticisms of Obama.) Cornel West has also ended his initial support and criticized Obama for his soft stand on race matters, for his continuation of America's imperial policies, and for his mild approach to class matters. More recently, West has been in the news for his criticism of Obama stemming from a vociferous debate with Al Sharpton on MSNBC's April 2011 special, "The Black Agenda," and a subsequent profile by Chris Hedges ("The Obama Deception: Why Cornel West Went Ballistic," truthdig.com, May 16, 2011, retrieved from www.truthdig.com/report/item/the_obama_deception_why_cornel_west_went_ballistic_20110516 [accessed March 31, 2013]).

85. Fredrick Harris, "The Price of a Black President," *New York Times*, October 27, 2012, retrieved from www.nytimes.com/2012/10/28/opinion/sunday/the-price-of-a-black-president.html?pagewanted=all (accessed March 31, 2013).

86. Michelle Obama has made some statements as First Lady that may be used against people of color.

87. During the campaign, MSNBC commentators Chris Matthews and Joe Scarborough, the first a Democrat and the second a Republican, pontificated in their shows about how irrelevant race had become in America. Matthews said many times that although he never attended school with blacks, his kids were color blind and had friends from all backgrounds. Scarborough, who is about twenty years younger than Matthews, mentioned often how people of his generation have no race issues and mingle with people from all racial background without hesitation. Interestingly, his TV and radio show are fundamentally "white shows."

88. Since his 2004 speech at the Democratic Convention, this line has become ubiquitous in Obama's campaign speeches.

89. Dylan Rodríguez, "Inaugurating Multiculturalist White Supremacy," Colorline, retrieved from http://colorlines.com/archives/2008/11/the_dreadful_genuis_of_the_oba.html.

90. Nicholas A. Valentino and Ted Brader, "The Sword's Other Edge: Perceptions of Discrimination and Racial Policy Opinion after Obama," *Public Opinion Quarterly* 75, no. 2 (November 2008): 201–26.

91. Michael Tesler, "The Spillover of Racialization into Health Care: How President Obama Polarized Public Opinion by Racial Attitudes and Race," *American Journal of Political Science* 56, no. 3 (2012): 690–704.

92. Sonya Ross and Jennifer Agiesta. "Racial Views: Poll Shows Majority Harbor Prejudice against Blacks," *Associated Press*, October 27, 2012, retrieved from www.huffingtonpost.com/2012/10/27/racial-views-new-polls-sh_n_2029423 .html?utm_hp_ref=fb&src=sp&comm_ref=false (accessed March 31, 2013).

93. Anti Defamation League, "White Supremacist Rage Boils Over after Obama Victory; Racist Site Crashes after Election," 2009, retrieved from www.adl .org/PresRele/Extremism_72/5387_72.htm (accessed March 31, 2013).

94. Coates, "Fear of a Black President."

95. Russell Goldman, "Donald 'Bombshell' Fails to Blow Up," ABC News, October 24, 2012, retrieved from http://abcnews.go.com/Politics/OTUS/donald -trump-fails-drop-bombshell-offers-cash-obama/story?id=17553670#.UJJ-y7t-0SaE (accessed March 31, 2013).

96. Joan Walsh, "When the Big Lie Works," *Salon*, September 13, 2012, retrieved from www.salon.com/2012/09/13/when_the_big_lie_works (accessed March 31, 2013).

97. Mike Dunford, "New York Post Editorial Cartoon Appears to Depict Obama as (Dead) Chimpanzee," *The Questionable Authority*, February 18, 2009, retrieved from http://scienceblogs.com/authority/2009/02/18/new-york-post -editorial-cartoo/ (accessed March 31, 2013).

98. Frances Martel, "Orange County, CA GOP Official Sends Email Saying Obama's Parents Were Monkeys," Mediaite, April 16, 2011, retrieved from www .mediaite.com/tv/orange-county-gop-official-solves-birther-mystery-presidents -parents-were-monkeys (accessed March 31, 2013).

99. CBS Minnesota, "Neighbors Speak Out against Chair-Lynching Display," October 31, 2012, retrieved from http://minnesota.cbslocal.com/2012/10/31/ neighbors-speak-out-against-chair-lynching-display (accessed March 31, 2013).

100. CBS Minnesota, "Neighbors Speak Out."

101. Victoria Cavaliere, "New Jersey Store Halloween Display Depicts Obama as a Witch Doctor in Loin Cloth, Bone through His Nose," *New York Daily News*, October 13, 2012, retrieved from www.nydailynews.com/news/national/obama -as-witch-doctor-photo-stokes-controversy-article-1.1182635 (accessed March 31, 2013).

102. Jilian Fama, "President Obama Witch Doctor Display 'Personal,' Not Racist, NJ Store Owner Says," ABC News, October 13, 2012, retrieved from http://abcnews.go.com/Politics/OTUS/president-obama-witch-doctor-display -personal-racist-nj/story?id=17463813#.UJKOILt0SaE (accessed March 31, 2013).

103. Charlie LaPlaca, "Anti-Obama Store Owner Says He's Not a Racist," *Manasquan-Belmar Patch*, October 12, 2012, retrieved from http://manasquan .patch.com/articles/anti-obama-store-owner-says-he-s-not-a-racist#c (accessed March 31, 2013).

104. Tim Arango, "Syrian War's Spillover Threatens a Fragile Iraq," *New York Times*, September 24, 2012, retrieved from www.nytimes.com/2012/09/25/world/ middleeast/iraq-faces-new-perils-from-syrias-civil-war.html?ref=world&_ r=0%20%20 (accessed March 31, 2013).

105. "US-Afghan Partnership Deal 'Agreed Upon,'" *Al Jazeera*, April 23 2012, retrieved from www.aljazeera.com/news/asia/2012/04/2012422171759880584 .html (accessed March 31, 2013).

106. Ben Farmer, "US Troops May Stay in Afghanistan until 2024," *Telegraph*, August 19 2011, retrieved from www.telegraph.co.uk/news/worldnews/asia/afghanistan/8712701/US-troops-may-stay-in-Afghanistan-until-2024.html (accessed March 31, 2013).

107. I point out here that no foreign power has ever been able to conquer Afghanistan, and the last one that tried (the Soviet Union) was forced out after eight years even though it maintained about 100,000 troops in the territory during its intervention.

108. David Cloud and Ken Dilanian, "U.S. Gathering Data on Suspects in Consulate Attack in Libya," *Los Angeles Times*, October 2, 2012, retrieved from http://articles.latimes.com/2012/oct/02/world/la-fg-libya-attack-20121003 (accessed March 31, 2013).

109. David Sanger, "Obama Order Sped Up Wave of Cyberattacks against Iran," *New York Times*, June 1, 2012, retrieved from www.nytimes.com/2012/06/01/world/middleeast/obama-ordered-wave-of-cyberattacks-against-iran.html?pagewanted=all (accessed March 31, 2013).

110. "US 'Building Missile Defence Radar' in Qatar," *Al Jazeera*, July 18 2012, retrieved from www.aljazeera.com/news/middleeast/2012/07/2012717203553999430.html (accessed March 31, 2013).

111. "Obama Aide Tells Israel of Iran Attack Plan—Paper," *Reuters*, July 29, 2012, retrieved from www.arabnews.com/middle-east/obama-aide-tells-israel-iran-attack-plan-%E2%80%94-paper (accessed March 31, 2013).

112. Jake Tapper and Amy Bingham, "Dems Quickly Switch to Include 'God,' 'Jerusalem,'" ABC News, September 5, 2012, retrieved from http://abcnews.go.com/Politics/OTUS/democrats-rapidly-revise-platform-include-god/story?id=17164108#.UEij2dCXQcg (accessed March 31, 2013).

113. Sean Rayment, "US And Britain Send Warships to the Persian Gulf to Prepare for an Israel Strike on Iran," *Business Insider*, September 16, 2012, retrieved from www.businessinsider.com/us-and-britain-sending-warships-to-gulf-2012-9 (accessed March 31, 2013).

114. Glenn Greenwald, "Iran Sanctions Now Causing Food Insecurity, Mass Suffering," *Guardian*, October 7, 2012, retrieved from www.guardian.co.uk/commentisfree/2012/oct/07/iran-santions-suffering (accessed March 31, 2013).

115. Saeed Kamali Dehghan, "Sanctions on Iran: 'Ordinary People Are the Target,'" *Guardian*, August 10, 2012, retrieved from www.guardian.co.uk/world/2012/aug/10/sanctions-iran-ordinary-people-target (accessed March 31, 2013).

116. Akbar Nasir Khan, "The US' Policy of Targeted Killing by Drones in Pakistan," *IPRI Journal* 11, no. 1 (Winter 2011): 21–40, retrieved from http://harvard.academia.edu/AkbarNasirKhan/Papers/157952/U.S._Policy_of_Targeted_Killing_by_Drones_in_Pakistan (accessed March 31, 2013).

117. Jo Becker and Scott Shane, "Secret 'Kill List' Proves a Test of Obama's Principles and Will," *New York Times*, May 29, 2012, retrieved from www.nytimes.com/2012/05/29/world/obamas-leadership-in-war-on-al-qaeda.html?pagewanted=all (accessed March 31, 2013).

118. International Human Rights and Conflict Resolution Clinic (Stanford Law School) and Global Justice Clinic (NYU School of Law), "Living Under Drones:

Death, Injury and Trauma to Civilians from US Drone Practices in Pakistan," Living Under Drones September 2012, retrieved from www.livingunderdrones .org/wp-content/uploads/2012/10/Stanford-NYU-LIVING-UNDER-DRONES .pdf (accessed March 31, 2013).

119. International Human Rights and Conflict Resolution Clinic and Global Justice Clinic, "Living Under Drones."

120. Joshua Hersh, "Hina Rabbani Khar, Pakistan Foreign Minister: Drones Are Top Cause Of Anti-Americanism," *Huffington Post*, September 28, 2012, retrieved from www.huffingtonpost.com/2012/09/28/hina-rabbani-khar -drones_n_1922637.html (accessed March 31, 2013).

121. Salman Masood, "Americans Join Pakistan Convoy to Protest Drone Strikes," *New York Times*, October 6, 2012, retrieved from www.nytimes .com/2012/10/07/world/asia/americans-join-pakistan-convoy-to-protest-drone -strikes.html?_r=0 (accessed March 31, 2013).

122. Matt Sledge, "Warrantless Electronic Surveillance Surges under Obama Justice Department," *Huffington Post*, September 28, 2012, retrieved from www.huffingtonpost.com/2012/09/28/warrantless-electronic-surveillance -obama_n_1924508.html (accessed March 31, 2013); Democracy Now, "Whistle-Blower: The NSA Is Lying—U.S. Government Has Copies of Most of Your Emails," April 20, 2012, retrieved from www.democracynow.org/2012/4/20/ whistleblower_the_nsa_is_lying_us (accessed March 31, 2013).

123. Jo Becker and Scott Shane, "Secret 'Kill List' Proves a Test of Obama's Principles and Will," *New York Times*, May 29, 2012, retrieved from www .nytimes.com/2012/05/29/world/obamas-leadership-in-war-on-al-qaeda .html?pagewanted=all (accessed March 31, 2013).

124. Greg Miller, "Plan for Hunting Terrorists Signals U.S. Intends to Keep Adding Names to Kill Lists," *Washington Post*, October 23, 2012, retrieved from www.washingtonpost.com/world/national-security/plan-for-hunting-terrorists -signals-us-intends-to-keep-adding-names-to-kill-lists/2012/10/23/4789b2ae-18 b3-11e2-a55c-39408fbe6a4b_print.html (accessed March 31, 2013).

125. Miller, "Plan for Hunting Terrorists."

126. This was highlighted when we heard, just before the 2012 election, that Obama's people were scrambling to establish rules and oversight for drone strikes, in case a Republican president inherited the program. When Romney lost, however, this plan "may have lost some urgency" (Scott Shane, "Elections Spurred a Move to Codify Drone Policy," *New York Times*, November 25, 2012, retrieved from www.nytimes.com/2012/11/25/world/white-house-presses-for -drone-rule-book.html?_r=0 [accessed March 31, 2013]).

127. Shiran Sadeghi, "Why the Republicans Ignored Afghanistan, Pakistan, Iraq & Iran at This Year's Convention," *Huffington Post*, August 30, 2012, retrieved from www.huffingtonpost.com/shirin-sadeghi/republican-convention-foreign -policy_b_1844100.html (accessed March 31, 2013).

128. Peter Finn, "Bush Trip to Switzerland Called Off amid Threats of Protests, Legal Action," *Washington Post*, February 5, 2011, retrieved from www.washing-tonpost.com/wp-dyn/content/article/2011/02/05/AR2011020502822.html (accessed March 31, 2013).

129. Agence France-Presse, "Obama Still Highly Popular in Europe: Poll," The Raw Story, September 4, 2011, retrieved from www.rawstory.com/rs/2011/09/14/obama-still-highly-popular-in-europe-poll (accessed March 31, 2013).

130. Jared Allen, "Black Lawmakers Irked by Obama's Diverse Cabinet," *The Hill*, December 22, 2008, retrieved from http://thehill.com/homenews/news/17479-black-lawmakers-irked-by-obamas-diverse-cabinet (accessed March 31, 2013).

131. Alain Sherter, "Citigroup Stint Shadows Obama's New Staff Chief," CBS News, January 10, 2012, retrieved from www.cbsnews.com/8301-505123_162-57355832/citigroup-stint-shadows-obamas-new-staff-chief (accessed March 31, 2013).

132. Peter Bergen and Jennifer Rowland, "John Brennan, Obama's Drone Warrior," CNN, January 7, 2013, retrieved from www.cnn.com/2013/01/07/opinion/bergen-brennan-drones/index.html (accessed March 31, 2013).

133. Jackie Calmes, "Study Looks at Tax Cut Lapse for Rich," *New York Times*, August 10, 2010, retrieved from www.nytimes.com/2010/08/11/us/politics/11tax.html (accessed March 31, 2013).

134. Ryan J. Donmoyer, "Would Ending Bush's Tax Cuts Hurt Small Business?" *Bloomberg Businessweek*, September 23, 2010, retrieved from www.businessweek.com/magazine/content/10_40/b4197030541676.htm (accessed March 31, 2013).

135. Obama taught law at Chicago and was influenced by the "Chicago School." Read Naomi Klein's incisive column in *The Nation* titled "Obama's Chicago Boys," June 12, 2008, where she documents the influence of the conservative, Milton Friedman–inspired Chicago School of Economics on Obama. The article can be found at www.thenation.com/doc/20080630/klein. See also David Leonhardt, "Obamanomics," *New York Times*, August 20, 2008, retrieved from www.nytimes.com/2008/08/24/magazine/24Obamanomics-t.html (accessed March 31, 2013).

136. Jonathan Chait, "Why Is Obama Caving on Taxes?," *New York Magazine*, December 2012, retrieved from http://nymag.com/daily/intelligencer/2012/12/why-is-obama-caving-on-taxes.html (accessed March 31, 2013).

137. The group Physicians for a National Health Care Program define single-payer as follows: "Single-payer national health insurance is a system in which a single public or quasi-public agency organizes health financing, but delivery of care remains largely private." See their website at www.pnhp.org/facts/single_payer_resources.php (accessed March 31, 2013).

138. NPR, "Sebelius: Single-Payer Health Care Not in Plans," NPR, June 16, 2009, retrieved from www.npr.org/templates/story/story.php?storyId=105442888 (accessed March 31, 2013).

139. Michael Vitez, "At Jefferson, Conyers Backs Obama Health Stand," *Philadelphia Enquirer*, March 7, 2009, retrieved from www.philly.com/philly/news/breaking/40898352.html (accessed March 31, 2013).

140. John Cassidy, "Obamacare by the Numbers, Part 1," *New Yorker*, March 24, 2010, retrieved from www.newyorker.com/online/blogs/johncassidy/2010/03/obamacare-by-the-numbers-part-1.html#ixzz22mBytI00 (accessed March 31, 2013).

141. Barack Obama, *The Audacity of Hope* (New York: Crown Publishers, 2006), 241.

142. Obama, *The Audacity of Hope*, 244–45.

143. Obama, *The Audacity of Hope*, 247. Like sociologist William Julius Wilson, who articulated this position in his books *The Declining Significance of Race* and *The Truly Disadvantaged*, Obama believes that a class-based or "universal" approach will help blacks and Latinos, as a good economy "will lift all boats." The problem with this policy is that it has not worked because even poor whites have racial advantages compared to poor blacks and Latinos and, accordingly, universal programs tend to benefit disproportionally not blacks but *whites*. It is noteworthy that Wilson changed his stand somewhat and now advocates for universal programs that are sensitive to race (see his shift in position in his 1996 book *When Work Disappears* and in his recent *More Than Just Race*). We cite below the work of john powell on this matter and urge interested parties to read the work of Princeton sociologist Marta Tienda on the limits of universal social policies. For a short statement on her findings, see Marta Tienda, "Diversifying the College Campus," *Contexts*, 2008, retrieved from http://contexts.org/articles/fall-2008/diversifying-the-college-campus (accessed March 31, 2013).

144. Obama, *The Audacity of Hope*, 254.

145. Obama, *The Audacity of Hope*, 255.

146. Obama, *The Audacity of Hope*, 255–57.

147. For a great discussion about how race affected how funds were dispersed in the New Deal, see Ira Katznelson, *When Affirmative Action Was White* (New York and London: W. W. Norton, 2005).

148. john powell, "Post-Racialism or Targeted Universalism?," *Denver University Law Review* 1 (February 2009), retrieved from www2.ohchr.org/english/bodies/hrcouncil/minority/docs/session3/statements/PostRacialismTargeted UniversalismbyJohnPowell.pdf (accessed March 31, 2013); Kirwan Institute for the Study of Race and Ethnicity, "Preliminary Report of the Impact of the Economic Stimulus Plan on Communities of Color," February 10, 2009, retrieved from www.abfe.org/FCDOCS/KirwanReport.pdf (accessed March 31, 2013).

149. Paul Butler, "Why Don't Black Leaders Demand More of the President?" *The Daily Beast*, September 24, 2012; Obama has since repeated this idea that he's not the president of black America multiple times. See Cornel West, in an interview with Jodi Kantor: "'It makes me want to vomit. . . . Did you say that to the business round table? . . . Do you say that to Aipac?' he said, referring to a pro-Israel lobbying group." Kantor, "For President, a Complex Calculus of Race and Politics."

150. White House, "Remarks by the President at Congressional Black Caucus Foundation Annual Phoenix Awards Dinner," September 24, 2011, retrieved from www.whitehouse.gov/the-press-office/2011/09/24/remarks-president-congres sional-black-caucus-foundation-annual-phoenix-a (accessed March 31, 2013).

151. Kenneth T. Walsh, "Obama: I'm Not the President of Black America," *U.S. News*, August 7, 2012, retrieved from www.usnews.com/news/blogs/Ken -Walshs-Washington/2012/08/08/obama-im-not-the-president-of-black-america (accessed March 31, 2013).

152. Seth James Wessler, "Food Stamp Bashing, Race, and the Bi-Partisan Attack on the Safety-Net," *Colorlines*, October 19, 2012, retrieved from http://

colorlines.com/archives/2012/10/food_stamp_bashing.html (accessed March 31, 2013).

153. Harris, "The Price of a Black President."

154. For great and in-depth coverage on voter suppression and intimidation during the 2012 election, see *Colorlines*'s *Voting Rights Watch* series by reporters Brentin Mock and Aura Bogado: http://colorlines.com/brentin-mock (accessed March 31, 2013).

155. James Ball, "At Black Caucus Dinner, Michelle Obama Urges Members to Get Out the Vote," *Washington Post*, September 22, 2012, retrieved from www.washingtonpost.com/politics/decision2012/at-cbcf-conference-faith-leaders-discuss-same-sex-marriage/2012/09/22/9cb60d0e-04ea-11e2-9146-c0cef8e81262_story.html (accessed March 31, 2013).

156. Gene Demby, "Michael Steele: Voter ID Rhetoric Is 'Irresponsible,' Party Needs New Approach to Black Voters," *Huffington Post*, August 31, 2012, retrieved from www.huffingtonpost.com/2012/08/31/michael-steele-voterid_n_1847623.html?utm_hp_ref=elections-2012 (accessed March 31, 2013).

157. Ari Berman, "Obama on Voter Suppression: 'It's a Problem,'" *The Nation Blog*, October 25, 2012, retrieved from www.thenation.com/blog/170830/obama-voter-suppression-its-problem# (accessed March 31, 2013).

158. Kantor, "For President, a Complex Calculus of Race and Politics."

159. Denise Stewart, "Strong Black Voter Turnout Translates to Obama Win," *Black America Web*, November 8, 2012, retrieved from www.rawstory.com/rs/2011/09/14/obama-still-highly-popular-in-europe-poll (accessed March 31, 2013); Tom Curry, "Voters Back President Obama Despite Economic Concerns, Polls Show," NBC News, November 6, 2012, retrieved from http://nbcpolitics.nbcnews.com/_news/2012/11/06/14979402-voters-back-obama-despite-economic-concerns-exit-polls-show?lite (accessed March 31, 2013).

160. Butler, "Why Don't Black Leaders Demand More of the President?"

161. For a good discussion on these matters, see chapter 6 in Street, *Barack Obama and the Future of American Politics*.

162. Elizabeth Flock, "Obama Campaign May Have Embraced Super PAC Earlier Than It Let On," *U.S. News*, September 7, 2012, retrieved from www.usnews.com/news/blogs/washington-whispers/2012/09/07/obama-campaign-may-have-embraced-super-pac-earlier-than-it-let-on (accessed March 31, 2013)

163. Amanda Terkel, "With 2012 Election Barely Over, Politicians Begin Fundraising for Next Cycles," *Huffington Post*, November 13, 2012, retrieved from www.huffingtonpost.com/2012/11/13/2012-election-fundraising_n_2126617.html (accessed March 31, 2013); T. W. Farnam, "Fundraising Starts Up Soon after Election, Filings Show," *Washington Post*, December 19, 2012, retrieved from http://articles.washingtonpost.com/2012-12-19/politics/35929528_1_leadership-pacs-election-day-shelley-moore-capito (accessed March 31, 2013).

164. Democracy Now, "'Effective Evil' or Progressives' Best Hope?"

165. Jonathan Martin and Carol E. Lee, "Obama: 'I Am a New Democrat,'" *Politico*, March 11, 2009, retrieved from www.politico.com/news/stories/0309/19862.html (accessed March 31, 2013).

166. Ali Gharib, "Obama Clear Winner in World Opinion." *International Press Service*, September 12, 2008, retrieved from www.commondreams.org/head

line/2008/09/12-2 (accessed March 31, 2013). But see also why a crucial segment of the world, the Muslim world, is not likely to be too impressed with Obama in Ala Al Aswany's piece, "Why the Muslim World Can't Hear Obama," *New York Times*, February 7, 2009, retrieved from www.nytimes.com/2009/02/08/opinion/08aswany.html (accessed March 31, 2013).

167. Kate Brower, "Obama Pitches Equal Pay to Win Women Even as Charges Drop," *Bloomberg News*, May 13, 2012, retrieved from www.bloomberg.com/news/2012-05-14/obama-pitches-equal-pay-to-win-women-even-as-charges-drop.html (accessed March 31, 2013).

168. Kate Brower and Elizabeth Dwoskin, "To Lure Women's Votes, Obama Turns to Lilly Ledbetter," *Bloomberg News*, May 17, 2012, retrieved from www.businessweek.com/articles/2012-05-17/to-lure-womens-votes-obama-turns-to-lilly-ledbetter (accessed March 31, 2013).

169. J. Bryan Lowder, "Campaign Love Notes: The Ballad of Lilly Ledbetter," *Slate Magazine*, May 15, 2012, retrieved from www.slate.com/blogs/xx_factor/2012/05/15/lilly_ledbetter_obama_and_women_is_the_act_being_overused_.html (accessed March 31, 2013).

170. Laura Bassett, "Gender Gap in 2012 Election Aided Obama Win," *Huffington Post*, November 7, 2012, retrieved from www.huffingtonpost.com/2012/11/07/gender-gap-2012-election-obama_n_2086004.html (accessed March 31, 2013).

171. Jennifer Loven, "Obama Seeks to Block Release of Abuse Photos," *AP White House Correspondent*, May 13, 2009, retrieved from www.dailyprogress.com/news/article_8c0d1d34-efdc-52a7-aa03-443ea13569b0.html (accessed March 31, 2013).

172. David Corn, "Obama and GOPers Worked Together to Kill Torture Probe," *Mother Jones*, December 1, 2010, retrieved from http://motherjones.com/politics/2010/12/wikileaks-cable-obama-quashed-torture-investigation (accessed March 31, 2013).

173. Lara Jakes, "Obama to Revive Military Tribunals for GITMO Detainees, with More Rights," *Huffington Post*, May 14, 2009, retrieved from www.huffingtonpost.com/2009/05/14/obama-to-revive-military-_n_203783.html (accessed March 31, 2013).

174. Charles Krauthammer, "Obama Denounced Enhanced Interrogation; Now He's Judge, Jury and Executioner," *Real Clear Politics*, May 29, 2012, retrieved from www.realclearpolitics.com/video/2012/05/29/krauthammer_obama_denounced_enhanced_interrogation_but_now_hes_judge_jury_and_executioner.html (accessed March 31, 2013).

175. Matt Negrin, "Guantanamo Bay: Still Open, Despite Promises," *ABC News*, July 3, 2012, retrieved from http://abcnews.go.com/Politics/OTUS/guantanamo-bay-open-promises/story?id=16698768 (accessed March 31, 2013).

176. Wayne Madsen, "Obama Authorizes Covert Economic War against Venezuela," *Center for Research on Globalization*, January 19, 2010, retrieved from www.globalresearch.ca/index.php?context=va&aid=17072 (accessed March 31, 2013).

177. Desmond Butler, "USAID Contractor Work in Cuba Detailed," *Business Week*, February 13, 2012, retrieved from www.businessweek.com/ap/financialnews/D9SSHGPG2.htm (accessed March 31, 2013).

178. Agence France-Presse, "US Working to Destabilise Morales Government: Bolivia," *Gulf Today*, January 7, 2013, retrieved from http://gulftoday.ae/portal/dbf649a1-cd27-42d9-ab6c-535fe6dbc59e.aspx (accessed March 31, 2013).

179. David Firestone, "What the Democrats Didn't Say," *New York Times*, September 5, 2012, retrieved from http://takingnote.blogs.nytimes.com/2012/09/05/what-the-democrats-didnt-say (accessed March 31, 2013).

180. Sam Stein, "Obama's Remarks on Employee Free Choice Act Make Labor 'Very Pleased,'" *Huffington Post*, February 12, 2009, retrieved from www.huffingtonpost.com/2009/02/12/obamas-remarks-on-employe_n_166345.html (accessed March 31, 2013).

181. Mike Allen and Eamon Javers, "Obama Announces New Fuel Standards," *Politico*, May 19, 2009, retrieved from www.politico.com/news/stories/0509/22650.html (accessed March 31, 2013).

182. Reddy Sudeep, "Obama Pushes for Legislation," *Wall Street Journal*, May 11 2009, retrieved from http://online.wsj.com/article/SB124186580127503661.html (accessed March 31, 2013).

183. Adam Sorensen, "Obama Passes Over Warren, Names Deputy to Run Consumer Agency," *Time*, July 17, 2012, retrieved from http://swampland.time.com/2011/07/17/obama-picks-former-ohio-ag-warren-deputy-to-head-consumer-bureau (accessed March 31, 2013).

184. Since early on, some black commentators who supported Obama expressed their concerns about how whites were framing this situation. Professor Roderrick J. Harrison, a demographer from Howard University, stated, "Historic as this moment is, it does not signify a major victory in the ongoing, daily battle." See Rachel L. Swarns, "Blacks Debate Civil Rights Risk in Obama's Rise," *New York Times*, August 24, 2008, retrieved from www.nytimes.com/2008/08/25/us/politics/25race.html (accessed March 31, 2013).

185. Rodríguez, "Inaugurating Multiculturalist White Supremacy."

186. Colin Powell fits many of the elements of the new type of post–civil rights minority politician. However, I must point out that on racial matters, Powell has maintained a decent record. Even during duress, he remained firm in his support for affirmative action and did not buy completely into the romantic view of America as a post-racial nation. See Colin L. Powell with Joseph E. Persico, *My American Journey* (New York: Random House, 1995).

187. Martin Plissner, "Ready for Obama Already," *New York Times,* February 7, 2007, retrieved from www.nytimes.com/2007/02/07/opinion/07plissner.html?_r??1&_r=0. (accessed March 31, 2013).

188. In his books, speeches, and interviews, Obama has insisted on these three matters: the need for bipartisanship, the limits of ideologically driven politics, and the desire for a pragmatic view on policies concerned with outcomes. For an early assessment on Obama's pragmatism, see David Ignatius's article in the *Washington Post*, "The Pragmatic Obama: He's Shaping the Debate on Foreign Policy," retrieved from www.washingtonpost.com/wp-dyn/content/article/2007/08/22/AR2007082202400.html (accessed March 31, 2013).

189. Leonhardt wrote this piece in August of 2008 and has since written two more long pieces based on interviews with now-president Obama.

190. David Leonhardt, "After the Great Recession," *New York Times*, April 28, 2009, retrieved from www.nytimes.com/2009/05/03/magazine/03Obama-t .html?pagewanted 6 (accessed March 31, 2013).

191. Ninety-four percent of black voters and 67 percent of Latinos supported Obama. The latter vote was more crucial as almost all past Democratic candidates in the last elections received upwards of 88 percent support (e.g., John Kerry received 90 percent of the black vote in 2004). Furthermore, the Latino vote was decisive in the all-important battleground states such as Pennsylvania, Virginia, and Nevada. For superb data on the elections, see the report by conservative analyst Joseph Gimpel, "Latino Voting in the 2008 Election: Part of a Broader Electoral Movement," for the anti-immigrant Center For Immigration Studies, which can be located at www.cis.org/latinovoting (sometimes the data talks more loudly than the ideology of those who produce it).

11

⌒

"The (Color-Blind) Emperor Has No Clothes"

Exposing the Whiteness of Color Blindness

> If there is no struggle, there is no progress. Those who profess to favor freedom, and yet deprecate agitation, are men who want crops without plowing up the ground. They want rain without thunder and lightning. They want the ocean without the awful roar of its many waters. This struggle may be a moral one, or it may be a physical one, or it may be both moral and physical, but it must be a struggle. Power concedes nothing without a demand. It never did and it never will.
>
> —Frederick Douglass, *My Bondage and My Freedom*

"I thought racism died in the sixties? But you guys keep talking, and talking, and talking about racism. Please stop using racism as a crutch!"

"Don't you think the best way of dealing with America's racial problems is by not talking about them? By constantly talking about racism you guys add wood to the racial fire, which is almost extinguished!"

"Race is a myth, an invention, a socially constructed category. Therefore, we should not make it 'real' by using it in our analyses. People are people, not black, white, or Indian. White males are just people."[1]

"A&M's tradition of focusing on race is a terrible mentality to teach a new generation. Dr. Eduardo Bonilla-Silva's book *White Supremacy & Racism in the Post–Civil Rights Era* is the latest evolution in this ritual that should have collapsed with the 1960s."[2]

"Is America's *main* problem still 'the color line' as W. E. B. DuBois put it 105 years ago? The very fact that the president is now black is a clear sign that it is no longer our *main* problem, and that we can, even as morally informed and socially concerned citizens, admit it."[3]

301

Statements such as these have become standard examples of how most whites think and talk about racism in contemporary America. The last one, by conservative black commentator John McWhorter, may be indicative of things to come, as a segment of the minority community has embraced, for reasons I articulate below, the dominant color-blind nonsense. Those of us who are minority professors in the academic trenches hear statements like these from students, staff, and colleagues. I personally have been accused of being a "racist" because I use the category race in my analysis (as if by closing our eyes, racial fractures would disappear from society and we would all just be "Americans") and of spreading "racist propaganda"[4] (in the color-blind era, those of us who write about race and racism are the ones accused of fostering racial divisions). These statements are all emblematic of the racial ideology that in this book I labeled "color-blind racism." At the heart of these statements—and of color blindness—lies a myth: the idea that race has all but disappeared as a factor shaping the life chances of all Americans. This myth is the central column supporting the house of color blindness. Remove this column and the house will collapse.

Removing this column, however, is not an easy task, because whites' racial views (views increasingly shared by a portion of the minority community) are not mere erroneous ideas to be battled in the field of rational discourse. They constitute, as I argued in this book, a racial ideology, a loosely organized set of ideas, phrases, and stories that help whites justify contemporary white supremacy;[5] they are the *collective representations*[6] whites have developed to explain, and ultimately justify, contemporary racial inequality. Their views, then, are not just a "sense of group position"[7] but *symbolic expressions of whites' dominance.* As such, they cannot be simply eradicated with "facts," because racial facts are highly contested. In the eyes of most whites, for instance, evidence of racial disparity in income, wealth, education, and other relevant matters becomes evidence that there is something wrong with minorities themselves; evidence of minorities' overrepresentation in the criminal justice system or on death row is interpreted as evidence of their overrepresentation in criminal activity; evidence of black and Latino underperformance in standardized tests is a confirmation that there is something wrong (maybe even genetically wrong)[8] with them.

Given that this ideology—like all ideologies—cannot be simply impugned with facts,[9] my main goal in this book was to decode the components of color blindness and explain their functions. But ideologies never float on thin air. They are always anchored in social systems. Thus, in chapter 2, I discussed the "new racism," the racial regime that has all but replaced the Jim Crow order of yesteryears. The mechanisms and practices associated with this new order are subtle, institutionalized, and seemingly nonracial. Not surprisingly, the ideology that accompanies this regime is as equally slippery and seemingly nonracial. In chapters 3, 4, and 5, I demonstrated how color-blind racism's frames, style, and racial stories help whites justify contemporary racial inequality. Whites use these components like "building blocks"[10] to manufacture accounts on a variety of racial matters. In general, their accounts amount to the statement "Race does not matter that much today, so let's move on." For example, when whites are asked about affirmative action, they resort to the frame of abstract liberalism to oppose it: "Why should we use discrimination to combat discrimination? Two wrongs don't make a right. We should judge people by their merits and let the best person get the job or promotion, or be admitted into a good college." When whites are confronted with the reality of the tremendous levels of residential and school segregation in the United States, they argue race has nothing to do with these matters. Many resort to the naturalization frame and say, "This is a natural thing. People prefer to be with people who are like them." Alternatively, they use the abstract liberalism frame and proclaim, "People have the right of choosing to live wherever they want to live. This is America, for God's sake!" When whites are faced with evidence of discrimination, they acknowledge its occurrence but label the episodes as "isolated incidents" and proceed to blame minorities for playing the "race card." Finally, when whites are questioned about the whiteness of their social networks, they rebut, "This has nothing to do with race. It's just the way things are." And if this does not work, they can project the problem onto minorities and say, "It's blacks who do not want to be with us. I have seen how they self-segregate in their neighborhoods and even when they attend our colleges." Others may be embarrassed by the makeup of their social networks and feel compelled to insert semantic moves ("Well, that's true, but some of my best friends are black") or personal stories ("My best buddy in Vietnam was Samoan!") to save face.

These frames, as I argued, set whites onto paths of no return. By regarding race-related matters as nonracial, "natural," or rooted in "people's choices," whites deem almost all proposals to remedy racial inequality necessarily as illogical, undemocratic, and "racist" (in reverse).

Besides examining the components of color-blind racism, I discussed two other important features in the color-blind era. First, I explored in chapter 6 the contradiction between whites claiming to be color blind and their almost-totally white pattern of social interaction. Second, I examined in chapter 8 the influence of color-blind racism on blacks. In chapter 7, I showed that whites, despite their professed color blindness, live in white neighborhoods, associate primarily with whites, befriend mostly whites, and choose whites as their mates. The contradiction between their professed life philosophy and their real practice in life is not perceived by whites as such because they do not interpret their hypersegregation and isolation from minorities (in particular blacks) as a *racial* outcome. For most whites, this is just "the way things are" or something that has nothing to do with race. In chapter 8, I concurred with most researchers[11] in showing that blacks exhibit a different attitudinal outlook on racial issues than whites. Blacks, unlike whites, believe discrimination is real and central in shaping their life chances and that the government must intervene in a number of areas to guarantee equality among the races (therefore, blacks are significantly more likely to support affirmative action, busing, and even reparations than whites). Blacks are also more likely than whites to engage in interracial friendship and intimacy. Nevertheless, I also documented how blacks are influenced by many of the frames of color blindness, directly and indirectly. Specifically, I underscored the large indirect effect of the frames of color blindness on blacks and how this blunts the oppositional character of their perspectives on racial matters. For example, many blacks endorse stereotypical views about themselves (e.g., blacks are lazy, less intelligent, or more athletic than whites), which leads them to adopt confusing standpoints (e.g., "Discrimination is very important, but we are a lazy people").

Finally, I examined "race traitors"—whites who do not dance to the tune of color blindness (see chapter 7). Unlike most social scientists, who posit that educated (mostly middle-class) white folks are racially tolerant and, hence, more likely to support the struggle for racial equality, my research suggested working-class women are significantly more likely than any other segment of the white population to be racially progressive. I also pointed out a number of other factors that racial progressives have in common that may explain their racial progressiveness, such as growing up in racially mixed neighborhoods, having extensive equal-status contacts with minorities, being center-to-left politically, and having dated across the color line. Although more research needs to be conducted to corroborate my findings, specify the set of circumstances (what sociologists call "variables") and the conditions that lead actors to become racially progressive, and determine why this segment of the white population is more progressive than others, I tentatively suggest that because working-class women experience at least two kinds of oppression (as workers and as women), they are more likely to empathize with racial minorities. In their narratives, many of these women used their own experiences as women to articulate their views on various hotly contested racial issues and, more specifically, to describe how discrimination occurs nowadays. Nevertheless, as in the case of blacks, I also showed that the "souls of [these] white folks"[12] are not pure, that is, that their racial progressiveness has some limits, as they too are influenced by color blindness.

The interview data in this book demonstrated that color-blind racism is central to old and young whites alike. Although older, working-class white respondents (mostly in the DAS sample) were less adept at using softer, more efficient versions of the frames and style of color-blind racism than were younger, middle-class, educated ones (mostly among the college student sample), both groups were attuned to this new ideology. Yet the fact that some whites are "compassionate conservatives" on race does not change in any way the reality that all are baptized in the waters of color-blind racism. Besides, even though younger, middle-class, educated whites seem better adept at using the arsenal of color blindness, many—particularly those who were already in the labor market or close to entering it—were as crude and unsophisticated as their poorer, less-educated brethren. To examine this matter more accurately, we need a panel study to follow college students over a ten-year period or so to assess whether or not, as they mature and deal with central life issues (e.g., getting a job, purchasing a house, getting married, having children), their color blindness becomes cruder.

The data also evinced that color-blind racism forms an impregnable yet elastic ideological wall that barricades whites off from America's racial reality—an impregnable wall because it provides them a safe, color-blind way to state racial views without appearing to be irrational or rabidly racist. And an elastic wall—and hence a stronger one—because this ideology does not rely on absolutes (it prefers statements such as "most blacks are" rather than "all blacks are"), admits a variety of ways of using its frames (from crude and direct to kinder and indirect), and allows whites to employ a variety of emotional tones for stating their views (from the angry "darned lazy blacks" to the compassionate conservative "poor blacks are trapped in their inferior schools in their cycle of poverty; what a pity").

Accordingly, my answer to the strange enigma of "racism without racists" is as follows. The United States does not depend on Archie Bunkers to defend white supremacy. (In truth, it never did, but that is *otros veinte pesos*.)[13] Modern racial ideology does not thrive on the ugliness of the past or on the language and tropes typical of slavery and Jim Crow. Today there is a sanitized, color-blind way of calling minorities niggers, spics, or chinks. Today most whites justify keeping minorities from having the good things of life with the language of liberalism ("I am all for equal opportunity; that's why I oppose affirmative action!"). And today, as yesterday, whites do not feel guilty about the plight of minorities (blacks in particular). Whites believe minorities have the opportunities to succeed and that, if they do not, it is because they do not try hard. And if minorities dare talk about discrimination, they are rebuked with statements such as "Discrimination ended in the sixties, man" or "You guys are hypersensitive."

The analysis of the interview data also sheds light on the methodological importance of using this kind of data for examining racial ideology.
Had I relied on my survey results to analyze whites' racial views, it would
have been difficult. Depending on which questions I had used to make
my case, I seemingly could have argued three totally different positions.[14]
Moreover, I could not have extracted from the survey data the stylistic
and narrative elements of color blindness. Although this does not mean
that surveys on racial attitudes are useless, it does mean that survey
researchers must strive to develop research projects with a qualitative dimension. Otherwise they may either produce an artificial image of racial
progress (see chapter 1) or miss central components of the contemporary
racial ideological constellation.

One set of questions that I could not answer properly with the data at
hand related to how color-blind racism affects other racial minorities and
how whites see other racial minorities in our new, more complex multiracial America. *Preliminarily*, although conceding that we lack data sets
that include all racial groups, involve questions on interethnic matters,
and include in-depth interviews with all the racial and ethnic groups, I
answer these questions as follows. First, the black-white continuum still
provides the bulk of the themes and imagery for the development of the
primary ideas associated with the dominant racial ideology.[15] Consequently, even when one asks generic questions about minorities, whites
are likely to focus on the black-white debate. Second, the practices of the
"new racism"—the post–civil rights set of arrangements that preserves
white supremacy in a mostly "kinder and gentler" way—affect *all* minorities, but the "race effect" seems to vary by the degree of closeness to
"whiteness" of the groups in question (phenotypically, culturally, and so
forth). For instance, although Latinos experience housing discrimination,
they are less likely to experience it if they are perceived as "white" than if
they are perceived as "black."[16] Similarly, although whites tend to marry
endogamously, when they cross the color line, they are more likely to do
so with Latinos (particularly with those of a lighter hue) and Asians than
with blacks. Lastly, the racial attitudes of racial minorities seem to fit their
"ranking" in the new racial hierarchy in America: Asians have views that
are closer to those of whites, Latinos' views are less like those of whites,
and blacks' are furthest from whites' views.[17] Therefore, because of the
aforementioned trends, I believe whites are already making important
distinctions among the various racial minorities; that such distinctions
have objective, subjective, and social interactional consequences for
minorities themselves; and that the degree of "color blindness" among
minorities correlates with their position in this new, more complex racial
stratification order.[18] Yet, on all these crucial issues for the future of race

relations in America, I claim, like most social scientists do, that more re-search needs to be done before we can adequately answer these questions.

Since I do not want to conclude this book on a pessimistic note, let me suggest a few of the political conditions necessary to fight color-blind racism. (Please see chapter 9 for a discussion of the politics and political strategies needed if the United States develops a Latin America–like racial stratification order.) First, blacks and their allies would be the core[19] of a new civil rights movement demanding equality of results.[20] I documented in chapter 8 that blacks, as a social collectivity, have a clear understand-ing of the basics of post–civil rights white supremacy and, therefore, their views and experiences ought to help guide this new movement. However, because color blindness has tainted their views, it is of cardinal importance that activists in the new movement educate the black masses on the nuances of color blindness. To launch a frontal attack on the "new racism" and its color-blind ideology, the black masses must be as racially conscious as the leaders of the new movement. In ideological terms, the movement must break with the hegemony color blindness has over all Americans.

Second, we need to nurture a large cohort of antiracist whites to begin challenging color-blind nonsense from within. Whites' collective denial about the true nature of race relations may help them feel good, but it is also one of the greatest obstacles to doing the right thing. In racial matters as in therapy, the admission of denial is the preamble for the beginning of recovery. Antiracist whites cannot just be "race traitors";[21] they must engage in struggles to end the practices and the ideology that maintain white supremacy. Individual racial treason without a political praxis to eliminate the system that produces racial inequality amounts to racial showboating.

These antiracist white activists,[22] as I suggested above, will most likely be working-class women. However, as in all social movements, the struggle needs to work to expand the coalition fighting the powers that be. This means that progressive activists need to work with all *vulnerable whites*: poor and working-class whites regardless of gender, whites in the lower middle class, and educated whites who in the past were so central to the struggle for civil rights in America. In order to persuade vulnerable whites to join the struggle, it is important to do ideological work with them (but see below). Hence, the third way of combating color blindness is for researchers and activists alike to provide counter-ideological argu-ments to *each* of the frames of color-blind racism. We need to counter whites' *abstract* liberalism with *concrete* liberal positions based on a real-istic understanding of racial matters and a concern with achieving racial equality. For example, whites' thesis of "We are for equal opportunity for everyone and that's why we oppose affirmative action" must be countered with the concrete argument that because discrimination (past and present) affects minorities negatively, race-based programs and massive programs on behalf of the poor are the only ways of guaranteeing racial equality.[23] The racially illiberal effects of the do-nothing social policy advocated by whites must be exposed and challenged.

Fourth, we need to undress whites' claims of color blindness before a huge mirror. That mirror must reflect the myriad facts of contemporary whiteness, such as whites living in white neighborhoods, sending their kids to white schools, associating primarily with whites, and having almost all their primary relationships with whites. And whites' absurd claim that these facts of whiteness are just a "natural thing" must be deflated with research and exposed by journalists showing the social and personal processes that produce each of these aspects of contemporary white supremacy. Researchers also need to turn the analytical lenses on *white* segregation and isolation from minorities and begin documenting how this isolation affects whites' views, emotions, and cognitions about themselves and about minorities.

Fifth, whiteness must be challenged wherever it exists; regardless of the social organization in which whiteness manifests itself (universities, corporations, schools, neighborhoods, churches), those committed to racial equality must develop a personal practice to challenge it. If you are a college student in a historically white college, you must raise hell to change your college; you must organize to change the racial climate and demography of your college. If you work in corporate America, you must wage war against subtle and covert racism; you must challenge the practices that track minorities into certain jobs and preserve high-paying ones for white males. If you are a parent who spends most of your time housebound, you need to begin a campaign for racial change in your family interactions and attitudes; you must engage with racial minorities, opt for a multiracial rather than a white church, and move from your white neighborhood into an integrated one.

Finally, the most important strategy for fighting "new racism" practices and the ideology of color blindness is to become militant once again. Changes in systems of domination and their accompanying ideologies are never accomplished by racial dialogues—the notion of "Can we all just get along?" or "workshops on racism"—through education, or through "moral reform"[24] alone. What is needed to slay modern-day racism is a new, in-your-face, fight-the-power civil rights movement, a new movement to spark change, to challenge not just color-blind whites but also minority folks who have become content with the crumbs they receive from past struggles. This new civil rights movement, as I have mentioned elsewhere,[25] must have at the core of its agenda the struggle for equality of results. Progressives cannot continue fighting for "equality of opportunity" when true equality cannot be achieved that way. It is time to demand equality now!

I realize many of these proposals are very idealistic. I know quite well most whites are not up to the challenge of working to develop a country without white supremacy. For example, few whites would engage in a social movement or in personal practices that would rock the foundation of the status quo and their everyday lives. The idea of moving from a "safe" neighborhood into a "dangerous" one, for instance, is anathema to most white Americans ("Honey, do you want our kids to attend *bad* schools? Do you want us to *lose our investment in this house?"*). However, social movements do not depend on mobilizing the masses to get started (yet, as I suggested above, successful movements must make *broad appeals* and, at least, gain the sympathy of the majority to be victorious).[26] The history of social mobilization shows that organized, active, resourceful, and creative movements have been able to challenge all kinds of oppressive structures.[27]

If this new civil rights movement begins a concerted campaign to fight "new racism" practices and color-blind idiocy, this movement has a chance. If the leaders of this movement begin to say to America, "We will no longer accept poverty and urban decay, substandard schools and housing, inferior jobs, old- as well as new-fashioned discrimination, and racial profiling, in short, we will no longer accept second-class citizenship in this country," then this movement has a chance. If liberal, progressive, and radical organizations join in this new civil rights movement to eliminate racial disparity in the United States once and for all, this movement has a chance. If progressive religious leaders of various denominations begin to preach about the need to complete the civil rights revolution we started years ago and derail the forces that want to turn back the racial clock, this movement has a chance. If the millions of conscientious college students across the nation wake up and do the right thing, as they did during the civil rights era, this movement has a chance. If young people and workers in the United States realize that racial inequality ultimately helps preserve other forms of inequality,[28] this movement has a chance. Activists and researchers alike need to realize the basic truth in Frederick Douglass's words, "If there is no struggle, there is no progress. . . . Power concedes nothing without a demand. It never did and it never will." Change is made, not theorized, written about, or orchestrated by policy makers or researchers. Only by demanding what seems impossible today (equality of results, reparations, and the end of all forms of racial discrimination), will we be able to achieve genuine racial equality in the future.

IMPORTANT ADDENDUM TO THE ORIGINAL CONCLUSION

The title of the original conclusion was "The (Color-Blind) Emperor Has No Clothes." Developments since the time I worked on that conclusion (1999–2000) suggest that a more fitting title for the chapter today would be "The (Color-Blind) Emperor Has *New* Clothes." The new "pants" of the emperor are from Latin America, by which I mean that racial stratification in the nation is becoming Latin America–like (the subject of chapter 9). The historical biracial order[29] (white-nonwhite) is morphing rather quickly into a more complex racial system. I suggest that three new "racial spaces"[30] are developing (white, honorary white, and the collective black) and that this order will allow people to make different choices not just about their "identity" but also about their race.[31] Given these new spaces, the likelihood of collective action from the traditional or historical "minority race groups" (blacks, Latinos, Asian Americans, and Native Americans) is decreasing as the new order fosters individual practices of racial mobility. For example, people who would have been regarded as "black" twenty or thirty years ago can now successfully manufacture a different place for themselves in America. Actors and performers such as "The Rock," Vin Diesel, Keanu Reeves, Jennifer Rubin, and Jennifer Tilly, all "racially mixed" (again, only in this moment is this claim possible, as during the Jim Crow period all of them would be assigned the "lower" race in the mix), work all sides of the racial spectrum as they can use their phenotypical capital (dare I say "honorary whiteness") to their advantage.[32]

This newly emerging racial landscape has received a boost from the new "shirt" the emperor began wearing since November 4, 2008: the Obama phenomenon. The election of *this* black man as president (and I will continue insisting on Obama's political and personal peculiarities) has accelerated the pace of the Latin-Americanization process and solidified further the house of color blindness. Why? Because Obama has worked the post-racial game and, as I argued in chapter 10, played perfectly the role whites have constructed for people of color (they "love" minority folks if they "behave," are nice to them, smile a lot, are "cool" and "respectable," and do not talk much about race). This game, which I argued is the true secret behind Obama's success, has placed a black person in power without altering that much the distribution of racial power or how social goods are distributed in the polity. Obama has helped establish what I called in the chapter a "multiracial white supremacy order"—a regime similar to those in the Americas or the Caribbean where people of color are in power without altering the "[racial] order of things."[33]

These two developments (the Latin Americanization of the racial order and the Obama phenomenon) will make the struggle for racial justice much harder in years to come. In *Obamerica* (see note 2 in chapter 10) several factors will buffer racial conflict and limit the likelihood of race-based frontal challenges. First, the traditional racial groups are becoming less "stable" or unified, as many members can now make legitimate claims to be something else. For example, immediately after Obama was elected president, many members of the "black elite" joined white America in their nonsensical preaching to poor blacks ("Folks, now you have a black president, so you have no more excuses") (see note 7 in chapter 10). This segment, which has always tried to distance itself from the "black majority," has now much more space to be something other than black. They can, as many formerly black and Indian people were able to do historically in the Americas and the Caribbean, struggle to create other classifications such as multiracial, biracial, or simply American. Thusly the strength of the "black" or "Latino" challenges will be diluted by this development.

Second, the segment or space I label "honorary white" will do a lot of the dirty work of policing racial boundaries and disciplining those in the "collective black." I expect to hear a lot of noise in the next decade about intra-racial or intra-ethnic struggle in the black, Latino, and Asian camps. That fight, however, will denote the efforts of segments within these communities to distance themselves from their groups of origin. And what may be read as intra-racial in the next years may soon become something else (for example, this "racial" discussion may become a "class" discussion among Americans about the behavior of the "poor"—likely to be the very dark segment of the population—and middle- and upper-middle-class honorary whites). The important thing to point out is that the dominant race in this society (whites) will no longer work alone in preserving the racial order, as honorary whites and some individuals[34] in the collective black space will help them maintain the coordinates of the new order.

Lastly, as of November 4, 2008, white America has shouted to the world: "(Finally) we are *all* Americans." They have now attained the upper hand in symbolic racial politics, as they can tell people of color, "We have a black president, what else do *you people* want?" Although some commentators are pointing out the limits of the notion of America as a "post-racial" nation, it is also true that the space for talking and debating race matters in the public has decreased tremendously.

But all empires have fractures and all emperors are eventually replaced. In the case of the new racial order, I outlined in chapters 9 and 10 the weaknesses of the system and suggested things we may do in the struggle for racial justice. I highlighted the urgent need for new social movements to challenge the "matrix of domination"[35] in contemporary America. I also called for doing active political work among the new emerging racial majority in the nation (the collective black), as that work might produce a new historical bloc to fight the current racial order. However, I also expressed my pesoptimism about these possibilities. On the Latin Americanization front, I mentioned that once this type of regime took hold in the Americas and the Caribbean, they became entrenched and posed formidable challenges to those at the bottom of the racial well. In the case of my call for social movements, I pointed out that—at least in terms of the Obama moment—political participation has been limited to electoral politics, which limits the likelihood of these movements ever developing. (I know there are many small movements dotting the political territory. My concern, however, is about how the massive participation of Americans—particularly the youth that threw itself into Obama—in mainstream politics has had the nefarious effect of *demobilizing* people and making them into political actors that do "politics" every four years.)

Notwithstanding my pesoptimism, history is what it is and no racial order can maintain itself forever. The oppressed (racially or otherwise) always resist domination and what seems like an insurmountable Mount Everest is always conquered (although some may die trying to reach its top). Accordingly, I end this fourth and hopefully *last* edition of this book mindful that slavery looked like a system that would never end and it did; that Jim Crow maintained people of color subjected for more than a hundred years[36] and it has all but died; and that the "new racism" with its Latin America–like extension looks like fast-setting cement, but it will eventually collapse, too. I just hope I am alive when this happens and that my bones allow me to celebrate the real "end of racism" in the country that will then be properly called America with no "k"s.

NOTES

1. A colleague said something like this to me almost verbatim a few years ago in response to a presentation I gave about racism in sociology. Later on, the same colleague uttered a statement along the same lines to challenge a graduate student's presentation on whiteness. Denying the *social reality* of race because of its constructed nature (see chapter 1), unfortunately, has become respectable in academia. This position, which has been uttered by conservatives such as David Horowitz, has now been adopted by liberals such as Todd Gitlin and even radicals (or former radicals) such as Paul Gilroy. For the latter, see Paul Gilroy, *Against Race* (Cambridge, Mass.: Belknap, 2000).

2. Matthew Maddox, "Institutionalized Racism Continues at A&M: Sociology Professor's Book Will Continue Tradition of Racist Ideology on Campus," *Battalion*, October 2, 2002.

3. John McWhorter, "The End of Racism?" Forbes.com, November 5, 2008, retrieved from www.forbes.com/2008/11/05/obama-racism-president-oped -cx_jm_1105mcwhorter.html.

4. Maddox, "Institutionalized Racist Ideology."

5. Charles W. Mills, *The Racial Contract* (Ithaca, N.Y.: Cornell University Press, 1997).

6. This is Emile Durkheim's term. However, *I* See Serge Moscovici, "The Coming Era of Soci *Approaches to Social Behaviour,* edited by J. P. Coc Nijhoff, 1982), 115–50.

7. Social psychologist Herbert Blumer conceive group position" and connected this "sense" to the hi Luigi Esposito and John W. Murphy, "Another Step in tions," *Sociological Quarterly* 41, no. 2 (2000): 171–87.

8. Although color-blind racism need not use biological arguments to maintain racial privilege, biological arguments creep back from time to time and have not yet been abandoned by at least a third of whites. For instance, in my own DAS, anywhere from 20 to 40 percent of whites believed biological stereotypes about blacks such as the idea that blacks are naturally more athletic than whites and blacks are sexually well endowed. For an academic incarnation of this tendency, see Richard J. Herrnstein and Charles Murray, *The Bell Curve* (New York: Free Press, 1994).

9. If ideologies are about "meaning in the service of power," as Thompson argues, they must be countered with power. Counter-ideological battles alone cannot ultimately erode power crystallized in institutions and practices to maintain white privilege. John B. Thompson, *Studies in Theory and Ideology* (Cambridge: Polity, 1984).

10. For data on New Zealand, see Margaret Wetherell and Jonathan Potter, *Mapping the Language of Racism* (New York: Columbia University Press, 1992).

11. See chapter 7 for references on blacks.

12. W. E. B. DuBois named one of his chapters "The Souls of White Folk," in *Darkwater* (Rahway, N.J.: Quinn and Boden, 1920).

13. "Otros veinte pesos" is a Puerto Rican expression that literally means "another twenty dollars" and is used to suggest that a side argument will take a long time to make and, therefore, that making it will distract from the main one.

14. See Eduardo Bonilla-Silva and Tyrone A. Forman, "'I Am Not a Racist, but . . .': Mapping White College Students' Racial Ideology in the USA," *Discourse and Society* 11, no. 1 (2000): 50–85.

15. On this point, see Joe R. Feagin, *Racist America: Roots, Realities, and Future Reparations* (New York: Routledge, 2000), 3.

16. On housing issues, see Douglas S. Massey and Nancy A. Denton, "Trends in the Residential Segregation of Blacks, Hispanics, and Asians: 1970–1980," *American Sociological Review* 52, no. 6 (1987): 802–25. On interracial relationships, see Zhenchao Qian and Daniel T. Lichter, "Measuring Marital Assimilation: Intermarriage among Natives and Immigrants," *Social Science Research* 30, no. 2 (2001): 289–312.

17. See Eduardo Bonilla-Silva and Karen Glover, "'We Are All Americans': The Latin Americanization of Race Relations in the USA," in *Changing Terrain of Race and Ethnicity,* edited by Maria Krysan and Amanda Lewis (New York: Russell Sage, 2004).

18. Bonilla-Silva and Glover, "'We Are All Americans.'"

19. On black social movements in America, see Cedric J. Robinson, *Black Movements in America* (New York: Routledge, 1997).

20. For more on this, see the conclusion to my *White Supremacy*.

21. For this concept and an elaboration of the politics behind it, see the journal *Race Traitor*.

22. For a study of white antiracists in American history, see Herbert Aptheker, *Anti-Racism in U.S. History: The First Two Hundred Years* (New York: Greenwood, 1992).

23. For a book focusing on the former, see David Ingram, *Group Rights: Reconciling Equality and Difference* (Lawrence: University Press of Kansas, 2000). For a policy suggestion that includes both, see William Julius Wilson, *When Work Disappears* (New York: Knopf, 1996).

24. Today, almost all religious groups in the United States abhor racism and have even denounced their past mistakes. For example, in 1995 the Southern Baptist Convention apologized to blacks for "condoning and/or perpetuating individual and systematic racism." Almost all religious groups advocate a moral crusade against racism, but few do anything beyond their occasional public statements. For a sensitive and intelligent analysis of religion and race in America, see Michael O. Emerson and Christian Smith, *Divided by Faith: Evangelical Religion and the Problem of Race in America* (New York: Oxford University Press, 2000).

25. Consult the conclusion of my *White Supremacy* for an argument on how this movement should be organized and a discussion of the need for a large movement agenda that includes class and gender concerns.

26. A good book for the basics of the social movement literature is Stanford M. Lyman, *Social Movements: Critiques, Concepts, Case-Studies* (New York: New York University Press, 1995). For a good book that argues that social movements need to make broad appeals and develop "connective structures" among different sectors, see Sidney Tarrow, *Power in Social Movements: Social Movements and Contentious Politics* (Cambridge: Cambridge University Press, 1998).

27. For an excellent collection of essays discussing the array of new and creative contemporary movements, see Enrique Larana, Hank Johnston, and Joseph R. Gusfield (eds.), *New Social Movements: From Ideology to Identity* (Philadelphia: Temple University Press, 1994). For examples of how to build multiracial coalitions, see John Anner (ed.), *Beyond Identity Politics: Emerging Social Justice Movements in Communities of Color* (Boston: Beacon, 1996).

28. This point has been made by, among others, Joe R. Feagin, in *Racist America* (New York: Routledge, 2000); in his newer book, *Systemic Racism: A Theory of Oppression* (New York: Routledge, 2006); and by Patricia Hill-Collins, in "Moving beyond Gender: Intersectionality and Scientific Knowledge," in *Revisioning Gender*, edited by Myra Marx Ferre, Judith Lorber, and Beth B. Hess, 261–84 (Thousand Oaks, Calif.: Sage, 1999).

29. The American racial order was never truly "biracial" if by that one means white-black. Across the nation other groups were part of the racial order and, in some places, were more significant than blacks (e.g., Mexican Americans throughout much of the Southwest and Native Americans in states such as Oklahoma). The point, however, is that in most of the nation the color line was fundamentally

structured around the white-nonwhite divide. However, see the work of Reginald Daniel, *More Than Black? Multiracial Identity and the New Racial Order* (Philadelphia: Temple University Press, 2002), for a discussion on "tri-racial isolates."

30. In the chapter here and in the previous edition I used terms such as "groups" and "strata" to refer to the three new collectivities I surmised were emerging. However, I also pointed out the inchoate and permeability of the boundaries of these groups. Lately (in truth, I used the term in 2004 in an article in the now-defunct *Race and Society* journal as well as in talks on this matter), I have referred to these collectivities as "racial spaces" to denote more clearly their "in itself" rather than "for itself." This is also the case of racial formations in Latin America and the Caribbean; that is, for many reasons, they seldom cohere as groups and act collectively. See Eduardo Bonilla-Silva, "Are the Americas 'Sick with Racism' or Is It a Problem at the Poles? A Reply to Christina A. Sue," *Ethnic and Racial Studies* 32, no. 6 (2009): 1071–82.

31. Sociologists of race and ethnicity make a distinction between "identity" as a mostly personal or subjective matter that may or may not correlate with your "race." Thus, a person that is regarded by most observers in a polity as "black" may call herself "white," "American," or "biracial." "Race" refers to the historico-political categories that are created in a racialized polity and have a strong externality; that is, actors are defined as such by others in the polity and have limited chances of challenging that characterization. In the above-mentioned case, for instance, the person self-identifying herself as white or any other identity would be viewed and treated by most as black.

32. For an interesting discussion on this matter as well as on the way that "multiculturalism" is used in cinema, see Mary C. Beltrán, "The New Hollywood Racelessness: Only the Fast, Furious, (and Multiracial) Will Survive," *Cinema Journal* 44, no. 2 (2005): 50–67.

33. Michel Foucault, *The Order of Things: An Archaeology of the Human Sciences* (New York: Vintage Books, 1973 [1970]).

34. I have suggested in chapter 8 and in many of my writings and presentations on this subject that many individuals in the collective black space may help buffer conflict in their efforts to be "anything but (part of the collective) black." It is to their *individual* advantage to distance themselves from those in their space if they wish to attain racial mobility and, hence, will likely step all over their brethren on their way up.

35. All modern societies exhibit a complex hierarchical order that includes class, gender, race, and other social categories. Thus, although I have focused mostly on the racial aspects of the American social order, I have also alluded to and included in some parts of my analyses the need for movements that are cognizant of the fact of this complexity. For a good discussion on this matter, read *anything* written by philosopher Charles W. Mills.

36. An impressive recent book describing the resistance of blacks to Jim Crow and the centrality of militant struggle is Hasan Kwame Jeffries, *Bloody Lowndes: Civil Rights and Black Power in Alabama's Black Belt* (New York and London: NYU Press, 2009).

Selected Bibliography

Aguirre, Adalberto, Jr. "Academic Storytelling: A Critical Race Theory Story of Affirmative Action." *Sociological Perspectives* 43, no. 2 (2000): 319–39.

Alexander, Michelle. *The New Jim Crow: Mass Incarceration in the Age of Colorblindness.* New York: The New Press, 2010.

Allen, Jared. "Black Lawmakers Irked by Obama's Diverse Cabinet." *The Hill*, December 22, 2008. Retrieved from http://thehill.com/homenews/news/17479 -black-lawmakers-irked-by-obamas-diverse-cabinet. Accessed March 31, 2013.

Allen, Mike, and Eamon Javers. "Obama Announces New Fuel Standards." *Politico*, May 19, 2009. Retrieved from www.politico.com/news/stories/0509/22650. html. Accessed March 31, 2013.

Allport, Gordon W. *The Nature of Prejudice.* New York: Doubleday/Anchor, 1958.

Alternet staff. "Outrage in Oakland after Cop Kills Unarmed Man: Piecing Together the Story." *Alternet*, January 13, 2009. Retrieved from www.alternet.org/story/119577/outrage_in_oakland_after_cop_kills_unarmed_man%3A_piec

America, Richard F. *Paying the Social Debt: What White America Owes Black America.* Westport, Conn.: Praeger, 1993.

Andersen, Margaret L. *Thinking about Women: Sociological Perspectives on Sex and Gender.* New York: Macmillan, 1988.

Anderson, Benedict. *Imagined Communities: Reflections on the Origin and Spread of Nationalism*, revised and extended. London and New York: Verso, 1991.

Anderson, Elijah. *Streetwise.* Chicago: University of Chicago Press, 1990.

Anner, John, ed. *Beyond Identity Politics: Emerging Social Justice Movements in Communities of Color.* Boston: Beacon, 1996.

Anti-Defamation League. *Highlights from an Anti-Defamation League Survey on Racial Attitudes in America.* New York: Anti-Defamation League, 1993.

———. "White Supremacist Rage Boils Over after Obama Victory; Racist Site Crashes after Election." 2009. Retrieved from www.adl.org/PresRele/Extrem ism_72/5387_72.htm. Accessed March 31, 2013.

Aptheker, Herbert. *Anti-Racism in U.S. History: The First Two Hundred Years.* New York: Greenwood, 1992.

Arango, Tim. "Syrian War's Spillover Threatens a Fragile Iraq." *New York Times,* September 24, 2012. Retrieved from www.nytimes.com/2012/09/25/world/ middleeast/iraq-faces-new-perils-from-syrias-civil-war.html?ref=world&_ r=0%20%20. Accessed March 31, 2013.

Argyle, Michael, and Monika Henderson. *The Anatomy of Relationships.* London: Routledge, 1985.

Armour, Jody David. *Negrophobia and Reasonable Racism: The Hidden Costs of Being Black.* New York: New York University Press, 1997.

Armstrong, Clairette P., and A. James Gregor. "Integrated Schools and Negro Character." In *White Racism and Black Americans,* edited by David G. Bromley et al., 101–49. Cambridge, Mass.: Schenkman, 1972.

Aronowitz, Stanley. *False Promises: The Shaping of American Working Class Consciousness.* Durham, N.C.: Duke University Press, 1991.

Auletta, Ken. *The Underclass.* Woodstock, N.Y.: Overlook, 1999.

Ayres, Ian. *Pervasive Prejudice?* Chicago: University of Chicago Press, 2002.

Baker, David V. "The Racist Application of Capital Punishment to African Americans." In *Racial Issues in Criminal Justice: The Case of African Americans,* edited by Marvin D. Free Jr.. Westport, Conn.: Praeger, 2003.

Baker, Dean, and Mark Weisbrot. *Social Security: The Phony Crisis.* Chicago: University of Chicago Press, 2001.

Baker, Houston A. "Scene . . . Not Heard." In *Reading Rodney King, Reading Urban Uprising,* edited by Robert Gooding-Williams, 38–50. New York: Routledge, 1993.

Balbus, Isaac D. *The Dialectics of Legal Repression; Black Rebels Before the American Criminal Courts.* New York: Russell Sage Foundation, 1974.

Baldi, Stéphane, and Debra Branch McBrier. "Do the Determinants of Promotion Differ for Blacks and Whites?" *Work and Occupations* 24 (1997): 478–97.

Baldus, David C., Charles A. Pulaski Jr., and George Woodworth. "Comparative Review of Death Sentences: An Empirical Study of the Georgia Experience." *Journal of Criminal Law & Criminology* 74 (1983): 661–753.

Ball, James. "At Black Caucus Dinner, Michelle Obama Urges Members to Get Out the Vote." *Washington Post,* September 22, 2012. Retrieved from www.washing tonpost.com/politics/decision2012/at-cbcf-conference-faith-leaders-discuss -same-sex-marriage/2012/09/22/9cb60d0e-04ea-11e2-9146-c0cef8e81262_ story.html. Accessed March 31, 2013.

Bartra, Roger. *Wild Men in the Looking Glass: The Mythic Origins of European Otherness.* Ann Arbor: University of Michigan Press, 1994.

Bassett, Laura. "Gender Gap in 2012 Election Aided Obama Win." *Huffington Post,* November 7, 2012. Retrieved from www.huffingtonpost.com/2012/11/07/ gender-gap-2012-election-obama_n_2086004.html. Accessed March 31, 2013.

Bauman, Zygmut. *Modernity and Ambivalence.* Ithaca, N.Y.: Cornell University Press, 1991.

Baumeister, Andrea T. *Liberalism and the "Politics of Difference."* Edinburgh: Edinburgh University Press, 2000.

Bay, Mia. *The White Image in the Black Mind: African-American Ideas about White People, 1830–1925.* New York: Oxford University Press, 2000.

Becker, Jo, and Scott Shane. "Secret 'Kill List' Proves a Test of Obama's Principles and Will." *New York Times,* May 29, 2012. Retrieved from www.nytimes.com/2012/05/29/world/obamas-leadership-in-war-on-al-qaedahtml?page wanted=all. Accessed March 31, 2013.

Bell, Derrick. *Faces at the Bottom of the Well.* New York: Basic Books, 1992.

———. *Race, Racism, and American Law.* Boston: Little, Brown, 1992.

Bellamy, Richard. "Liberalism." In *Contemporary Political Ideologies,* edited by Roger Eatwall and Anthony Wright, 23–49. Boulder, Colo.: Westview, 1993.

Benokratis, Nijole. "Racial Exclusion in Juries." *Journal of Applied Behavioral Science* 18 (1982): 29–47.

Berg, John C. *Class, Gender, Race, and Power in the U.S. Congress.* Boulder, Colo.: Westview Press, 1994.

Bergen, Peter, and Jennifer Rowland. "John Brennan, Obama's Drone Warrior." CNN, January 7, 2013. Retrieved from www.cnn.com/2013/01/07/opinion/bergen-brennan-drones/index.html. Accessed March 31, 2013.

Berman, Ari. "Obama on Voter Suppression: 'It's a Problem.'" *The Nation Blog,* October 25, 2012. Retrieved from www.thenation.com/blog/170830/obama-voter-suppression-its-problem#. Accessed March 31, 2013.

Berry, Mary France. *Black Resistance, White Law: A History of Constitutional Racism in America.* London: Allen Lane/Penguin Press, 1994.

Bishop, Donna M. "The Role of Race and Ethnicity in Juvenile Justice Processing." In *Our Children, Their Children: Confronting Racial and Ethnic Differences in American Juvenile Justice,* edited by Darnell F. Hawking and Kimberly Kempf-Leonard. Chicago and London: University of Chicago Press, 2005.

Blanchard, Janice, and Nicole Lurie. "R-e-s-p-e-c-t: Patient Reports of Disrespect in the Health Care Setting and Its Impact on Care." *Journal of Family Practice* 53 (2004): 721–31.

Blauner, Robert. *Black Lives, White Lives: Three Decades of Race Relations in America.* Berkeley: University of California Press, 1989.

Blinder, Scott. "Dissonance Persists: Reproduction of Racial Attitudes among Post–Civil Rights Cohorts of White Americans." *American Politics Research* 35, no. 3 (2007): 299–335.

Bobo, Lawrence D., and Devon Johnson. "Racial Attitudes in a Prismatic Metropolis: Mapping Identity, Competition, and Views on Affirmative Action." In *Prismatic Metropolis: Inequality in Los Angeles,* edited by Lawrence D. Bobo et al., 81–163. New York: Russell Sage Foundation, 2000.

Bobo, Lawrence D., and James Kluegel. "Opposition to Race-Targeting: Self-Interest, Stratification Ideology, or Racial Attitudes?" *American Sociological Review* 58, no. 4 (1993): 443–64.

Bobo, Lawrence D., James A. Kluegel, and Ryan A. Smith. "Laissez-Faire Racism: The Crystallization of a Kinder, Gentler, Antiblack Ideology." In *Racial Attitudes in the 1990s: Continuity and Change,* edited by Steven A. Tuch and Jack K. Martin, 15–44. Westport, Conn.: Praeger, 1997.

Bobo, Lawrence D., and Fred Licari. "Education and Political Tolerance: Testing the Effects of Cognitive Sophistication and Target Group Affect." *Public Opinion Quarterly* 53, no. 5 (1989): 285–308.

Bobo, Lawrence D., and Susan Suh. "Surveying Racial Discrimination: Analyses from a Multiethnic Labor Market." In *Prismatic Metropolis: Inequality in Los Angeles*, edited by Lawrence D. Bobo et al., 523–60. New York: Russell Sage Foundation, 2000.

Bonilla-Silva, Eduardo. "Rethinking Racism." *American Sociological Review* 62, no. 3 (1997): 465–80.

———. "'This Is a White Country': The Racial Ideology of the Western Nations of the World-System." *Sociological Inquiry* 70, no. 2 (2000): 188–214.

———. *White Supremacy and Racism in the Post–Civil Rights Era*. Boulder, Colo.: Rienner, 2001.

Bonilla-Silva, Eduardo, and Amanda E. Lewis. "The 'New Racism': Toward an Analysis of the U.S. Racial Structure, 1960–1990s." In *Race, Nation, and Citizenship*, edited by Paul Wong, 100–150. Boulder, Colo.: Westview, 1999.

Bonilla-Silva, Eduardo, and David Dietrich. "The Sweet Enchantment of Color-Blind Racism in Obamerica." *The ANNALS of the American Academy of Political and Social Science* 634 (March 2011): 190–206.

Bonilla-Silva, Eduardo, and Ashley Doane Jr., eds. "New Racism, Color-Blind Racism, and the Future of Whiteness in America." In *Whiteout: The Continuing Significance of Racism and Whiteness*. New York: Routledge, 2003.

Bonilla-Silva, Eduardo, and Tyrone A. Forman. "'I Am Not a Racist, but . . .': Mapping White College Students' Racial Ideology in the USA." *Discourse and Society* 11, no. 1 (2000): 50–85.

Bonilla-Silva, Eduardo, and Karen S. Glover. "'We Are All Americans': The Latin Americanization of Race Relations in the USA." In *The Changing Terrain of Race and Ethnicity: Theory, Methods and Public Policy*, edited by Amanda E. Lewis and Maria Krysan. New York: Russell Sage Foundation, 2004.

Bonilla-Silva, Eduardo, Tyrone A. Forman, Amanda E. Lewis, and David G. Embrick. "'It Wasn't Me': How Will Race and Racism Work in 21st Century America." *Research in Political Sociology* 12 (2003): 111–34.

Bordieau, Pierre. *Distinction*. Cambridge, Mass.: Harvard University Press, 1984.

———. *Pascalian Meditations*. Stanford, Calif.: Stanford University Press, 1997.

———. "Social Space and Symbolic Power." *Sociological Theory* 7 (Spring 1980): 12–25.

Boston, Thomas D. *Race, Class, and Conservatism*. Boston: Unwin Hyman, 1988.

Bouie, Jamelle. "Pennsylvania Admits It: No Voter Fraud Problem." *Washington Post*, July 24, 2012. Retrieved from www.washingtonpost.com/blogs/plum line/post/pennsylvania-admits-it-no-voter-fraud-problem/2012/07/24/gJQAHNVt6W_blog.html. Accessed March 29, 2013.

Bourgeois, Philippe. *In Search of Respect: Selling Crack in El Barrio*. New York: Cambridge University Press, 1995.

Bradford, Calvin. *Risk or Race? Racial Disparities in the Subprime Refinance Market*. Washington, D.C.: Center for Community Change, 2002.

Brewster, Zachary W. "Racially Discriminatory Service in Full-Service Restaurants: The Problem, Cause, and Potential Solutions." *Cornell Hospitality Quarterly* 53, no. 4 (2012): 274–85.

Brodkin, Karen. *How Jews Became White Folks and What That Says about Race in America.* New Brunswick, N.J.: Rutgers University Press, 1998.

Brooks, Roy. *Integration or Separation? A Strategy for Racial Equality.* Cambridge, Mass.: Harvard University Press, 1996.

———. *Rethinking the American Race Problem.* Berkeley: University of California Press, 1990.

Brower, Kate. "Obama Pitches Equal Pay to Win Women Even as Charges Drop." *Bloomberg News,* May 13, 2012. Retrieved from www.bloomberg.com/news/2012-05-14/obama-pitches-equal-pay-to-win-women-even-as-charges-drop.html. Accessed March 31, 2013.

Brower, Kate, and Elizabeth Dwoskin. "To Lure Women's Votes, Obama Turns to Lilly Ledbetter." *Bloomberg News,* May 17, 2012. Retrieved from www.businessweek.com/articles/2012-05-17/to-lure-womens-votes-obama-turns-to-lilly-ledbetter. Accessed March 31, 2013.

Brown, Lee P. "Crime in the Black Community." *The State of Black America,* edited by Janet Dewart, 95–113. New York: National Urban League, 1988.

Bush, Roderick. *We Are Not What We Seem: Black Nationalism and Class Struggle in the American Century.* New York: New York University Press, 1999.

Butler, Desmond. "USAID Contractor Work in Cuba Detailed." *Business Week,* February 13, 2012. Retrieved from www.businessweek.com/ap/financial news/D9SSHGPG2.htm. Accessed March 31, 2013.

Butler, Paul. "Why Don't Black Leaders Demand More of the President?" *The Daily Beast,* September 24, 2012.

Caditz, Judith. *White Liberals in Transition: Current Dilemmas of Ethnic Integration.* New York: Spectrum Publications, 1976.

Calmes, Jackie. "Analysis Looks at Effect of Letting Tax Cuts Lapse for Rich." *New York Times,* August 10, 2010. Retrieved from www.nytimes.com/2010/08/11/us/politics/11tax.html. Accessed March 31, 2013.

Campbell, Angus, and Howard Schuman. *Racial Attitudes in Fifteen American Cities.* Ann Arbor, Mich.: Survey Research Center, June 1968.

Canellos, Peter. "On Affirmative Action, Obama Intriguing but Vague." Boston.com, April 29, 2008. Retrieved from www.boston.com/news/nation/articles/2008/04/29/on_affirmative_action_obama_intriguing_but_vague. Accessed March 31, 2013.

Cardwell, Diane. "Daring to Believe, Blacks Savor Obama Victory." *New York Times,* January 5, 2008. Retrieved from www.nytimes.com/2008/01/05/us/politics/05race.html. Accessed March 31, 2013.

Carson, Clayborne. *Malcolm X: The FBI File.* New York: Carroll and Graf Editors, 1991.

Cashin, Sheryll. *Failures of Integration: How Race and Class Are Undermining the American Dream.* New York: Public Affairs, 2004.

Cassidy, John. "Obamacare by the Numbers, Part 1." *New Yorker,* March 24, 2010. Retrieved from www.newyorker.com/online/blogs/johncassidy/2010/03/

obamacare-by-the-numbers-part-1.html#ixzz22mBytI00. Accessed March 31, 2013.

Cavaliere, Victoria. "New Jersey Store Halloween Display Depicts Obama as a Witch Doctor in Loin Cloth, Bone through His Nose." *New York Daily News*, October 13, 2012. Retrieved from www.nydailynews.com/news/national/ obama-as-witch-doctor-photo-stokes-controversy-article-1.1182635. Accessed March 31, 2013.

CBS Minnesota. "Neighbors Speak Out against Chair-Lynching Display." October 31, 2012. Retrieved from http://minnesota.cbslocal.com/2012/10/31/ neighbors-speak-out-against-chair-lynching-display. Accessed March 31, 2013.

Center for Responsible Lending. "Lost Ground, 2011: Disparities in Mortgage Lending and Foreclosures." November 17, 2011. Retrieved from www.respon siblelending.org/mortgage-lending/policy-legislation/regulators/facing-the -foreclosure-crisis.html. Accessed March 31, 2013.

Chait, Jonathan. "Why Is Obama Caving on Taxes?" *New York Magazine*, December 2012. Retrieved from http://nymag.com/daily/intelligencer/2012/12/ why-is-obama-caving-on-taxes.html. Accessed March 31, 2013.

Chambliss, Theresa. "The Growth and Significance of African American Elected Officials." In *From Exclusion to Inclusion: The Long Struggle for African American Political Power*, edited by Ralph C. Gomes and Linda Faye Williams. New York: Greenwood Press, 1992.

Cheng, Cheng, and Mark Hoekstra. *Does Strengthening Self-Defense Law Deter Crime or Escalate Violence? Evidence from Castle Doctrine*. Cambridge, Mass.: National Bureau of Economic Research, 2012.

Chideya, Farai. *Don't Believe the Hype: Fighting Cultural Misinformation about African-Americans*. New York: Penguin Books, 1995.

Childress, Sarah. "Is There Racial Bias in 'Stand Your Ground' Laws?" *Frontline*, July 31, 2012. Retrieved from www.pbs.org/wgbh/pages/frontline/criminal -justice/is-there-racial-bias-in-stand-your-ground-laws. Accessed March 29, 2013.

Churchill, Ward, and Jim Vander Wall. *Agents of Repression: The FBI's Secret Wars against the Black Panther Party and the American Indian Movement*. Boston: South End Press, 1988.

Clinton, Catherine. *The Plantation Mistress*. New York: Pantheon, 1982.

Cloud, Cathy, and George Galster. "What Do We Know about Racial Discrimination in Mortgage Markets?" *The Review of Black Political Economy* 21 (1993): 101–20.

Cloud, David, and Ken Dilanian. "U.S. Gathering Data on Suspects in Consulate Attack in Libya." *Los Angeles Times*, October 2, 2012. Retrieved from http:// articles.latimes.com/2012/oct/02/world/la-fg-libya-attack-20121003. Accessed March 31, 2013.

Coates, Ta-Nehisi. "Fear of a Black President." *The Atlantic*, September 2012. Retrieved from www.theatlantic.com/magazine/archive/2012/09/fear-of-a -black-president/309064. Accessed March 31, 2013.

Coll, Stephen. *Ghost Wars: The Secret History of the CIA, Afghanistan, and bin Laden, from the Soviet Invasion to September 10, 2001*. New York: Penguin, 2004.

Collins, Sharon. *Black Corporate Executives: The Making and Breaking of a Black Middle Class.* Philadelphia: Temple University Press, 1997.
———. "The Making of the Black Middle Class." *Social Problems* 30 (1983): 369–82.
Cooper, Anderson. "The Full Story Behind Rev. Jeremiah Wright's 9/11 Sermon." *AC360*, March 21, 2008. Retrieved from http://AC360.blogs.cnn.com/2008/03/21/the-full-story-behind-rev-jeremiah-wrights-911-sermon. Accessed March 31, 2013.
Cooper, John L. *The Police and the Ghetto.* Port Washington, N.Y., and London: Kennikat Press, 1980.
Corn, David. "Obama and GOPers Worked Together to Kill Torture Probe." *Mother Jones*, December 1, 2010. Retrieved from http://motherjones.com/politics/2010/12/wikileaks-cable-obama-quashed-torture-investigation. Accessed March 31, 2013.
Cose, Ellis. *The Rage of a Privileged Class: Why Are Middle-Class Blacks Angry? Why Should America Care?* New York: HarperCollins, 1993.
Cotton, Jeremiah. "Opening the Gap: The Decline in Black Economic Indicators in the 1980s." *Social Science Quarterly* 70 (1989): 803–19.
Crosby, Faye. *Affirmative Action Is Dead: Long Live Affirmative Action.* New Haven, Conn.: Yale University Press, 2004.
Cruse, Harold. *Plural but Equal: A Critical Study of Blacks and Minorities and America's Plural Society.* New York: Morrow, 1987.
Curry, Tom. "Voters Back President Obama Despite Economic Concerns, Polls Show." NBC News, November 6, 2012. Retrieved from http://nbcpolitics.nbcnews.com/_news/2012/11/06/14979402-voters-back-obama-despite-economic-concerns-exit-polls-show?lite. Accessed March 31, 2013.
Darity, William A., Jr. "Stratification Economics: The Role of Intergroup Inequality." *Journal of Economics and Finance* 29, no. 2 (Summer 2005): 144–53.
Darity, William A., Jr., Jeremiah Cotton, and Herbert Hill. "Race and Inequality in the Managerial Age." In *African Americans: Essential Perspectives*, edited by Wornie L. Reed, 33–80. Westport, Conn.: Auburn House, 1993.
Darity, William A., Jr., and Samuel L. Myers. "Changes in the Black-White Income Inequality, 1968–1978: A Decade of Progress?" *The Review of Black Political Economy* 10 (1980): 365–92.
Davis, Allison, Burleigh B. Gardner, and Mary R. Gardner. *Deep South: A Social Anthropological Study of Caste and Class.* Chicago: University of Chicago Press, 1941.
Davis, Dernoral. "Toward a Socio-Historical and Demographic Portrait of Twentieth-Century African Americans." In *Black Exodus: The Great Migration from the American South*, edited by Alferdteen Harrison, 1–19. Jackson, Miss., and London: University of Mississippi Press, 1991.
Dawson, Michael C. *Behind the Mule: Race and Class in African American Politics.* Princeton, N.J.: Princeton University Press, 1994.
———. *Black Visions: The Roots of Contemporary African-American Political Ideologies.* Chicago: University of Chicago Press, 2001.
Day, Jennifer Cheeseman, and Eric Newburger. *The Big Payoff: Educational Attainment and Synthetic Estimates of Work-Life Earnings.* Washington, D.C.: U.S. Census Bureau, 2002.

Dehghan, Saeed Kamali. "Sanctions on Iran: 'Ordinary People Are the Target,'" *Guardian*, August 10, 2012. Retrieved from www.guardian.co.uk/world/2012/aug/10/sanctions-iran-ordinary-people-target. Accessed March 31, 2013.

Demby, Gene. "Michael Steele: Voter ID Rhetoric Is 'Irresponsible,' Party Needs New Approach to Black Voters." *Huffington Post*, August 31, 2012. Retrieved from www.huffingtonpost.com/2012/08/31/michael-steele-voterid_n_1847623 .html?utm_hp_ref=elections-2012. Accessed March 31, 2013.

Democracy Now. "'Effective Evil' or Progressives' Best Hope? Glen Ford vs. Michael Eric Dyson on Obama Presidency." September 7, 2012. Retrieved from www.democracynow.org/2012/9/7/effective_evil_or_progressives_best_ hope. Accessed March 31, 2013.

———. "Whistleblower: The NSA Is Lying—U.S. Government Has Copies of Most of Your Emails." April 20, 2012. Retrieved from www.democracynow .org/2012/4/20/whistleblower_the_nsa_is_lying_us. Accessed March 31, 2013.

DeMott, Benjamin. *The Trouble with Friendship: Why Americans Can't Think Straight about Race.* New York: Atlantic Monthly Press, 1995.

Demuth, Stephen, and Darrell Steffensmeier. "Ethnicity Effects on Sentence Outcomes in Large Urban Courts: Comparisons among White, Black, and Hispanic Defendants." *Social Science Quarterly* 85 (2004): 994–1011.

DeNavas-Walt, Carmen, Bernadette D. Proctor, and Jessica C. Smith. "Income, Poverty, and Health Insurance Coverage in the United States: 2011." U.S. Census Bureau, September 2012. Retrieved from www.census.gov/prod/2012pubs/ p60-243.pdf. Accessed March 31, 2013.

Denzin, Norman K. *The Research Act.* Englewood Cliffs, N.J.: Prentice Hall, 1989.

Denzin, Norman K., and Yvonna S. Lincoln. *Handbook of Qualitative Research.* Thousand Oaks, Calif.: Sage, 2000.

Desena, Judith N. "Local Gatekeeping Practices and Residential Segregation." *Sociological Inquiry* 64, no. 3 (1994): 307–21.

Doane, Ashley W. "White Identity and Race Relations in the 1990s." In *Perspectives on Current Social Problems,* edited by Gregg Lee Carter, 151–59. Boston: Allyn and Bacon, 1997.

Dollard, John. *Caste and Class in a Southern Town.* New York: Doubleday, 1957.

Domhoff, William. *Who Rules America?* Englewood Cliffs, N.J.: Prentice Hall, 2006.

Donmoyer, Ryan J. "Would Ending Bush's Tax Cuts Hurt Small Business?" *Bloomberg Businessweek,* September 23, 2010. Retrieved from www.businessweek .com/magazine/content/10_40/b4197030541676.htm. Accessed March 31, 2013.

Dorn, Edward. *Rules and Racial Equality.* New Haven, Conn.: Yale University Press, 1979.

Dovidio, John F., and Samuel L. Gaertner. "Changes in the Expression and Assessment of Racial Prejudice." In *Openmind Doors,* edited by Harry J. Knopke et al., 119–50. Tuscaloosa: University of Alabama Press, 1991.

Dowding, Keith. *Power.* Minneapolis: University of Minnesota Press, 1996.

Drew, Christopher, and Mike McIntire. "After 2000 Loss, Obama Built Donor Network from Roots Up." *New York Times,* April 3, 2007. Retrieved from www .nytimes.com/2007/04/03/us/politics/03obama.html?_r1. Accessed March 31, 2013.

D'Souza, Dinesh. *The End of Racism: Principles for a Multiracial Society*. New York: Free Press, 1995.

DuBois, W. E. B. *The Souls of Black Folk*. New York: Penguin, 1995.

Duke, David. Retrieved from www.duke.org. Accessed December 8, 2002.

Duke, Lynne. "How Big a Stretch? For Barack Obama, Winning the White House Would Mean Bridging the Biggest Gap of All." *Washington Post*, May 7, 2007. Retrieved from www.washingtonpost.com/wp-dyn/content/article/2007/05/06/AR2007050601255.html. Accessed March 31, 2013.

Dunford, Mike. "New York Post Editorial Cartoon Appears to Depict Obama as (Dead) Chimpanzee." *The Questionable Authority*, February 18, 2009. Retrieved from http://scienceblogs.com/authority/2009/02/18/new-york-post-editorial-cartoo. Accessed March 31, 2013.

Dunn, Thomas L. "The New Enclosures: Racism in the Normalized Community." In *Reading Rodney King, Reading Urban Uprising*, edited by Robert Gooding-Williams, 178–95. New York: Routledge, 1993.

Edin, Kathryn. *Making Ends Meet: How Single Mothers Survive Welfare and Long-Wage Work*. New York: Russell Sage Foundation, 1997.

Edsall, Thomas, and Mary D. Edsall. *Chain Reaction: The Impact of Race, Rights, and Taxes on American Politics*. New York: Norton, 1992.

Eliasoph, Nina. "'Everyday Racism' in a Culture of Political Avoidance: Civil Society, Speech, and Taboo." *Social Problems* 46, no. 4 (1997): 479–502.

Emerson, Michael O., and Christian Smith. *Divided by Faith: Evangelical Religion and the Problem of Race in America*. New York: Oxford University Press, 2000.

Epstein, J. L. "After the Bus Arrives: Resegregation in Desegregated Schools." *Journal of Social Issues* 41, no. 3 (1985): 23–43.

Esposito, Luigi, and John W. Murphy. "Another Step in the Study of Race Relations." *Sociological Quarterly* 41, no. 2 (2000): 171–87.

Essed, Philomena. *Diversity: Gender, Color, and Culture*. Amherst: University of Massachusetts Press, 1996.

Esses, Victoria, John Dividio, and Gordon Hodson. "Public Attitudes toward Immigration in the United States and Canada in Response to the September 11, 2001 'Attack on America.'" *Analyses of Social Issues and Public Policy* 2 (2002): 69–85.

Fair, Bryan K. *Racial Caste Baby: Color Blindness and the End of Affirmative Action*. New York: New York University Press, 1997.

Fairclough, Norman. *Critical Discourse Analysis: The Critical Study of Language*. London: Longman, 1995.

———. *Language and Power*. London: Longman, 1989.

Fama, Jilian. "President Obama Witch Doctor Display 'Personal,' Not Racist, NJ Store Owner Says." ABC News, October 13, 2012. Retrieved from http://abcnews.go.com/Politics/OTUS/president-obama-witch-doctor-display-personal-racist-nj/story?id=17463813#.UJKOILt0SaE. Accessed March 31, 2013.

Farley, Reynolds. *Blacks and Whites: Narrowing the Gap?* Cambridge, Mass., and London: Harvard University Press, 1984.

———. "The Common Destiny of Black and Whites: Observations about the Social and Economic Status of the Races." In *Race in America: The Struggle for Equality*, edited by Herbert Hill and James E. Jones Jr. Madison: University of Wisconsin Press, 1993.

———. *The New American Reality*. New York: Russell Sage Foundation, 1996.

Farley, Reynolds, and Walter R. Allen. *The Color Line and the Quality of Life in America*. New York: Russell Sage Foundation, 1987.

Farmer, Ben. "US Troops May Stay in Afghanistan until 2024." *Telegraph*, August 19 2011. Retrieved from www.telegraph.co.uk/news/worldnews/asia/afghanistan/8712701/US-troops-may-stay-in-Afghanistan-until-2024.html. Accessed March 31, 2013.

Farnam, T. W. "Fundraising Starts Up Soon after Election, Filings Show." *Washington Post*, December 19, 2012. Retrieved from http://articles.washingtonpost.com/2012-12-19/politics/35929528_1_leadership-pacs-election-day-shelley-moore-capito. Accessed March 31, 2013.

Fay, Brian. *Contemporary Philosophy of Social Science*. Oxford: Blackwell, 1996.

Feagin, Joe R. "The Continuing Significance of Race: Antiblack Discrimination in Public Places." *American Sociological Review* 56, no. 1 (1991): 101–16.

———. *Racist America: Roots, Realities, and Future Reparations*. New York: Routledge, 2000.

Feagin, Joe R., and Karen D. McKinney. *The Many Costs of Racism*. Lanham, Md.: Rowman & Littlefield, 2003.

Feagin, Joe R., and Melvin Sikes. *Living with Racism: The Black Middle-Class Experience*. Boston: Beacon, 1994.

Feagin, Joe R., and Hernán Vera. *White Racism: The Basics*. New York: Routledge, 1995.

Feagin, Joe R., Hernán Vera, and Nikitah Imani. *The Agony of Education: Black Students at White Colleges and Universities*. New York: Routledge, 1996.

Fehr, Beverly. *Friendship Process*. Newbury Park, Calif.: Sage, 1996.

Fine, Michelle, and Lois Weis. *The Unknown City: Lives of Poor and Working-Class Young Adults*. Boston: Beacon, 1998.

Finn, Peter. "Bush Trip to Switzerland Called Off amid Threats of Protests, Legal Action." *Washington Post*, February 5, 2011. Retrieved from www.washingtonpost.com/wp-dyn/content/article/2011/02/05/AR2011020502822.html. Accessed March 31, 2013.

Firebaugh, Glenn, and Kenneth E. Davis. "Trends in Antiblack Prejudice, 1972–1984: Region and Cohort Effects." *American Journal of Sociology* 94 (1988): 251–72.

Firestone, David. "What the Democrats Didn't Say." *New York Times*, September 5, 2012. Retrieved from http://takingnote.blogs.nytimes.com/2012/09/05/what-the-democrats-didnt-say. Accessed March 31, 2013.

Fix, Michael, and Raymond J. Struyk. *Clear and Convincing Evidence: Measurement of Discrimination in America*. Washington, D.C.: Urban Institute, 1993.

Flippen, Chenoa. "Unequal Returns to Housing Investments? A Study of Real Housing Appreciation among Black, White, and Hispanic Households." *Social Forces* 82, no. 4 (2004): 1523–51.

Flock, Elizabeth. "Obama Campaign May Have Embraced Super PAC Earlier Than It Let On." *U.S. News*, September 7, 2012. Retrieved from www.usnews.com/news/blogs/washington-whispers/2012/09/07/obama-campaign-may-have-embraced-super-pac-earlier-than-it-let-on. Accessed March 31, 2013.

Foner, Philip S. *Organized Labor and the Black Worker, 1619–1981*. New York: International Publishers, 1981.

Fontana, Andrea, and James H. Frey. "The Interview: From Structured Questions to Negotiated Text." In *Handbook of Qualitative Research*, edited by Norman K. Denzin and Yvonna S. Lincoln, 645–72. Thousand Oaks, Calif.: Sage, 2000.

Forman, Tyrone A., and Amanda E. Lewis. "Racial Apathy and Hurricane Katrina: The Social Anatomy of Prejudice in the Post–Civil Rights Era." *Du Bois Review* 3, no. 1 (2006): 175–202.

Foucault, Michel. *The Order of Things: An Archeology of the Human Sciences*. New York: Random House, 1973.

France-Presse, Agence. "Obama Still Highly Popular in Europe: Poll." *The Raw Story*, September 4, 2011. Retrieved from www.rawstory.com/rs/2011/09/14/obama-still-highly-popular-in-europe-poll. Accessed March 31, 2013.

———. "US Working to Destabilise Morales Government: Bolivia." *Gulf Today*, January 7, 2013. Retrieved from http://gulftoday.ae/portal/dbf649a1-cd27-42d9-ab6c-535fe6dbc59e.aspx. Accessed March 31, 2013.

Frankenberg, Ruth. *White Women, Race Matters*. Minneapolis: University of Minnesota Press, 1993.

Fraser, James, and Edward Kick. "The Interpretive Repertoires of Whites on Race-Targeted Policies: Claims Making of Reverse Discrimination." *Sociological Perspectives* 43, no. 1 (2000): 13–28.

Fredrickson, George. *Black Image in the White Mind: The Debate on Afro-American Character and Destiny, 1817–1914*. New York: Evanston; San Francisco and London: Harper Torchbooks, 1973.

———. *White Supremacy: A Comparative Study in American and South African History*. New York: Oxford University Press, 1981.

Friedersdorf, Conor. "Why I Refuse to Vote for Obama." *The Atlantic*, September 26, 2012. Retrieved from www.theatlantic.com/politics/archive/2012/09/why-i-refuse-to-vote-for-barack-obama/262861. Accessed March 31, 2013.

Gabbidon, Shaun, and Steven A. Peterson. "Living While Black: A State-Level Analysis of the Influence of Select Social Stressors on the Quality of Life among Black Americans." *Journal of Black Studies* 37, no. 1 (2008): 83–102.

Gallagher, Charles A. "Interracial Dating and Marriage: Fact, Fantasy and the Problem of Survey Data." In *Quality and Quantity of Contact: African Americans and Whites on College Campuses*, edited by Robert Moore, 240–54. New York: University Press of America, 2002.

Garrow, David J. *The FBI and Martin Luther King*. New York: Penguin Books, 1983.

Garwood, Alfred N. *Black Americans: A Statistical Sourcebook*. Boulder, Colo.: Numbers and Concepts, 1991.

Gharib, Ali. "Obama Clear Winner in World Opinion." *International Press Service*, September 12, 2008. Retrieved from www.commondreams.org/headline/2008/09/12-2. Accessed March 31, 2013.

Gilroy, Paul. *Against Race*. Cambridge, Mass.: Belknap, 2000.

Gittleman, Maury, and Edward N. Wolff. "Racial Differences in Patterns of Wealth Accumulation." *Journal of Human Resources* 39 (2004): 193–227.

Glaster, George C. "Racial Steering by Real Estate Agents: Mechanisms and Motives." *The Review of Black Political Economy* 19, no. 1 (Spring 1990): 39–61.

Goad, Jim. *The Redneck Manifesto*. New York: Touchstone, 1997.

Goldberg, David T. *Racist Culture: Philosophy and the Politics of Meaning.* Cambridge: Blackwell, 1993.

Goldfield, David R. *Black, White, and Southern: Race Relations and Southern Culture, 1940 to the Present.* Baton Rouge: Louisiana State University Press, 1990.

Goldfield, Michael. *The Color of Politics: Race and the Mainsprings of American Politics.* New York: New York Press, 1997.

Goldman, Russell. "Donald 'Bombshell' Fails to Blow Up." ABC News, October 24, 2012. Retrieved from http://abcnews.go.com/Politics/OTUS/donald-trump -fails-drop-bombshell-offers-cash-obama/story?id=17553670#.UJJ-y7t0SaE. Accessed March 31, 2013.

Gossett, Thomas. *Race: The History of an Idea in America.* Dallas: Southern Methodist University Press, 1963.

Gouldner, Helen, and Mary Strong. *Speaking of Friendship: Middle-Class Women and Their Friends.* New York: Greenwood, 1987.

Graham, Lawrence Otis. *Member of the Club.* New York: HarperCollins, 1995.

Graves, Earl. "State of Black America." *Black Enterprise,* April 8, 2009. Retrieved from www.blackenterprise.com/blogs/2009/04/08/state-of-black-america -wealth-for-life. Accessed March 21, 2013.

Gray, John. *Liberalism.* Minneapolis: University of Minnesota Press, 1986.

Greene, Lorenzo, and Carter G. Woodson. *The Negro Wage Earner.* New York: Association for the Study of Negro Life and History, 1930.

Greenwald, Glenn. "Iran Sanctions Now Causing Food Insecurity, Mass Suffering." *Guardian,* October 7, 2012. Retrieved from www.guardian.co.uk/commen- tisfree/2012/oct/07/iran-santions-suffering. Accessed March 31, 2013.

Grier, Peter, and James N. Thurman. "Youth's Shifting Attitudes on Race." *Christian Science Monitor,* August 18, 1999.

Grodsky, Eric, and Devah Pager. "The Structure of Disadvantage: Individual and Occupational Determinants of the Black-White Wage Gap." *American Sociological Review* 66 (2001): 542–67.

Gross, Samuel R., and Robert Mauro. *Death and Discrimination: Racial Disparities in Capital Sentencing.* Boston: Northeastern University Press, 1989.

Hall, Stuart. "The Narrative Construction of Reality." *Southern Review* 17 (1984): 3–17.

Hallinan, Maureen, and Richard A. Williams. "The Stability of Student's Interracial Friendships." *American Sociological Review* 52, no. 2 (1987): 653–64.

Hamilton, Charles. *The Black Political Experience in America.* New York: Capricorn Books, 1973.

Hanchard, Michael G. *Orpheus and Power.* Princeton, N.J.: Princeton University Press, 1994.

Haney, Craig. "On the Selection of Capital Juries: The Biasing of the Death-Qualification Process." *Law and Human Behavior* 8 (1984): 121–32.

Harrington, Michael. *The Other America: Poverty in the United States.* New York: Macmillan, 1962.

Harris, C. *Flying While Black: A Whistleblower's Story.* Los Angeles: Milligan, 2001.

Harris, David A. "Driving While Black: Racial Profiling on Our Nation's Highways." American Civil Liberties Union Special Report. *American Civil Liberties*

Union, June 1999. Retrieved from http://archive.aclu.org/profiling/report/index.html. Accessed December 8, 2002.

Harris, Fredrick. "The Price of a Black President." *New York Times,* October 27, 2012. Retrieved from www.nytimes.com/2012/10/28/opinion/sunday/the-price-of-a-black-president.html?pagewanted=all. Accessed March 31, 2013.

Harrison, Alferdteen. *Black Exodus: The Great Migration from the American South.* Jackson: University Press of Mississippi, 1991.

Harrison, Bennett, and Barry Bluestone. *The Great U-Turn: Corporate Restructuring and the Polarizing of America.* New York: Basic Books, 1988.

Hartigan, John, Jr. *Racial Situations: Class Predicaments of Whiteness in Detroit.* Princeton, N.J.: Princeton University Press, 1999.

Hartmann, Paul. *Racism and the Mass Media: A Study of the Role of the Mass Media in the Formation of White Beliefs and Attitudes in Britain.* Totowa, N.J.: Rowman & Littlefield, 1974.

Heckman, James J., and Brooks S. Payner. "Determining the Impact of the Federal Antidiscrimination Policy on the Economic Status of Blacks: A Study of South Carolina." *American Economic Review* 79, no. 1 (1992): 138–72.

Helderman, Rosalind S. "The 113th Congress Is the Most Diverse in History." *Washington Post,* January 3, 2013. Retrieved from www.washingtonpost.com/politics/113th-congress-has-more-women-minorities-than-ever/2013/01/03/7d1aaf30-55e5-11e2-8b9e-dd8773594efc_story.html. Accessed March 29, 2013.

Henri, Florette. *Black Migration: Movement North, 1900–1920.* New York: Anchor Press, Doubleday, 1975.

Herrnstein, Richard J., and Charles Murray. *The Bell Curve: Intelligence and Class Structure in American Life.* New York: Free Press, 1994.

Hersh, Joshua. "Hina Rabbani Khar, Pakistan Foreign Minister: Drones Are Top Cause of Anti-Americanism." *Huffington Post,* September 28, 2012. Retrieved from www.huffingtonpost.com/2012/09/28/hina-rabbani-khar-drones_n_1922637.html. Accessed March 31, 2013.

Hill-Collins, Patricia. *Black Feminist Thought.* New York: Routledge, 1990.

———. "Moving beyond Gender: Intersectionality and Scientific Knowledge." In *Revisioning Gender,* edited by Myra Marx Ferre, Judith Lorber, and Beth B. Hess, 261–84. Thousand Oaks, Calif.: Sage, 1999.

Hing, Julianne. "Remembering Oscar Grant on the Day of Johannes Mehserle's Release." *Colorlines,* June 14, 2011. Retrieved from http://colorlines.com/archives/2011/06/remembering_oscar_grant_on_the_day_of_johannes_mehserles_release.html. Accessed March 29, 2013.

Hoberman, John. *Darwin's Athletes.* Boston: Houghton Mifflin, 1997.

Hochschild, Jennifer. *Facing Up to the American Dream.* Princeton, N.J.: Princeton University Press, 1995.

Horton, Hayward Derrick, and Lori Latrice Sykes. "Toward a Critical Demography of Neo-Mulattoes: Structural." In *Skin Deep: How Race and Complexion Matter in the "Color-Blind" Era,* edited by Cedric Herring, Verna Keith, and Hayward Derrick Horton, 159–73. Urbana: University of Illinois Press, 2004.

Hughes, Michael. "Symbolic Racism, Old-Fashioned Racism, and Whites' Opposition to Affirmative Action." In *Racial Attitudes in the 1990s: Continuity and*

Change, edited by Steven A. Tuch and Jack K. Martin, 45–75. Westport, Conn.: Praeger, 1997.

Hunt, Darnell. *O. J. Simpson Facts and Fictions: News Rituals in the Construction of Reality*. Cambridge: Cambridge University Press, 1999.

———. *Screening the Los Angeles "Riots": Race, Seeing, and Resistance*. Cambridge: Cambridge University Press, 1996.

Hunt, Matthew O., Pamela Barboy Jackson, Brian Powell, and Lala Carr Steelman. "Color Blind: The Treatment of Race and Ethnicity in Social Psychology." *Social Psychology Quarterly* 63, no. 4 (2000): 352–64.

Hwang, Sean-Shong, Rogelio Saenz, and Benigno E. Aguirre. "Structural and Individual Determinants of Outmarriage among Chinese-, Filipino-, and Japanese-Americans in California." *Sociological Inquiry* 64, no. 4 (1994): 396–414.

Ignatiev, Noel. *How the Irish Became White*. New York: Routledge, 1995.

Ingram, David. *Group Rights: Reconciling Equality and Difference*. Lawrence: University Press of Kansas, 2000.

International Human Rights and Conflict Resolution Clinic (Stanford Law School) and Global Justice Clinic (NYU School of Law). "Living Under Drones: Death, Injury and Trauma to Civilians from US Drone Practices in Pakistan." Livingunderdrones.org, September 2012. Retrieved from www.livingunderdrones.org/wp-content/uploads/2012/10/Stanford-NYU-LIVING-UNDER-DRONES.pdf. Accessed March 31, 2013.

Jackman, Mary R. *The Velvet Glove: Paternalism and Conflict in Gender, Class, and Race Relations*. Berkeley: University of California Press, 1994.

Jackman, Mary R., and Marie Crane. "'Some of My Best Friends Are Black . . .': Interracial Friendship and Whites' Racial Attitudes." *Public Opinion Quarterly* 50 (Winter 1986): 459–86.

Jackson, Pamela I. *Minority Group Threat, Crime, and Policing*. New York, Westport, Conn., and London: Praeger, 1989.

Jakes, Lara. "Obama to Revive Military Tribunals for GITMO Detainees, with More Rights." *Huffington Post*, May 14, 2009. Retrieved from www.huffingtonpost.com/2009/05/14/obama-to-revive-military-_n_203783.html. Accessed March 31, 2013.

Jaynes, Gerald D., and Robin M. Williams. *A Common Destiny: Blacks and American Society*. Washington, D.C.: National Academy Press, 1989.

Jennings, James. *The Politics of Black Empowerment: The Transformation of Black Activism in Urban America*. Detroit: Wayne State University Press, 1992.

Johnson, Charles S. *Patterns of Negro Segregation*. New York: Harper & Brothers, 1943.

———. *Racial Attitudes: Interviews Revealing Attitudes of Northern and Southern White Persons, of a Wide Range of Occupational and Educational Levels, toward Negroes*. Nashville, Tenn.: Social Science Institute, Fisk University, 1946.

Johnson, Monica Kirkpatrick, and Margaret Mooney Marini. "Bridging the Racial Divide in the United States: The Effect of Gender." *Social Psychology Quarterly* 61, no. 3 (1998): 247–58.

Judis, John B. "Creation Myth." *The New Republic*, September 10, 2008. Retrieved from www.newrepublic.com/article/creation-myth-0. Accessed March 31, 2013.

Jung, Mon-Kie, João H. Costa Vargas, and Eduardo Bonilla-Silva, eds. *State of White Supremacy: Racism, Governance, and the United States*. Stanford, Calif.: Stanford University Press, 2011.

Kalmijn, Matthijs. "Intermarriage and Homogamy: Causes, Patterns, Trends." *Annual Review of Sociology* 24 (1998): 395–421.

Kane, Emily W. "Racial and Ethnic Variations in Gender-Related Attitudes." *Annual Review of Sociology* 26 (2000): 419–39.

Kantor, Jodi. "For President, a Complex Calculus of Race and Politics." *New York Times*, October 23, 2012. Retrieved from www.nytimes.com/2012/10/21/us/politics/for-president-obama-a-complex-calculus-of-race-and-politics.html?pagewanted=2&_r=1&smid=fb-share. Accessed March 31, 2013.

Keen, Sam. *Faces of the Enemy: Reflections of the Hostile Imagination*. New York: Harper & Row, 1986.

Kelley, Robin D. G. *Yo' Mama's Disfunktional: Fighting the Culture Wars in Urban America*. Boston: Beacon, 1997.

Khan, Akbar Nasir. "The US' Policy of Targeted Killing by Drones in Pakistan." *IPRI Journal* 11, no. 1 (Winter 2011): 21–40. Retrieved from http://harvard.academia.edu/AkbarNasirKhan/Papers/157952/U.S._Policy_of_Targeted_Killing_by_Drones_in_Pakistan. Accessed March 31, 2013.

Kinchelor, Joel L., and Peter McLaren. "Rethinking Critical Theory and Qualitative Research." In *Handbook of Qualitative Research*, edited by Norman K. Denzin and Yvonna S. Lincoln, 279–314. Thousand Oaks, Calif.: Sage, 2000.

Kinder, Donald R., and David O. Sears. "Prejudice and Politics: Symbolic Racism versus Racial Threats to the Good Life." *Journal of Personality and Social Psychology* 40, no. 1 (1981): 414–31.

Kinder, Donald R., and Lynn M. Sanders. *Divided by Color: Racial Politics and Democratic Ideals*. Chicago: University of Chicago Press, 1996.

King, Martin Luther, Jr. *A Call to Conscience: The Landmark Speeches of Dr. Martin Luther King, Jr.* Edited by Clayborne Carson and Kris Shephard. New York: Intellectual Properties Management, in association with Warner Books, 2001.

Kirschenman, Joleen, and Kathryn M. Neckerman. "'We'd Love to Hire Them, but . . .': The Meaning of Race for Employers." In *Race and Ethnic Conflict*, edited by Fred L. Pincus and Howard J. Erlich. Boulder, Colo.: Westview Press, 1994.

Kirwan Institute for the Study of Race and Ethnicity. "Preliminary Report of the Impact of the Economic Stimulus Plan on Communities of Color." February 10, 2009. Retrieved from www.abfe.org/FCDOCS/KirwanReport.pdf. Accessed March 31, 2013.

Klein, Naomi. *The Shock Doctrine: The Rise of Disaster Capitalism*. New York: Metropolitan Books, 2007.

Kochhar, Rakesh, Richard Fry, and Paul Taylor. "Wealth Gaps Rise to Record Highs Between Whites, Blacks and Hispanics." Pew Research Center, July 26, 2011. Retrieved from http://pewresearch.org/pubs/2069/housing-bubble-subprime-mortgages-hispanics-blacks-household-wealth-disparity. Accessed March 31, 2013.

Kovaleski, Serge, and Sewell Chan. "D.C. Cabs Still Bypass Minorities, Study Finds: City Crackdown Called Sporadic, Inadequate." *Washington Post*, October

7, 2003. Retrieved from www.highbeam.com/doc/1P2-313833.html. Accessed March 31, 2013.

Kovel, Joel. *White Racism: A Psychohistory*. New York: Columbia University Press, 1984.

Kozol, Jonathan. *Savage Inequalities*. New York: Crown, 1992.

Krauthammer, Charles. "Obama Denounced Enhanced Interrogation; Now He's Judge, Jury and Executioner." *Real Clear Politics*, May 29, 2012. Retrieved from www.realclearpolitics.com/video/2012/05/29/krauthammer_obama_de nounced_enhanced_interrogation_but_now_hes_judge_jury_and_executioner .html. Accessed March 31, 2013.

Krugman, Paul. "Played for a Sucker." *New York Times*, November 16, 2007. Retrieved from www.nytimes.com/2007/11/16/opinion/16krugman.html?_r=0. Accessed March 31, 2013.

Krysan, Maria, Mick P. Couper, Reynolds Farley, and Tyrone A. Forman. "Does Race Matter in Neighborhood Preferences? Results from a Video Experiment." *American Journal of Sociology* 115, no. 2 (2009): 527–59.

Lacy, Karyn. "All's Fair? The Foreclosure Crisis and Middle-Class Black (In)Stability." *American Behavioral Scientist* 56, no. 11 (2012): 1565–80.

Lafer, Gordon. *The Job Training Charade*. Ithaca, N.Y.: Cornell University Press, 2002.

LaPlaca, Charlie. "Anti-Obama Store Owner Says He's Not a Racist." *Manasquan-Belmar Patch*, October 12, 2012. Retrieved from http://manasquan.patch.com/ articles/anti-obama-store-owner-says-he-s-not-a-racist#c. Accessed March 31, 2013.

Larana, Enrique, Hank Johnston, and Joseph R. Gusfield, eds. *New Social Movements: From Ideology to Identity*. Philadelphia: Temple University Press, 1994.

Lee, Suevon. "Everything You've Ever Wanted to Know about Voter ID Laws." *ProPublica*, November 5, 2012. Retrieved from www.propublica.org/article/ everything-youve-ever-wanted-to-know-about-voter-id-laws. Accessed March 29, 2013.

Leiman, Melvin M. *Political Economy of Racism*. London and Boulder, Colo.: Pluto Press, 1992.

Leonhardt, David. "After the Great Recession." *New York Times*, April 28, 2009. Retrieved from www.nytimes.com/2009/05/03/magazine/03Obama-t .html?pagewanted6. Accessed March 31, 2013.

———. "Obamanomics." *New York Times*, August 20, 2008. Retrieved from www .nytimes.com/2008/08/24/magazine/24Obamanomics-t.html. Accessed March 31, 2013.

Lerner, Gerda. *The Grimké Sisters from South Carolina: Pioneers for Woman's Rights and Abolition*. New York: Schocken, 1967.

Levin, Jack, and Jack McDevitt. *Hate Crimes: The Rising Tide of Bigotry and Bloodshed*. New York: Plenum, 1993.

Lewis, Oscar. *The Children of Sanchez: Autobiography of a Mexican Family*. New York: Random House, 1961.

———. *La Vida: A Puerto Rican Family in the Culture of Poverty—San Juan and New York*. New York: Random House, 1966.

Lichter, Daniel T. "U.S. Far from an Interracial Melting Pot." CNN Opinion, June 16, 2010. Retrieved from www.cnn.com/2010/OPINION/06/14/lichter.interracial.marriage/index.html. Accessed March 29, 2013.

Lipset, Seymour. *American Exceptionalism.* New York: Norton, 1996.

Liptak, Adam. "U.S. Imprisons One in 100 Adults, Report Finds." *New York Times*, February 29, 2008. Retrieved from www.nytimes.com/2008/02/29/us/29prison.html. Accessed March 29, 2013.

Liska, Allen E. Joseph J. Lawrence, and Michael Benson. "Perspectives on the Legal Order: the Capacity for Social Control." *American Journal of Sociology* 87 (1981): 413–26.

Lizote, Alan J. "Extra-Legal Factors in Chicago's Criminal Courts: Testing the Conflict Model of Criminal Justice." *Social Problems* 25 (1978): 564–80.

Logan, John R. "Ethnic Diversity Grows, Neighborhood Integration Lags." In *Redefining Urban and Suburban America: Evidence from Census 2000*, edited by Bruce Katz and Robert Lang. Washington, D.C.: Brookings Institution Press, 2003.

Loven, Jennifer. "Obama Seeks to Block Release of Abuse Photos." *AP White House Correspondent*, May 13, 2009. Retrieved from www.dailyprogress.com/news/article_8c0d1d34-efdc-52a7-aa03-443ea13569b0.html. Accessed March 31, 2013.

Lowder, J. Bryan. "Campaign Love Notes: The Ballad of Lilly Ledbetter." *Slate Magazine*, May 15, 2012. Retrieved from www.slate.com/blogs/xx_factor/2012/05/15/lilly_ledbetter_obama_and_women_is_the_act_being_overused_.html. Accessed March 31, 2013.

Lusane, Clarence. *African Americans at the Crossroads: The Restructuring of Black Leadership and the 1992 Elections.* Boston: South End Press, 1994.

Lyman, Stanford M. *Social Movements: Critiques, Concepts, Case-Studies.* New York: New York University Press, 1995.

Maddox, Matthew. "Institutionalized Racism Continues at A&M: Sociology Professor's Book Will Continue Tradition of Racist Ideology on Campus." *Battalion*, October 2, 2002.

Madsen, Wayne. "Obama Authorizes Covert Economic War against Venezuela." *Center for Research on Globalization*, January 19, 2010. Retrieved from www.globalresearch.ca/index.php?context=va&aid=17072. Accessed March 31, 2013.

Marable, Manning. *How Capitalism Underdeveloped Black America.* Boston: South End Press, 1981.

———. "Jackson and the Rise of the Rainbow Coalition." *New Left Review* 1, no. 149 (1989). Retrieved from http://newleftreview.org/I/149/manning-marable-jackson-and-the-rise-of-the-rainbow-coalition. Accessed March 31, 2013.

———. *Race, Reform, and Rebellion: The Second Reconstruction in Black America, 1945–1990.* Jackson: University Press of Mississippi, 1991.

Marks, Carole. "The Social and Economic Life of Southern Blacks during the Migration." In *Black Exodus: The Great Migration from the American South*, edited by Alferdteen Harrison, 36–50. Jackson, Miss., and London: University of Mississippi Press, 1991.

Marsh, Taylor. "Barack Obama's Progressive Cannibalism." *Huffington Post*, December 8, 2007. Retrieved from www.huffingtonpost.com/taylor-marsh/barack-obamas-progressiv_b_75933.html. Accessed March 31, 2013.

Marshall, Ray. "Industrialisation and Race Relations in the Southern United States." In *Industrialisation and Race Relations: A Symposium*, edited by Guy Hunter, 61–96. London and New York: Oxford University Press, 1965.

Martel, Frances. "Orange County, CA GOP Official Sends Email Saying Obama's Parents Were Monkeys." Mediaite, April 16, 2011. Retrieved from www .mediaite.com/tv/orange-county-gop-official-solves-birther-mystery-presidents -parents-were-monkeys. Accessed March 31, 2013.

Martin, Jonathan, and Carol E. Lee. "Obama: 'I Am a New Democrat.'" *Politico*, March 11, 2009. Retrieved from www.politico.com/news/stories/0309/19862 .html. Accessed March 31, 2013.

Marx, Karl. *The German Ideology*. Edited by C. J. Arthur. New York: International, 1985.

Masood, Salman. "Americans Join Pakistan Convoy to Protest Drone Strikes." *New York Times*, October 6, 2012. Retrieved from www.nytimes.com/2012/10/07/ world/asia/americans-join-pakistan-convoy-to-protest-drone-strikes.html?_ r=0. Accessed March 31, 2013.

Massey, Douglas S., and Nancy A. Denton. *American Apartheid: Segregation and the Making of the Underclass*. Cambridge, Mass.: Harvard University Press, 1993.

———. "Trends in the Residential Segregation of Blacks, Hispanics, and Asians: 1970–1980." *American Sociological Review* 52, no. 6 (1987): 802–25.

Massey, Douglas S., R. Alarcon, J. Durand, and H. Gonzalez. *Return to Aztlan: The Social Process of International Migration from Western Mexico*. Berkeley: University of California Press, 1997.

Mauer, Marc, and Ryan S. King. "Uneven Justice: State Rates of Incarceration by Race and Ethnicity." The Sentencing Project, June 2007.

McConahay, John B. "Modern Racism, Ambivalence, and the Modern Racism Scale." In *Prejudice, Discrimination, and Racism*, edited by John F. Dovidio and Samuel L. Gaertner, 91–126. New York: Academic, 1986.

McConahay, John B., and J. C. Hough. "Symbolic Racism." *Journal of Social Issues* 32, no. 2 (1976): 23–46.

McCullough, Mary W. *Black and White as Friends: Building Cross-Race Friendships*. Cresskill, N.J.: Hampton, 1998.

McLellan, David, ed. *Karl Marx: Selected Writings*. London: Oxford University Press, 1982.

McWhorter, John. "The End of Racism?" *Forbes*, November 5, 2008. Retrieved from www.forbes.com/2008/11/05/obama-racism-president-oped-cx_ jm_1105mcwhorter.html.

Mead, Lawrence M. *Beyond Entitlement: The Social Obligations of Citizenship*. New York: Free Press, 1986.

Media Action Network for Asian Americans. "Restrictive Portrayals of Asians in the Media and How to Balance Them." A Memo from MANAA to Hollywood: Asian Stereotypes. 2001. Retrieved from www.manaa.org/asianstereotypes .html. Accessed December 8, 2002.

Meehan, Albert, and Michael Ponder. "Race and Place: The Ecology of Racial Pro- filing African American Motorists." *Justice Quarterly* 19 (2002): 399–430.

Meizhu, Lui, Barbara J. Robles, Betsy Leondar-Wright, Rose M. Brewer, and Rebecca Adamson. *The Color of Wealth: The Story Behind the U.S. Racial Wealth Divide*. New York: The New Press, 2006.

Mendell, David. *Obama: From Promise to Power.* New York: HarperCollins, 2007.

Miller, Greg. "Plan for Hunting Terrorists Signals U.S. Intends to Keep Adding Names to Kill Lists." *Washington Post,* October 23, 2012. Retrieved from www .washingtonpost.com/world/national-security/plan-for-hunting-terrorists -signals-us-intends-to-keep-adding-names-to-kill-lists/2012/10/23/4789b2ae -18b3-11e2-a55c-39408fbe6a4b_print.html. Accessed March 31, 2013.

Mills, Charles W. *Blackness Visible.* Ithaca, N.Y.: Cornell University Press, 1998.

———. *The Racial Contract.* Ithaca, N.Y.: Cornell University Press, 1997.

Moran, Rachel. *Interracial Intimacy: The Regulation of Race and Romance.* Chicago: University of Chicago Press, 2001.

Morris, Aldon. *The Origins of the Civil Rights Movement: Black Communities Organizing for Change.* New York: The Free Press, 1984.

Morrow, Joseph J. "American Negroes—a Wasted Resource." *Harvard Business Review* January–February 1957, 65–74.

Moscovici, Serge. "The Coming Era of Social Representations." In *Cognitive Approaches to Social Behaviour,* edited by J. P. Codol and J. P. Leyens, 115–50. The Hague: Nijhoff, 1982.

Moss, Phillip, and Chris Tilly. *Stories Employers Tell: Race, Skill, and Hiring in America.* New York: Russell Sage Foundation, 2001.

Moss, Yvonne E., Wornie L. Reed, Alphonso Pinkney, James Turner, and Sidney Wilhelm. "Black Political Participation: The Search for Power." In *African Americans: Essential Perspectives,* edited by Wornie L. Reed. Westport, Conn.: Auburn House, 1993.

Moynihan, Daniel P., ed. *On Understanding Poverty: Perspectives from the Social Sciences.* New York: Basic, 1969.

Murdock, Steve H., and David R. Ellis. *Applied Demography: An Introduction to Basic Concepts, Methods, and Data.* Boulder, Colo.: Westview Press, 1991.

Murray, Charles A. *Losing Ground: American Social Policy, 1950–1980.* New York: Basic, 1984.

Myrdal, Gunnar. *An American Dilemma: The Negro Problem and Modern Democracy.* New York: Harper & Brothers, 1944.

Neal, Patrick. *Liberalism and Its Discontents.* New York: New York University Press, 1997.

Negrin, Matt. "Guantanamo Bay: Still Open, Despite Promises." ABC News, July 3, 2012. Retrieved from http://abcnews.go.com/Politics/OTUS/guantanamo bay-open-promises/story?id=16698768. Accessed March 31, 2013.

Nelson, Dana D. *National Manhood: Capitalist Citizenship and the Imagined Fraternity of White Men.* Durham, N.C.: Duke University Press, 1998.

Nelson, William E. "Black Mayoral Leadership: A Twenty-Year Perspective." In *Black Electoral Politics,* edited by Lucius Barker, 188–95. New Brunswick, N.J., and London: Transaction Publishers, 1990.

Newman, Katherine S. *Declining Fortunes: The Withering of the American Dream.* New York: Basic, 1993.

Nopper, Tamara. "Barack Obama's Community Organizing as New Black Politics." Special issue of *Political Power and Social Theory,* "Rethinking Obama," edited by Eduardo Bonilla-Silva and Louise Seamster, vol. 22 (2011): 51–73. Retrieved from http://tamaranopper.com/wp-content/uploads/2012/01/

barack-obamas-community-organizing-as-new-black-politics-nopper-2011.pdf. Accessed March 31, 2013.

Northrup, Herbert R. "Industry's Racial Employment Policies." In *Employment, Race, and Poverty*, edited by Arthur M. Ross and Herbert Hill, 290–307. New York: Harcourt, Brace, and World, 1967.

NPR. "Sebelius: Single-Payer Health Care Not in Plans." NPR, June 16, 2009. Retrieved from www.npr.org/templates/story/story.php?storyId=105442888. Accessed March 31, 2013.

Oakes, Jeannie, Molly Selvin, Lynn Karoly and Gretchen Guiton. *Educational Matchmaking: Academic and Vocational Tracking in Comprehensive High Schools*. Santa Monica, Calif.: Rand, 1992.

"Obama Aide Tells Israel of Iran Attack Plan—Paper." *Reuters*, July 29, 2012. Retrieved from www.arabnews.com/middle-east/obama-aide-tells-israel-iran -attack-plan-%E2%80%94-paper. Accessed March 31, 2013.

Obama, Barack. *The Audacity of Hope*. New York: Crown Publishers, 2006.

Odum, Howard W. *American Social Problems*. New York: Holt, 1939.

Ogbu, John. *Minority Education and Caste: The American System in Cross-Cultural Perspective*. New York: Academic, 1978.

O'Hare, William, Kelvin Pollard, Taynia Mann, and Mary Kent. "African Americans in the 1990s." *Population Bulletin* 46, no. 1 (1991).

Oliver, Melvin, James H. Johnson, and Walter C. Farrell Jr. "Anatomy of a Rebellion: A Political-Economic Analysis." In *Reading Rodney King, Reading Urban Uprising*, edited by Robert Gooding-Williams, 117–41. New York and London: Routledge, 1993.

Oliver, Melvin, and Thomas Shapiro. *Black Wealth/White Wealth: A New Perspective on Racial Inequality*. New York: Routledge, 1995.

Omi, Michael, and Howard Winant. *Racial Formation in the United States*. New York: Routledge, 1994.

Orbuch, Terri L. "People's Account Count: The Sociology of Accounts." *Annual Review of Sociology* 23 (1997): 455–78.

Orfield, Gary. *Must We Bus? Segregated Schools and National Policy*. Washington, D.C.: Brookings Institution Press, 1978.

———. "School Desegregation after Two Generations: Race, Schools and Opportunity in Urban Society." In *Race in America*, edited by Herbert Hill and James E. Jones. Madison: University of Wisconsin Press, 1993.

Orfield, Gary, and Carol Ashkinaze. *The Closing Door: Conservative Policy and Black Opportunity*. Chicago: University of Chicago Press, 1991.

Orfield, Gary, Susan Eaton, and the Harvard Project on School Desegregation. *Dismantling Desegregation: The Quiet Reversal of* Brown v. Board of Education. New York: New York Press, 1996.

Orfield, Gary, and Chungmei Lee. "Why Segregation Matters: Poverty and Educational Inequality." Harvard University, The Civil Rights Project, 2005.

Orfield, Gary, and Franklin Monfort. *Status of School Desegregation: The Next Generation*. Alexandria, Va.: National School Boards Association, 1992.

Orwell, George. "In Front of Your Nose." In *The Collected Essays, Journalism, and Letters of George Orwell*, vol. 4, edited by S. Orwell and I. Angus. New York: Harcourt, Brace, and World, 1946.

Pager, Devah. "The Mark of a Criminal Record." *American Journal of Sociology* 108 (2003): 937–75.

Pager, Devah, and Lincoln Quillian. "Walking the Talk? What Employers Say versus What They Do." *American Sociological Review* 70, no. 3 (2005): 355–80.

Park, Robert E. *Race and Culture.* Glencoe, Ill.: Free Press, 1950.

Parker, Frank R. "Eradicating the Continuing Barriers to Effective Minority Voter Participation." In *From Exclusion to Inclusion: The Long Struggle for African American Political Power,* edited by Ralph C. Gomes and Linda Faye Williams. New York: Greenwood Press, 1992.

Passel, Jeffery S., Wendy Wang, and Paul Taylor. "Marrying Out: One-in-Seven New US Marriages Is Interracial or Interethnic." Pew Research Center, June 8, 2010. Retrieved from www.pewtrusts.org/our_work_report_detail .aspx?id=59361. Accessed March 29, 2013.

Patterson, Ernest. *City Politics.* New York: Dood, Mead, 1974.

Peffley, Mark, and Jon Hurwitz. "Whites' Stereotypes of Blacks: Sources and Political Consequences." In *Perception and Prejudice: Race and Politics in the United States,* edited by Jon Hurwitz and Mark Peffley, 58–99. New Haven, Conn.: Yale University Press, 1998.

Penner, Louis A., John F. Dovidio, Donald Edmondson, Rhonda K. Dailey, Tsveti Markova, Terrance L. Albrecht, and Samuel L. Gaertner. "The Experience of Discrimination and Black-White Health Disparities in Medical Care." *Journal of Black Psychology* 35 (2009): 180–203.

Perry, Huey L. "The Evolution and Impact of Biracial Coalitions and Black Mayors in Birmingham and New Orleans." In *Racial Politics in American Cities,* edited by Rufus P. Browning, Dame Rogers Marshall, and David H. Tabb. New York: Longman, 1990.

Pettigrew, Thomas F. "New Patterns of Prejudice: The Different Worlds of 1984 and 1964." In *Race and Ethnic Conflict,* edited by Fred L. Pincus and Howard J. Erlich. Boulder, Colo.: Westview Press, 1994.

Pettigrew, Thomas F., and Joanne Martin. "Shaping the Organizational Context for Black American Inclusion." *Journal of Social Issues* 43, no. 1 (1987): 41–78.

Pew Research Center. "Blacks Upbeat About Racial Progress, Prospects a Year after Obama's Election." January 12, 2010. Retrieved from www.pewsocialtrends .org/2010/01/12/blacks-upbeat-about-black-progress-prospects. Accessed March 31, 2013.

Pincus, Fred. *Reverse Discrimination: Dismantling the Myth.* Boulder, Colo.: Lynne Reinner Publishers, 2003.

Pinkney, Alphonso. *The Myth of Black Progress.* Cambridge: Cambridge University Press, 1984.

Piven, Frances Fox. *Challenging Authority: How Ordinary People Change America.* Lanham, Md.: Rowman & Littlefield, 2006.

Piven, Frances Fox, and Richard Cloward. *Poor People's Movements.* New York: Vintage, 1978.

Plissner, Martin. "Ready for Obama Already." *New York Times,* February 7, 2007. Retrieved from www.nytimes.com/2007/02/07/opinion/07plissner .html?_r??1&_r=0. Accessed March 31, 2013.

Pomer, Marshall. "Labor Market Structure, Intragenerational Mobility, and Discrimination: Black Male Advancement Out of Low-Paying Occupations, 1962–1973." *American Sociological Review* 51 (1986): 650–59.

Poulantzas, Nicos. *Political Power and Social Classes.* Translation by Timothy O'Hagan. London: Verso, 1984.

Powell, Colin L., with Joseph E. Persico. *My American Journey.* New York: Random House, 1995.

Powell, John. "Post-Racialism or Targeted Universalism?" *Denver University Law Review* 1 (February 2009). Retrieved from www2.ohchr.org/english/bodies/hrcouncil/minority/docs/session3/statements/PostRacialismTargetedUniversalismbyJohnPowell.pdf. Accessed March 31, 2013.

Powell, Michael. "Obama Addresses Critics on 'Centrist' Moves." *New York Times,* July 8, 2008. Retrieved from http://thecaucus.blogs.nytimes.com/2008/07/08/obama-addresses-critics-on-centrist-moves. Accessed March 31, 2013.

Pruitt, Charles R., and James Q. Wilson. "A Longitudinal Study of the Effect of Race in Sentencing." *Law and Society Review* 7 (1983): 613–35.

Public Agenda. "'Walking on Eggshells': Observations on How Americans Discuss Race." 1998. Retrieved from www.publicagenda.org/specials/moveon/moveon8.htm. Accessed December 8, 2002.

Qian, Zhenchao, and Daniel T. Lichter. "Measuring Marital Assimilation: Intermarriage among Natives and Immigrants." *Social Science Research* 30 (2001): 289–312.

Quillian, Lincoln. "Group Threat and Regional Change in Attitudes toward African-Americans." *American Journal of Sociology* 102, no. 3 (1996): 816–60.

Radelet, Michael L., and Glenn L. Pierce. "The Role of Victim's Race and Geography on Death Sentencing." In *From Lynch Mobs to the Killing State,* edited by Charles J. Ogletree Jr. and Austin Sarat. New York: New York University Press, 2006.

Rawick, George P. *From Sundown to Sunup: The Making of the Black Community.* Westport, Conn.: Greenwood, 1972.

Rayment, Sean. "US and Britain Send Warships to the Persian Gulf to Prepare for an Israel Strike on Iran." *Business Insider,* September 16, 2012. Retrieved from www.businessinsider.com/us-and-britain-sending-warships-to-gulf-2012-9. Accessed March 31, 2013.

Reed, Adolph. "The Curse of Community." *Village Voice,* January 16, 1996—reprinted in *Class Notes: Posing as Politics and Other Thoughts on the American Scene.* New York: New Press, 2000.

———. "Sitting This One Out." *The Progressive,* November 2007. Retrieved from www.progressive.org/mag_reed1107. Accessed March 31, 2013.

Reed, Wornie L., and Bertin M. Louis. "'No More Excuses': Problematic Responses to Barack Obama's Election." *Journal of African American Studies* 13, no. 1 (2009): 97–109.

Reese, Renford. *Prison Race.* Durham, N.C.: Carolina Academic Press, 2006.

Reich, Michael. *Racial Inequality: A Political-Economic Analysis.* Princeton, N.J.: Princeton University Press, 1981.

Reskin, Barbara, and Irene Padavic. *Women and Men at Work.* Thousand Oaks, Calif.: Pine Forge, 2002.

Ridgeway, Cecilia, Elizabeth Heger Boyle, Kathy J. Kuipers, and Dawn T. Robinson. "How Do Status Beliefs Develop? The Role of Resources and Interactional Experience." *American Sociological Review* 63 (1998): 331–50.

Ridgeway, Cecilia, and James Balkwell. "Group Processes and the Diffusion of Status Beliefs." *Social Psychology Quarterly* 60, no. 1 (1997): 14–31.

Rieder, Jonathan. *Canarsie: The Jews and Italians of Brooklyn against Liberalism.* Cambridge, Mass.: Harvard University Press, 1985.

Rivera, Amaad, Jeannette Huezo, Christina Kasica, and Dedrick Muhammad. "State of the Dream 2009: The Silent Depression." United for a Fair Economy, January 15, 2009. Retrieved from www.faireconomy.org/files/pdf/state_of_dream_2009.pdf. Accessed March 31, 2013.

Robinson, Cedric J. *Black Marxism: The Making of the Black Radical Tradition.* Chapel Hill: University of North Carolina Press, 2000.

———. *Black Movements in America.* New York: Routledge, 1997.

Roediger, David. *Colored White: Transcending the Racial Past.* Berkeley: University of California Press, 2000; London: Verso, 2002.

———. *The Wages of Whiteness.* London: Verso, 1994.

Roscigno, Vincent J. *The Face of Discrimination: How Race and Gender Impact Work and Home Lives.* Lanham, Md.: Rowman & Littlefield, 2007.

Rose, Sonya O. "Class Formation and the Quintessential Worker." In *Reworking Class,* edited by John R. Hall, 133–66. Ithaca, N.Y.: Cornell University Press, 1997.

Rosentraub, Mark S., and Karen Harlow. "Police Policies and the Black Community: Attitude toward the Police." In *Contemporary Public Policy Perspectives and Black Americans,* edited by Mitchell F. Rice and Woodrow Jones Jr., 107–21. Westport, Conn., and London: Greenwood Press, 1984.

Ross, Sonya, and Jennifer Agiesta. "Racial Views: Poll Shows Majority Harbor Prejudice against Blacks." *Associated Press,* October 27, 2012. Retrieved from www.huffingtonpost.com/2012/10/27/racial-views-new-polls-sh_n_2029423.html?utm_hp_ref=fb&src=sp&comm_ref=false. Accessed March 31, 2013.

Rosynsky, Paul T. "BART Officer Admits Oscar Grant III Posed No Threat Before Mehserle Shot Him." *The Oakland Tribune,* June 3, 2009. Retrieved from www.highbeam.com/doc/1P2-20356411.html. Accessed March 29, 2013.

Royster, Deirdre A. *Race and the Invisible Hand: How White Networks Exclude Men from Blue-Collar Jobs.* Berkeley: University of California Press, 2003.

Rubin, Lillian B. *Families on the Fault Line: America's Working Class Speaks about the Family, the Economy, Race, and Ethnicity.* New York: HarperCollins, 1994.

———. *Just Friends: The Role of Friendship in Our Lives.* New York: HarperCollins, 1985.

Rugh, Jacob S., and Douglass Massey. "Racial Segregation and the American Foreclosure Crisis." *American Sociological Review* 75, no. 5 (2010): 629–51.

Rusche, Sarah E., and Zachary W. Brewster. "'Because They Tip for Shit!': The Social Psychology of Everyday Racism in Restaurants." *Sociology Compass* 2, no. 6 (2008): 2008–29.

Russell, Gregory D. *The Death Penalty and Racial Bias: Overturning Supreme Court Assumptions.* Westport, Conn., and London: Greenwood Press, 1994.

Russell, Katheryn K. *The Color of Crime: Racial Hoaxes, White Fear, Black Protectionism, Police Harassment, and Other Macroaggressions.* New York: New York University Press, 1998.

Ryan, William A. *Blaming the Victim.* New York: Random House, 1976.

Sabini, John. *Social Psychology.* New York: Norton, 1992.

Sadeghi, Shiran. "Why the Republicans Ignored Afghanistan, Pakistan, Iraq and Iran at This Year's Convention." *Huffington Post,* August 30, 2012. Retrieved from www.huffingtonpost.com/shirin-sadeghi/republican-convention-foreign-policy_b_1844100.html. Accessed March 31, 2013.

Sanger, David. "Obama Order Sped Up Wave of Cyberattacks against Iran." *New York Times,* June 1, 2012. Retrieved from www.nytimes.com/2012/06/01/world/middleeast/obama-ordered-wave-of-cyberattacks-against-iran.html?pagewanted=all. Accessed March 31, 2013.

Savage, Charlie. "Wells Fargo Will Settle Mortgage Bias Charges." *New York Times,* July 12, 2012. Retrieved from www.nytimes.com/2012/07/13/business/wells-fargo-to-settle-mortgage-discrimination-charges.html. Accessed March 31, 2013.

Schuman, Howard, Eleanor Singer, Rebecca Donovan, and Claire Selltiz. "Discriminatory Behavior in New York Restaurants: 1950 and 1981." *Social Indicators Research* 13, no. 1 (1983): 69–83.

Schuman, Howard, Charlotte Steeh, Lawrence Bobo, and Maria Krysan. *Racial Attitudes in America: Trends and Interpretations.* Cambridge, Mass.: Harvard University Press, 1997.

Sears, David O. "Symbolic Racism." In *Eliminating Racism: Profiles in Controversy,* edited by Phylis A. Katz and Dalmas A. Taylor, 53–84. New York and London: Plenum Press, 1988.

Sears, David O., and Donald R. Kinder. "Racial Tensions and Voting in Los Angeles." In *Los Angeles: Viability and Prospects for Metropolitan Leadership,* edited by Werner Z. Hirsch, 55–75. New York: Praeger, 1971.

Sewell, William H., Jr. "The Concept(s) of Culture." In *Beyond the Cultural Turn,* edited by Victoria E. Bonnell and Lynn Hunt, 35–61. Berkeley: University of California Press, 1999.

Shane, Scott. "Elections Spurred a Move to Codify Drone Policy." *New York Times,* November 25, 2012. Retrieved from www.nytimes.com/2012/11/25/world/white-house-presses-for-drone-rule-book.html?_r=0. Accessed March 31, 2013.

Sharkey, Patrick. "The Intergenerational Transmission of Context." *American Journal of Sociology* 113 (2008): 931–69.

Sheatsley, Paul B. "White Attitudes toward the Negro." In *The Negro American,* edited by Talcott Parsons and Kenneth B. Clark, 303–24. Boston: Houghton Mifflin, 1966.

Sherman, Lawrence W. "Execution Without Trial: Police Homicide and the Constitution." *Vanderbilt Law Review* 33 (1980): 71–100.

Sherter, Alain. "Citigroup Stint Shadows Obama's New Staff Chief." CBS News, January 10, 2012. Retrieved from www.cbsnews.com/8301-505123_162-57355832/citigroup-stint-shadows-obamas-new-staff-chief. Accessed March 31, 2013.

Sidanius, Jim, et al. "It's Not Affirmative Action, It's the Blacks." In *Racialized Politics: The Debate about Racism in America,* edited by David O. Sears, Jim Sidanius, and Lawrence Bobo, 191–235. Chicago: University of Chicago Press, 2000.

Siegel, Paul M. "On the Cost of Being a Negro." *Sociological Inquiry* 35, no. 1 (1965): 41–57.

Siegelman, Peter. "Racial Discrimination in 'Everyday' Commercial Transactions: What Do We Know, What Do We Need to Know, and How Can We Find Out." In *A National Report Card on Discrimination in America: The Role of Testing,* edited by Michael Fix and Margery Austin Turner, 69–98. Washington, D.C.: Urban Institute, 1998. Retrieved from www.urban.org/UploadedPDF/report—card .pdf. Accessed December 8, 2002.

Sigelman, Lee, and Susan Welch. *Black Americans' View of Racial Inequality: The Dream Deferred.* Cambridge: Cambridge University Press, 1991.

Silverstein, Ken. "Barack Obama, Inc.: The Birth of a Washington Machine." *Harper's,* November 2006. Retrieved from www.harpers.org/archive/2006/11/0081275. Accessed March 21, 2013.

Slack, Jennifer Daryl. "The Theory and Method of Articulation in Cultural Studies." In *Stuart Hall: Critical Dialogues in Cultural Studies,* edited by David Morley and Kuan-Hsing Chen, 112–27. London: Routledge, 1996.

Sledge, Matt. "Warrantless Electronic Surveillance Surges under Obama Justice Department." *Huffington Post,* September 28, 2012. Retrieved from www .huffingtonpost.com/2012/09/28/warrantless-electronic-surveillance-obama_ n_1924508.html. Accessed March 31, 2013.

Sloan, Irving J. *Our Violent Past: An American Chronicle.* New York: Random House, 1970.

Smith, Douglas, Christy A. Visher, and Laura Davidson. "Equity and Discretionary Justice: The Influence of Race on Police Arrest Decisions." *Journal of Criminal Law and Criminology* 75 (1984): 234–49.

Smith, James P., and Finnis R. Welch. *Closing the Gap, Forty Years of Economic Progress for Blacks.* Santa Monica, Calif.: Rand Corporation, 1986.

Smith, Robert C. "'Politics' Is Not Enough: The Institutionalization of the African American Freedom Movement." In *From Exclusion to Inclusion: The Long Struggle for African American Political Power,* edited by Ralph C. Gomes and Linda Faye Williams, 97–126. New York and London: Greenwood Press, 1992.

———. *Racism in the Post–Civil Rights Era, Now You See It, Now You Don't.* New York: State University of New York Press, 1995.

Smith, Tom W. "Intergroup Relations in Contemporary America." In *Intergroup Relations in the United States: Research Perspectives,* edited by Wayne Winborne and Renae Cohen, 69–106. New York: National Conference for Community and Justice, 1998.

———. "Measuring Inter-Racial Friendships: Experimental Comparisons." Paper presented at the annual meeting of the American Sociological Association, August 6, 1999, in Chicago.

Smith, William A., Walter Allen, and Lynnette Danley. "'Assume the Position . . . You Fit the Description': Psychosocial Experiences and Racial Battle Fatigue among African American Male College Students." *American Behavioral Scientist* 51, no. 4 (2007): 551–78.

Sniderman, Paul M., and Edward G. Carmines. *Reaching beyond Race*. Cambridge, Mass.: Harvard University Press, 1997.

Sniderman, Paul M., and Thomas Piazza. *The Scar of Race*. Cambridge, Mass.: Harvard University Press, 1993.

Somers, Margaret. "The Narrative Constitution of Identity: A Relational and Network Approach." *Theory and Society* 23, no. 3 (1994): 605–49.

Sorensen, Adam. "Obama Passes Over Warren, Names Deputy to Run Consumer Agency." *Time*, July 17, 2012. Retrieved from http://swampland.time .com/2011/07/17/obama-picks-former-ohio-ag-warren-deputy-to-head-con sumer-bureau. Accessed March 31, 2013.

Sowell, Thomas. *Civil Rights: Rhetoric of Reality?* New York: Morrow, 1984.

Spero, Sterling D., and Abraham L. Harris. *The Black Worker: The Negro and the Labor Movement*. New York: Atheneum, 1974.

Spohn, Cassia. "Crime and the Social Control of Blacks: Offender/Victim Race and the Sentencing of Violent Offenders." In *Inequality, Crime, and Social Control*, edited by George S. Bridges and Martha A. Myers, 249–68. Boulder, Colo., San Francisco, and Oxford: Westview Press, 1994.

Stein, Sam. "Obama's Remarks on Employee Free Choice Act Make Labor 'Very Pleased.'" *Huffington Post*, February 12, 2009. Retrieved from www.huffington-post.com/2009/02/12/obamas-remarks-on-employe_n_166345.html. Accessed March 31, 2013.

Steinberg, Stephen. *The Ethnic Myth*. Boston: Beacon, 1989.

Stewart, Denise. "Strong Black Voter Turnout Translates to Obama Win." *Black America Web*, November 8, 2012. Retrieved from www.rawstory.com/ rs/2011/09/14/obama-still-highly-popular-in-europe-poll. Accessed March 31, 2013.

St. Jean, Yanick. "Let People Speak for Themselves: Interracial Unions and the General Social Survey." *Journal of Black Studies* 28, no. 3 (1998): 398–414.

Stouffer, S. A. *The American Soldier*, vols. 1 and 2. Princeton, N.J.: Princeton University Press, 1949.

Street, Paul. *Barack Obama and the Future of American Politics*. Boulder, Colo., and London: Paradigm Publishers, 2009.

Sudeep, Reddy. "Obama Pushes for Legislation." *Wall Street Journal*, May 11, 2009. Retrieved from http://online.wsj.com/article/SB124186580127503661.html. Accessed March 31, 2013.

Sue, Derald Wing, Christina M. Capodilupo, Gina C. Torino, Jennifer M. Bucceri, Aisha M. B. Holder, Kevin L. Nadal, and Marta Esquilin. "Racial Microaggressions in Everyday Life: Implications for Clinical Practice." *American Psychologist* 62, no. 4 (2007): 271–86.

Swarns, Rachel L. "Blacks Debate Civil Rights Risk in Obama's Rise." *New York Times*, August 24, 2008. Retrieved from www.nytimes.com/2008/08/25/us/ politics/25race.html. Accessed March 31, 2013.

Sweet, Lynn. "Obama's Selma Speech. Text as Delivered." *Chicago Sun Times*, March 5, 2007. Retrieved from http://blogs.suntimes.com/sweet/2007/03/ obamas_selma_speech_text_as_de.html. Accessed March 31, 2013.

Taguieff, Pierre-André, ed. *Face au Racisme, Tome II: Analyse, Hypotheses, Perspectives*. Paris: La Découverte, 1991.

———. *The Force of Prejudice: Racism and Its Doubles*. Minneapolis: University of Minnesota Press, 2001.

Tanur, Judith, ed. *Questions about Questions*. New York: Russell Sage Foundation, 1994.

Tapper, Jake, and Amy Bingham. "Dems Quickly Switch to Include 'God,' 'Jerusalem.'" ABC News, September 5, 2012. Retrieved from http://abcnews.go.com/Politics/OTUS/democrats-rapidly-revise-platform-include-god/story?id=17164108#.UEij2dCXQcg. Accessed March 31, 2013.

Tarrow, Sidney. *Power in Social Movements: Social Movements and Contentious Politics*. Cambridge: Cambridge University Press, 1998.

Tatum, Beverly Daniel. *"Why Are All the Black Kids Sitting Together in the Cafeteria?": And Other Conversations about Race*. New York: Basic, 1997.

Taylor, Paul, Rakesh Kochhar, Richard Fry, Gabriel Velasco, and Seth Motel. "Wealth Gaps Rise to Record Highs between Whites, Blacks and Hispanics." *Pew Research Center, Social and Demographic Trends*. Retrieved from www.pewsocialtrends.org/files/2011/07/SDT-Wealth-Report_7-26-11_FINAL.pdf. Accessed March 29, 2013.

Terkel, Amanda. "With 2012 Election Barely Over, Politicians Begin Fundraising for Next Cycles." *Huffington Post*, November 13, 2012. Retrieved from www.huffingtonpost.com/2012/11/13/2012-election-fundraising_n_2126617.html. Accessed March 31, 2013.

Terkel, Studs. *Race: How Blacks and Whites Feel and Think about the American Obsession*. New York: Doubleday, 1993.

Tesler, Michael. "The Spillover of Racialization into Health Care: How President Obama Polarized Public Opinion by Racial Attitudes and Race." *American Journal of Political Science* 56, no. 3 (2012): 690–704.

Thai, Xuan, and Ted Barrett. "Biden's Description of Obama Draws Scrutiny." CNN, January 31, 2007. Retrieved from http://articles.cnn.com/2007-01-31/politics/biden.obama_1_braun-and-al-sharpton-african-american-presidential-candidates-delaware-democrat?_s=PM:POLITICS. Accessed March 31, 2013.

Thomas, Alexander, and Samuel Sillen. *Racism and Psychiatry*. New York: Brunner/Mazel, 1972.

Thomas, Melvin. "Anything but Race: The Social Science Retreat from Racism." *African American Research Perspectives* (Winter 2000): 79–96.

Thompson, John B. *Studies in the Theory of Ideology*. Cambridge: Polity, 1984.

Thompson, Phillip J., III. *Double Trouble: Black Mayors, Black Communities, and the Call for a Deep Democracy*. Oxford: Oxford University Press, 2006.

Tolnay, Stewart, and E. M. Beck. "Rethinking the Role of Racial Violence in the Great Migration." In *Black Exodus: The Great Migration from the American South*, edited by Alferdteen Harrison, 20–35. Jackson, Miss., and London: University of Mississippi Press, 1991.

Trujillo, Melissa. "Henry Louis Gates Arrested, Police Accused of Racial Profiling." *Huffington Post*, July 20, 2009. Retrieved from www.huffingtonpost.com/2009/07/20/henry-louis-gates-jr-arre_n_241407.html. Accessed March 31, 2013.

Tuch, Steven, and Michael Hughes. "Whites' Racial Policy Attitudes in the Twenty-First Century: The Continuing Significance of Racial Resentment." *The ANNALS of the American Academy of Political and Social Science* 634 (2011).

Turner, Margery A., Raymond Struyk, and John Yinger. *The Housing Discrimination Study.* Washington D.C.: The Urban Institute, 1991.

Turner, Margery A., Stephen L. Ross, George C. Glaster, and John Yinger. *Discrimination in Metropolitan Housing Markets: National Results from Phase 1 HDS.* Washington, D.C.: The Urban Institute, 2002.

Tuttle Jr., William M. "Labor Conflict and Racial Violence: The Black Worker in Chicago, 1894–1919." In *Black Labor in America*, edited by Milton Cantor, 86–110. Westport, Conn.: Negro Universities Press, 1970.

Unzueta, Miguel M., Brian S. Lowery, and Eric D. Knowles. "How Believing in Affirmative Action Quotas Protects White Men's Self-Esteem." *Organizational Behavior and Human Decision Processes* 105, no. 1 (2007): 1–13.

"US-Afghan Partnership Deal 'Agreed Upon,'" *Al Jazeera*, April 23 2012. Retrieved from www.aljazeera.com/news/asia/2012/04/2012422171759880584 .html. Accessed March 31, 2013.

"US 'Building Missile Defence Radar' in Qatar." *Al Jazeera*, July 18 2012. Retrieved from www.aljazeera.com/news/middleeast/2012/07/2012717203533999430 .html. Accessed March 31, 2013.

U.S. Department of Labor, Bureau of Labor Statistics. *The Employment Situation— October 2012.* Retrieved from www.bls.gov/news.release/archives/empsit_ 11022012.pdf. Accessed March 31, 2013.

Valentino, Nicholas A., and Ted Brader. "The Sword's Other Edge: Perceptions of Discrimination and Racial Policy Opinion after Obama." *Public Opinion Quarterly* 75, no. 2 (November 2008): 201–26.

Van Dijk, Teun A. *Communicating Racism: Ethnic Prejudice in Cognition and Conversation.* Amsterdam: Benjamins, 1987.

———. *Ideology: A Multidisciplinary Approach.* Thousand Oaks, Calif.: Sage, 1998.

———. *News as Discourse.* Hillsdale, N.J.: Erlbaum Associates, 1988.

———. *Prejudice in Discourse: An Analysis of Ethnic Prejudice in Cognition and Conversation.* Amsterdam: Benjamins, 1984.

———. *Racism and the Press.* London: Routledge, 1991.

Vigil, James Diego. *Barrio Gangs: Street Life and Identity in Southern California.* Austin: University of Texas Press, 1988.

Vitez, Michael. "At Jefferson, Conyers Backs Obama Health Stand." *Philadelphia Enquirer*, March 7, 2009. Retrieved from www.philly.com/philly/news/breaking/40898352.html. Accessed March 31, 2013.

Voloshinov, Vladimir N. *Freudianism: A Marxist Critique.* New York: Academic, 1976.

Waddoups, Jeffrey. "Racial Differences in Intersegment Mobility." *Review of Black Political Economy* 20, no. 2 (1991): 23–43.

Walsh, Joan. "When the Big Lie Works." *Salon*, September 13, 2012. Retrieved from www.salon.com/2012/09/13/when_the_big_lie_works. Accessed March 31, 2013.

Walsh, Kenneth T. "Obama: I'm Not the President of Black America." *U.S. News*, August 7, 2012. Retrieved from www.usnews.com/news/blogs/Ken-Walshs

-Washington/2012/08/08/obama-im-not-the-president-of-black-america. Accessed March 31, 2013.

Walters, Ronald. *White Nationalism, Black Interests: Conservative Public Policy and the Black Community*. Detroit: Wayne State University Press, 2003.

Warner, W. Lloyd. "American Class and Caste." *American Journal of Sociology* 42, no. 2 (1936): 234–37.

Weber, Max. "Objectivity in Social Science and Social Policy." In *Max Weber on the Methodology of the Social Sciences*, edited and translated by Edward A. Shils and H. A. Finch, 50–112. New York: The Free Press, 1949.

Webster, Yehudi O. *The Racialization of America*. New York: St. Martin's, 1992.

Weitzer, Ronald, and Steven Tuch. "Race and Perception of Police Misconduct." *Social Problems* 51 (2004): 305–25.

Wellman, David T. *Portraits of White Racism*. Cambridge: Cambridge University Press, 1993.

Wessler, Seth James. "Food Stamp Bashing, Race, and the Bi-Partisan Attack on the Safety-Net." *Colorlines*, October 19, 2012. Retrieved from http://colorlines .com/archives/2012/10/food_stamp_bashing.html. Accessed March 31, 2013.

West, Cornel. *Race Matters*. Boston: Beacon, 1993.

Wetherell, Margaret, and Jonathan Potter. *Mapping the Language of Racism*. New York: Columbia University Press, 1992.

White House. "Remarks by the President at Congressional Black Caucus Foundation Annual Phoenix Awards Dinner." September 24, 2011. Retrieved from www .whitehouse.gov/the-press-office/2011/09/24/remarks-president-congressional -black-caucus-foundation-annual-phoenix-a. Accessed March 31, 2013.

Wicker, Tom. *Tragic Failure*. New York: Morrow, 1996.

Willie, Charles V. *Caste and Class Controversy on Race and Poverty: Round Two of the Willie/Wilson Debate*. New York: General Hall, 1989.

Wilson, William Julius. *The Declining Significance of Race*. Chicago: University of Chicago Press, 1978.

———. *The Truly Disadvantaged: The Inner City, the Underclass, and Public Policy*. Chicago: University of Chicago Press, 1987.

———. *When Work Disappears*. New York: Norton, 1996.

Wingfield, Adia-Harvey. "Are Some Emotions Marked 'Whites Only'? Racialized Feeling Rules in Professional Workplaces." *Social Problems* 57, no. 2 (2010): 251–68.

Wise, Tim. "School Shootings and White Denial." 2001. Retrieved from www .timwise.org/2001/03/school-shootings-and-white-denial. Accessed March 29, 2013.

Witte, Rob. *Racist Violence and the State*. London and New York: Longman, 1996.

Wong, Paul, ed. *Race, Nation, and Citizenship*. Boulder, Colo.: Westview Press, 1999.

Woodward, C. Vann. *The Strange Career of Jim Crow*, 2d ed. New York: Oxford University Press, 1966.

Wynn, Neil A. *The Afro-American and the Second World War*. New York: Holmes and Meir, 1993.

Yinger, John. *Closed Doors, Opportunities Lost: The Continuing Costs of Housing Discrimination*. New York: Russell Sage Foundation, 1995.

——. "Housing Discrimination and Residential Segregation as Causes of Poverty." In *Understanding Poverty*, edited by Sheldon H. Danziger and Robert H. Haveman, 359–91. New York: Russell Sage Foundation, 2001.

Zinn, Howard. *A People's History of the United States*. New York: HarperCollins, 1980.

Zuberi, Tukufu. "Deracializing Social Statistics: Problems in the Quantification of Race." *Annals of the American Academy of Political and Social Science* 568 (March 2000): 172–85.

Index

abstract liberalism: black color
  blindness with, 74, 201, *202*, 203,
  204, 211, 219, 222n6; color-blind
  racism with, 74, 76, 78–84, 95, 201,
  202, 203, 204, 211, 219, 222n6, 303,
  307
accommodationist, Obama as, 262–63,
  286n46
Adams, John, 257, 283n4
affirmative action: attack on, 233; black
  color blindness and, 199, 201–3,
  209, 213–14, 218, 220; color-blind
  racism and, 74, 76, 81, 82, 84, 95,
  108, 109–10, 112–14, 115, 118; new
  racism and, 37, 42, 54, 56; racial
  progressives and, 179, 180, 182,
  185, 187, 188, 190–92, 196n7; racial
  stories and, 125, 126, 127, 128, 129,
  133, 134, 136, 145, 146; racism and,
  1, 4, 6, 10, 14, 15, 19n23; whites'
  attitude about, 238, 303
affirmative action, during Obama
  presidency, 264, 265, 287n57
Afghanistan, 272, 293n107
African Americans: businesses
  owned by, 39; classification
  of, 75; economic life of, 53–56;

underemployment of, 54;
  unemployment of, 54. *See also*
  blacks
aggressive, blacks as, 59, 115, 135, 136,
  146
Ali, José, 237
America: as post-racial nation, 311;
  power structure of, 261, 285n33. *See
  also* race, in contemporary America
American Apartheid (Massey and
  Denton), 32, 152
American Creed, 6, 78, 199
Americanism, 199
American Legislative Exchange
  Council, 47
Americas, racial stratification in,
  229–31
ANC, 31
Anglo-Saxon American culture, 225
antiblack stereotypes, 221
antiracists, 15, 307
"anything but race," 110–11
apartheid, 29, 31
Arab Americans, 186, 242, 243, 246
Archie Bunkers, 143, 179–97, 305
Argentines, 231, 236
arrest rate, 49–51

347

Asian Americans, 183, 193, 226,
    237, 239, 244; Latinos and, *238*;
    mean per capita income of, *234*;
    racial attitudes of, 238, 306; racial
    distinctions among, 236, 250n32;
    racial stratification of, 241, 242;
    residential segregation among, 241,
    251n56
Asian Indians, 227, 242
Asian women, 166, 176n39
assimilation process, 244
The Audacity of Hope (Obama), 261,
    265, 277, 295n143
Auletta, Ken, 151
aversive racism, 259

bad behavior, 147, 149n27
Baldus, David C., 48
Barndt, Joseph, 151
Baucus, Max, 276
"being a white male . . . ," 181–82
Berg, John C., 40
Beyond Good and Evil (Nietzsche), 255
Biden, Joe, 268
biracial people, 226, 247n6, 310, 314n29
"birther" movement, 270
black acquaintances, 188
black color blindness, 199–224;
    abstract liberalism with, 74, 201,
    202, 203, 204, 211, 219, 222n6;
    affirmative action and, 199, 201–3,
    209, 213–14, 218, 220; color-blind
    racism frames and, 73–99, 200–211,
    202; color-blind racism style and,
    212–17; cultural racism with, 205–7;
    DAS on, 199, 214; discrimination
    with, 208–11, 218, 222n9; interracial
    marriage and, 215–16, 223n16;
    minimization of racism with, 208–
    11; naturalization of racial matters,
    207–8; preferred neighborhoods
    of, 199; racial stories of, 217–18;
    rhetorical incoherence and, 214–17;
    school, residential segregation and,
    203–5; studies of, 199–200
black elite, 245, 262, 311
Black Enterprise, 257

black ghetto life, 151
black officials, 38; limited possibilities
    of, 40–41; structural barriers
    to election of, 39–40, 260;
    underrepresentation of, 40
Black Panthers, 51, 52
blacks: as aggressive, 59, 115, 135, 136,
    146; collective, *228*, 231, 235, 238–39,
    240, 242, 243, 311, 315n34; cultural
    limitations of, 2, 18n16; cultural
    racism and, 205–7; cultural status
    of, 206; disproportional arrest rate
    of, 49–51; housing of, 2, 203, 204,
    258–59; impolite treatment of, 2; Jim
    Crow employment pattern of, 28;
    Latinos and, *238*; managerial views
    of, 59–60; Obama and, 256–58,
    268–69; occupational distribution
    of, *27*; in politics, 38; power of, 221,
    224nn24–25; racial profiling of, 2;
    racial strata of, 233–34; as racists,
    220; self-segregation of, 128, 142,
    145, 163, 179, 303; social control of,
    25, 29, 42–53; social life of, 2, 28,
    36–37; stereotypes of, 206. *See also*
    African Americans; testimonies
black-white continuum, 306
blanqueamiento, 230
Blau, Judith, 152
Bobo, Lawrence, 6, 7, 98n23, 239
Bolivians, 234, 249n25, 281
Bonilla-Silva, Eduardo, 301
Booker, Cory, 261
Brennan, John, 275
"Broken Borders," 225
Brown, H. Rap, 52
Brown, John, 179
Brown v. Board of Education, 82
Bureau of Labor Statistics, 257, 258
Bush, George W., 243, 272, 274, 279
businesses, of African Americans, 39
busing, 82–83, 187, 199, 238
Byrd, James, Jr., 77

Cablanasian, 226
Cairo United Front, 52
California Racial Privacy, 232

Cambodians, 227
Canellos, Peter S., 265
capital punishment: lynching and, 47–49; racial bias with, 47
Caribbean nations, 227, 235, 237, 245, 310, 312
Carmichael, Stokely, 51, 52
Carmines, Edward, 5
Cassidy, John, 276
Center for Responsible Lending, 258
Central Americans, 235, 240, 244
Central Intelligence Agency (CIA), 273, 274, 275
"change we can believe in," 264
Changing Race (Rodriguez), 237
Chavez, Hugo, 280
Chicago School, 275, 295n135
Child, Lydia Maria, 179
children, of interracial marriage, 170, 182–84, 193
Chileans, 231, 235
China, 226
Chinese Americans, 181, 227, 236, 238, 240, 244
CIA. *See* Central Intelligence Agency
CIC, 29
Civil Rights Act, 58
civil rights era, 102, 309
civil rights movement, 31, 42, 51–53, 76, 179, 180, 268
civil rights movement, new, 307
Civil Rights Project, at Harvard University, 35
Clark, Kenneth, 4
class, 195, 197n25
Class and Caste in a Southern Town (Dollard), 73
classical liberalism, 75
Cleaver, Emanuel, 278
Clinton, Bill, 192
Clinton, Hilary, 274
COINTELPRO, 52
Cold War, 29
collective blacks: disciplining of, 311, 315n34; in racial stratification, 228, 231, 235, 240, 242, 243; whites' racial attitudes and, 238–39

collective representations, 302, 313n6
college, cross-racial interaction in, 157–58, 171, 175n27
college students, as racial progressives, 181–86
color blindness, style of, 101–21; DAS on, 103, 104, 105, 106, 108, 109, 111, 113, 117, 118, 120; diminutives, 114–15; language of, 101–2, 120n2, 170; "nigger," 102–4; projection, 102, 111–14, 120n12; rhetorical incoherence and, 102, 115–18; rhetorical maze of, 104–11; semantic moves in, 102, 212–14
color blindness, white house of, 151–77; interracial marriage, 164–71, 165, 175nn37–38; "just the way things were," 159–64, 303. *See also* whites' racial segregation and isolation
color blindness, whiteness of, 301–15; collective representations of, 302, 313n6; degree of, 306; myths relating to, 301–2; racial ideology of, 302–3, 313nn8–9; reality of, 303; sense of group position, 302, 313n7; symbolic expressions of whites' dominance, 302
color-blind racism, 2–4, 7, 13, 15, 16, 221, 302; abstract liberalism with, 74, 76, 78–84, 95, 201, 202, 203, 204, 211, 219, 222n6, 303, 307; affirmative action and, 74, 76, 81, 82, 84, 95, 108, 109–10, 112–14, 115, 118; of all ages, 305; components of, 303; cultural racism, 74, 75, 87–90, 95, 202; DAS on, 74, 78, 82, 84, 86, 87, 89, 91, 93, 94; ideology of, 179, 232, 305; minimization of, 74, 77, 88, 91–95; naturalization, 74, 76, 84–87, 95, 202, 207; by racial progressives, 190; reasonable racism, 78–84, 98n22; study of, 11–12. *See also* frames, of color-blind racism
color-blind racism fight: antiracist whites in, 307; counter-ideological arguments for, 307–8; moral

reform in, 308, 314n24; new civil rights movement for, 307, 308–9; whiteness challenged in, 308; white segregation viewed in, 307–8

color-blind racism style, blacks and, 212–17; semantic moves of, 202, 212–14

"colored," 103, 140, 144

color gradations, 227

colorism, 230, 245

communicative interaction, 11, 22n64

compassionate conservatives, 305

competitive racism, 259

Congressional Black Caucus, 42, 277

conservative cabinet, of Obama presidency, 274–75

conservatives, compassionate, 305

Conyers, John, 276

CORE, 29

Cose, Ellis, 36

Costa Ricans, 235

costs, of residential segregation, 33

counter-ideological arguments, 307–8

Craig, Gregory, 262

credit card industry control, 281

cross-racial interaction, in college, 157–58, 171, 175n27

Cubans, 231, 235, 237, 240, 241

cultural inferiority, 7

cultural limitations, 2, 18n16

cultural racism: blacks and, 205–7; frame of, 74, 75, 87–90, 95, 202

cultural status, of blacks, 206

culture: Anglo-Saxon American, 225; pathological, 13, 23n74; of poverty, 87, 99n35, 151; of residential segregation, 152

Daley, William, 274

dark-skinned Latinos, 227

DAS. *See* 1998 Detroit Area Study

data: on race, in contemporary America, 12–13; on racial ideology, 302, 305, 306; on racial stratification future, 233–35

dating. *See* interracial dating

Davis, Angela, 267

Davis, Kenneth, 5

death penalty, 49, 239

The Death Penalty and Racial Bias: Overturning Supreme Court Assumptions (Russell), 48

Declining Fortunes (Newman), 77

declining significance, of race thesis, 91–95

The Declining Significance of Race (Wilson), 91

defensive beliefs, 143

Democratic party, 42, 260–61, 282; Obama and, 262, 276, 279

demography: of interracial dating/marriage, 226, 247n9; of racial progressives, 180

Denton, Nancy, 32, 152

Department of Housing and Urban Development, 33

Despite the Best Intentions: Why Racial Inequality Thrives in Good Schools (Lewis and Diamond), 35

Detroit area residents, racial progressive profiles of, 186–92

Diamond, John B., 35

diminutives, 114–15

discrimination, 25, 62n1, 95; aspects of, 259; with black color blindness, 208–11, 218, 222n9; detection of, 61; economic inequality and, 56, 57; with education, 35; group-based, 83–84; isolated incidents of, 303; in jobs, 93; of minorities, 179, 182, 183; racial progressives and, 180, 182, 188, 190; research on, 61–62, 194; reverse, 131–35, 179, 184, 212, 223n15, 266; "smiling face," 3, 259; systemic, 74, 149n23, 202

disenfranchisement, 3, 29

diversity, 4, 185, 186

Divided by Color (Kinder and Sanders), 6

Doane, Ashley, 264

Dobbs, Lou, 225, 243, 246n3

Dole, Bob, 282

Dollard, John, 73, 143

dominance: social, 259; by whites, 302
dominant class ideology, 219
dominant race, 9, 311; ideology of, 219; racial status quo of, 10–11, 77, 98n18; social cleavage of, 10
domination, matrix of, 311, 315n35
Dominicans, 235, 240, 241, 244
Douglass, Frederick, 301, 309
Dreams of My Father (Obama), 265
Drew, Christopher, 262
drones, 273
DuBois, W. E. B., 114, 301

Eastwood, Clint, 271
economic inequality, 25, 53–60; discrimination and, 56, 57; income differentials, 54–55; interracial social interaction in, 38; in labor market, 56–58, 258–59; managerial views, of blacks, 59–60; occupational mobility and segmentation, 55–56; wage differentials, 54–55; in wealth, 58–59
economic life, of African Americans, 53–56
education: discriminatory practices with, 35; government intervention for, 192, 193; interracial social interaction in, 34–36; minority status in, 79, 80, 95, 182; predictions and scorecard of, 278; quality of, 35; quantity of, 35
elected black mayors, 41
election, of Obama. *See* Obama, Barack, election of
electoral participation, as entrapment, 41–42
elite: black, 245, 262, 311; white, 262
Emanuel, Rahm, 279
emission and mileage standards, 281
emotions, 146, 149n23
Employee Free Choice Act, 281
employment: audit of, 57; pattern of, 28
enhanced interrogation techniques, 256, 280

enigma, of race, in contemporary America, 1–24
entrapment, 41–42
Equal Employment Opportunity Commission, 131
equality of opportunity, 309
equal opportunity, 79–80, 98n24, 219
The Ethnic Myth (Steinberg), 131
European humanism, 75
European racism, 87
executive power, during Obama presidency, 273

Farrakhan, Louis, 51
FBI, 51–52
Federal Reserve Bank of Boston study, 34
Fenty, Adrian, 261
"fight or flight mode," 259, 285n27
Filipinos, 227
Firebaugh, Glenn, 5
FISA. *See* Foreign Intelligence Surveillance Act
Flores-Gonzales, Nilda, 237
Ford, Glen, 267
Ford, Harold, 261
Foreign Intelligence Surveillance Act (FISA), 263, 273, 286n47
foreign policy, of Obama presidency, 126, 274, 294
Fox News commentators, 225
frames, of color-blind racism, 73–99, 200–211; abstract liberalism, 74, 76, 78–84, 95, 201, 202, 203, 204, 211, 219, 222n6, 303, 307; cultural racism, 74, 75, 87–90, 95, 202; influences of, 220; minimization of racism, 74, 77, 88, 91–95; naturalization, 74, 76, 84–87, 95, 202, 207, 303
Friedersdorf, Conor, 267
friendships: interracial, 304; "I used to have very good black friends," 144–45; "some of my best friends are . . . ," 105–6; whites' racial segregation and isolation and, 155–56, 158–59, 174n18, 175nn29–31

Garveyism, 29
Gates, Henry Louis, 42, 51, 269, 290n82
Gates, Robert, 274
gay community, 279
Geithner, Timothy, 274
The German Ideology (Marx), 9
Gillian, Daniel, 42, 265
global racial reality, 232
government intervention, 25, 128,
    218; for education, 192, 193; for
    housing, 203, 204; for jobs, 209; for
    minorities, 33, 34, 127, 129, 130, 204,
    208, 209; opposition to, 79, 83
Grant, Oscar, III, 46
Graves, Earl, Jr., 257
Gray, John, 74
Greenwald, Glenn, 273
Grimke sisters, 179
group-based discrimination, 83–84
Grutter v. Bollinger, 233
Guantanamo, 280

Hagel, Chuck, 275
Haley, Nikki, 261
"hand extended to rival nations," 280
Harris, Fredrick, 269
health care plan, 276, 281, 295n137
hegemonic rule, 9, 22n60, 74, 97n5, 307
Heran, Joyce, 268
hierarchical racial order, 238–39, *239*
Hispanics, 59, 107, 160, 186, 190, 193,
    237
Home Mortgage Disclosure Act, 34
honorary whites, 227, *228*, 311; racial
    strata, 233–34, 240, 242, 245, 246,
    253n67; social identity of, 235–36
housing, 2, 203, 204, 258–59
Housing Discrimination Study, 33
humanism: European, 75; liberal,
    74–75, 97n9
Huntington, Samuel, 225, 227
Hutchings, Vincent, 264
Hyman, Herbert, 4
hypersegregation, 156, 159, 304

"I am not black, so I don't know,"
    106–8

"I am not prejudiced," 105–6
identity: with race, 310, 315n31. *See
    also* social identity
ideology: of color-blind racism, 179,
    232, 305; dominant class, 219;
    dominant racial, 219; racial, 10–11,
    15, 29, 74, 219; style of, 101
"I did not get a job/promotion/
    college admittance because of a
    minority," 131–35, 145, 148n20, 217
"I didn't own any slaves," 127–30, 145,
    217
"if Jews, Italians, and Irish have made
    it, how come blacks have not,"
    130–31, 145, 217
immigrants: Latinos, 236; new, 244
incoherence. *See* rhetorical incoherence
income differentials, 54–55
individualism, 83–84, 99n29
individual racism, 270
industrialization, 30–31
inequality. *See* economic inequality;
    racial inequality
integrated neighborhoods, 238
integration: of institutions, 2, 18n7,
    35; residential, 83, 99n28, 203–5; of
    schools, 83, 85, 86, 156, 238; survey
    on, 153, *154*, 173n10, 173nn12–13
intermediate racial group, 230, 231,
    248n18
internal stratification, 242
interpretation, of race, 13–15, 23n72,
    24nn77–78
interracial dating: demography of,
    226, 247n9; of minorities, 144, 146,
    184–86, 194; whites in, 226
interracial friendships, 304
interracial hostility, 7
interracial lifestyle, 153, 165, 166
interracial marriage, 36, 164–71,
    175nn37–38; black color blindness
    and, 215–16, 223n16; children of,
    170, 182–84, 193; demography of,
    226, 247n9; increase in, 226, 247n8;
    opposition to, 165, *165*, 169–70;
    racial progressives and, 180, 181,
    183, 185, 186, 187, 189; reservations

towards, 165, *165*, 167–68; support of, 164, *165*, 166, 167; whites in, 226
interracial relationships, 182–84
interracial social interaction: in economic inequality, 38; education, 34–36; new racism, 2, 3, 28, 31–38, 86–87; residential segregation, 3, 32–34, 86–87; in social life, 2, 28, 36–37
interrogation techniques, 256, 280
Iran, 272–73
Iraq, 272
Irish, 130–31
isolation: of minorities, 151–77. *See also* whites' racial segregation and isolation
Israel, 273
Italians, 110, 120n10, 130–31
"I used to have very good black friends," 144–45

Jackman, Mary, 7
Jackson, Jesse, 260, 268
Japanese Americans, 226, 227, 240, 242–43
Jefferson, Thomas, 75
Jews, 126, 130–31
Jim Crow, 127, 145; demise of, 31; employment pattern of, 28; era of, 3, 5, 11, 25, 77, 79, 125, 310, 312; new racism and, 260–63, 302; racism of, 2, 3, 4, 5, 11, 15, 27, 43, 73, 75, 243, 259; support of, 15; violence of, 30; white attitudes about, 4
Jindal, Bobby, 261
jobs, 93, 158
Johnson, Lyndon B., 282
Jordan, Vernon, 262
"just the way things were," 159–64, 303

Karenga, Ron, 51
Karzai, Hamid, 272
Kentucky Human Rights Commission study, 33
Khan, Imran, 273

kill list, 273, 280
Kinder, Donald, 6
King, Martin Luther, Jr., 1, 17n2, 51, 52, 96, 267
King, Rodney, 46, 77
Kluegel, Kames, 7
Koen, Charles, 52
Korean Americans, 227, 238, 244
Krauthammer, Charles, 280
Ku Klux Klan, 29, 62, 142

labor market: minorities in, 57–58, 77, 91, 92, 131–35, 145, 148n20; racial inequality in, 56–58, 258–59
laissez-faire racism, 7, 20n45, 78, 81, 164
Lang, Katie, 268
language: of color blindness, 101–2, 120n2, 170; of liberalism, 305; of segregation, 152
Laotians, 184, 227
Latin America-like United States race struggle, 244–46, 253n69, 310
Latin Americanization, 228, 231–33, 240, 246, 253n68, 310, 312
Latin American nations, 227; racial stratification in, 229–31, 245
Latinoamericanos, 231; as racial others, 237
Latinos, 2, 33, 147, 152, 166, 239, 247n10; Anglo-Saxon American culture and, 225; Asians and, *238*; blacks and, *238*; dark-skinned, 227; immigrant, 236; light-skinned, 227; mean per capita income of, *234*; Obama and, 257–58; population explosion of, 225, 226; racial attitudes of, 236–37, 305; racial self-classification of, *235*; racial stratification of, 241, 242, 243, 244; residential segregation among, 241; social interaction of, 240–41; study of, 236–37; white, 227, 233, 235, 236–37, 249n28
lazy, minorities as, 90, 131, 187, 188, 206
Lehman, Melvin M., 30

Leonhardt, David, 282
Lew, Jack, 274
Lewis, Amanda E., 35, 152
Lewis, John, 260
liberal humanism, 74–75, 97n9
liberalism: abstract, 74, 76, 78–84, 95,
    201, *202*, 203, 204, 211, 219, 222n6;
    classical, 75; language of, 305
liberals: Obama and, 256, 259, 267,
    285n30; tradition of, 75–76, 97n14
Liberating Our White Ghetto (Barndt),
    151
Libya, 172
light-skinned Latinos, 227
light-skinned multiracial people, 227
Lilly Ledbetter Fair Pay Act, 280
Lipset, Seymour, 5
"living while black," 259, 284n26
Lou Dobbs Tonight, 225
lynching, 29, 47–49

Malcolm X, 51, 52
managerial views, of blacks, 59–60
marriage: of minorities, 144, 146, 226.
    See also interracial marriage
Martin, Trayvon, 42, 47
Martinez, Susana, 261
Marx, Karl, 9, 172, 177n46
Massey, Douglas, 32, 152
matrix of domination, 311, 315n35
McCain, John, 264
McClesky, Warren, 48
McClesky v. Kemp, 49
McDermott, George, 77
McIntire, Mike, 262
McWhorter, John, 302
Mead, Lawrence, 87, 151
mean per capita income, *234*
Medicaid, 281
Member of the Club (Otis Graham), 37
Memmi, Albert, 1
men, working-class, 193, 197n16
Mendell, David, 262
meritocracy, 80–81
mestizaje, 229, 230–31
Mexicans, 186, 235, 237, 240, 241, 244
Middle East, 263–69

Middle Eastern Americans, 227
migration, 30
mileage standards, 281
military policies, of Obama, 272, 273
Mill, John Stuart, 75
Miller, Greg, 273
minimization, of racism, 74, 77, 88,
    91–95; with black color blindness,
    208–11
minorities: dating of, 144, 146, 184–86,
    194; death penalty for, 49, 239;
    discrimination against, 179, 182,
    183; educational status of, 79, 80,
    95, 182; government intervention
    for, 33, 34, 127, 129, 130, 204, 208,
    209; isolation of, 151–77; in labor
    market, 57–58, 77, 91, 92, 131–35,
    145, 148n20; as lazy, 90, 131, 187,
    188, 206; marriage of, 144, 146, 226;
    opportunities of, 305; profiling of,
    179; reverse discrimination with,
    131–35, 179, 184, 212, 223n15, 266;
    talking about, 101–21; in their
    place, 25, 26, 27, 125. *See also* "I did
    not get a job/promotion/college
    admittance because of a minority"
minority politician, 260, 282, 285n32
minority race groups, 310
miracle, of Obama election, 256
miscegenation, 229–30
mob violence, 29
modern racial ideology, 305
modern racism, 259, 285n29
moral reform, 308, 314n24
Morris, Alden, 50
MOVE Organization, 51
Muhammad, Elijah, 51, 52
multiracial people, 226, 247nn6–7;
    light-skinned, 227
multiracial white supremacy, 270,
    310
Murray, Charles, 87, 151
Muslim, Obama as, 271
My Bondage and My Freedom
    (Douglass), 301
Myrdal Gunnar, 30
myths, of color blindness, 301–2

National Association for the Advancement of Colored People (NAACP), 29, 34, 62
National Urban League, 29, 62
Nation of Islam, 52
Native Americans, 75, 181, 183, 240, 243
naturalization: of color-blind racism frames, 74, 76, 84–87, 95, 202, 207, 303; of racial matters, 207–8
negative interactions, with blacks, 135–38, 146
"Negroes," 103, 212
negrophobia, 165, 196n10
The Negro American (Parsons and Clark), 4
neighborhoods: integrated, 238; preferred, 199; segregation of, 159–63, 204–5, 207, 222n8
new civil rights movement, 307, 308–9; agenda of, 309; blacks and allies at core of, 307; campaign of, 309
new Democrat, Obama as, 279
new immigrants, 244
Newman Katherine, 77
new racial structure, in 1960s, 27–31
new racism, 16, 25–72, 73, 256; affirmative action and, 37, 42, 54, 56; continuing racial economic inequality, 25, 53–60; eventual collapse of, 312; interracial social interaction, 2, 3, 28, 31–38, 86–87; introduction to, 25–27; Jim Crow and, 260–63, 302; new racial structure, in 1960s, 27–31; political structure of, 38–42; practices of, 306, 309; social control, of blacks since 1960s, 25, 29, 42–53
Newton, Huey P., 51
Nietzsche, Friedrich, 255
"nigger," 102–4, 210, 237, 305
1997 Survey of Social Attitudes of College Students, 12–13
1998 Detroit Area Study (DAS), 12–13, 16; on black color blindness, 199, 214; on color blindness style, 103, 104, 105, 106, 108, 109, 111, 113, 117,

118, 120; on color-blind racism, 74, 78, 82, 84, 86, 87, 89, 91, 93, 94; on racial progressives, 180, 186; on racial stories, 126, 128, 130, 132, 133, 135, 139, 140, 142, 143; on whites' segregation, 153, 155, 156, 157, 159, 161, 162, 163, 164, 165
Nobel Peace Prize, for Obama, 274
nonracist, 15
nonwhite, 237
Nopper, Tamara K., 267
North, 28, 29, 30

Obama, Barack: as accommodationist, 262–63, 286n46; blacks and, 256–58, 268–69; concerns about, 263–64, 268; Democratic party and, 262, 276, 279; image of, 279–80; individual racism against, 270; interview with, 265, 287n59; liberals and, 256, 259, 267, 285n30; as Muslim, 271; as new Democrat, 279; Nobel Peace Prize received by, 274; post-racialism of, 17, 255, 261, 264, 265, 266, 267, 269, 290nn77–78, 290nn83–84; pragmatism of, 281–82, 299n188; progressiveness of, 263; progressives and, 256, 259, 267, 272, 274, 285n30; as pro-growth Democrat, 279; race speech of, 266–67, 288nn65–66; racial resentment against, 270; racist images of, 271; success of, 310; supporters of, 264; as symbol, 258, 289n74; universalist position of, 277; as "University of Chicago Democrat," 282
Obama, Barack, election of, 299n191, 310; as foundational event, 255; meaning of, 246; miracle of, 256; as new racism, 256; question of victory of, 256–59
Obama, Barack, presidency of: affirmative action during, 264, 265, 287n57; blacks under, 256–58; criticism of, 42, 256; drones used during, 273; enhanced interrogation

techniques during, 256, 280; executive power during, 273; foreign policy of, 126, 274, 294; from Jim Crow to new racism, 260–63; kill list under, 273, 280; Latinos under, 257–58; madness, 256; Middle East during, 263–69; politics of, 263–69; predictions and scorecard of, 269–81, 291n87; race lite stand during, 265; racial disparity under, 258; scrutiny of, 256; torture during, 280; unemployment under, 257–58, 269, 278; wealth disparity under, 257–58, 269

Obama, Michelle, 261, 269, 278, 291n86

Obamacare, 281

Obamania, 267, 289n68

Obamerica, 255, 271, 281, 283n1, 311

Obeler, Suzanne, 237

objectivity, with race, 13–15, 23n72, 24nn77–78

occupational distribution, 27

occupational mobility, segmentation and, 55–56

occupational race-typing, 55

official state brutality, 45–47

Omi, Michael, 220, 223n21, 224n21

On Liberty (Mill), 75

Orwell, George, 256

Otis Graham, Lawrence, 37

otros veinte pesos, 305, 313n13

PAC Priorities USA, 279

paid community organizer, 261, 285n36

Pakistan, 272, 273

Parsons, Talcott, 4

"the past is the past," 125–27, 145, 148n10, 217

pathological cultures, 13, 23n74

Patrick, Deval, 261

people of color, 3, 29, 103

personal stories, 143–45, 146

pesoptimism, 312. *See also* racial pesoptimist

Pettigrew, Tom, 264

Pew Research Center, 36, 268–69, 271

pigmentocracy, 228, 230

plural racial stratification systems, 230

political racial inequality, 25

political scandals, 226, 247n5

political structure, of new racism, 38–42

politics: blacks in, 38; of Obama presidency, 263–69; with race, 13–15, 23n72, 24nn77–78

population explosion, of Latinos, 225, 226

Portraits of White Racism (Wellman), 8

positive interactions, with blacks, 138–40, 146

post–civil rights era, 88, 104, 231, 232; story lines of, 125. *See also* whites' racial attitudes, in post–civil rights era

post–civil rights minority politician, 282

post–civil rights social control, 53

post-racialism, of Obama, 17, 255, 261, 264, 265, 266, 267, 269, 290nn77–78, 290nn83–84

post-racial nation, America as, 311

poverty, 277–78; culture of, 87, 99n35, 151; rate of, 258

Powell, Colin, 40, 282, 299n186

power, of blacks, 221, 224nn24–25

power structure, of America, 261, 285n33

pragmatism, of Obama, 281–82, 299n188

predictions and scorecard, of Obama presidency, 269–81, 291n87; about Afghanistan, 272, 293n107; on conservative cabinet, 274–75; credit card industry control, 281; on education, 278; on Employee Free Choice Act, 281; about end of racism, 270; enhanced interrogation techniques cessation, 256, 280; in foreign policy, 274, 294; "hand extended to rival nations," 280; on health care plan, 276, 281, 295n137; about Iraq, 272; Lilly Ledbetter

Fair Play Act, 280; about military policies, 272, 273; on money, 279; about multiracial white supremacy, 270, 310; new emission and mileage standards, 281; about Pakistan, 272, 273; on race-specific policies, 276–77, 278; about racial stratification, 269–70; on tax compromises, 275

preferred neighborhoods, 199

prejudice, 7, 105–6, 220, 221, 229

prison, 43–45, *44*

privilege, 180

"probably because of racism," 189–90

profiles: of Detroit area residents, 186–92; of racial progressives, 181–92

profiling, 2, 179

progressiveness, of Obama, 263

progressives: Obama and, 256, 259, 267, 272, 274, 285n30. *See also* racial progressives

pro-growth Democrat, Obama as, 279

projection, as rhetorical tool, 102, 111–14, 120n12

Puerto Ricans, 231, 237, 240, 241

al-Qaeda, 273

race, 8–11; decrease in, 26; differences in, 8, 21n54; identity with, 310, 315n31; notion of, 8, 21n51, 26; problem of, 1; as socially constructed category, 8, 21n52; social reality of, 8–9, 21n55. *See also* dominant race

race, in contemporary America: caveat with, 15–17; color-blind racism study, 11–12; data sources for, 12–13; enigma of, 1–24; key terms with, 8–11; politics, interpretation, and objectivity with, 13–15, 23n72, 24nn77–78; racism, without racists, 1–4, 19n24

Race and Politics (Saito), 236

race card, 1, 77, 271, 303

"race effect," 306

Race in the Schools: Perpetuating White Dominance (Blau), 152

Race in the Schoolyard: Negotiating the Colorline in Classrooms and Communities (Lewis), 152

race lite stand, of Obama, 265

race relations, 184, 281, 299

race riots, 29, 52

race-specific policies, of Obama, 276–77, 278

race speech, of Obama, 266–67, 288nn65–66

race talk, 212

race traitors, 304, 307

race-typing, occupational, 55

racial attitudes: of Asian Americans, 238, 306; of Latinos, 236–37, 305; of racial strata, 236–39; of whites, 238–39. *See also* whites' racial attitudes, in post–civil rights era

racial bias, 47

racial considerations, 2

racial contract, 10, 22n63

racial disparity, under Obama, 258

racial distinctions, among Asian Americans, 236, 250n32

racial diversity, 4, 185, 186

racial equality, 304

Racial Formation in the United States (Omi and Winant), 220, 223n21

racial gerrymandering, 39

racial ideology, 10–11, 15, 29, 74, 219; of color blindness, 302–3, 313nn8–9; data about, 302, 305, 306

racial inequality, 2, 3, 9, 22n58, 258; economic, 25; political, 25; racial progressives and, 187; social, 25; social control, 25, 29, 42–53

racially mixed actors and performers, 310

racial matters, naturalization of, 207–8

racial microaggressions, 37

racial optimists, 4

racial order, 212, 222n13

racial others, 237

racial pesoptimist, 5–6

racial pluralism, 84

racial practices, in labor market, 56–58, 258–59

racial progressives, 167; affirmative action and, 179, 180, 182, 185, 187, 188, 190–92, 196n7; college students as, 181–86; color-blind racism by, 190; contradictions of, 188; DAS on, 180, 186; demography of, 180; Detroit area residents, 186–92; discrimination and, 180, 182, 188, 190; interracial marriage and, 180, 181, 183, 185, 186, 187, 189; profiles of, 181–92; racial inequality and, 187; working-class women, 180, 194, 195nn4–5, 304, 307

racial resentment, against Obama, 270

racial retreat, 233

racial self-classification, of Latinos, *235*

racial situation, heart of, 220

racial species, 310, 315n30

racial status quo, 10–11, 77, 98n18

racial stories, 123–49, 147n7; affirmative action and, 125, 126, 127, 128, 129, 133, 134, 136, 145, 146; black color blindness and, 217–18; DAS on, 126, 128, 130, 132, 133, 135, 139, 140, 142, 143; testimonies, 124, 135–46. *See also* story lines

racial strata: blacks, 233–34; honorary whites, 233–34, 240, 242, 245, 246, 253n67; phenotype, 233, 249n24; racial attitudes of, 236–39; residential segregation among, 240–41; social interaction among, 240–41; subjective standing of, 234–35; whites, 233–34

racial stratification, in Latin America, 245; *blanqueamiento*, 230; colorism, 230; Latinoamericanos, 231; mestizaje, 229, 230–31; miscegenation, 229–30; pigmentocracy, 230; plural, 230

racial stratification, predictions and scorecard of, 269–70

racial stratification future, 225–53, 251nn58–59; in Americas, 229–31; of Asian Americans, 241, 242; collective blacks in, *228*, 231, 235, 240, 242, 243; data about, 233–35;

discussion about, 241–46; honorary whites, social identity of, 235–36; Latin Americanization, 228, 231–33, 240, 246, 253n68; of Latinos, 241, 242, 243, 244; racial attitudes of, 236–39; social interaction of, 240–41

racial stratification systems, plural, 230

racial structure, 9–10, 21n56, 22n58; in 1960s, 27–31; elements of, 26; ideologically influenced by, 15; materially influenced by, 15; reorganization of, 60

racial tolerance, 11

racial unfairness, equal opportunity and, 79–80, 98n24, 219

racism, 186–87; affirmative action and, 1, 4, 6, 10, 14, 15, 19n23; aversive, 259; competitive, 259; concept of, 220–21; cultural, 74, 75, 87–90, 95, *202*; decrease in, 26; definition of, 102; end of, 226, 256, 270, 312; individual, 270; of Jim Crow, 2, 3, 4, 5, 11, 15, 27, 43, 73, 75, 243, 259; laissez-faire, 7, 20n45, 78, 81, 164; modern, 259, 285n29; without racists, 1–4, 19n24, 305; structure of, 26; subtle, 259; symbolic, 6–7, 20n36. *See also* color-blind racism; new racism; "probably because of racism"

Racism (Memmi), 1

racist image, of Obama, 271

racist propaganda, 302

racists, 196n9; blacks as, 220; disclosure stories of, 140–43, 146; racism without, 1–4, 19n24, 305; terminology of, 104. *See also* antiracist; nonracist

rainbow coalition, 260

Reaching beyond Race (Sniderman and Carmines), 5

Reed, Adolph, 261, 267, 289n69

reorganization, of racial structure, 60

reparations, 79, 127, 129, 145, 179, 219

repression, Civil Rights Movement and, 51–53

Republican party, 232, 247, 260, 261, 279
research, on discrimination, 61–62, 194
residential choices, 11, 22n67
residential integration, 83, 99n28, 203–5
residential segregation, 219; among Asian Americans, 241, 251n56; costs of, 33; culture of, 152; decline of, 32; government's role on, 208; as interracial social interaction, 3, 32–34, 86–87; among Latinos, 241; among racial strata, 240–41; schools and, 203–5; studies of, 33, 153
reverse discrimination, 131–35, 179, 184, 212, 223n15, 266
Revolutionary Action Movement, 51
rhetorical incoherence, 102, 115–18; black color blindness and, 214–17
rhetorical maze, of color blindness, 104–11; "anything but race," 110–11; "I am not black, so I don't know," 106–8; "I am not prejudiced," 105–6; "some of my best friends are . . . ," 105–6; "yes and no, but . . . ," 108–10
rhetorical tool, projection as, 102, 111–14, 120n12
Riot Control Act, 53
Rodriguez, Clara, 237
Romney, George, 39, 271, 276, 277
Rove, Karl, 268
Rubio, Marco, 38, 261
Rush, Bobby, 262
Russell, Gregory D., 48–49

Saito, Leland, 236
Sanders, Lynn, 6
schools: integration of, 83, 85, 86, 156, 238; residential segregation and, 203–5
Schuman, Howard, 5–6, 36
Scientific American, 4
SCLC. *See* Southern Christian Leadership Conference
Scott, Tim, 38

Seale, Bobby, 51
Sears, David, 6
Sebelius, Kathleen, 276
segmentation, 55–56
segregated schools, 35
segregation, 82, 85, 96, 203; hypersegregation, 156, 159, 304; language of, 152; neighborhoods, 159–63, 204–5, 207, 222n8; self-segregation, 86, 116, 117, 138, 142, 145, 159, 163, 179. *See also* residential segregation; whites' racial segregation and isolation
self-segregation, 116, 117; of blacks, 128, 142, 145, 163, 179, 303; universal process of, 86; of whites, 159, 307–8
semantic moves, 102, 212–14
sense of group position, 7, 302, 313n7
Sharpton, Al, 268
Sheatsley, Paul B., 4
Showell, Andre, 265
Sidanius, Jim, 7
Silverstein, Ken, 262
sincere fictions, of whites, 2, 17n5
slavery, 77, 79, 129, 148nn12–13, 218, 312
Smiley, Tavis, 269
"smiling face" discrimination, 3, 259
SNCC. *See* Student Nonviolent Coordinating Committee
Sniderman, Paul, 5
social change, 82–83, 98nn26–27
social cleavage, 10
social control, since 1960s, 25, 29, 42–53; official state brutality and, 45–47; prison and, 43–45, 44; state as enforcer of, 43–45
social distance questions, 153, 154
social dominance, 259
social identity: of honorary whites, 235–36; tradition of, 171, 176nn40–44
social inequality, 25
social interaction: of Latinos, 240–41; among racial strata, 240–41. *See also* interracial social interaction

social life, 2, 28, 37; intermarriage, 36; studies of, 36
socially constructed category, of race, 8, 21n52
social reality, of race, 8–9, 21n55
social scientists, 8, 26, 151, 269
"some of my best friends are . . . ," 105–6
The Souls of Black People (DuBois), 114
South, 28, 29, 30
South Africa, 31
South Americans, 240, 241
Southeast Asia, 226, 241, 246n4
Southern Christian Leadership Conference (SCLC), 51
Southern Regional Council, 29
"spic," 103, 237, 305
"stage Negroes," 212
"stage whites," 212
state, as enforcer, 43–45
"State of Black America 2009," 257
"State of the Dream 2009: The Silent Depression," 257
status quo, racial, 10–11, 77, 98n18
Steele, Michael, 260, 278
Steinberg, Stephen, 131, 233
Stephanopoulos, George, 265
stereotypes, 206, 221
Stevens, Thaddeus, 179
stories: of disclosure, of a racist, 140–43, 146; of interactions with blacks, 135; personal, 143–45, 146. *See also* racial stories; story lines
Stormfront, 270
story lines, 124, 219; "I did not get a job/promotion/college admittance because of a minority," 131–35, 145, 148n20, 217; "I didn't own any slaves," 127–30, 145, 217; "if Jews, Italians, and Irish have made it, how come blacks have not," 130–31, 145, 217; of post–civil rights era, 125; "the past is the past," 125–27, 145, 148n10, 217
stratification, internal, 242
Street, Paul, 262, 267

structural barriers, to election of blacks, 39–40, 260
structure: new racial structure, in 1960s, 27–31; political, of new racism, 38–42; of racism, 26. *See also* racial structure
Student Nonviolent Coordinating Committee (SNCC), 51, 52
studies: of black color blindness, 199–200; of color-blind racism, 11–12; Federal Reserve Bank of Boston, 34; *Housing Discrimination Study*, 33; Kentucky Human Rights Commission, 33; of Latinos, 236–37; of residential segregation, 33, 153; of social life, of blacks, 36. *See also* 1998 Detroit Area Study
style: of ideology, 101. *See also* color blindness, style of
subtle racism, 259
Summers, Larry, 274
Sumner, Charles, 179
super PAC, 279
surveys: on integration, 153, *154*, 173n10, 173nn12–13; 1997 Survey of Social Attitudes of College Students, 12–13; on white's racial attitudes, 4, 11–12
symbolic expressions, of whites' dominance, 302
symbolic racism, 6–7, 20n36
systemic discrimination, 74, 149n23, *202*

Taguieff, Pierre-André, 87, 99n33
Taliban, 273
targeted universalism, 277
tax compromises, of Obama presidency, 275
Tea Party, 27, 62, 270
terminology, of racists, 104
testimonies, 124; "I used to have very good black friends," 144–45; negative interactions, with blacks, 135–38, 146; personal stories, 143–45, 146; positive interactions, with blacks, 138–40, 146; someone close

to me married or dated a minority, 144, 146; stories of disclosure, of a racist, 140–43, 146; stories of interactions with blacks, 135
Texaco case, 77, 98n21
Thomas, Clarence, 38, 40
torture, during Obama presidency, 280
triracial system, 227–28, *228*, 242
Trump, Donald, 270
Turner, Margery A., 33
2012 Democratic National Convention, 281

underemployment, 54
underrepresentation, of black officials, 40
unemployment, 54
unemployment, during Obama presidency, 257–58, 269, 278
universalist position, of Obama, 277
"University of Chicago Democrat," 282
urbanization, 30–31
Uruguay, 231
USAID, 280

Venezuela, 231
Vickerman, Milton, 245
Vietnamese, 227, 241, 244
Volker, Paul, 274
voter ID laws, 39, 278
vulnerable whites, 307

wage differentials, 54–55
Walters, Ronald, 269
War and the Reconstruction (1865-1877), 28
"War on Terror," 243, 272, 279
wars: Cold War, 29; War and the Reconstruction (1865-1877), 28; "War on Terror," 243, 272, 279; World War I, 28, 29, 131; World War II, 29, 30, 139, 226, 243
Waters, Maxine, 42
wealth disparity, 58–59; under Obama presidency, 257–58, 269

welfare leavers, 57
welfare reform, 239, *239*
Wellman, David, 8
Wells Fargo, 34
West, Allen, 260
West, Cornel, 87, 151
West Indians, 245
white elite, 262
white habitus, 152, 171–72, 173n7
white Latinos, 227, 233, 235, 236–37, 249n28
white males, 301, 312n1
whiteness, 193, 196n12; color-blind racism fight and, 308. *See also* color blindness, whiteness of
whitening, 230, 231, 248n17
white racial progressives. *See* racial progressives
whites, 1, 17n3, *228*, 242; affirmative action attitude of, 238, 303; as compassionate conservatives, 305; dominance by, 302; interracial dating/marriage of, 226; Jim Crow attitudes of, 4; racial attitudes of, 238–39; racial strata of, 233–34; self-segregation of, 159, 307–8; sincere fictions of, 2, 17n5; souls of, 304; "stage whites," 212; vulnerable, 307. *See also* honorary whites
whites' racial attitudes, in post–civil rights era, 3, 8; communicative interaction of, 11, 22n64; racial optimists, 4; racial pesoptimist, 5–6; residential choices relating to, 11, 22n67; sense of group position, 7; surveys on, 4, 11–12; symbolic racism, 6–7, 20n36
whites' racial segregation and isolation: cross-racial interaction, in college, 157–58, 171, 175n27; DAS on, 153, 155, 156, 157, 159, 161, 162, 163, 164, 165; facts of, 153–59; friendship and, 155–56, 158–59, 174n18, 175nn29–31; jobs and, 158; social distance questions about, 153, *154*

white supremacist organizations, 1, 17n1, 77
white supremacy, 9, 22n57, 28, 232, 302, 306; multiracial, 270, 310
White Supremacy & Racism (Bonilla-Silva), 301
"white traitors," 180, 195n2
Who Are We? The Challenges to America's National Identity (Huntington), 225, 246n2
Who Is White? Latinos, Asians, and the New Black/Nonblack Divide (Yancey), 243
Williams, Mike, 262
Wilson, William Julius, 26, 87, 91, 151
Winant, Howard, 220, 223n21, 224n24
Wise, Tom, 46

women, 219; Asian, 166, 176n39; working-class, 180, 194, 195nn4–5, 304, 307
Woods, Tiger, 226
Woodward, C. Vann, 28
working-class men, 193, 197n16
working-class women, 180, 194, 195nn4–5, 304, 307
World War I, 28, 29, 131
World War II, 29, 30, 139, 226, 243
Wright, Jeremiah, 266, 288n62

Yancey, George, 243
"yes and no, but . . . ," 108–10
Yinger, John, 33

Zubrinsky, Charles, 241

About the Author

Eduardo Bonilla-Silva is currently a professor and the chair of the sociology department at Duke University. Bonilla-Silva challenged social scientists in his 1997 article, "Rethinking Racism: Toward a Structural Interpretation," in the *American Sociological Review,* as he asked them to abandon the sterile soil of the prejudice problematic. He is the author of several books, among them, *White Supremacy and Racism in the Post–Civil Rights* Era (2001), co-winner of the 2002 Oliver C. Cox Award; *White Out* (2003), with Woody Doane; *White Logic, White Methods: Racism and Methodology* (2008), with Tukufu Zuberi, co-winner of the 2009 Oliver C. Cox Award; and *The State of White Supremacy: Racism, Governance, and the United States* (2011), with Moon-Kie Jung and Joao H. Costa Vargas. He received the 2007 Lewis A. Coser Award for theoretical agenda-setting given by the theory section of the American Sociological Association and is currently working on a book titled *The Invisible Weight of Whiteness: The Racial Grammar of Everyday Life in the USA.*